D0406850

Managing Software Engineering Knowledge

Springer
Berlin
Heidelberg
New York
Hong Kong
London
Milan
Paris
Tokyo

Aybüke Aurum   Ross Jeffery
Claes Wohlin   Meliha Handzic (Eds.)

Managing Software
Engineering Knowledge

With 47 Figures and 23 Tables

 Springer

Editors:

Aybüke Aurum
School of Information Systems,
Technology and Management
University of New South Wales
Sydney, NSW, 2052 Australia

Ross Jeffery
School of Computer Science
and Engineering
University of New South Wales
Sydney, NSW, 2052 Australia

Claes Wohlin
Dept. of Software Engineering and
Computer Science
Blekinge Institute of Technology
Box 520 SE-372 25 Ronneby, Sweden

Meliha Handzic
School of Information Systems,
Technology and Management
University of New South Wales
Sydney, NSW, 2052 Australia

Library of Congress Cataloging-in-Publication Data applied for

Bibliographic information published by *Die Deutsche Bibliothek*
Die Deutsche Bibliothek lists this publication in the *Deutsche
Nationalbibliografie;* detailed bibliographic data is available in the
Internet at <http://dnb.ddb.de>.

ACM Subject Classification (1998): D.2.8 D.2.9 J.4 K.6.1 K.6.3 K.6.4

ISBN 3-540-00370-3 Springer-Verlag Berlin Heidelberg New York

Springer-Verlag Berlin Heidelberg New York
a member of BertelsmannSpringer Science+Business Media GmbH

© Springer-Verlag Berlin Heidelberg 2003
Printed in Germany

The use of designations, trademarks, etc. in this publication does not imply, even in the absence of a specific statement, that such names are exempt from the relevant protective laws and regulations and therefore free for general use.

Cover Design: KünkelLopka, Heidelberg
Typesetting: Computer to film by author´s data
Printed on acid-free paper   45/3142XT 5 4 3 2 1 0

Foreword

H. Dieter Rombach

Software development is a human-based knowledge-intensive activity. In addition to sound methodology and technology, the success of a software project depends heavily on the knowledge and experience brought to the project by its developers. In the past, developers have mostly depended upon implicit knowledge. This resulted in problems when experienced people left a project and new developers entered. The implicit knowledge was not owned by the development organization, and therefore the necessary learning curve for novice developers resulted in a significant lowering of the software quality and developer productivity. The concept of continuous improvement remained commercially nonattractive as no improvements could be sustained in the face of personnel turnover.

For too long knowledge management and software engineering existed as separate communities with different paradigms and terminology. The knowledge management community developed models and methods for handling knowledge in many areas, however, they did not adequately address the specific needs of human-based development activities such as software engineering. On the other hand, the software engineering community understood the requirements of software engineering tasks and in an "amateur-style", reinvented many of the knowledge management models and methods. Only in the past ten years have these two communities begun to grow together.

Knowledge management is comprised of the elicitation, packaging and management, and reuse of knowledge in all its different forms. Explicit software engineering knowledge includes all types of software engineering artifacts, ranging from traditional software artifacts such as code, design and requirements to process knowledge in the form of models, data and standards, and lessons learned. In that sense, reuse of knowledge can be viewed as the most comprehensive form of reuse possible. One of the most important aspects of knowledge management is therefore the focus on reuse scenarios.

The blind population of knowledge repositories will not lead to success. Rather, the careful and goal-oriented inclusion and packaging of knowledge for specific reuse scenarios should be aimed for. The "store and hope for reuse" paradigm has failed in the past in its attempts to get code artifacts reused; it also will fail in the attempt to get comprehensive knowledge reused. The term "packaging" is related to the important distinction between data, information and knowledge. Whereas most definitions use the terms "data" and "information" interchangeably, "knowledge" is mostly referred to as information in a reusable context.

Finally, software process improvement people tend to refer to "experience" as a specific form of knowledge resulting from "actually doing it in your own environment". The advantage is that the context is clear, and consequently the credibility and acceptance of experience is high. For example, it is clear that effort estimation models based on data from one's own environment are better accepted than estimation models imported from foreign environments.

This book aims to provide a comprehensive overview of the state-of-the-art and practices in knowledge management and its application to software engineering. It is structured in four parts addressing the motives for knowledge management, the concepts and models used in knowledge management, its application to software engineering, and practical guidelines for managing software engineering knowledge. The editors have included authors from many research groups actively involved in the interdisciplinary area between knowledge management and software engineering. This book has the potential to serve as a benchmark for the state-of-the-art practices in this important interdisciplinary area. I am convinced it will become one of the most important background materials to graduate students, practitioners and researchers. I compliment the editors on an important service to the software engineering community. Well done!

Author Biography

Dr. H. Dieter Rombach is a full professor in the Department of Computer Science, Universität Kaiserslautern, Germany. He holds a chair in software engineering and is executive director of the Fraunhofer Institute for Experimental Software Engineering (IESE). His research interests are in software methodologies, modeling and measurement of the software process and resulting products, software reuse, and distributed systems. He has more than 120 publications in international journals and conference proceedings. Prior to his current position, Dr. Rombach held faculty positions with the Computer Science Department and University of Maryland Institute for Advanced Computer Studies, University of Maryland, USA, and was a member of the Software Engineering Laboratory.

He has a Ph.D. in computer science from the University of Kaiserslautern, Federal Republic of Germany. In 1990 he received the prestigious Presidential Young Investigator Award from the National Science Foundation, USA, in recognition of his research accomplishments in software engineering. In 2000 he was awarded the Service Medal of the State of Rhineland-Palatinate, Germany, for his accomplishments in software engineering research and his contributions to the economic development of the state through the establishment of a Fraunhofer institute.

Dr. Rombach heads several research projects funded by the German Government, European Union and Industry. He currently is the lead principal of a federally funded project (ViSEK) aimed at building up a German repository of knowledge about innovative software engineering technologies. He consults for numerous companies on issues including quality improvement, software measurement, software reuse, process modeling, and software technology in general, and he is an advisor to federal and state government on software issues. He is an associate editor of the Kluwer journal *Empirical Software Engineering* and serves on the editorial boards of numerous other journals and magazines. He is a member of GI and ACM, and a Fellow of IEEE.

Preface

Aybüke Aurum, Ross Jeffery, Claes Wohlin, Meliha Handzic

A recent trend in software engineering is the management of software engineering knowledge. The articles in this book explore the interdisciplinary nature of this area and portray the current status of management of software engineering knowledge. This book introduces researchers' and practitioners' knowledge management principles in the field of software engineering in a way that will capture their interest, excite and provoke them.

An Introduction to Knowledge Management in Software Engineering

Software development is a complex problem-solving activity where the level of uncertainty is high. There are many challenges concerning schedule, cost estimation, reliability, security, defects and performance due to great increases in software complexity and quality demands. Furthermore, high staff turnover, volatile software requirements, competitive environments, dynamics of team members' psychology and sociology as individuals - as well as in groups - are only a few examples of the challenges that face software developers.

Increasing application complexity and changing technology provide, opportunities for the utilization of available experience and knowledge. There is a need to collect software engineering experiences and knowledge, and reuse them for software process improvement. Thus, developing effective ways of managing software knowledge is of interest to software developers. However, it is not well understood how to implement this vision. On a higher level, a knowledge repository can improve an organization's professional image and can also create a competitive advantage. Knowing and learning how to manage software engineering knowledge directly address this perception.

In what way can knowledge management assist software development? To discuss this question, it is necessary to first define knowledge and knowledge management.

Knowledge and Knowledge Management

A variety of definitions of knowledge have been presented in the literature. Knowledge is a broad and abstract notion. The Australian Webster's dictionary defines knowledge as "the act, fact, or state of knowing; the body of facts, principles, accumulated by mankind".

Nonaka [3] distinguishes between implicit (tacit) and explicit knowledge. Explicit knowledge is stored in textbooks, software products and documents.

Implicit knowledge is stored in the minds of people in the form of memory, skills, experience, education, imagination and creativity. Choo [2] adds cultural knowledge to Nonaka's classification. On the other hand, Spender [5] classifies knowledge in terms of implicit, explicit, individual and collective knowledge. There is a common agreement that both implicit and explicit knowledge are important, however, implicit knowledge is more difficult to identify and manage.

The terms "knowledge" and "data" are often used interchangeably in both information systems and software engineering literature. Knowledge is seen a type of information that is attached to a particular context. Alavi and Leidner [1] speculate that information becomes knowledge once it is processed in the mind of an individual, which then becomes information once it is articulated and communicated to others in the form of text, software product or other means. The receiver can then cognitively process the information so that it is converted back into tacit knowledge.

Wilson and Snyder [6] define two types of information: support information and guidance information. Support information includes descriptive explanations that provide a basic understanding of a product or process by answering questions such as who, what, when, where and why. The information on guidance illustrates how to accomplish a task. In order to be able to accomplish a task, to solve a problem or to answer questions we need to be able to access both types of information so that we can cognitively process and interpret it.

Information has an economic value derived from its accuracy, timeliness and exclusivity. According to the economists G.A. Akerloff, A.M. Spence and J.E. Stiglitz, who won the 2001 Nobel Prize in economics, asymmetric information can distort economic behavior and is seen as a competitive advantage [7]. Basic intellectual capital management strategies are based on beliefs that value creation comes from people. Furthermore, ideas are the source of beliefs, and corporate growth is a natural process and derived from skill transfer. Thus, knowledge is considered a crucial resource for organizations and it should be managed carefully.

The management of knowledge is regarded as a main source of competitive advantage for organizations. Keeping organizational knowledge up-to-date is seen as a competitive strategy, especially when the knowledge at hand helps to generate considerably significant returns [4].

In essence, the objective of knowledge management is to transfer implicit knowledge to explicit knowledge, as well as to transfer explicit knowledge from individuals to groups within the organization. Hence, knowledge management is concerned with creating, preserving and applying the knowledge that is available within organizations. This implies that knowledge management requires an appropriate infrastructure for creating and managing explicit as well as implicit knowledge about artifacts and processes.

The Role of Knowledge in Software Development

Software developers possess highly valuable knowledge relating to product development, the software development process, project management and technologies. As knowledge intensive work, software development requires various forms of explicit as well as implicit knowledge. This knowledge is dynamic and evolves with technology, organizational culture, and the changing needs of the organization's software development practices. There are cases where the knowledge is created at irregular intervals and the value of its use can only be displayed over time. There are also cases where the knowledge for the task is well defined and reusable. Improving software products, software processes and resources are special cases of knowledge management. For instance, process support includes improved processes and their results, well-defined tasks, improved communication and guiding people to perform their task. The use of the Internet facilitates the storage and utilization of activities, thus improving the quality of the software development process. Experience also plays a major role in knowledge-related activities. Software development can be improved by recognizing the related knowledge content and structure as well as the required appropriate knowledge, and performing planning activities.

What Can We Learn from Knowledge Management to Support Software Development?

Knowledge management is an area that has much to offer to software developers because it takes a multidisciplinary approach to the various activities of gathering and managing knowledge. The knowledge management viewpoint draws from well established disciplines such as cognitive science, ergonomics, computer science and management. Most importantly, it views the management of knowledge as a human endeavor and acknowledges the fact that human assets are buried in the minds of individual software developers and leverages it into a team asset that can be used, learned and shared by other team members.

A knowledge management system in a software organization provides an opportunity to create a common language of understanding among software developers so that they can interact with each other, negotiate and share their knowledge and experiences. A knowledge management system supports the ability to systematically manage innovative knowledge in software development. It facilitates an organizational learning approach to software development by structuring and assisting knowledge transfer at the project-organization level. This system has a knowledge repository that stores long-term reusable solutions and illustrates how novel problems can be solved by adapting similar solutions that fit the organization's technical and business context. It provides "lessons learned" functions for solving specific problems e.g. knowledge acquired from past projects for customer-specific solutions or for handling similar tasks such as planning for software projects. It aids in the development of an organizational memory bank for practitioners. In this way it facilitates repetitive administrative oriented as well as knowledge-intensive tasks (also known as workflow management) in a software development environment.

Finally a knowledge management system repository fosters the use of fault measurement processes and continuous improvement, and encompasses the development of generic standards as well as specific development methods. It acts as a facilitator at both individual and collective levels, for example, by defining relevant qualitative and quantitative measurements, and by establishing regular feedback.

Potential Issues

Although the idea of creating a system that allows software developers to share knowledge is an attractive idea, the literature is filled with questions that software developers need to address. What kind of knowledge would be useful to store for software system design? What kind of problems can we solve in software development by using knowledge management principles? How do you acquire and represent software development knowledge?

There are number of obstacles to the introduction of knowledge management into software engineering communities. First, a knowledge management system in a software organization essentially involves the development of a technical and organizational infrastructure. This requires significant effort for the development of knowledge content, filtering and organizing knowledge, capturing intellectual assets and capturing processes. The system needs continuous updating and monitoring of knowledge resources. Furthermore, training of software developers for timely, effective and efficient reuse of experience in subsequent projects is a necessity. The communication of knowledge for accessibility and its application to support effective software development is expensive and time consuming. In other words, a considerable amount of investment is required for the application of knowledge management principles in a software development environment, where the effort is critical to its success.

In addition to the above, a lack of awareness of knowledge management practices among software developers, or their reluctance to share knowledge because they are afraid that sharing and transferring their knowledge to colleagues decreases their value and job security are only few examples of dilemmas that software practitioners face.

Software developers commonly agree that software engineering can benefit from knowledge management solutions. It is important to remember that software team members need encouragement and support to share information and learn from each other. They need an interactive environment where they can continuously learn in an everyday environment and improve job performance.

Aims of the Book and Target Audience

Management of knowledge and experience are key means for systematic software development and process improvement. This book illustrates several examples of how to get this vision to work in theory as well as how to apply these solutions to industrial practice. Furthermore, it provides an important collection of articles for researchers and practitioners on knowledge management in software development. It is hoped that this book will become a useful reference for postgraduate students undertaking research in software development. Although it is recommended that the readers have a sound background in software development, this book offers new insight into the software development process for both novice software developers as well as experienced professionals.

Book Overview

This book is organized into four major parts. Each part contains three to five chapters. Although it is preferable to first familiarize yourself with the first chapter of Part 1, or at least with portions of other chapters in Part 1, the book is designed to permit reading of the parts in many different orders, depending on readers' interests.

Part 1: Motives for Knowledge Management Initiatives

Challenge: Why manage software engineering knowledge?

There may be many different motives for starting knowledge management initiatives in organizations. These motives may be grouped into two broad categories: survival and advancement. The difference is in the focus on existing or new knowledge. Survival strategies concentrate on knowledge management initiatives around capturing and locating valuable company knowledge and making the maximum use of the existing knowledge through transferring and sharing practices. Advancement strategies, on the other hand, focus on generation of new knowledge and processes necessary for enabling successful innovations.

Articles in Part 1 of this book cover several major motivational aspects of knowledge management in software engineering from three different perspectives: people, process and product. The three chapters are by John. S. Edwards (Aston Business School, Birmingham, UK); June M. Verner and William M. Evanco (College of Information Science and Technology, Drexel University, USA); Torgeir Dingsøyr (SINTEF Telecom and Informatics, Norway) and Reidar Conradi (Norwegian University of Science and Technology, Norway).

Part 2: Supporting Structures for Managing Software Engineering Knowledge

Challenge: Need to clarify concepts and models

Some observers predict that knowledge management is a vague concept that will neither deliver what it promises nor add to the bottom line. Part 2 examines the existing knowledge management frameworks, focusing on those that may potentially be helpful for managing software engineering knowledge. Existing problems of managing software engineering knowledge will be addressed.

The five chapters are by Mikael Lindvall and Ioana Rus (Fraunhofer Center for Experimental Software Engineering Maryland, USA); Tore Dybå (SINTEF Telecom and Informatics, Norway); Gary R. Oliver, John D'Ambra and Christine Van Toorn (University of New South Wales, Australia); Allen Dutoit (Informatics Department of Technische Universitaet Muenchen, Germany), Barbara Paech, (Fraunhofer Institute for Experimental Software Engineering, Germany); and David Lowe (University of Technology, Sydney Australia).

Part 3: Application of Knowledge Management in Software Engineering

Challenge: The use of knowledge management in software engineering

Knowledge Management is not a single technology but instead a collection of indexing, classifying, retrieval and communication technologies coupled with methodologies designed to achieve results desired by the user. Part 3 covers the applications of knowledge management in software engineering

The five chapters are by Martin Shepperd (Bournemouth University, UK); Sira Vegas, Natalia Juristo (Universidad Politécnica de Madrid, Spain) and Victor Basili (University of Maryland, USA); Stefan Biffl (Vienna University of Technology) and Michael Halling (Johannes Kepler University, Austria); Linda H. Rosenberg (Goddard Flight Space Center, NASA, USA); and Klaus-Dieter Althoff and Dietmar Pfahl (Fraunhofer Institute of Experimental Software Engineering, Germany).

Part 4: Practical Guidelines for Managing Software Engineering Knowledge

Challenge: Lack of standards

Some industry observers say that the lack of standards is fragmenting deployment of enterprise-wide knowledge management products. Many organizations, including Standards Australia, are working on standardizing various aspects of knowledge management functionality. Part 4 concludes the book by looking at the industrial practices in software development.

The four chapters are by Rini van Solingen (CMG Technical Software Engineering, The Netherlands), Rob Kusters (Eindhoven University of

Technology and Open University, The Netherlands), Jos Trienekens (Eindhoven University of Technology, The Netherlands); Christof Ebert, Jozef De Man and Fariba Schelenz (Alcatel, France); and Pankaj Jalote (Department of Computer Science and Engineering, I.I.T., India).

Acknowledgement

There are many people whom we would like to thank for their help and support. We wish to thank all the authors for their hard work and effort in creating this book. We are especially grateful to Fethi Rabhi, Adrian Gardiner, Peter Parkin and Paul Scifleet for their participation in the external review process and for their valuable comments. We would also like to thank Liming Zhu for his assistance in creating the Web site and formatting this book and Irem Sevinç for assisting with the proof reading. A special thanks goes to Ralph Gerstner of Springer, Germany for providing professional advice during the publishing process. Finally, a big thank you is due to our families for enduring the lengthy editing process. This book is dedicated to our families.

References

1. Alavi M., Leidner D. (1999) Knowledge management systems: emerging views and practices from the field. In: Proceedings of 32nd annual Hawaii international conference on system sciences, Maui, Hawaii, USA, 11p.
2. Choo C.W. (1998) The knowing organization. Oxford university press, New York, NY
3. Nonaka I. (1994) A dynamic theory of organizational knowledge creation. Organization science, 5: 14-37
4. Schulz M., Lloyd A.J. (2001) Codification and tacitness as knowledge management strategies: an empirical exploration. Journal of high technology management research, 12: 139-165
5. Spender J.C. (1998) Pluralist epistemology and the knowledge-based theory of the firm. Organization science, 5: 233-256
6. Wilson, L.T., Snyder C.A. (1999) Knowledge management and IT: how are they related? IT Professional, 1: 73 -75
7. Williams J. (2002) Practical issues in knowledge management. IT Professional, 4: 35-39

Contents

List of Contributors

Klaus-Dieter Althoff
Fraunhofer IESE, Sauerwiesen 6
D-67661 Kaiserslautern, Germany
althoff@iese.fhg.de

Aybüke Aurum
School of Information Systems, Technology and Management
University of New South Wales
NSW, 2052 Australia
aybuke@unsw.edu.au

Victor Basili
Department of Computer Science
University of Maryland
College Park, MD 20742, USA
basili@cs.umd.edu

Stefan Biffl
Institute for Software Technology
Vienna University of Technology
Karlsplatz 13, A-1040 Vienna, Austria
Stefan.Biffl@tuwien.ac.at

Reidar Conradi
Norwegian University of Science and Technology
NO-7491 Trondheim, Norway
Reidar.Conradi@idi.ntnu.no

John D'Ambra
School of Information Systems, Technology and Management
University of New South Wales
NSW 2052 Australia
j.dambra@unsw.edu.au

Jozef De Man
Alcatel
Fr.-Wellesplein 1, B-2018 Antwerpen, Belgium
jozef.de_man@alcatel.be

Torgeir Dingsøyr
SINTEF Telecom and Informatics
SP Andersens vei 15
NO-7465 Trondheim, Norway
Torgeir.Dingsoyr@sintef.no

Allen Dutoit
Technische Universität München, Institut für Informatik, Boltzmannstraße 3
D-85748 Garching b. München, Germany
dutoit@in.tum.de

Tore Dybå
SINTEF Telecom and Informatics
S.P. Andersensv. 15, NO-7465 Trondheim, Norway
tore.dyba@sintef.no,

Christof Ebert
Alcatel
54 rue La Boetie, 75008 Paris, France
Christof.Ebert@alcatel.com

John S. Edwards
Aston Business School
Birmingham, B4 7ET, UK
j.s.edwards@aston.ac.uk

William Evanco
College of Information Science and Technology
Drexel University
3141 Chestnut St, Philadelphia, PA 19104, USA
William.evanco@cis.drexel.edu

Michael Halling
Dept. of Systems Engineering and Automation
Johannes Kepler University
Linz Altenbergerstr. 69, A-4040 Linz, Austria
Michael.Halling@univie.ac.at

Meliha Handzic
School of Information Systems, Technology and Management
University of New South Wales
NSW, 2052, Australia
m.handzic@unsw.edu.au

Pankaj Jalote
Department of Computer Science and Engineering
Indian Institute of Technology Kanpur
Kanpur, India 208016
Jalote@iitk.ac.in

Ross Jeffery
School of Computer Science and Engineering
University of New South Wales
NSW, 2052 Australia
rossj@cse.unsw.edu.au

Natalia Juristo
Facultad de Informática. Universidad Politécnica de Madrid
Campus de Montegancedo
28660 Boadilla del Monte, Madrid, Spain
natalia@fi.upm.es

Rob Kusters
Eindhoven University of Technology,
Den Dolech 2, 5600 MB Eindhoven, The Netherlands,
R.J.Kusters@tm.tue.nl

Mikael Lindvall
Fraunhofer Center for Experimental Software Engineering Maryland
4321 Hartwick Rd, Suite 500
College Park, MD 20740, USA
mlindvall@fc-md.umd.edu

David Lowe
University of Technology, Sydney
PO Box 123, Broadway
NSW, 2007, Australia
david.lowe@uts.edu.au

Gary Oliver
Australian Graduate School of Management
University of New South Wales
NSW, 2052, Australia
gary@agsm.edu.au

Barbara Paech
Fraunhofer IESE, Sauerwiesen 6
D-67661 Kaiserslautern, Germany
paech@iese.fhg.de

Dietmar Pfahl
Fraunhofer IESE, Sauerwiesen 6
D-67661 Kaiserslautern, Germany
pfahl@iese.fhg.de

Dieter Rombach
Fraunhofer IESE, Sauerwiesen 6
D-67661 Kaiserslautern, Germany
rombach@iese.fhg.de

Linda H. Rosenberg
Goddard Space Flight Center, NASA
Greenbelt, MD 20771, USA
Linda.H.Rosenberg@nasa.gov

Ioana Rus
Fraunhofer Center for Experimental Software Engineering Maryland
4321 Hartwick Rd, Suite 500
College Park, MD 20740, USA
irus@fc-md.umd.edu

Fariba Schelenz
Alcatel
54 rue La Boetie, 75008 Paris, France
fariba.schelenz@alcatel.fr

Martin Shepperd
Empirical Software Engineering Research Group
School of Design, Engineering and Computing, Bournemouth University
Bournemouth, BH1 3LT, UK
mshepper@bmth.ac.uk

Jos Trienekens
Eindhoven University of Technology
Den Dolech 2, 5600 MB Eindhoven, The Netherlands
J.J.M.Trienekens@tm.tue.nl

Rini van Solingen
LogicaCMG Technical Software Engineering
P. O. Box 8566, 3009 AN Rotterdam, The Netherlands
Rini.van.Solingen@cmg.nl

Christine Van Toorn
School of Information Systems, Technology and Management
University of New South Wales
NSW 2052 Australia
c.vantoorn@unsw.edu.au

Sira Vegas
Facultad de Informática. Universidad Politécnica de Madrid
Campus de Montegancedo
28660 Boadilla del Monte, Madrid, Spain
svegas@fi.upm.es

June Verner
College of Information Science and Technology
Drexel University
3141 Chestnut St., Philadelphia, PA 19104, USA
june.verner@cis.drexel.edu

Claes Wohlin
Department of Software Engineering and Computer Science
Blekinge Institute of Technology
Box 520, SE-372 25 Ronneby, Sweden
Claes.Wohlin@bth.se

Part 1
Why Is It Important to Manage Knowledge?

Meliha Handzic

> *Investment in knowledge pays best interest.*
> — Benjamin Franklin

Rapid change and competition for customer loyalty have forced firms to seek sustainable competitive advantage in order to distinguish themselves from their competitors. Business leaders view knowledge as the chief asset of organizations and the key to sustaining a competitive advantage [4]. For this reason, companies have started to focus more on what they know, and less on what they own. It is therefore not surprising that knowledge has been identified as the new basis for competition and as the only unlimited resource, the one asset that grows with use.

Many firms have also come to understand that they require more than just a casual approach to corporate knowledge if they are to succeed in the new economy [2]. Companies have to find out where their business-specific knowledge is, and how to transform it into valuable products and services that differentiates them from the rest of the market. Good knowledge management can foster the creation of new knowledge to meet new challenges and enables the effective and rapid application of knowledge to create value.

The main purpose of knowledge management is to make sure that the right people have the right knowledge at the right time. In particular, knowledge management needs to ensure that people have the necessary talents, skills, knowledge and experiences to implement corporate strategies. Implementations of knowledge management also need to provide structures and systems that enable people to share and apply their knowledge to support decisions, to present services to the customer, to support customers' needs, to develop solutions required and expected by the customer, as well as to stay in business and to secure employability.

It is argued here that there is a need for holistic approaches that can help practitioners to understand the sorts of knowledge management initiatives or investments that are possible and to identify those that make sense in their context [1]. Accordingly, Part 1 brings together various perspectives on motives for knowledge management.

While there may be many different individual reasons for starting knowledge management initiatives in organizations, they can be grouped into three broad categories: *minimizing risk*, *seeking efficiency* and *enabling innovation* which ensure business survival or advancement.

If the prime motive for knowledge management is minimizing risk, the response typically involves identifying and holding onto the core competencies of a company. Thus, risk minimization is closely related to knowledge initiatives aimed at locating and capturing valuable company knowledge [5]. In software engineering, people have been recognized as key holders of valuable knowledge content. Therefore, identifying, locating and capturing what is known by individuals and groups of software developers is of critical importance for software businesses survival.

In today's complex economy, businesses are constantly confronted with the need to operate more efficiently in order to stay competitive and satisfy increasing market demands. Seeking efficiency usually relates to knowledge initiatives for transferring experiences and best practices throughout the organization in order to avoid unnecessary duplication and to reduce cost. Technology is often an important part of achieving efficiency improvements [5]. In particular, companies that develop software are under increasing pressure from their customers to deliver software solutions faster and cheaper. Therefore, researchers and practitioners in the field of software engineering need to turn their attention to new ways and tools for improving the software development process as a possible means for achieving enhanced efficiency and sustaining the competitive advantage of software firms.

There is a growing belief that knowledge can do more than improve efficiency. The new products and services resulting from knowledge and technology may bring profound changes in the way businesses operate and compete in the new economy. The unifying thread among various theoretical views is the perception that innovation is the key driver of an organization's long-term economic success. Innovation of products, processes and structures has been assessed as a critical component in the success of new-age firms.

Typically, innovative organizations focus both on new knowledge and on knowledge processes. They constantly engage and motivate people, creating the overall enabling context for knowledge creation. These organizations take a strategic view of knowledge, formulate knowledge visions, tear down knowledge barriers, develop new corporate values and trust, catalyze and coordinate knowledge creation, manage various contexts involved, develop conversational culture and globalize local knowledge [3].

The greatest challenge for software engineering companies is to move in a knowledge-enabling direction by consciously and deliberately addressing knowledge management. By nurturing knowledge, enabling its sharing and use, getting knowledge out of individual minds into the social environment, and by turning individual creativity into innovativeness for everyone, software firms can ensure their long-term advancement and business success.

The review of literature on knowledge management reveals large gaps in the body of knowledge in this area. The ultimate challenge is to determine the best strategies to improve the development, transfer and use of organizational knowledge at the individual and collective levels. We believe that the integrated approach adopted in this book can help make sense of many different issues and theoretical concepts, and provide an underlying framework that can guide future research and practice.

The overall field of knowledge management can accommodate a wide range of themes and approaches. Articles in Part1 of this book cover several major motivational aspects of knowledge management in software engineering from three different perspectives. These include people, process and product viewpoints.

Software engineering has been recognized as one of the most knowledge intensive professions. In the first article, John Edwards takes a closer look at software engineers (people) and identifies major issues involved in managing these professional knowledge workers. He then uses this as a framework to discuss how knowledge management may be relevant to further advancing the software engineering profession.

Despite extensive research into project failure and the many guidelines for successful software development that have been proposed, projects still fail. Therefore, in the second article, June Verner and William Evanco specifically address the improvement of software development (process), focusing primarily on project risk management because of its major influence on project success. First, the authors describe the current state of the practice and identify critical success factors. Then, they propose a preliminary knowledge-based model to predict future software project success.

Software is often a major part of most innovative products and services or is an innovative product in its own right. In the third article, Torgeir Dingsøyr and Reidar Conradi illustrate the importance of innovative knowledge management software (product) as an engine of a learning software organization. In particular, the article shows the need for software organizations to work with both codification and personalization strategies to achieve effective knowledge management.

References

1. Handzic M. (2001) Knowledge management: a research framework. In: Proceedings of the 2nd European conference on knowledge management, Bled, Slovenia, pp. 219-229
2. Nonaka I. Takeuchi H. (1995) The knowledge creating company: How Japanese companies create the dynamics of innovation. Oxford university press, New York, USA
3. Nonaka I., Nishiguchi T. (2001) Knowledge emergence. Oxford university press, New York, USA
4. Raich M. (2000) Managing in the knowledge based economy. Raich Ltd., Zurich, Switzerland
5. Von Krogh G., Ichijo K., Nonaka I. (2000) Enabling knowledge creation. Oxford university press, New York, USA

Editor Biography

Dr. Meliha Handzic is a senior lecturer at the School of Information Systems, Technology and Management, University of New South Wales. She is the founder and the group leader of knowledge management research group (kmRg) in the University of New South Wales. Her main research interest is Knowledge

Management, more specifically processes and enablers of knowledge creation, sharing, organization and discovery. Her other interests include forecasting and decision support. She has published over 50 research papers on these topics. Presently she is regional editor of the journal *Knowledge Management Research and Practice*, and on the editorial boards of *In Thought and Practice* and *Journal of Information Technology Education*.

1 Managing Software Engineers and Their Knowledge

John S. Edwards

Abstract: This chapter begins by reviewing the history of software engineering as a profession, especially the so-called software crisis and responses to it, to help focus on what it is that software engineers do. This leads into a discussion of the areas in software engineering that are problematic as a basis for considering knowledge management issues. Some of the previous work on knowledge management in software engineering is then examined, much of it not actually going under a knowledge management title, but rather "learning" or "expertise". The chapter goes on to consider the potential for knowledge management in software engineering and the different types of knowledge management solutions and strategies that might be adopted, and it touches on the crucial importance of cultural issues. It concludes with a list of challenges that knowledge management in software engineering needs to address.

Keywords: Knowledge management, Software engineering, Software process improvement, Learning, Expertise, Knowledge management strategy

1.1 Introduction

Software engineering is one of the most knowledge-intensive professions. Knowledge and its management are relevant to several aspects of software engineering at different levels, from the strategic or organizational to the technical. These include:

- Estimation of costs and time scales
- Project management
- Communicating with clients and users
- "Problem solving" in system development
- Reuse of code
- Training and staff development
- Maintenance and support

It might therefore be expected that software engineers would be well advanced in the practice of knowledge management. However, there are few signs that this is being the case. Although the general knowledge management literature contains many examples of knowledge management systems in successful use in information technology - related companies, relatively few are specifically for software engineering. Most reported systems in these companies address areas such as overall company performance, sales and marketing, or perhaps trouble-shooting hardware failures. Mouritsen et al. [40] for example, give a very detailed account of knowledge management in the form of producing an intellectual capital statement for a software engineering firm, Systematic Software Engineering. However, there is virtually nothing in their article that is specific to software engineering.

One reason for the lack of "visibility" of software engineering in the wider knowledge management literature is the tendency for discussion of such topics to take place at conferences for the software engineering community. These include the Learning Software Organizations Workshop, the International Conference on Software Engineering, the International Conference on Software Engineering and Knowledge Engineering and the European Software Process Improvement Conference. Thus there is an active knowledge management community in software engineering, but it is interesting that much of their work is distanced from the knowledge management mainstream.

In this chapter, we begin by reviewing the history of software engineering as a profession, to provide a background for discussing the issues involved in knowledge management in software engineering. We then look at the aspects of software engineering that may make knowledge management problematic, but equally are often the reasons why it is important. We next consider what has been done so far by way of knowledge management in software engineering, and in particular the question of whether knowledge management has been taking place, but under other names. Finally, we look at the potential for knowledge management in software engineering by offering a framework for discussing knowledge management, including the cultural issues that most influence this profession. We conclude by identifying the principal challenges for knowledge management in software engineering and by arguing for a "complementary" strategy to address them.

1.2 History of the Profession

In this section, we review some of the key features of the history of software engineering, both as an activity and a profession. This serves to introduce the relevance of knowledge management to software engineering. The topics include the impression given of perpetual crisis, efforts at software process improvement, what software engineers actually do in technical/functional terms, and whether or not software engineering is knowledge work.

1.2.1 Perpetual Crisis?

At one level, the history of software engineering gives the impression of a profession in perpetual crisis. Even before the 1968 NATO conference on software engineering, which brought the term into common use [41], back in the days of punched cards and paper tape, the development of software was regarded as being problematic. Indeed, it is asserted [47] that the term software engineering was chosen for this conference title deliberately in order to be provocative. The tendency for commercial and governmental systems to be delivered late, over budget and lacking functionality was already becoming apparent. There was a need for the development of computer systems to be performed with the rigor and discipline associated with branches of engineering.

More than 30 years later and in another century, not much seems to have changed, as the paper by Bryant indicates [12]. Granted, the majority of software development now takes places in specialized companies rather than in the in-house departments of large organizations, but the problems relating to cost, time and quality still seem to be similar. One might therefore conclude that nothing much has changed in software engineering over this period. Yet the situation is not as simple as this. Recent major successes of software engineering, such as avoiding (for the most part) any major Y2K problems and coping with the introduction of the euro, have earned the profession little credit either externally or internally. The profession presents itself in a strange light, presumably because this is how it sees itself—a crisis of identity, at least. Indeed, one of the UK's weekly magazines for professionals in this field has a reputation for almost always headlining a negative story. Bryant rightly questions whether software engineering as a profession is part of the solution or part of the problem.

Towards the middle of the period we have been discussing, Andrew Friedman (with Dominic Cornford) produced an influential account of the history of software engineering [22]. One of the frameworks used for this analysis was a model based on three phases, derived from "the story so far" up to the late 1980s. The phases were dominated by hardware constraints, software issues and user needs, respectively. Baxter [7] argues that if Friedman's time-based phasing model had been correct, then "by now software writing would be unproblematic", but that this does not seem to be the case, as we would agree. However, Friedman himself said that phase three (dominated by user needs) would not necessarily give way to a phase four, and that "one possibility…is to revert back to the domination of earlier phase concerns". Programming issues still have a great influence on what software is created, rather than just the requirements of the users. Baxter points out that "beta versions", "patches" and "bugs" are all commonplace in the software world, but, as she puts it "can the reader imagine having a "beta" set of wheels on their car?"

The view within the software engineering department is no more reassuring. For example, Perlow [46] refers to the "fast paced, high-pressure, crisis-filled environment in which software engineers work". If a general expectation that software will not work properly and a crisis-filled environment are reasonable indications, then software engineering is indeed a profession in a continuing state of crisis.

1.2.2 Software Process Improvement

The comments in Sect. 1.2.1 should not be taken as evidence that nothing has been done to improve matters. On the contrary, many systematic attempts have been made to produce software that is more reliable and of higher quality. One way to do this is simply to improve the testing procedures, but we will not consider this further here for two reasons. First, this approach goes against all the principles of total quality management, since it is far cheaper and easier to avoid errors rather than to find and correct them. Second, the ever-increasing complexity of modern software [23] makes it much harder to test than, say, a piece of mechanical equipment. The emphasis has therefore rightly been on producing software that is more reliable and of higher quality by methods that are more predictable and robust. These approaches are generally grouped under the heading of software process improvement. A good review of various different improvement "technologies" is given by the experienced commentator on the field, Robert Glass [24].

In this section we concentrate on those improvement methods termed "process models" by Glass, since these have the greatest relevance to the management aspects of the software engineering profession, as opposed to the technical aspects. If improvements are left solely to the technical level, then the best that is likely to be achieved will be isolated "islands of knowledge". This is a widely recognized problem in knowledge management. Among these process models are the Capability Maturity Model (CMM), the Quality Improvement Paradigm (QIP), Software Process Improvement and Capability dEtermination (SPICE), and the ISO 9000 series of internationally agreed standards.

1.2.2.1   The Software Capability Maturity Model

One of the most widely recognized frameworks for looking at the extent of professionalism in a software engineering company or unit is the software Capability Maturity Model [33, 44, 45]. This was developed at Carnegie Mellon University's Software Engineering Institute (SEI). The CMM for software (there are now other related CMMs) is organized into five maturity levels:

1. *Initial*: The software process is characterized as ad hoc, and occasionally even chaotic. Few processes are defined, and success depends on individual effort and heroics.
2. *Repeatable*: Basic project management processes are established to track cost, schedule, and functionality. The necessary process discipline is in place to repeat earlier successes on projects with similar applications.
3. *Defined*: The software process for both management and engineering activities is documented, standardized and integrated into a standard software process for the organization. All projects use an approved, tailored version of the organization's standard software process for developing and maintaining software.
4. *Managed*: Detailed measures of the software process and product quality are collected. Both the software process and products are quantitatively understood and controlled.

5. *Optimizing*: Continuous process improvement is enabled by quantitative feedback from the process and from piloting innovative ideas and technologies.

Here we see the progression from a "let's run the program and see what happens" approach to the technically rigorous and managerially disciplined approach that an engineering discipline should have. Perlow frequently refers to "individual heroics" in discussing the organization that he studied [46]; clearly it belongs at level 1. Knowledge management is by definition nonexistent in a level 1 unit, but becomes increasingly important as the level rises. Indeed, it could be argued that more effective knowledge management is one of the hallmarks distinguishing the higher levels of capability maturity.

1.2.2.2   Quality Improvement Paradigm

The Quality Improvement Paradigm (QIP) is an approach that draws on the field of Total Quality Management (TQM). One of the pioneers of this approach was the Software Engineering Laboratory at NASA's Goddard Space Flight Center [6]. The phrase coined for the resulting organization is the "experience factory". The relationship between the QIP and the experience factory is well described by Basili and Caldiera [5]. They also explain why manufacturing-based total quality approaches have not worked well in software engineering. Such approaches do not deal well enough with the nature of a software product. For example, any particular piece of software is only developed once, so that statistical quality control approaches are impossible. Some of the lessons learned at the Goddard Space Flight Center are described in Chap. 12 of this book [48].

1.2.2.3   Software Process Improvement and Capability Determination

Software process improvement and capability dEtermination (SPICE) is an initiative intended to produce an international standard for software process assessment [31]. This covers not only software development and operation, but also procurement and support as related to packaged software. Extensive trials have occurred for some years. Thus far it has reached the status of a technical report (ISO/IEC TR 15504: 1998) published by the international organization for standardization (ISO), with the intention that this will evolve into a full international standard. More general international quality standards are covered in the Sect. 1.2.2.4.

1.2.2.4   ISO 9000 Series Standards

The ISO 9000 series of standards [30] relates to quality management systems of all kinds in organizations, but some parts of the software engineering industry have been particularly attracted by the idea of systems designed to deliver products that meet customer needs. In many industries, ISO 9000 certification is either a source of competitive advantage or an essential qualifier in order to be considered as a supplier at all. Software consultancies, therefore, have shown great interest in becoming accredited under ISO 9000. A particular point of commonality with the other methods mentioned is that the latest version, ISO 9000:2000, is constructed around the idea of viewing a business in terms of its processes, and separating those into the "realization processes", which form the core of what the organization does, and support processes. Thus in a software house or consultancy, developing software is a core realization process. However, in an organization whose business is making diesel engines or selling insurance, it would be a support process.

1.2.3 What Functions Do Software Engineers Carry Out?

In this section, we look at the functional or technical activities carried out by software engineers, to complement the "management" perspective of the previous section. Historically, attempts to describe what software engineers do have usually gone hand in hand with attempts to formalize the process by which they do it. Thus the "waterfall" led to the life cycle approaches and then to structured methods, also sometimes called methodologies; see [22]. Similarly, prototyping, once the ultimate in "make it up as you go along" approaches, has acquired far more structure and transferability in recent years because of initiatives such as the development of dynamic systems development method (DSDM).

As an example of a structured method, we shall use the UK government-approved structured systems analysis and design method (SSADM) [59]. In its most recent version (4.3), SSADM comprises five modules: feasibility study, requirements analysis, requirements specification, logical system specification, and physical design.

DSDM by its very nature has a more complex structure than the hierarchical one of SSADM. At the top level, the project process has five phases: feasibility study, business study, functional model iteration, design and build iteration, implementation. In addition, there are the preproject and postproject phases, making seven in all. The authoritative source for information on DSDM can be found at http://www.dsdm.org (last accessed November 1, 2002). From this, it is clear that in DSDM, the term project refers to the actual system development, not to its maintenance or support. SSADM, unusually for a structured method, is even more restricted, stopping before even the programming, let alone the implementation or maintenance.

This is not just an issue of semantics, however. In principle, a software development project may be cancelled at any time before its completion. Often, the method being used includes specific points at which a "stop/go" decision is to be taken. However, Baxter [7] points out that in fact there is in reality only one gate (as she terms such decision points), at the end of what she terms the feasibility phase. As she puts it, "projects are never cancelled once started". Our own experience supports this view. Thus there is a very specific knowledge management issue in identifying knowledge relevant to this single gate.

There are many other methods for systems development; some of the principal ones are reviewed and compared in [26]. Drawing on these together with SSADM and DSDM, we obtain the following list of ten activities involved in systems development and maintenance: investigation, determine feasibility, systems analysis, system design, programming, testing, training, documentation, implementation, and maintenance/support.

Figure 1.1 gives an idea of the relationship between these various technical and functional activities of software engineers. It is not intended to be an exact representation, because the time spent on activities varies from one project to the next, and there will be loops back. Also shown in Fig. 1.1, there are in addition two higher-level activities: project management, control, and people management (users, clients, project team). For the remainder of this chapter, we shall keep this list in our minds as our description of "what software engineers do".

1.2.4 Is Software Engineering Knowledge Work?

Let us now consider whether software engineering qualifies as knowledge work at all. Newell et al. suggest [42] that knowledge work has three particular distinctive characteristics. The first two of these are autonomy and co-location. Autonomy of the workers is a consequence of the creativity and problem-solving aspects of the work. Creativity and problem solving have long been recognized as vital elements of software engineering. Clearly, therefore, this feature is present. Co-location is described by Newell et al. as "the need to work remote from the employing firm, typically physically located at the client firm". This does not apply to all software engineers, but it is a definite feature of the profession, as seen in the widespread use of contractors and the outsourcing of either or both of development and maintenance work. Newell et al. comment that "The client firm might therefore be in direct competition with the employing firm for the services of knowledge workers" will strike a chord with many in the IT industry.

The third feature identified by Newell et al. is that knowledge workers are "gold collar" workers, a term coined by Kelley [35]. Such workers need to be "provided with excellent working conditions and generally afforded exceptional, or at least very good, terms and conditions of employment". No doubt many software engineering professionals would challenge the notion that their pay and conditions are excellent as a matter of principle, but by and large they do receive a better remuneration and benefits package than their opposite numbers in many other jobs. For example, the average salary for graduates entering IT jobs in the UK is typically 10% higher than the average for all graduates.

We can safely conclude, therefore, that software engineering is knowledge work, and hence that knowledge management is of high importance in software engineering—or at least it should be. We now go on to look at the problematic issues in software engineering and its management.

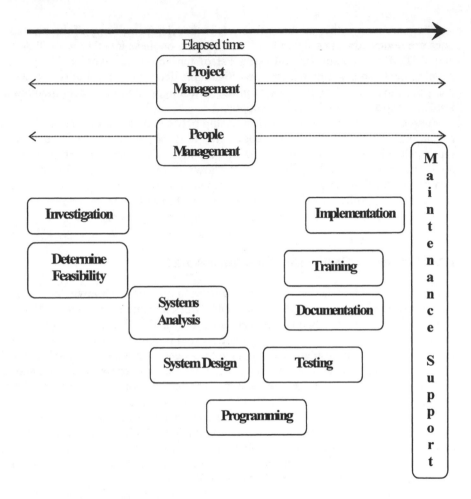

Fig. 1.1. Software engineering activities

1.3 Problematic Areas in Software Engineering

Various authors have studied software engineers and software engineering over many years [5, 7, 28, 36, 39, 46, 63]. Combining their views with our own experience, we see that among the problematic features particular to this profession are:

- The tension between systems development and maintenance/support work
- A combination of organizational and technical aspects
- The nature of team working

- A combination of generic skills and extremely specific skills
- Constant change, some of it externally imposed
- The need for a quick response coupled with long system lifetimes

1.3.1 The Tension Between Systems Development and Maintenance/Support Work

Fundamentally, the work of software engineering splits into two parts—development and maintenance. These can be characterized (or perhaps caricatured) as the creative, interesting, exciting part and the boring, routine, annoying part, respectively. Glass [23] points out that software engineering theory tended to ignore maintenance for many years, perhaps for this reason. Naturally, as with almost all such categorizations, there is a grey area in the middle where the two overlap. An important consequence of this division in the work, however, is that in many cases there is a corresponding split into separate teams. This is a distinct obstacle to successful knowledge management, because it is as important to share knowledge between the two "functions" as within them. The maintenance team needs access to knowledge about how a system was developed, but equally the development team might well benefit from knowledge of maintenance issues relating to a similar system developed previously. Sharing knowledge across teams is bound to be more difficult than within teams.

1.3.2 A Combination of Organizational and Technical Aspects

The discussion in the Sect. 1.2 identified that that there are both technical and organizational or managerial aspects to a software engineer's work. It is also important to realize that very few of those involved in software engineering have only technical or only organizational or managerial responsibilities. Table 1.1 shows a broad characterization of the relationship between these responsibilities and the activities identified earlier. This balance, or indeed tension, between technical and organizational activities is an issue to which we shall return later.

1.3.3 The Nature of Team Working

Another relevant feature is that software engineers—and especially software *developers*—normally work in groups. However, compared to similar groups in other professions, software development groups change very rapidly. For this reason, Baxter [7] prefers to call them coalitions rather than teams. Perlow [46] reports that although individuals worked together, success meant doing high-visibility work, and that this was associated with the individual rather than the team. The knowledge management implications of this are readily apparent. Sharing knowledge is necessary to get the work done, but the rapidly changing membership of the team/coalition means that the basis of the knowledge is often an individual rather than a group. As Perlow found, helping others is often seen as a distraction rather than something that is rewarded by management.

Table 1.1. The different aspects of various software engineering activities

Activity	Main responsibilities (in descending order)
Investigation	Organizational
Determine feasibility	Organizational
Systems analysis	Organizational, technical
System design	Technical, organizational
Programming	Technical, managerial
Testing	Technical, managerial, organizational
Training	Organizational, managerial
Documentation	Technical, managerial
Implementation	Organizational, technical, managerial
Maintenance/support	Technical, organizational, managerial
Project management and control	Organizational, managerial
People management	Managerial

1.3.4 A Combination of Generic Skills and Extremely Specific Skills

Skills possessed by software engineers are a curious combination of the very general and the very specific. A database administrator, for example, needs to have not only generic knowledge about the principles of database design and structure, but also very detailed specific knowledge about the particular software package version, hardware configuration and operating system for which she is responsible [4]. This is by no means unique to software engineers; a similar problem applies to automobile mechanics, for example. However, the balance between the general and the specific seems far less clear in software engineering than in many other professions. For example, when does knowledge about a particular facet of database design in Oracle 8I on a Unix platform override more general knowledge of database design principles?

1.3.5 Constant Change, Some of It Externally Imposed

Change increases the importance of knowledge management whilst simultaneously making it more difficult to do it effectively. A further degree of control over potential change is lost because most of the changes faced by software engineers are, to a greater or lesser extent, externally imposed. At the highest level, if a government decides to change the way in which a particular tax is calculated, then all systems relating to that tax have to be amended. However, in another sense, most of what software engineers do is externally determined, because it is client driven. Thus there is the need to anticipate change, as well as to react to it.

1.3.6 The Need for a Quick Response Coupled with Long System Lifetimes

This raises an issue of what knowledge to keep, and what to discard. At one extreme, keep everything, and the response provided to a query or problem is likely to get slower and slower. At the other, keep only what is used daily, and you will soon find yourself in trouble for example, when reports or procedures that are only run annually come along. The tradition that documentation is the poor relation in software development does not help matters here.

1.4 Previous Work on Knowledge Management in Software Engineering

As we said at the start of the chapter, there are relatively few "mainstream" articles about knowledge management in software engineering, for example, as defined by the result of a keyword search. However, the situation is beginning to change, including eight articles in a special May/June 2002 issue of *IEEE Software*. The article by the guest editors for that issue, Rus and Lindvall [49], gives a good overview of the present state of the art, as does Chap. 4 of this book, contributed by the same authors [38].

Carter [13] interviews Kathy Schoenherr, a software engineering manager about knowledge management in her organization, an American insurance company. Schoenherr identifies three categories of activity in software engineering where knowledge management can contribute:

- Problem tracking and resolution
- Method documentation
- Human resource issues

She also argues that effective use of knowledge management would allow more *sharing* of analysis and design from previous applications. (Again, the remainder of the article is about knowledge management more generally, not specifically knowledge management in software engineering.)

Hellstrom et al. [27] use a software engineering firm as an example of what they call the "decentralized management of knowledge work". They argue that top-down approaches to knowledge management are inappropriate in such circumstances, and propose instead that "semiorganized" knowledge exchange, or brokerage, between individuals is most effective. This approach resonates with the view sometimes heard expressed that managing software engineers is like herding cats!

Kautz et al. also look at knowledge management, specifically knowledge creation, in a small Danish software house [34]. They look in particular at the role of IT systems in knowledge management and discuss various tasks as knowledge processes, especially quality assurance for the software. They conclude that the IT systems played "an important, yet subordinate role". Openness, trust and mutual respect were vital in enabling learning to take place.

Doctoral theses (which have an inevitable three- or four-year time lag) are also beginning to appear in the area of knowledge management in software engineering, for example those of Birk [8], Dingsøyr [16] and van Aalst [57]. Some of Dingsøyr's work may also be found in Chap. 3 of this book [17].

1.4.1 Knowledge Management by Another Name?

As well as the research outlined above, there is also much work that is relevant to knowledge management in software engineering that does not actually call itself knowledge management, either by choice (especially in the case of some of the conferences referred to earlier), or because the term was not current when the article was written. There are three strands of relevant work, one being that on professional expertise in software engineering, a second on learning and experience in software engineering, and the third on the use of knowledge-based systems in software engineering.

1.4.1.1 Professional Expertise in Software Engineering

We have already drawn on this literature in our earlier discussions, including [22]. The work in this strand stresses that knowledge is socially constructed. Although there must be limits to the extent to which this affects, say, a work-around for a bug in a COBOL compiler, the organizational dimension of software engineering knowledge management is clearly dependent on this. Scarbrough [51] explains this position well.

Williams and Procter discuss IT expertise in a bank, using an extended case study [60]. They use a typology developed by Winstanley [61] to identify four different situations for the software engineer, according to the power that their expertise possesses in internal (within their own organization) and external labor markets. This is shown in Table 1.2.

Table 1.2. Winstanley's typology [61]

	Undeveloped internal labor market	Developed internal labor market
Positive worker power in external labor market	A. Independent mobile professional	B. Company professional
Negative worker power in external labor market	C. Insecure contract worker	D. Dependent worker

Expertise in this context appears to mean the same as what we have termed knowledge. The external labor market has a strong component of technical knowledge. The internal labor market has a strong element of organizational knowledge. Williams and Procter identified three teams of software engineers (including all roles from programmers up to management) within the bank who fell into three different categories in the typology. The first team was very technically oriented, and their knowledge related mainly to programming languages and technology. They thus fell into category A, independent mobile professionals. A second team, although possessing strong programming knowledge, relied even more on its internal reputation—earned by knowledge of the bank's systems. They come into category B, company professionals. The third team had a much broader range of knowledge, but not the same in-depth knowledge of any area as the other two. They came under category D, dependent workers.

Newell et al. [42] continue to draw on this school of work, although nowadays with an explicit knowledge management label. They remark that IT experts are increasingly subject to market pressures, because of developments such as the rise in outsourcing and the use of consultants, and that this tends to dilute the role of the profession in regulating abstract knowledge. In the Williams and Procter/Winstanley terms, software engineers are being pushed from category A to category C, and from category B to category D. This substantially increases the knowledge management problems for user organizations, who are becoming more and more dependent on their "providers" for software knowledge. It will also have adverse effects on the attitude of the software engineers towards sharing their knowledge, especially for those in category C.

Where the outsourcing or consultancy is provided from another country, the problems will be still more acute. Davenport and Prusak [15] explain the need for face-to-face meetings to facilitate knowledge sharing. Edwards and Kidd [20] describe some of the additional problems of cross-border knowledge management.

1.4.1.2   Learning and Experience in Software Engineering

A central element of this strand is the "experience factory" work referred to earlier [5]. More recent papers drawing on the earlier work [52, 29] describe DaimlerChrysler's implementation of an Experience Center in software engineering. These ideas have now spread widely; for an Australian example see [37], and also [11, 14]. The thrust of this work involves robust processes with a strong emphasis on managing the people as well as the software systems. There are strong connections between this strand of work and the extensive literature on learning organizations, much of which was inspired by the work of Senge [54].

1.4.1.3   Knowledge-Based Systems in Software Engineering and More Generally

This strand of work also has a long history, although just as most knowledge management research about software engineering firms is not specifically related to software engineering, so most knowledge-based systems in software engineering firms are not specifically related to software engineering either. One of the themes that carries over into knowledge management work has been that of understanding the nature of what software engineers do. See, for example, all eight of the articles in Part I of the collection edited by Partridge [43].

The more important lessons from past research or applications in this strand are often not the knowledge-based systems that were created (or even in some cases that failed to be created), but the processes of knowledge elicitation and representation that the developers, experts and users went through. For example, the issues of work in teams and the balance between general and specific knowledge were central to the work of Barrett and Edwards [4] on a system for database design and maintenance. No fewer than eight layers of expertise, from the most general to the most specific, were identified. Different experts proposed different solutions to a problem, and some means of "adjudicating" between them was necessary. A "knowledge czar" approach—nominating someone as the senior expert—was chosen.

A great deal of knowledge-based systems work in software engineering has been carried out at the Fraunhofer Institute for Experimental Software Engineering (IESE). Examples of this can be found in [10] and in some of the papers in [2], and Chap. 11 of this book gives the current position [3].

More generally in the knowledge-based systems field, one of the most widely used methods for building knowledge-based systems, CommonKADS, an extension of the earlier KADS [53, 58], is based on a philosophy of knowledge modeling. CommonKADs incorporates no fewer than six types of model: organizational, task, agent, expertise, communication, and design. There are libraries of common problem-solving methods and extensive ontologies. Knowledge modeling surely is one approach to knowledge management, but the knowledge management literature makes virtually no reference to KADS or CommonKADS at all.

1.5 Potential for Knowledge Management

Let us now attempt gradually to bring these diverse themes together. Picking up the earlier theme from Kautz et al. [34], there have been many studies over the years of the psychological profiles and personality traits of computer programmers and software engineers. A relatively recent example by Wynekoop and Walz [62] is interesting in that it considers programmers, systems analysts and project managers separately. Many previous studies have either considered only one of these groups, or have combined all of them together. Wynekoop and Walz found that the three groups differed both from each other, and from the general population:

> The picture that emerges is that IS personnel are more conventional, conscientious, diligent, dependable, organized, logical, and analytical than the general population. However, systems analysts and managers also possess more leadership characteristics, and are more ambitious hardworking and creative with more self-confidence and a stronger self-image. Programmers, on the other hand, are more inflexible and predictable and less social than the general population.

Assuming that we can equate "IS personnel", as identified by Wynekoop and Walz, with software engineers, a further important point is that their results confirmed earlier findings that software engineers *are* innovative and creative [55]. Thus both innovative/creative and analytical/technical dimensions of knowledge are present in software engineering, and both may benefit from being managed.

In order to proceed further, we present in Fig. 1.2 a model that we have used before [18]. This model takes an organizational viewpoint regarding what happens to a particular element of knowledge. First, knoeledge is created/acquired; then it goes through a cycle of retain, use and refine/update (any of these activities may be temporary, or indeed missing entirely). It may also be shared with/transferred to those outside the circle of people who originally created/acquired it, in parallel with this retain - use - refine cycle.

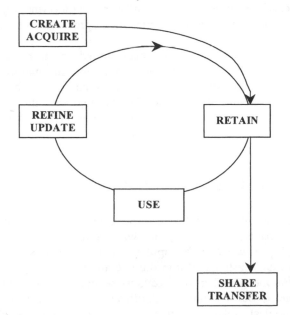

Fig. 1.2. A view of the knowledge management process

These five knowledge activities need to be considered in relation to the list of software engineering activities Sect. 1.2.3. In principle, there needs to be a process to carry out each of the knowledge activities effectively for each of the software engineering activities. In general, there can be no rules as to which is more important or easiest to do. Knowledge management must be situated in an organizational context; these priorities must be determined for any given software engineering unit at any given time.

Types of Solution: An investigation into the approaches that managers believe should be used in knowledge management [21] identified that, broadly speaking, there are three types of "solution" that can be applied in knowledge management. These are technological, people and process solutions. Although this research looked at knowledge management in general, we believe that the categories apply to knowledge management in software engineering.

Technological solutions are concerned with installing new technology or making better use of existing technology. Specific technologies in the study included data mining, databases or intranet access. Activities included standardization of hardware or software, eliminating duplicate systems or data, and in one case trying to discourage the use of privately owned personal organizers and laptops, which were seen as a barrier to sharing information and knowledge.

People solutions are concerned with staff retention and motivation, training, debriefing and networking. One organization identified the need to rely less on "training through osmosis". Significantly for software engineering, another thought the processes should involve removing their previous "culture of confidentiality".

Process solutions are concerned partly with paper-based specifications and process instructions but also with the mix between formal and informal methods of sharing knowledge. The emphasis is on "working smarter". In the study mentioned above, these solutions tended to be favored by the smaller organizations—the ones in which, at least in principle, everyone knew who everyone else was.

1.6 Overall Knowledge Management Strategy

The last element in our framework is that, broadly speaking, there are two overall strategies in knowledge management: codification and personalization, as pointed out by Hansen et al. [25]. These may be applied either separately or, more profitably, in a complementary fashion. Within the overall strategy, any or all of the three types of solution mentioned in the previous section may be deployed. Certain combinations tend to occur naturally. Codification strategies tend to be associated with technological solutions such as intranets and knowledge repositories. Personalization strategies more often favor people-based solutions such as communities of practice (CoPs) and storytelling. A more complementarist approach may favor process-based solutions, especially those that integrate top-down and bottom-up knowledge management concerns; see Edwards and Kidd [19] for further discussion of the latter. We now look at the possibilities for each of these three strategies in software engineering knowledge management.

1.6.1 Codification Strategies

Some software engineers might be more sympathetic to a codification strategy. The work of Wynekoop and Walz [62] suggests that this ought to be especially true of programmers. Codification strategies seem appropriate when the "right answer" from one context is easily transferable to another. Thus sharing knowledge about programming issues should be suited to this strategy. There has indeed been a considerable amount of work on tools to support programming and design work (two of the most technical activities from Table 1.1). These include so-called Computer Aided System Engineering (CASE) tools and designer workbenches. These are most useful for retain, share and use activities in knowledge management; they provide little support for refining knowledge and none for creating knowledge.

Problem tracking and resolution, and method documentation, identified earlier as categories of knowledge management activity, also seem to be targets for codification strategies. There is, however, a snag here: Much of this work has concentrated on retaining and sharing knowledge within a single project. As was argued by Schoenherr [13], effective sharing of analysis and design knowledge *between* applications is a major potential benefit.

The more concrete products of the knowledge-based systems work on software engineering mentioned earlier also correspond to a codification approach to knowledge management.

1.6.2 Personalization Strategies

Having identified codification strategies as best suited to the more technical activities within software engineering, personalization strategies by implication are more suited to the managerial and/or organizational activities. Personalization strategies can be very effective for creating and refining knowledge, and also effective for sharing and retaining it. They provide less direct help in using it.

Human resource issues in software engineering are clearly candidates for a personalization strategy for knowledge management. Most of the discussion by Hellstrom et al. [27] concerns successful personalization strategies. The professional expertise and learning and experience strands of research into software engineering also ally themselves naturally with this viewpoint. We would argue that the managerial activities (i.e. those relating directly to the people involved with the project) are those where a personalization strategy is likely to be most successful, along with higher-level technical activities such as those in analysis and implementation where Creating and Refining knowledge is crucial, i.e. existing solutions aren't good enough.

1.6.3 Complementary Strategies

Our view is that, while codification and personalization both have their place, a complementary strategy is the most effective. This must involve process-based solutions, often to link technological- and people-based ones. How, for example, does an organization ensure that knowledge created in a community of practice is then successfully retained? What elements can be stored in some kind of repository, and what cannot? Post mortems, as advocated by Birk, Dingsøyr and Stålhane [9], are useful under all types of strategy. In a personalization strategy, a post mortem aids both individual and group understanding, while in a codification strategy, it assists in determining what documents, databases and so on are worth keeping.

The paper by Kautz et al. [34] is a good example of a complementary strategy towards knowledge management using IT for codification where it is appropriate, but also employing a range of other approaches. The knowledge-based systems work where the emphasis was on elicitation of the knowledge rather than building a system also fits well into this category.

1.6.4 The Importance of Cultural Issues

Although we come to this heading last, research suggests that in many ways culture generally is the most important aspect of knowledge management [50, 42]. Software engineering should be no exception, because most of the emphasis in the process improvement and experience approaches is on understanding and controlling the process and the product. This must be a shared rather than an individual understanding, or else there is no guarantee that the process will be repeatable. Individuals may excel in creating or using knowledge (to use the Fig. 1.2 terminology), but successful knowledge management in software engineering means an emphasis on retaining and sharing knowledge, whether the overall strategy is codification, personalization, or both. This can only be achieved with an appropriately supportive knowledge-sharing culture [56, 32]. Such a culture may not come naturally to all software engineers or their departments, given the findings of Wynekoop and Walz [62] that programmers are less social than average, and the rewarding of individual heroics found by Perlow [46].

Crucially, such a culture needs to be generated both from the top down, from management expectations and leadership, and from the bottom up, from the community of software engineers within the organization [19].

A final cultural issue is that knowledge management in software engineering may not involve just the software engineers. The culture of the users may be important too. Al-Karaghouli et al. [1] discuss a system to help what they term the system developers and their customers to understand and communicate with each other. However, such a technological solution will be of little help unless the customers also trust the developers, whether they are external consultants, or in-house colleagues.

1.7 Conclusion and Summary

The way in which software engineering is organized has changed substantially over the past 35 years, but many of the knowledge management issues have not. Software engineers face issues connected with technical, managerial and organizational activities. The balance between these activities depends both on the particular individual's job, and the context they are working in at any given time. Among the principal challenges to be faced are:

- Software engineering is knowledge work. Effective knowledge management is therefore vital in improving the professionalism of a software engineering department or unit. Analysis and design knowledge particularly needs to be shared between projects.
- The fact that projects are rarely cancelled except at the end of the feasibility study makes retaining knowledge about how to make this stop/go decision crucial.
- The division between development and maintenance can easily become a split with dire consequences if knowledge management is not performed well, especially sharing knowledge between individuals and teams.
- Rapid turnover of staff makes it important to retain continuity of knowledge. However, the high workloads that are in part a consequence of this high turnover mean a lack of time for knowledge sharing and for reflective activities such as knowledge refinement.
- Software engineering knowledge contains an unusually complex combination of different layers of expertise, from the very general to the very specific. This is especially problematic when using knowledge.
- The culture of the department or unit, and indeed the organization it is part of, must encourage a bottom up "buy in" to knowledge management activities that matches the knowledge management strategies employed from the top down.

Despite the many problems, effective knowledge management in software engineering is possible. There are technological, people and process-based solutions, and the best approach is surely a combination of all three within an overall knowledge management strategy that includes both personalization and codification elements. At least any obstacles facing software engineers are not related to technical issues of computer support for knowledge management, since using computer-based tools poses few such problems for software engineers. The most important aspect overall, however, is to develop a culture that encourages both knowledge sharing and reflection.

References

1. Al-Karaghouli W., Fitzgerald G., Alshawi S. (2002) Knowledge requirements systems: an approach to improving and understanding requirements. In: Coakes E., Willis D. Clarke S. (Eds.), Knowledge management in the sociotechnical world: the graffiti continues, Springer, Berlin Heidelberg New York, pp. 170-184
2. Althoff K.-D., Feldmann R., Müller W. (Eds.) (2001) Advances in learning software organizations. Springer, Berlin Heidelberg New York
3. Althoff K.-D., Pfahl D. (2003) Integrating experience-based knowledge management with sustained competence development. In: Aurum A., Jeffery R., Wohlin C.,

Handzic, M. (Eds), Managing software engineering knowledge, Springer, Berlin Heidelberg New York

4.   Barrett A.R., Edwards J.S. (1995) Knowledge elicitation and knowledge representation in a large domain with multiple experts. Expert systems with applications, 8: 169-176

5.   Basili V.R., Caldiera G. (1995) Improve software quality by reusing knowledge and experience. Sloan management review, 37: 55-64

6.   Basili V.R., Caldiera G., McGarry F., Pajerski R., Page G., Waligora S. (1992) The software engineering laboratory: An operational software experience factory. In: Proceedings of the 14th international conference on software engineering, Melbourne, Australia, pp. 370-381

7.   Baxter L.F. (2000) Bugged: The software development process. In: Prichard C., Hull R., Chumer M., Willmott H. (Eds.), Managing knowledge: critical investigations of work and learning, Macmillan, Basingstoke, pp. 37-48

8.   Birk A. (2000) A knowledge management infrastructure for systematic improvement in software engineering. Dr. Ing Thesis, University of Kaiserslautern, Germany

9.   Birk A., Dingsøyr T., Stålhane T. (2002) Postmortem: never leave a project without it. IEEE Software, 19: 43-45

10. Bomarius F., Althoff K.-D., Müller W. (1998) Knowledge management for learning software organizations. Software process: improvement and practice, John Wiley and Sons, West Sussex, UK, pp. 89-93

11. Brössler P. (1999) Knowledge management at a software house: An experience report. In: Learning software organizations: methodology and applications. In: Ruhe G. Bomarius F. (Eds.) Lecture Notes in Computer Science, Springer Berlin, Heidelberg New York, 1756: 163-170

12. Bryant A. (2000) It's engineering Jim; but not as we know it: software engineering, solution to the software crisis or part of the problem? In: Proceedings of 22nd international conference on software engineering Limerick, Ireland, pp. 78-87

13. Carter B. (2000) The expert's opinion: knowledge management. Journal of database management, 11: 42-43

14. Chatters B. (1999) Implementing an experience factory: maintenance and evolution of the software and systems development process. In: Proceedings of the IEEE International conference on software maintenance, Oxford, UK, pp. 146-151

15. Davenport T.H., Prusak L. (1998) Working knowledge: how organizations manage what they know. Harvard business school press, Boston, USA

16. Dingsøyr T. (2002) Knowledge management in medium-sized software consulting companies. PhD Thesis, Norwegian University of Science and Technology, Norway

17. Dingsøyr T., Conradi R. (2003) Usage of intranet tools for knowledge management in medium-sized software consulting companies. In: Aurum A., Jeffery R., Wohlin C. Handzic M. (Eds.), Managing software engineering knowledge, Springer, Berlin Heidelberg, New York

18. Edwards J.S. (2000) Artificial intelligence and knowledge management: How much difference can it really make? In: Proceedings of KMAC2000, (Eds), Edwards J.S., Kidd J.B. (Eds.) Operational research society, Aston university, Birmingham, UK, pp. 136-147

19. Edwards J. S., Kidd J.B. (2001) Knowledge management when "the times they are a-changing". In: Proceedings of 2nd European conference on knowledge management, Bled, Slovenia, 171-183

20. Edwards J.S., Kidd J.B. (2003) Knowledge management sans frontières. Journal of the operational research society, 54: 130-139
21. Edwards J.S., Shaw D., Collier P.M. (2002) Group perceptions of knowledge management. In: Proceedings of 3rd European conference on knowledge management, Dublin, Ireland pp. 209-222
22. Friedman A.L., Cornford D.S. (1989) Computer systems development, history, organization and implementation. John Wiley and Sons, Chichester, UK
23. Glass R.L. (1996) The relationship between theory and practice in software engineering. Communications of the ACM, 39: 11-13
24. Glass R.L. (1999) The realities of software technology payoffs. Communications of the ACM, 42: 74-79
25. Hansen M.T., Nohria N., Tierney T. (1999) What's your strategy for managing knowledge? Harvard business review, 77: 106-116.
26. Harry M.J.S. (2001) Business information: A systems approach. Financial times, Prentice Hall, Harlow
27. Hellstrom T., Malmquist U., Mikaelsson J. (2001) Decentralizing knowledge: managing knowledge work in a software engineering firm. Journal of high technology management research, 12: 25-38
28. Hohmann L. (1997) Journey of the software professional: a sociology of software development. Prentice Hall, New Jersey
29. Houdek F., Schneider K., Wieser E. (1998) Establishing experience factories at Daimler-Benz: an experience report. In: Proceedings of the 20th international conference on software engineering, Kyoto, Japan, pp. 443-447
30. Hoyle D. (2001) ISO 9000 quality systems handbook. Butterworth-Heinemann, London UK
31. http://www.sqi.gu.edu.au/SPICE/ The software process improvement and capability dEtermination Website, (accessed November 6, 2002)
32. Huber G.P. (2000) Transferring sticky knowledge: Suggested solutions and needed studies. In: Proceedings of knowledge management beyond the hype: looking towards the new millennium, Edwards, J.S., Kidd, J.B. (Eds.), Operational research society, Birmingham, pp. 12-22
33. Humphrey W.S. (1989) Managing the software process. Addison-Wesley, Reading, MA, USA
34. Kautz K., Thaysen K., Vendelø M.T. (2002) Knowledge creation and IT systems in a small software firm. OR Insight, 15: 11-17
35. Kelley R. (1990) The gold collar worker: harnessing the brainpower of the new workforce. Addison-Wesley, Reading, MA
36. Kidder T.L. (1981) The soul of a new machine. Avon, New York
37. Koennecker A., Jeffery R., Low G. (2000) Implementing an experience factory based on existing organizational knowledge. In: Proceedings of the Australian software engineering conference, Canberra Australia, pp. 53-62
38. Lindvall M., Rus I. (2003) Knowledge management in software engineering. In: Aurum A., Jeffery R., Wohlin C., Handzic M. (Eds.), Managing software engineering knowledge, Springer, Berlin Heidelberg New York
39. Moody F. (1990) I sing the body electric: a year with Microsoft on the multimedia frontier. Viking, New York

40. Mouritsen J., Larsen H.T., Bukh P.N., Johansen M.R. (2001) Reading an intellectual capital statement: describing and prescribing knowledge management strategies. Journal of intellectual capital, 2: 359-383
41. Naur P., Randell B. (Eds.) (1969) Software engineering: report on a conference sponsored by the NATO science committee, Garmisch, Germany
42. Newell S., Robertson M., Scarbrough H., Swan J. (2002) Managing knowledge work. Palgrave, Basingstoke
43. Partridge D. (Ed.) (1991) Artificial intelligence and software engineering. Ablex, Norwood, NJ, USA
44. Paulk M.C., Curtis B., Chrissis M.B., Weber C.V. (1993) Capability maturity model, Version 1.1. IEEE Software, 10: 18-27
45. Paulk M.C., Weber, C.V., Curtis B. (1995) The capability maturity model: guidelines for improving the software process. Addison-Wesley, Reading, MA
46. Perlow L.A. (1999) The time famine: Toward a sociology of work time. Administrative science quarterly, 44: 57-81
47. Randell B. (1996) The 1968/69 NATO software engineering reports. Presented at Dagstuhl-Seminar 9635: "History of software engineering", Schloss Dagstuhl, Germany, 26-30 August, 1996
48. Rosenberg L.H. (2003) Lessons learned in software quality assurance. In: Aurum A., Jeffery R., Wohlin C., Handzic M. (Eds.), Managing software engineering knowledge, Springer, Berlin Heidelberg New York
49. Rus I., Lindvall M. (2002) Knowledge management in software engineering. IEEE Software, 19: 26-38
50. Scarbrough H. (1996a) The management of expertise. Macmillan Business, Basingstoke
51. Scarbrough H. (1996b) Strategic IT in financial services: the social construction of strategic knowledge. In: Scarbrough H. (Ed.), The management of expertise Macmillan, Basingstoke, pp. 150-173
52. Schneider K., von Hunnius J.-P., Basili V.R. (2002) Experience in implementing a learning software organization. IEEE Software, 19: 46-49
53. Schreiber A.T., Wielinga B.J., Akkermans J.M., van de Velde W., de Hoog R. (1994) CommonKADS: a comprehensive methodology for KBS development. IEEE Expert, 9: 28-37
54. Senge P.M. (1990) The fifth discipline, the art and practice of the learning organization. Doubleday, New York
55. Sitton S., Chmelir G. (1984) The intuitive computer programmer. Datamation, 30: 137-140
56. Snowden D. (2000) Cynefin, a sense of time and place: an ecological approach to sense making and learning in formal and informal communities. In: Proceedings of KMAC2000, Edwards J.S., Kidd J.B. (Eds.), Operational research society, Birmingham, UK, pp. 1-11
57. van Aalst J.-W. (2001) Knowledge management in courseware development. PhD Thesis, Delft University of Technology, Delft, The Netherlands
58. van Heijst G., Schreiber A.T., Weilinga B.J. (1997) Using explicit ontologies in KBS development. International journal of human-computer studies, 46: 183-292
59. Weaver P.L. (1993) Practical SSADM 4. Pitman, London

60. Williams R., Procter, R. (1998) Trading places: a case study of the formation and deployment of computing expertise. In: Williams R., Faulkner W., Fleck, J. (Eds.), Exploring expertise: issues and perspectives, Macmillan, Basingstoke, pp. 197-222
61. Winstanley D. (1986) Recruitment strategies as a means of managerial control of technical labor. In: Proceedings of labor process conference, Aston University, Birmingham, UK
62. Wynekoop J.L., Walz D.B. (1998) Revisiting the perennial question: are IS people different? Database for advances in information systems, 29: 62-72
63. Zachary G.P. (1994) Showstopper! the breakneck race to create Windows NT and the next generation at Microsoft. Free Press, New York

Author Biography

John S. Edwards is Professor of Operational Research and Systems at Aston Business School, Birmingham, UK. His principal research interests are in knowledge management and decision support, especially methods and processes for system development. He has published more than 60 research papers on these topics, and two books, *Building Knowledge-Based Systems* and *Decision Making with Computers*. Current work includes the transferability of best practices in knowledge management, linking knowledge-based systems with simulation models to improve organizational learning, and an investigation of knowledge management in organizations using group facilitation techniques. He is also editor of the journal *Knowledge Management Research and Practice*.

2 An Investigation into Software Development Process Knowledge

June M. Verner and William M. Evanco

Abstract: Knowledge management elevates individual knowledge to the organizational level by capturing and sharing information and turning it into organizational knowledge. In order to provide a better understanding of the most serious software project risks and the interrelations among risks, we collected software project data from developers. This data includes information about senior management, customers and users, requirements, estimation and scheduling, the project manager, the software development process, and development personnel. In order to elevate our data to organizational knowledge we conducted a variety of studies on this data and found that the most critical success factor was good requirements. Other critical success factors were either influenced by the requirements, or themselves influenced the development of the requirements.

Keywords: Software project success, Critical success factors, Software development, Developer perspective

2.1 Introduction

Developing software systems is an expensive, often difficult process with high failure rates. While one recent study found that 20% of software projects failed, and 46% experienced cost and schedule overruns or significantly reduced functionality [41], another study suggested that failure rates for software development projects are as high as 85% [31]. Software development projects are plagued with too many problems, such as poor project management, cost and schedule overruns, poor software quality, and under-motivated developers [5, 9, 65]. Development failures lead to a lack of credibility and to communication problems among software developers, senior management, customers, and users, which in turn makes software development an even more difficult task [23, 24].

Despite extensive research into and many guidelines for successful software development, systems still fail [7, 42, 46, 51]. The majority of organizations have software development practices that keep them at level 1 on the Software Engineering Institute's capability maturity model (CMM) scale [32]. Few project post mortems are conducted [65], little understanding is gained from the results of previous projects within the organization, and past mistakes continue in new projects. Too frequently, key development practices are ignored and early warning signs that lead to project failure are not understood. Of course, it is hard to capture lessons learned and there are few incentives to use prior knowledge, especially when the project manager is under pressure [57].

Much of the literature regarding project failure is from the customer/user perspective [22, 33, 72]. But it is just as important to recognize the effect that project failure has on development staff. Troubled projects cause developers to suffer long hours of unpaid overtime, loss of motivation, and burnout, leading to excessive staff turnover and its associated costs. Developers have acquired valuable individual experience from each project with which they have been involved. Organizations and individuals could gain much insight if they could share such knowledge [59].

From the discussion above, it is clear that the ability of the project manager to understand the consequences of actions taken during the development process and the effect that various decisions have on the development outcome are critical to project success. Identifying project success and failure factors and their consequences as early as possible may provide valuable clues that help the project manager to improve the software development process.

A quantitative approach to software development is in alignment with the 1998 NSF Software Research Program for the 21st Century Workshop findings [3, 6, 45]. The participants at this workshop suggested that future research activities should "develop the empirical science underlying software as rapidly as possible" and to "analyze how some organizations have learned to build no-surprise systems in stable environments. By extracting principles from these analyses, empirical research can help enlarge the no-surprise envelope." Our research fits into this quantitative approach providing a better understanding of the most serious project risks, the interrelations among risk factors, and their impacts on project failure probabilities.

Factors affecting software project success and failure can be classified as risks, critical success factors, and mitigants. Risks involve events in the development environment or situations in the external environment that threaten project success. Knowledge management can be viewed as a risk prevention and mitigation strategy because it addresses risks that are too often ignored [59]. Critical success factors are the handful of factors that the development team must ensure are present; in their absence, failure of the project is highly probable[1]. Mitigants are actions or activities in which the development team can engage once a risk appears to be likely.

2.2 Software Development Process Research

Risks, critical success factors, and mitigants are related to project success and failure in a very complex fashion. It is the long-range goal of our research to use knowledge management to shed light on these complex interrelationships and to provide a tool that project managers can use to better manage their development projects. Knowledge management elevates individual knowledge to the

---

[1] This is a probabilistic definition of critical success factors rather than the deterministic definition often used.

organizational level by capturing and sharing this information and turning it into knowledge that the organization can access [59]. The development of automated tools could provide the project manager with more objective criteria for the prediction of project outcomes and an early warning of potential problems. Our thesis is that there will be fewer software development failures if project managers improve their understanding of the project success determinants at a conceptual level. An automated project management tool could help project managers and software development teams evaluate the likelihood of a successful project outcome and better understand the risks associated with a project. They would be able to perform "what if" analyses that would enable them to determine areas in which the concentration of scarce resources will ensure the best project outcomes.

Our research approach is unique in its focus on software practitioners and their perspectives. From industry interviews, we know that the software practitioner perspective is extremely valuable to the discipline of software engineering in general, and to the management of the software development process in particular. Support for this approach is provided by a number of process quality improvement models (e.g., CMM, ISO 9000 and Software Process Improvement and Capability dEtermination (SPICE)) which are based on the widely held belief that improving the software development process improves the quality of the software product [50, 66].

We are engaged in a series of research projects and are in the process of developing comprehensive statistical models that relate software development risks, critical success factors, and mitigants to help project managers predict software project success or failure. The data used to calibrate our models come from extensive case studies of real life projects, interviews with software practitioners, and survey questionnaires. Methodologies based on multiple and logistic regression, principal component analysis, and Bayesian belief networks serve as a basis for the development of the predictive models.

Our research agenda fits with that suggested by Fenton and Neil [21]. They noted that the future for software metrics lies in using relatively simple existing metrics to build management decision-support tools that combine different aspects of software development and testing. This will enable managers to make many kinds of predictions, assessments, and trade-offs during the software life-cycle. They note that we need to handle the key factors largely missing from the usual metrics approaches, namely: causality, uncertainty, and combining different (sometimes subjective) evidence. Thus, they suggest that the way forward for software metrics research lies in causal modeling, empirical software engineering, and multi criteria decision aids. The causal model *tells the story* that is missing from the naïve approach. It can be used to help make intelligent decisions for risk reduction and to identify factors that can be controlled or influenced.

The rest of our discussion is organized as follows. We review the background to our work and other related research; this is followed by a section that reviews the general background to our work and other related research. Sect. 2.4 discusses our research approach. We then provide an outline of research completed to date and the results obtained from this research. Finally, we conclude with a discussion of our findings thus far and future research.

2.3 Background and Related Research

In Sect. 2.3.1, we review and discuss research related to the definition of software project success. In Sect. 2.3.2, we discuss the factors influencing project success and failure.

2.3.1 Project Success

Many studies have shown that project success or failure is a question of perception, and that the criteria may vary from project to project [34, 35, 48, 68, 69]. Glass [26] noted a profound difference of opinion between managers and team members concerning software project success, and our recent research agrees with his views [54]. In Linberg's [41] study of several projects, the criteria for success that had strong agreement among all the involved parties were "meets user requirements, achieves purpose, meets time scale, meets budget, happy users, and meets quality". Other researchers cite successful software development projects as having met agreed upon business objectives and being completed on time and within budget [2, 36, 41, 49, 61, 70, 71]. Still other definitions of success include the degree to which the project achieved its goals; reliability, maintainability and meeting of user requirements; user satisfaction; effective project teamwork; professional satisfaction on the part of the project manager [28, 52]; and the extent to which the software is actually used [14, 25]. Another important consideration for management is that a successful project does not result in cancellation [38, 39].

2.3.2 Factors Affecting Project Success or Failure

Factors leading to project failure are summarized below [41, 52]:

- *Estimation and scheduling failures*: Resource failures leading to conflicts of people and time, and schedule pressure
- *Requirements failures*: Poor specification of requirements, poor scope definitions, and goal failures caused by inadequate statement of project goals by management
- *Communication failures*: User contact failures including the inability to communicate with the customer/user, organizational failures caused by poor organizational structure, lack of leadership, lack of top-level management support, or excessive span of control, people management failures involving a lack of effort, stifled creativity, and personality clashes
- *Process failures*: Technology failures including failure to meet specifications, technique failures caused by the failure to use effective software development approaches and poor business processes, methodology failures with a failure to perform necessary activities; planning and control failures characterized by vague assignments and use of inadequate project management and tracking

tools; and size failures with projects that are too large for the performing organization

Although there is a significant amount of risk management literature [8, 10, 11, 30], this review is necessarily brief because of space limitations. Many researchers have investigated the components of software risk; for example, Boehm [8] suggested ten risk categories while Ropponen and Lyytinen [58] identified six categories of risk.

Based on an extensive review of the risk literature, we identified seven categories of software project risk: (1) senior management, (2) customers and users, (3) requirements, (4) estimation and scheduling, (5) the project manager, (6) software development process, and (7) development personnel [65, 63, 54, 55]. In the following paragraphs, we further discuss the seven major risk categories.

Senior management/sponsor: Inadequate management[2] practices have far-reaching implications for project success [1]. A serious project risk is lack of sponsor support [50]. Inadequate senior management and sponsor support can lead to a lack of commitment on the part of customer/users and their availability. Serious consequences may also result from interference by senior management that leaves a project manager without the authority to properly manage the project. Arbitrarily changing the project manager during the project may also have serious project consequences.

Customer/users: Lack of end-user involvement in any of the phases of the development life cycle will also have a negative impact on project success [1, 44]. While customer/user problems are one of the major contributors to failed projects [65], realistic customer expectations can reduce conflict which in turn, supports the perception of project success from both the developer and managerial standpoint [42].

Requirements: Understanding requirements is an essential critical success factor in the development of a system; a poor understanding of both the problem and its scope leads to poorly defined requirements and serious project risk [60]. If there is no clear agreement on the part of customers and users regarding the project's requirements, unrealistic expectations regarding software projects often surface [51]. Requirements continue to be a huge problem for IT development, and poor requirements are involved in most project failures [4, 26, 60]. Requirements gathering early in the development process using well-defined methodologies that result in well-documented requirements understood by all stakeholders reduces project risk [12]. In addition, well-defined procedures for changes to those requirements increase the probability of project success.

Effort estimation and scheduling: Much has been written about the detrimental effects of underestimated schedules on the development process and the resulting shortchanging of development activities [8, 50, 51]. A poor estimate of effort and schedule is often found to be a major contributor to software project failure [7].

---

[2] When we refer to management, we are referring to corporate management. Where appropriate, we will explicitly refer to a project manager.

Brooks [9] stated that more projects have gone awry for lack of calendar time than from all other causes combined. Since the late 1970s there has been on-going research into effort and schedule estimation. DeMarco [17] suggested that "the software cost estimation problem is solved" and "though software managers know what to do, they just don't do it." More recent research by Verner and Evanco [63] also shows that although many cost estimation models are available, they are not in general use. Poor requirements gathering can result in poor effort estimation, hence poor resource estimation, stressed developers, and shortchanged project activities; testing activities are usually the main casualty. Unfortunately, senior management does not always permit project managers to be involved in project estimates [63]. Perhaps if project managers were better educated in estimation techniques and methodologies, they might improve their effort and schedule estimation credibility and thus be permitted to have more involvement.

Project management: A project without a project manager, or one who does not have the appropriate background and experience, is at serious risk [65]. Inadequate project management practices also have far-reaching implications for software project success [1]. Many key project risks are associated with the management process itself, and much of good management practice is the control of pervasive and fundamental process risks [67]. Good managers do not merely accept, or worse, ignore risky aspects of the development project. However, during project execution many project managers become so busy and subject to mounting resource and time pressures that they neglect risk control procedures [56].

Effective project management is focused on people, problems, and process [19, 51]. Though most managers admit that they face more people-related problems than those of a technical nature, managers seldom manage that way [18] as they are generally not schooled in managing the sociological aspects of software development [16].

Developers: The impact of developers on the software development process is critical both in terms of what they do and with whom they interact. Lack of project control that results in developers working long hours without adequate rewards, and the associated negative effects on their personal lives, are serious risks to the success of a project [15]. Most productivity studies have found that motivation is a stronger influence on productivity than any other contributing factor [7, 42]. Properly motivated employees will also more readily support the achievement of broader organizational-level goals [18].

Software development process: Project risk management is just one facet of the development process. However, the analysis, tracking, and control of risks are weak areas of the development process [56]. Risk can be reduced through the improvement of the development process [32]. The idea behind the CMM is to place the process of developing software under statistical control to make it more predictable. Inappropriate life-cycle models, poor planning, monitoring, and control, and inadequate change-management procedures add significantly to project risk.

2.4 Research Approach

Our research approach is divided into pilot studies and questionnaires; each of these is described below.

2.4.1 Pilot Studies

The objective of our pilot studies was to investigate software project success, project success risk factors, and their relationships to obtain a better understanding of the success components. Such studies are instrumental in the preliminary identification of the critical success factors associated with project success.

Structured interviews formed the basis of this part of the research. The procedures used in Wohlin et al. [70] and Wohlin [71] to study the relationships between project characteristics and project success using subjective evaluation factors form the basis of some of this work. Several structured discussions with software developers from a variety of organizations took place. Initial discussions were with 25 software practitioners who were employed in the same organization. These discussions covered a number of important software development topics. Following the initial discussions, we had further discussions with another group of 21 software development personnel from a large financial/insurance institution. We identified a comprehensive list of critical success factors, risks, and mitigants. The success components identified during these discussions were later used to develop a comprehensive project success questionnaire.

2.4.2 Questionnaires

As noted above, after our structured discussions, we developed a comprehensive software project success questionnaire. All the respondents to our questionnaire were software developers. The questionnaire, which dealt with completed software projects and the factors that led to the success or otherwise of these projects, was organized under the seven headings described in Sect. 2.3.2 above, namely (1) senior management, (2) customers and users, (3) requirements, (4) estimation and scheduling, (5) project manager, (6) software development process, and (7) development personnel.   In addition, we asked (1) "Did senior management in the organization consider the project to be a success?" and (2) "Do you (the developer) consider this project was a success?" When we refer to management's perception of success, we are actually describing the developer's perception of senior management's view. Although this may appear a little strange, at the time this work was done we did not have access to a sufficient base of senior managers to obtain their views directly. As a result of this work, we discovered that developers appear to have a different view of project success from other software project stakeholders and that their perspectives on a successful project needed to be further investigated. Each of the 21 respondents from the large financial/insurance institution answered two questionnaires, one that focused on a successful project and the other on an unsuccessful project. Data from 42 software projects was thus gathered (data set 1). The software development projects in data set 1 involved from 5 to 500 software practitioners.

We subsequently held discussions with software practitioners from a number of U.S. (data set 2) organizations and asked them to complete our questionnaire. Data Set 2 includes 78 projects from a diverse group of practitioners. These respondents were from different organizations, ranging from small business IT departments to large firms that are contractors to the US Government. The employing organizations ranged from level 1 to level 4 on the CMM scale. A colleague collected data set 3, which consisted of 43 Australian projects.

We then developed a small pilot study questionnaire to investigate factors that contribute to practitioners' perceptions of project success. Twenty-nine questions relating to success were included in this questionnaire [55]. Statistical analysis including correlation analysis and factor analysis was used to develop a success definition [13, 29, 37, 40, 43]. Note that our focus is on the developer perspective.

During our pilot discussions, we collected over 80 pages of comments related to the developers' definitions of project success and factors that lead to software project success and failure. Though we have completed some data analysis, as described below, further investigation of this data is warranted.

2.5 Results

Our results are organized as follows: definition of project success, issues raised during discussions, and data analysis.

2.5.1 Definition of Project Success

A notable result of our pilot study is that software developers have a different definition of project success from that usually cited in the literature. Our results show that the practitioner view of project success consists of two parts, namely personal factors associated with the work and customer/user factors.

1. The personal factor includes a sense of achievement while working on a project, a good job was done (i.e., quality was delivered), the project work was satisfying, and the project resulted in professional growth.
2. The customer/user factors include whether the customer/users were involved, if they had realistic expectations, and whether the project met all of their requirements.

We note that there is nothing in this definition that mentions budget or schedule. Details of this part of the study can be found in [55].

2.5.2 Issues Raised During the Discussions

Discussions of software projects with the developer groups were wide ranging and resulted in the following factors being perceived as having major impacts on project success:

1. Little or no senior management support
2. Customer and user problems
3. Poor requirements
4. Project management problems, including inadequate management skills, the lack of a project manager, and midstream changes of the project manager
5. Estimation and scheduling problems, including short-changed testing and poor-quality products
6. The development process itself, including problems with the life-cycle model used, and with project monitoring and control
7. Lack of a change control system

Notably, not a single respondent addressed risk assessment, or the lack of it, when discussing failed projects. This suggests to us that, in the organizations we studied, risk assessment is not routinely part of the development process. Other findings from the discussions showed that management regarded staff turnover as a major contributor to the failure of software development projects.

2.5.3 Data Analysis

We have not conducted a complete analysis of all the data. Rather we have focused our attention thus far on management support, customers and users, requirements, and estimation and scheduling. We now describe the investigations we have completed to date. Some of the investigations involve a single data set, while other investigations analyze all three data sets.

2.5.3.1 Investigations into Estimation and Scheduling

Data set 1: Chi-square analyses related estimation and scheduling responses to success outcomes, i.e., developers' views of the success of the project and their perceptions of management's view of the projects' success. In addition, logistic regression was used to predict success from both developers' and management's views. Estimation and scheduling critical success factors significantly associated with developer's views of success were as follows:

1. Project estimates were based on appropriate requirements information
2. The ability of the project manager and developers to have input into the schedule
3. Goodness of the effort estimates

The only estimation and scheduling critical success factor that was associated with management's view of success was that the customers/users had input into the schedule [63].

Data sets 1 and 2: What was striking about the data was that in two thirds of the projects, the project manager was not involved in the initial project estimates, and in only half of these projects was the project manager able to negotiate schedule changes [63].

For the combined data (120 projects), 3 additional estimation and schedule critical success factors emerged, namely:

1. Good project estimates
2. Adequate staff
3. No late staff additions to meet an aggressive schedule

Critical success factors perceived to be important to management's view of success included: the project manager had input into the schedule and the quality of the estimates.

Logistic regression was used to predict project success for the first 42 projects (i.e., data set 1, all respondents from the same organization), and these results were compared with the 78 projects (data set 2, the diverse group of respondents). Equations developed for data set 1 were used to predict success for Data Set 2, and vice versa. The prediction equation developed from Data Set 2 was the better predictor of success for both data sets showing that the results were generalizable in this instance. It is illuminating to note that two thirds of the projects that the respondents suggested had "estimates of average quality" were underestimated, which suggests that the respondents were so accustomed to underestimates that they did not consider this to be unusual. Even worse, 85% of those projects that supposedly had above average estimates were underestimated.

Data Sets 1, 2 and 3: In order to conduct a more comprehensive analysis, the additional project data set (set 3) was added to the database of projects, the details of which are reported in [64]. This data was used to investigate the generalizability of some of the estimation and scheduling prediction equations. The majority of projects in our samples were estimated with unclear requirements. In view of the fact that 69% of our projects were underestimated, our results reiterate that it is still true that we are optimistic and assume that things will go well. Inadequate requirements severely handicap the project team's ability to apply estimation techniques and methodologies that might provide reasonable cost and schedule estimates. The most surprising results of this study are that (1) project manager involvement in the initial effort and schedule estimates was not significantly correlated with project success from either the management or developer point of view and (2) developer input to the estimates was negatively correlated with the quality of the estimates and with both success variables. While many factors impinge on project success and failure, this investigation suggests that the most important of the estimation and scheduling factors are:

1. Project estimates were based on appropriate requirements information
2. Goodness of the effort estimates
3. Taking staff leave into account
4. The effect of adding staff late to meet an aggressive schedule

Commonsense tells us that poor requirements are unlikely to lead to good effort estimates. The lack of risk assessment affects the development process, with schedule and cost underestimates leading to inadequate staffing. Staffing itself then becomes a major risk factor. Adding staff late to meet an aggressive schedule is still a problem and is perceived by both managers and developers as leading to project failure.

2.5.3.2 Investigations of Management Support, Customers and Users, and Requirements

Data Set 1: Analysis of data set 1 resulted in the identification of the following management, customer/user, and requirements critical success factors from the developers' perspective:

1. Lasting sponsor commitment
2. The level of customer/user confidence in the development team
3. Level of customer involvement
4. Customers/users stayed through the project
5. Realistic customer expectations
6. Requirements were completed adequately, were good overall
7. Customers/users involved in requirements gathering

Data Sets 1 and 2: In a study of the combined data set of 120 projects, described in detail in Procaccino et al. [53], developers' views of success were explained by the following critical success factors:

1. The level of customer/user confidence in the development team
2. Level of customer involvement
3. Customers/users involved in requirements gathering
4. The size of the project was large and affected requirements elicitation

Management's view of success was explained only by the scope of the project being well-defined. Because the data consisted of two data sets, we were able to investigate the generalizability of our results. Logistic regression models developed from data set 1 and applied to data set 2 correctly predicted 80% of the successful projects from the developers' point of view and 57% of the successful projects from management's point of view. Regression models calibrated from data set 2 and then applied to data set 1 correctly predicted 73% of the projects with regard to developer success and 88% of the projects with regard to management success. "Good" prediction was suggested by Boehm [7] to be within 25% of actual values at least 75% of the time. Hence, predictions of 80% and 88% can be considered good from Boehm's perspective.

Data Sets 1 and 2, path analysis: Further research by Evanco et al. [20] applied a number of statistical techniques including tetrachoric correlation analysis, path analysis, probit regression analysis, and Bayesian belief networks to the data from data sets 1 and 2. These methodologies allowed us to investigate cause/effect models within the software development process.

Path analysis, like any other statistical technique cannot prove causality, but it can serve to test the goodness-of-fit of a theorized causal model based on correlation among independent and dependent variables. The steps we used in developing our path analysis diagrams were as follows: based on our extensive review of the literature and the results of the previously cited studies, we constructed an a priori theoretical model of relationships among a number of dichotomous variables (i.e., yes/no or high/low) with their proposed causal linkages supported by tetrachoric correlational analysis.

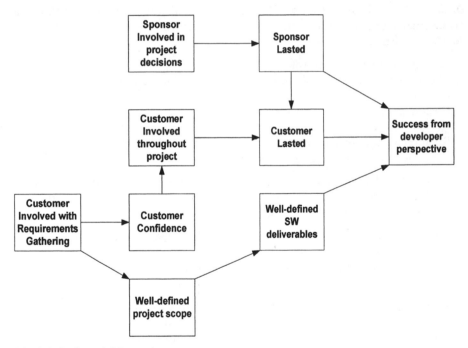

Fig. 2.1. Path model for project success

The path model is depicted graphically in Fig. 2.1. As shown in Fig. 2.1, if customers/users devote adequate time to the requirements gathering process, we might expect a higher probability of a well-defined project scope. In turn, a well-defined project scope will lead to well-defined software deliverables. Involvement in requirements gathering and interaction with the developers will also instill greater confidence on the part of the customer/user with respect to the development team. Customer/user confidence, in turn, may result in a greater level of customer involvement throughout the rest of the project. This involvement can include milestone and progress reviews, user interface testing, development of test cases, and acceptance testing.

If the sponsor is involved in project decisions, we might expect the probability that the sponsor remains committed throughout the project to increase. Similarly, both the level of customer involvement in various aspects of the development process and the sponsor remaining committed throughout the project, increases the probability that the customer will last through the project. Finally, from the point of view of the project developers, project success is governed by both the sponsor and customer lasting through the project and the ability to produce well-defined software deliverables.

A test of the overall model fit is the generalized squared multiple correlation [62, 47], whose value was calculated to be 0.64. We also ran a probity regression analysis for the success variable with the eight variables included without regard to causality. We found an $R^2=0.40$, which is substantially less than the generalized square multiple correlation. The model's generalized squared multiple correlation being greater than the R^2 for the overall regression model is evidence that our proposed model is a *good* fit based on the overall correlation of the observed data.

Finally, from the probity estimates for the various paths, we computed the probabilities for each of the two dichotomous dependent variables. These probabilities were used in a Bayesian belief network model to compute the probabilities of success given the possible values of the independent dichotomous variables, *customer involved with requirements gathering* and *sponsor involved in project decisions*. The probabilities ranged from 55% when both variables had "no" answers to 68% when both variables had "yes" answers. Thus, customer and sponsor involvement increase the likelihood of project success.

2.6 Discussion

The analyses we have conducted thus far focused on data relating to only four of the seven major software project success categories we identified earlier, namely senior management, customers/users, requirements, and estimation and scheduling. The data for the other four categories still requires detailed analysis.

Using knowledge management techniques that can elevate individual knowledge to the organizational level, we have identified a number of critical success factors for software development projects. Our investigations suggest that the most important of the estimation and scheduling factors are:

1. Project estimates were based on appropriate requirements information
2. Goodness of the effort estimates
3. Taking staff leave into account
4. The effect of adding staff late to meet an aggressive schedule

It is notable that input by developers into the estimates was negatively correlated with project success and with good estimates. The most important factors in the categories of management support, customers/users, and requirements are:

1. The level of customer/user confidence in the development team
2. Level of customer involvement
3. Customers/users involved in requirements gathering
4. The size of the project was large and affected requirements elicitation

The path analysis shows that in addition to the first three variables above, other variables affecting success were:

1. Sponsor is involved in project decisions
2. Customer is involved throughout the project
3. Both sponsor and customer lasted throughout the project
4. There was a well-defined project scope
5. Software deliverables were well-defined

Note that the variable, "the size of the project was large and affected requirements elicitation," did not enter our path analysis.

The most critical success factor was good requirements. Other critical success factors were either affected by the requirements, or themselves affected the development of good requirements. The above results make it clear that a project manager needs to consider seriously the risk to a project if the requirements are poor. Good project estimates and the number of staff assigned to the project depend on good requirements. Critical success factors, such as sponsor involvement in project decisions and a well-defined project scope, influence the development of good requirements.

We have shown that a project manager must juggle many factors that influence project success and that many project managers are unable to do this. Better project management education and more guidance, based on both successful and unsuccessful project experiences, will help project managers who are ill prepared to deal with so many diverse factors. It is noteworthy that good requirements and issues related to good requirements are so important in predicting project success.

Three observations impacting future studies are significant from the above studies: increasing the size of the respondent population leads to more robust statistical results; for most analyses, fewer variables tend to be related to management success when compared to developers' view of project success; and many of the explanatory variables derived from our questionnaire are correlated. The fact that not a single respondent addressed risk assessment, or the lack of it, when discussing either successful or failed projects suggests that risk assessment is not routinely part of the development process.

2.7 Further Work

Our next step is to add estimation and scheduling variables to our path analysis model to develop a more comprehensive path model. This will be followed in turn by analysis of each of the other categories—namely, the software development process, the development personnel, and the project manager—and the integration of their critical success factors into an increasingly comprehensive path model.

Because we found it very interesting that software developers have a different definition of project success from that usually cited in the literature, we have developed a revised project success questionnaire to investigate further the definition of project success. We are collaborating with several international researchers in order to discover if, or how, cultural factors affect developers' definition of software project success.

The lack of risk assessment for the projects in our samples surprised us. The practice of risk assessment in real-world environments, when and how often it is done, and how formal or informal the process is, needs further investigation.

References

1. Amoako-Gyampah K., White K.B., (1997) When is user involvement not user involvement. Information strategy: the executive's journal, 13: 40-45
2. Baccarini D., (1999) The logical framework method for defining project success. Project management journal, 30: 25-32
3. Basili V, Belady L., Boehm B., Brooks F., Browne J., DeMillo R., Feldman S.I., Green C., Lampson B., Lawrie D., Leveson N., Lynch N., Weiser M., Wing J. (1999) Final report. In: NSF workshop on a software research program for the 21st century, software engineering notes, 24: 3
4. Beizer B. (1984) Software system testing and quality assurance. Van Nostrand Reinhold Company, New York, USA
5. Bennatan E.M. (2000) On time, within budget. John Wiley and Sons, UK
6. Boehm B.W., Basili V., (2000) Gaining intellectual control of software development. IEEE Software, 33: 27-33
7. Boehm B.W., (1981) Software engineering economics. Prentice Hall, Englewood Cliffs, NJ, USA
8. Boehm B.W. (1991) Software risk management: principles and practices. IEEE Software, 1: 32-41
9. Brooks F.P. Jr., (1975) The mythical man month. Essays on software engineering, Addison Wesley, USA
10. Carr M.J., Konda S., Monarch I., Ulrich C., Walker C. (1993) Taxonomy-based risk identification. Software engineering institute, Carnegie-Mellon university, technical report CMU/SEI-93-TR-6
11. Charette R.N., (1989) Engineering risk analysis and management. McGraw-Hill New York, USA
12. Clavadetscher C. (1998) User involvement key to success. IEEE Software, 15: 30-32
13. Cohen J. (1960) A coefficient of agreement for nominal scales. Educational and psychological measurement, 20: 37-46

14. Davis F.D. (1989) Perceived usefulness, perceived ease of use and user acceptance of information technology. MIS quarterly, 13: 319-339
15. DeMarco T. (2001) Keynote speech at the international conference on software metrics, London, April 4
16. DeMarco T., (1991) Non-technical issues in software engineering. In: Proceedings of IEEE Conference on software engineering, Austin, Texas, pp. 149-150
17. DeMarco T., (1995) What "lean and mean" really means. IEEE Software, 12: 101-102
18. DeMarco T., Lister T. (1989) Software development: state of the art vs state of the Practice. In: Proceedings of IEEE conference on software engineering, Pittsburgh, USA, pp. 271-275
19. DeMarco T., Lister T. (1999) Peopleware: productive projects and teams. Dorset House Publishing Co. New York, NY
20. Evanco W., Procaccino J.D., Verner J.M. (2002) Software project success: a path analysis. Submitted to IEEE transaction on engineering management
21. Fenton N.E., Neil M. (2002) Software metrics: roadmap. In: Finkelstein A. (Ed.), The future of software engineering, 22nd international conference on software engineering, ACM press, pp. 357-370
22. Garrity E.J., Saunders G.L. (1998) Introduction to information systems success measurement. In: Garrity E., Saunders L. (Eds.), Information system success measurement, Idea publishing group, Hershey, Pennsylvania, pp. 1-12
23. Gefen D. (2000) It is not enough to be responsive: the role of cooperative intentions in MRP II Adoption. The DATA BASE for advances in information systems, 31: 65-79
24. Gefen D., Keil M. (1998) The impact of developer responsiveness on perceptions of usefulness and ease of use: an extension of the technology acceptance model. The DATA BASE for advances in information systems, 29: 35-49
25. Gefen D., Straub D. (2000) The relative importance of perceived ease-of-use in IS adoption: a study of e-commerce adoption. JAIS, 1: 1-30
26. Glass R.L., (1998) Software runaways. Prentice-Hall, Upper Saddle River, New Jersey
27. Glass R.L. (1999) Evolving a new theory of project success. Communications of the ACM, 42: 17-19
28. Hagerty N. (2000) Understanding the link between IT project manager skills and project success: research in progress. In: Proceedings of SIGCPR conference, Evanston, IL, USA, pp. 192-195
29. Hair J.F., Jr., Anderson R.E., Tatham R.L., Black W.C. (1995) Multivariate data analysis with readings. Prentice Hall, Englewood Cliffs, NJ
30. Higuera R., Haimes Y. (1996) Software risk management. Software engineering institute, Technical report, CMU/SEI-TR-012
31. Hoffman T. (1999) Study: 85% of IT departments fail to meet business needs. Computerworld, 33: 24
32. Humphrey W.S. (1988) Characterizing the software process: a maturity framework. IEEE Software, 5: 73-79
33. Ishman M. (1998) Measuring information systems success at the individual level in cross-cultural environments. In: Garrity E., Saunders L. (Eds.), Information system success measurement, Idea publishing group, Hershey, Pennsylvania, pp. 60-68
34. Johnston J. (1999): (The Standish group), Turning CHAOS into success. Software magazine, 19: 30-39
35. Johnston J. (1999): (The Standish group) The ghost of Christmas future: small movements spell where big shifts will come. Software magazine, 19: 15-17

36. Jones C, (1995) Patterns of large systems failure and success. IEEE Computer, 28: 86-87
37. Katchigan S.K. (1986) Statistical analysis - an introduction to interdisciplinary introduction to Univariate and multivariate methods. Radius press, New York, USA
38. Keil M., (1995) Pulling the plug: software project management and the problems of project escalation. MIS quarterly, 19: 421-444
39. Keil M., Montealegre R. (2000) Cutting your losses: extricating your organization when a big project goes awry. Sloan management review, 41: 55-68
40. Kellner M.I. (1991) Non-technical numbers in software engineering (Panel Session Overview). ICSE, Austinn, USA, pp. 149-150
41. Linberg K.R. (1999) Software developer perceptions about software project failure: a case study. Journal of systems and software, 49: 177-192
42. McConnell S. (1996) Rapid development. Microsoft Press, Redmond, Washington
43. Miles M., Huberman M. (1994) Qualitative data analysis: an expanded sourcebook, Sage Publication, USA
44. Nolan A.J. (1999) Learning from success. IEEE Software, 16: 97-105
45. NSF (2000) Final report. In: NSF workshop on a software research program for the 21st century http://www.cs.umd.edu/projects/SoftEng/tame/nsfw98/FinalRep.rtf (accessed 17th April, 2003)
46. Paulk M., Curtis B., Chrissis M., Webster C. (1993) Capability maturity model for software. In: Technical report, CMU/SEI-93-TR-024, Software engineering institute, Carnegie Mellon, Pittsburgh, USA
47. Pedhazur E.J. (1982) Multiple regression in behavioral research: explanation and prediction. Holt, Rinehart and Winston, New York, NY, USA
48. Pinto J.K., Mandel S.J. (1990) The causes of project failure. IEEE transactions on engineering management, 34: 269-276
49. Pinto J.K., Slevin D.P. (1988) Project success: definitions and measurement techniques. Project management journal, 19: 67-72
50. Pfleeger S.L. (1998) Software engineering: theory and practice. Prentice-Hall, (Englewood Cliffs, NJ
51. Pressman R. (1996) Software engineering: a practitioners approach, McGraw Hill, London, UK
52. Pressman R. (1998) Fear of trying: the plight of rookie project managers. IEEE Software, 15: 50-54
53. Procaccino J.D., Verner J.M. (2000) Early risk factors for software development. In: Proceedings of the 12th European software control and metrics conference, London, pp.107-116
54. Procaccino J.D., Verner J.D., Overmyer S.P., Darter, M. (2002) Case study: factors For early prediction of software development success. Information and software technology, 44: 53-62
55. Procaccino J.D., Verner J.D. (2002) Software practitioner's perception of project success: a pilot study. International journal of the computer, the Internet and management, 10: 20-30
56. Raz T., Michael E. (2002) Use and benefits for project risk management. International journal of project management, 19: 9-12
57. Reifer D.J. (2002) A little bit of knowledge is a dangerous thing. IEEE Software, 19: 14-15

58. Ropponen J., Lyytinen K. (2000) Components of software development risk: how to address them? A project manager survey. IEEE transactions on software engineering, 26: 98-112
59. Rus I., Lindvall M. (2002) Knowledge management in software engineering. IEEE Software, 19: 26-38
60. Schenk K.D., Vitalari N.P., Shannon D. (1998) Differences between novice and expert systems analysts: what do we know and what do we do? Journal of management information systems, 15: 9-51
61. Standish Group (1994) CHAOS, http://www.pm2go.com/sample_research (accessed date 17th April)
62. Schumacker R.E., Richard G.L. (1996) A beginner's guide to structural equation modeling. Lawrence Erlbaum Associates, Mahwah, NJ, USA
63. Verner J., Evanco W. (2000) The state of the practice of software effort estimation in business organizations. In: Proceedings of ESCOM-SCOPE, Munich, Germany, pp. 229-237
64. Verner J.,W., Evanco W., Cerpa N. (2002) How important is effort estimation to software development success? Submitted to the journal of empirical software engineering research
65. Verner J.M, Overmyer S.P., McCain, K.W. (1999) In the 25 years since the mythical man-month what have we learned about project management? Information and software technology, 4: 1021-1026
66. Wang Y., Court I., Ross M., Staples G., King G., Dorling A. (1997) Quantitative evaluation of SPICE, CMM, ISO 9000 and BOOTSTRAP. In: Proceedings of the 3rd IEEE international symposium on software engineering standards, IEEE computer society press, USA, pp.57-68
67. Ward S.C., Chapman C.B. (1995) Risk management perspective on the project lifecycle. International journal of project management, 13: 145-149
68. Wateridge J. (1995) IT projects: a basis for success. International journal of project management, 13: 169-172
69. Wateridge J. (1998) How can IS/IT projects be measured for success? International journal of project management, 16: 59-63
70. Wohlin C., Mayrhauser A. von, Host M., Regnell B. (2000) Subjective evaluation as A tool for learning from software project success. Information and software technology, 42: 983-992
71. Wohlin C., Amscheler Andrews A. (2001) Assessing project success using subjective evaluation factors. Software quality journal, 9: 43-70
72. Woodroof J., Kasper G.M. (1998) A conceptual development of process and outcome user satisfaction. In: Garrity E., Saunders L. (Eds.), Information system success measurement, Idea publishing group, Hershey, PA, pp. 122-132

Author Biography

Dr June Verner is a Professor of Information Systems in the College of Information Science and Technology at Drexel University, Philadelphia. She has been involved in research into software quality, software process improvement, software project management, and software metrics for many years. Dr. Verner has published over 50 research papers and is a member of the Technical Council on Software Engineering. Dr. Verner's received her Ph.D. in software engineering from Massey University NZ.

Dr. William Evanco has a Ph.D. from Cornell University. He is currently on the faculty of the College of Information Science and Technology at Drexel University. Before Dr. Evanco joined Drexel he was on the technical staff of Mitre Corp in Washington, DC. He has many years of IT consulting experience with US industry and government agencies. His research interests are in software quality, software testing, and software project management and risk analysis.

3 Usage of Intranet Tools for Knowledge Management in a Medium-Sized Software Consulting Company

Torgeir Dingsøyr and Reidar Conradi

Abstract: Many software companies have invested in or developed knowledge management tools. This chapter examines intranet-based knowledge management tools in a medium-sized software consulting company. We present four tools: the Project Guide, a structured knowledge repository designed to help developers and managers carry out projects; the "Well of Experience", an unstructured knowledge repository containing more than 600 experience notes; the Competence Block manager for organizing internal courses; the Skills Manager, which gives an overview of employee competence. In addition to presenting the tools, we describe how developers and managers use the tools, and find that knowledge management tool usage depends on what work tasks an employee has, as well as the employee's personal preferences. We argue that medium-sized software companies should choose a knowledge management strategy that supports the actual work tasks and personal preferences of employees.

Keywords: Knowledge management tools, Intranet, Knowledge cartography, Knowledge repository and library, Personalization, Codification.

3.1 Introduction

This chapter describes how intranet-based knowledge management tools are used in a medium-sized software consulting company. Medium-sized software consulting companies are interesting because there are relatively few studies of knowledge management in this type of company. Also, many companies belong to this category, and they often use other technical solutions than those used by larger companies. By studying how knowledge management tools work, we can learn how to improve them.

The company Alpha Consulting focuses on knowledge engineering and has 150 employees. The company has chosen a knowledge management strategy that relies on both *codification*, to represent knowledge in written form and *personalization*, to foster the exchange of tacit knowledge. Alpha Consulting has developed tools to support both of these strategies, and we describe four tools, including how they are used, based on 14 interviews with employees in different groups in the company. We analyze how the tools support company strategies, and argue that the synergy between personalization and codification work particularly well in this medium-sized company.

First, we first present details of Alpha Consulting and then continue with a discussion of knowledge management tools in general. We focus on the knowledge management tools at Alpha in particular and how they are used, and end by discussing this usage. A more detailed description of knowledge management at Alpha Consulting can be found in [2]. For a survey of other case studies of knowledge management initiatives in software companies, see also Dingsøyr and Conradi [3].

3.2 Alpha Consulting

Alpha Consulting ("Alpha") is a software consulting company based in Norway, develops knowledge-based systems for a variety of customers. When it was founded in 1985, it was a spin-off of a larger, more general consulting company, and according to a Norwegian newspaper, "an international staff of specialists will develop expert systems that above all will cover the needs of the demanding oil industry". The newspaper continues: the company shall "offer services in industrial use of knowledge-based expert systems, and software in the field of artificial intelligence".

Since then, the company has grown organically, from just a few employees in the beginning; to approximately 150 in 2002 both by increasing staff and through and acquisition in 2000. The company has also extended their services and market.

In the annual report for 1999, they state that their vision is to "make knowledge sharing in organizations more effective, and thereby contribute so that knowledge is refined and used to achieve the organization's goal". Their mission is to

> Deliver services, solutions and products to organizations and individuals who wish to make their business more effective through innovative use of information technology. The company's core competence is knowledge management, process-support and implementation of intelligent systems for knowledge-based behavior and knowledge processes. Within this business area, Alpha will seek international activity based on their role as a leading vendor in Norway.

In July 2001, the company discussed with a major aircraft company about delivering a system for modeling software and organizations.

The important technologies for delivering these solutions include network and database technology, document management and search, Web technology, work process support, co-ordination technology, artificial intelligence and data mining. The underlying technology is Java, Microsoft and SmallTalk technology.

Customers come from the public, marine and industry sector. Projects for these customers typically include 3 - 10 people working for at least half a year, and in some cases for several years. In projects, the participants take on different roles, as "project manager", "technical manager", and "customer contact". In addition to these projects, the company has a record of participating in cooperative research projects, from highly applied research to more advanced research in EU- and Norwegian Research Council-funded projects.

The company is organized around "processes" and "projects". The "process organization" means that they have defined important areas for the company, which has one "process manager", usually with support from a small team. Examples of processes are management, delivery and support, and also knowledge management. Many employees in the company are responsible for some process issues while working on a project. Most employees have a university degree in computer science, and some have doctoral degrees, specifically in artificial intelligence.

The knowledge management process at Alpha hands out a prize to the "knowledge sharer of the month" in order to promote knowledge management. This prize has been given to people who share their knowledge through Alpha's knowledge management tools, or through oral communication.

On first sight, the organization seems very flat with people rotating between different process manager positions. But as one employee told us, "of course, there is a hierarchy here as well, it is just not written down any place".

While working on projects, most of the development has traditionally been done in-house rather than at the customer's site. However, situation where employees work at the customer's sites are becoming more frequent. When we visit the company, approximately 20% of the staff were working elsewhere outside the main company building.

3.3 Knowledge Management Strategies and Tools

Here we present what strategies a company can choose when applying knowledge management, and then present categories of tools that support these strategies.

3.3.1 Knowledge Management Strategies

There are essentially two main strategies for knowledge management [7]:

- *Codification*: To systematize and store information that represents the knowledge of the company, and make this available for the people in the company.
- *Personalization*: To support the flow of information in a company by storing information about knowledge sources, like a "yellow pages" of who knows about what in a company.

Hansen et al. [7] argue that companies should focus on just one of these strategies. We wish to add however, that the codification strategy does not fit all types of knowledge. In situations where knowledge is very context-dependent and where the context is difficult to encode and transfer, it can be dangerous to reuse knowledge without analyzing it critically. For some examples of problems with this strategy, see Jørgensen and Sjøberg [8].

Another alternative to the two strategies could be to support the growth of knowledge, that is, creation of new knowledge by arranging for innovation through special learning environments or expert networks, but we will not discuss that here. Note that some have referred to these strategies by other names: Codification can also be called "exploitation", and personalization "exploration" [9].

3.3.2 Knowledge Management Tools

In terms of tools for knowledge management, we mean tools that have several users and are widely available for employees in an organization. This is usually what we call intranet tools [11] which support knowledge management in "at least three ways: 1) providing compression of time and space among the users. 2) offering the flexibility to exchange information, and 3) supporting information transfer and organizational networking independent of direct contacts between the users".

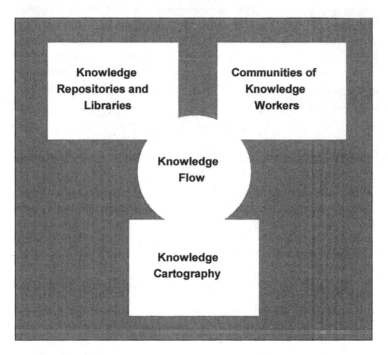

Fig. 3.1. Types of knowledge management tools [1]

There are many dimensions for describing knowledge management tools. Ruggles [10] mentions tools that *generate knowledge*, for example, tools for data mining that discover new patterns in data. Further, we have *knowledge codification tools* to make knowledge available for others, and *knowledge transfer tools* to decrease problems with time and space when communicating in an organization. Another dimension is whether the tools are *active* [6] or *passive*. By active tools, we mean tools that notify users when it is likely that users require some kind of knowledge. Passive tools require a user to actively seek knowledge without any system support. We now categorize the tools according to a model from the book Information Technology for Knowledge Management [1], because it is widely known. The authors divide technology for a "corporate memory" into four parts, shown in Fig. 3.1:

- *Knowledge repositories and libraries*: Tools for handling repositories of knowledge in form of documents
- *Communities of knowledge workers*: Tools to support communities of practice in work; like organizing workspaces for communities for online discussions and distributed work
- *Knowledge cartography*: Tools for mapping and categorizing knowledge, from core competence in a company to individual expertise; what we can refer to as "metaknowledge"
- *The flow of knowledge*: Here we find tools for supporting the interaction between tacit knowledge, explicit knowledge and metaknowledge that is, that combines the three parts above

3.4 Research Method

The aim of the research reported in this chapter is to investigate how intranet-based knowledge management tools are used in a medium-sized software consulting company. We selected Alpha as a case company because we know that they have many knowledge management tools and have been working internally on knowledge management for several years.

To obtain the data for the research reported in this article, we used a method inspired by ethnography [5]. For the analysis, we relied on a grounded theory approach. We spent four weeks at Alpha, obtained access to their intranet systems and attended all meetings where all the employees were invited as well as meetings concerning one project.

3.4.1 Data Collection

We used the following data sources:

- *Interviews*: We used semistructured interviews with open-ended questions. The interviews were transcribed in full, and in total we obtained 120 pages of transcripts for analysis.
- *Usage logs*: We collected logs from the usage of the knowledge management system on the intranet Web pages.
- *Documents*: We gathered documents about the design and intent of the Knowledge Management tools.
- *Screenshots*: We gathered screenshots from different areas of the knowledge management system.
- *Pictures*: We took pictures of people in normal work-situations to get a better understanding of the workplace and work processes.
- *Logbook*: We registered observations from everyday life in the company in a logbook, together with memorandums from conversations, meetings and presentations.

3.4.2 Data Analysis

We analyzed the qualitative data using the principles of grounded theory [12]. We also kept quantitative data in logs, which first had to be preprocessed before we could plot them for analysis.

How did we organize the analysis of the data that was collected? First, we gathered the qualitative material that was collected on each knowledge management tool. We constructed a database[1] with information from the interviews, documents and our own logbook observations. We tagged the information to show what kind of source it came from, and categorized the people who interviewed: managers, project managers, developers, and people responsible for knowledge management.

We then searched this database for areas of interest, and gathered information from the different sources. For example, a search in the database for the keyword "skill" resulted in 43 occurrences in 10 documents.

After that, we analyzed (and "coded") the chunks of information to find interesting categories that might later contribute to theory building. Would there be any special patterns in what the people were saying? A triangulation approach was used to see if there were differences between groups of people or between what people were saying and logs or collected documents.

3.5   Usage of Knowledge Management Tools at Alpha

We now present some of the knowledge management tools at Alpha, and divide them into two groups: *knowledge repositories and libraries* and *knowledge cartography tools*. We do not discuss other types of tools because there has been more work on tools supporting communities of knowledge workers. Also, there were no tools that we can describe as *knowledge flow* tools at Alpha. All the tools that we examined were "passive" knowledge management tools.

The usage situations found for each tool are presented, as well as the types of user groups. We start by giving a general overview of the front page on the intranet system, then present knowledge repository tools, knowledge cartography tools, and finally, we give a general assessment of the tools.

3.5.1 Knowledge Management Tools in General

At the main Web page of the knowledge management system at Alpha, there are links to several different subsystems. The first page provides company-internal news. Above that, there is a calendar, which shows the current events. On the left, there are links to several other Web pages: The skills manager, competence blocks, the knowledge repository WoX and several other tools.

---

[1] Using N5, a tool for analysis of non-numerical data from (QSR international, Australia)

On the top of the page, there are links to each employee's timesheet, a telephone list, the external Web pages, and the possibility to send an e-mail to the Webmaster. On the right-hand side, there is a "tip" about a knowledge management magazine, and a link to an informal "newspaper" that covers social events in the company. At the bottom of the screen, there is a "quiz of the day" and viewers may answer this quiz in a box below.

When we asked employees in the company how often they would use the tools for knowledge management, most of the employees from Alpha said that they were used it several times a day. A developer said he used it "between five to ten times a day", and another said "a couple of times a week to register hours. [since] it is always something you must do... look at news. If you want to follow what is happening in the company, you have to look at it a couple of times a day. When I open Internet Explorer, it is the first page I get". Of other people we spoke to at Alpha, it seemed that most were using the tools "several times a day", some "daily" and a few "weekly".

3.5.2 Knowledge Repository and Library Tools

With this group, the following tools are highlighted: the project guide and the well of experience.

3.5.2.1 Project Guide

This is a practical guide to assist project work that contains descriptions of different processes that are common, such as project start-up and closure, how to do testing and so on. It contains templates for documents that are normally produced during project execution, as well as examples. Different company roles, such as developer, manager and customer contact, have different views to the guide.

According to one manager this tool "has a form that is very nice—initiatives on peptalks when projects start and such. It is really a step in the right direction, that things are triggered by the system, and that people do not just know how to do things". Another manager commented that the tool was the" result of a lot of projects, and some routines and terms around it is an indirect result".

Many people at Alpha indicated that they do not use this tool very often. One manager said, "I must say that this is a tool that I might have used more. And when I say that, I suppose there are other people as well that could have used it more". A developer said "No, I do not use that... or at least not deliberately, but I suppose that there are many things that we do that you can find in the project guide". Another developer said, "No, there is no need for me to use it. It is maybe aimed more towards project managers, but to be honest I have not used it as project manager either. Maybe because the projects have been too small. Or that it has been clever people on the projects that have not needed any training". Another developer had problems with the form of the project guide: "I do not like it a lot, maybe because it is available electronically". This developer felt that he lost overview when reading hypertext documents, for example, when investigating "acceptance tests, it was a long list of subpoints that you could click on. But you never get through such a list—it is too much! And I am a bit uncertain because it looks like a whole book, and if I pick out a piece to read it, do I have to read everything before it?" A third developer said she felt "angry when using it", because it did not contain a complete set of information, and is difficult to navigate in.

Overall we found that people mainly used the tool to obtain tips and advice in project start up and execution. A manager said that he "used it as a daily support – in order to solve projects in general, and when we needed an acceptance test earlier in the project, we had a look there to see what tips and advice we could find".

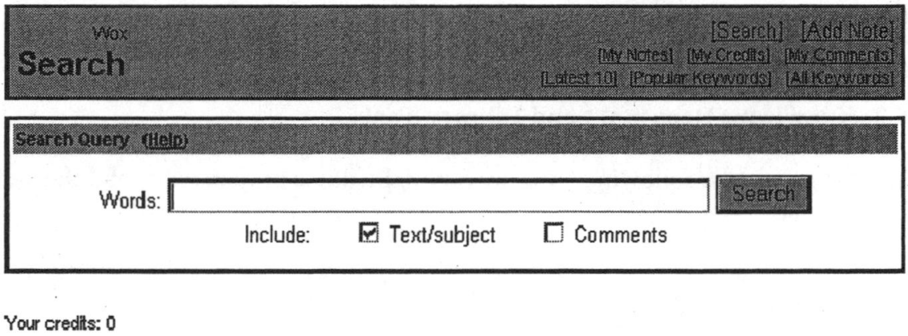

Your credits: 0

Fig. 3.2. The well of experience (WoX) search interface for the knowledge repository of experience notes

3.5.2.2   Knowledge Repository: The WoX

The Well of Experience WoX,, is a small tool for capturing knowledge that would normally be written on yellow stickers, what the company calls "collective yellow stickers". It contains everything from the phone number of the pizza restaurant on the corner, to "how you set up SmallTalk on a special platform". You find information by searching an unstructured database (Fig. 3.2), and you can give "credits" to notes that you find useful. Notes with more accumulated credits about an issue show up before notes with less. The tool contains a mechanism to give feedback to the person who wrote the note, and there has been a kind of competition in the company to get the most credits. One developer described this module as "quite useful; it is simple enough to be used in practice". When we visited the company, it contained around 600 "experience notes".

Examples of such notes are "how to reduce the size of your profile in Windows NT", "how to remove garbage from an image in SmallTalk", "technical problems with cookies" and "an implementation of the soundex algorithm in Java".

According to one developer, "People are very good at submitting notes when they think that something can be useful for others." A manager described the notes in terms of "a behavioral arena that people use in different ways, to create a culture of knowledge sharing, and [the tool] lets people experience that others make use of their knowledge". The tool is promoted by posters, which can be found in frequently visited places like the one in Fig. 3.3, located just outside the staff restaurant.

Fig. 3.3. "I've been WoX'ing today, have you?" One of several posters promoting the use of the WoX knowledge repository at Alpha

When we asked employees to describe what kind of tools they were using in their work, almost all of the developers mentioned that they were using WoX. All developers but one (seven out of eight) said that they have written experience notes, and all of them have tried to search for experience notes. The managers were not as active in using the notes as others. Three out of six managers did not mention WoX when we asked about knowledge management tools in the company.

We found five different types of usage of the knowledge repository, to

1. Solve a specific technical problem
2. Get an overview of problem areas
3. Avoid rework in having to explain the same solution to several people
4. Improve individual work situation by adjusting technical tools
5. Find who has a specific competence in the company

We describe each of these types of usage in more depth:

Solve a specific technical problem: The most prominent use of this tool seemed to be in "problem solving". As one developer explains "If you run into a problem, then you can use WoX to see if anyone else in the company has had a similar problem", or it can be used "when you sit with a problem that you can't solve, or a strange bug, or if you do not understand why the computer does not behave the way it should".

Another developer says: "It happens that I have been searching and have found things in WoX. And then you do not have to search in other places, and maybe spend two or three days".

As one developer mentioned, the problem with the notes is that "the person that writes something has a certain background, and with that background they presume that when they write 'first you do this, then that...', the others will also know what to do". This, however, is not always the case, especially in more complicated situations.

Get an overview of problem areas: One employee said, "If I am stuck and wonder about something, usually, I remember that it was written somewhere in WoX, and then I go back and find it". One developer, for example, tends to refer back to notes about project startup, particularly at a startup phase, which happens every six months or so. Another developer and another manager also said that they would look almost every day to see what was new on WoXso I know what is in there, and do not have to search for things".

But people do not write about all types of problems as experience notes. Notes about issues that are "unofficial knowledge", or as one developer put it "not things that are unethical, but things that you do that could easily be interpreted wrongly by customers" do not appear and that knowledge is transferred through informal oral communication.

Avoid rework in having to explain the same solution to several people: One developer said: "When the third person comes and asks about the same thing, then you realize that it is about time to document it". He would then later tell people who were asking about the topic to look it up in WoX.

Improve individual work situation by adjusting technical tools: Some said that they would find information on how to improve the tools that they use in their daily work, like Outlook, to make them more easy to use. Another example is "how to reduce your profile in Windows NT", which reduces the booting-time of your operating system quite a bit. A third example of a small improvement is a note on how to burn CDs for customers. This note in particular explains how to design covers for the CDs so that they look more professional when delivering a final software product.

Find who has a specific competence in the company: "Newbies get a short-cut to discover things that I have spent some time to build up. If they browse WoX a bit, they can find that 'this person knows a lot about low-level Windows-patching' and that 'this person is good at Apache Webserver set up'", one developer said.

3.5.3 Knowledge Cartography Tools

At Alpha we examined two cartography tools: Competence Blocks and the Skills Manager.

3.5.3.1 Competence Blocks

The Competence Blocks is a list of company-internal courses that are open for assigning and viewing, and the courses may be evaluated after completion. A brief description of each course is given, together with schedule information and who is responsible. Most of the courses are given in a day or less. Sometimes, courses from other suppliers are also offered through this system. A manager described it as a "very valuable supplement (to normal on-the-job-training), with blocks that can be composed specifically". According to a developer, the management "encourage people to organize competence blocks". This tool is used when someone wants to participate in a course, or plan a course (or Competence Block).

We found six people who mentioned this tool in interviews. This is a tool that people do not use very often, but must use if they want to participate in a course. A developer said that this tool "suits me very well—I prefer oral communication to written".

3.5.3.2 Skills Manager

This is a system where all employees can state what level of knowledge they have in different areas that are of interest to the company, like object-oriented technology or the ability to program in Visual Basic. It can be used to indicate which level you want to be at, so if you are interested in learning more about Visual Basic, you can state it in this tool. The tool is used for staffing projects, and many people in the company also use it to find someone who can help them to solve a problem. As one developer said: "I can say that I need a person that knows HTML, and then I will get a list of people, and see what level of knowledge they have." For a wider discussion of this tool, see Dingsøyr and Røyrvik [4].

Managers, project managers as well as developers said in our interviews that they used this tool. From the interviews, we have divided the usage of this tool into four categories, some with subcategories, to

1. Search for competence to solve problems
2. Allocate resources
3. Find projects and external marketing
4. Develop competence

We discuss each of these uses more in detail below:

Search for competence to solve problems: The developers often need to know something about a topic they are not very skilled in themselves. We can then distinguish between two types of usage of the skills management system. First, people use it to find other people in the company who have knowledge about a specific problem that they have to solve i.e. short-term usage. Second, people increase their overall insight in to the core competencies of the company i.e. long-term usage.

Let us look at first the short-term usage. One developer says, "It happens (that I use it), if I suddenly have a specific problem in an area that I do not know much about. Then it sometimes helps to go in there and find someone who knows about it. I have in fact done that once...". Another developer seems to use it more often: "of course, when I wonder if there is anyone who can help me with something, I look up in the skills management system to see if anyone has the knowledge that I need." In Fig. 3.4, we show a screenshot of the skills management system, giving an overview of skills in object-oriented development. Here, you can also e-mail people who have a required competence in a specific area, or you can just print a list of people and ask them yourself, as another developer has done: "I find a list, and look at what level they have ... and then I go around in the building and ask them". Of course, this depends on people-to-rate themselves in a honest way. One developer used the skills management system to find people, but after asking the believed "experts" she found that she "did not get the answers that I needed, so I had to go to someone else. It depends very much on people to update their skills correctly. To describe a skill level is not that easy, so some overrate themselves and others underrate themselves strongly." Another developer is critical of the categories of competence in the skills management system: "what you can get information about now is if someone knows about Web– and that contains quite a lot! Maybe it is not that general, but not too far off. It is based on the core competency areas of the company, but when it comes to more detailed things, like who in fact can write a computer program, and who can find a solution, you do not find that there."

When we looked at long-term usage, we found very little material in our interviews. One developer, however, often finds a group that knows something about a subject on the skills management system, and asks them questions by e-mail. But "if it then happens that you have asked questions about SQL to ten gurus, and it is always the same two that answers, then you start to go to them and talk. You learn after a while who it is worth to attempt to get anything out of".

Allocate resources: In our empirical material from Alpha, we can see some patterns of the practical uses of the skills management system, in terms of resource allocation.

As one new employee said, "contrary to a lot of other companies that use such a system, here at Alpha we really use the system for resource planning." Another comment is on the same track "I think that the Skills Manager is a useful tool, but a tool that still has got a lot of potential when it comes to practical use. Those who do the resource management already use the tool a lot in the daily resource allocation work."

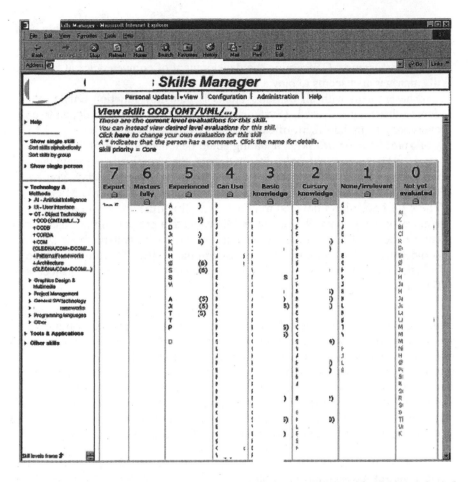

Fig. 3.4. An example of a result after querying for competence on "object-oriented development" in the Skills Manager. The names of people have been removed

A third Alpha employee comments on the Skills Manager as an important tool for resource allocation, but also for the strategic development of the company: "The tools I use the most are ... the competence block manager and the Skills Manager. Definitely! I'm responsible for the content in many databases, and partly the skills management base. And the Skills Manager is a tool that is very important for the resource allocation process. Therefore, many employees come up with suggestions to new content, new elements, in the skills database."

Find projects and external marketing: Another use of the system is for the sales department. One manager said that "even sales can use it (the skills management system), to find new directions to go in", or rather to find what types of projects suit the company well. We can also think of another use that we did not hear from anyone, probably because we did not talk to people in the sales department, namely to use the system as external marketing; that is as proof of a highly skilled workforce.

Develop competence: Concerning the development of competencies at Alpha, the skills manager also seems to play a part.

The problem with all of our systems is that they function only to the degree that they are used. (Systems) like the Skills Manager depends on everybody to update them often and objectively. That could be solved by work-process support. Skills updating could be a natural part of the closing of a project, for example by updating the involved competencies, particularly those that have been in use during the project. Today, you are allocated to projects on the basis of what you have in the Skills Manager. There we have views devoted to people with free time and the competence required in the project. When you are allocated to a project on the basis of a competence profile, then there is also knowledge in the system about which competencies that are expected to be used in the project. Therefore it would be natural to ask for an update on those competencies when the project is finished.

Another employee sees the Skills Manager in light of intellectual capital: Such tools are very good indicators for accounting intellectual capital. You are able to see what kind of competencies we will need in the long term, evaluate it, and compare it to what competence we already have in the firm. Then, you can say that we have that many person months with C++ or Java competence, and we see that there is an increase in this competence, and then we can evaluate that.

In the skills management system at Alpha, the employees can use this tool to state what they want to learn about in the future, not only what they know now. In that way, people can develop their competence by working on relevant projects.

3.5.4 General Assessment of Tools

When we asked people to assess the tools that they have available for knowledge management in their daily work, we got a variety of answers. Some said that the tools that exist now are "primitive", and far from what the company thinks should be possible to use. Others said they worked "fine", while others think that they were impractical.

Several people in the company believe in more technically advanced knowledge management tools. One manager said, If we were allowed to set up a project with more of our skilled people, and followed up in the same way as we do against customers, then we would have had a (set of knowledge management tools) that are much more functional, support our employees better, and support knowledge management at Alpha better than what we have today." Another manager said: "It (the knowledge management system) is characterized by when it was made, and the need that has been in the organization at different times. That is, it has been developed once, and has been patched-up a bit afterwards." As a result, the technical condition of the system is not something that the company would sell to an external customer. This view is also supported by a developer, who said, "We have a number of tools that represent some good ideas, but the tools' condition today is not the ultimate. We see a lot of possibilities for improvement, especially on technology. What really could have made a difference is that we could have had much better integration between the tools". An example of tools that could be integrated better are the Skills Manager and the WoX. Another possible integration is between the Skills Manager and the Competence Blocks.

Other people emphasized that the tools are under constant development. A manager said "It is under constant development, really, and when you get something new, you discover at once the need for something more".

Several people mention that they would appreciate a more "active" kind of knowledge management, like one manager who said:

> The problem is not that we do not document enough experience, but to make the experience appear when it is needed. It is ok in those situations when an employee recognizes that 'now I need knowledge about something' - we could have improved the indexing possibilities [in internal knowledge repositories] ... But if we had done so, it would be like that if I was thrown into a new project - or a newly employed was - and you are to do a relatively specific thing, then it could happen that you do some searches for knowledge on the essence on the job, but all the side-experience you have, you would not search for [knowledge that does not fit the search criteria]. I see it like the essence of the border of passive knowledge management [that the knowledge management system supports].

One developer said: "I only use the knowledge management system for registering hours, and doing smaller stuff. I do not think it is easy to find information there." This was because this developer would normally need information whilst working on software development, and she felt it was time-consuming to start a browser and look up a Web page for the internally developed framework she was mostly working with. Also, she meant that these Web pages were usually not updated, so she preferred to read code to find answers to problems. Another user said, "I think the knowledge management system is a bit messy. I do not really know what is in there, because I have never had the time to go through everything".

Others were critical of an extensive use of tools: "Some people talk warmly about 'taking our own medicine' by using work processes in development and things like that. That is just bullshit! Maybe it is a good thing for in-house training, but work processes is not the most effective way of working." This developer said that if you are an expert user, you have your own way of working that is probably much better. Work processes would force you into a work pattern that does not suit you, because the way the company is modeling work patterns is "extremely static".

Another developer said that the contents of the tools are "much more up to date than you would expect". He thinks this is because much of the information is generated from databases that are easier to maintain than Web pages.

Over the time period we collected measurements, we found that the front page was accessed an average of 2032 times per week, which is approximately 14 times per week per employee.

3.6 Discussion

The structure of this discussion highlights again the types of tools and strategies described in the previous paragraphs. We have focused on two main strategies for knowledge management: codification and personalization. We investigated two types of tools: knowledge repositories and libraries and knowledge cartography tools. We now discuss how these tools were used for codification and personalization in the company, then we examine what kind of learning that takes place as a result of these tools.

3.6.1 Knowledge Repositories and Libraries

When we go on to ask about how these knowledge repository and library tools are used for transferring knowledge between development projects, we divide the usage into two types. First, we look at usage of codified knowledge from the tools in terms of what corresponds to the codification strategy that we have presented in Sect. 3.3.1. Second, we notice that some types of usage are more suitable to the personalization strategy.

3.6.1.1 Codification Strategy

For the knowledge repository and library tools, we found the following usage situations (with the corresponding tool in parentheses):

- Get tips and advice in project startup and execution (Project guide)
- Solve a specific technical problem (Well of Experience)
- Avoid rework in having to explain the same solution to several people (Well of Experience)
- Improve work situation by adjusting technical tools (Well of Experience)

From the interviews it seemed that the Project Guide was in use by different employee groups and with a different frequency than the Well of Experience. The Project Guide seemed to be mostly in use by some project managers, and not very much in use by developers. The Well of Experience on the other hand, seems to be used by many employees, and at a much higher frequency. We note that it was mainly developers who said that they actively contributed to the contents of the Well of Experience, and not employees who acted as project managers or managers.

Why do we see this difference between the usage of these tools? Is it because of the intended focus of the knowledge in the tools, or the way the tools can be used? The Project Guide is intended to be a support in project work and contains abstracted knowledge from previous projects. The Well of Experience has no structure and may contain any type of information. Yet, it seems that it is the developers that use the tool and fill it with technical information, either to make it easier for others to solve a problem, or to avoid rework oneself by having to explain the same thing several times, or to adjust technical tools to increase performance.

The user interfaces of the tools are quite different: The Project Guide can display knowledge according to different roles in a development project, and is browsable. The Well of Experience is a small search engine containing company-relevant information.

It might be that developers require more specific information to solve most of their daily problems. When they have a specific problem, the solution is often in a "bug fix", or a technical description on how to change something. The solution is not found in an abstract way to reason on such problems, which is what you might expect from the Project Guide. Maybe the type of abstract knowledge found there is better suited in situations that require overall decisions, but not in concrete problem situations.

3.6.1.2 Personalization Strategy

When asking employees about usage, we found two uses of Knowledge Repositories/ Libraries that are part of the personalization strategy

- Get an overview of problem areas (Well of Experience)
- Find who has a specific competence in the company (Well of Experience)

Here, the employees did not use the knowledge found in the Well of Experience directly. They saw the available knowledge and who made it, then used that information for getting an overview of problem areas the company faced often. They also saw who frequently posted tips on topics: persons who could be considered some kind of expert. It is an interesting point that the tools with codified knowledge can be seen as having an additional purpose other than pure "codification" and "distribution".

3.6.2 Knowledge Cartography

We now discuss how the knowledge cartography tools supported personalization at Alpha. We did not find any usage types that we classified as codification. Of the cartography tools, we found the Skills Manager to be in use for four different purposes:

- Searching for competence to solve problems (Skills Manager)
- Resource allocation (Skills Manager)
- Finding projects and external marketing (Skills Manager)
- Competence development (Skills Manager)

Only two employees mentioned that they were using the Competence Blocks. From the interviews it seems that this tool is used much less than the Skills Manager that almost everyone mentioned, where most employees had updated their skill levels.

Developers said they were using the Skills Manager for solving problems and competence development. Managers and administration used it for resource allocation, to find external projects and to market the company externally.

3.6.3 Learning at Alpha

We now go on to discuss what kind of learning the different usage types at Alpha resulted in. We found some of the usage types resulted in problem solving:

- Solve a specific technical problem (Well of Experience)
- Searching for competence to solve problems (Skills Manager)

We also found use in avoiding rework and improving the work situation:

- Avoid rework in having to explain the same solution to several people (Well of Experience)
- Improve work situation by adjusting technical tools (Well of Experience)

Other types of use were to obtain orientation in the company, and for making some work processes more effective:

- Getting an overview of problem areas (Well of Experience)
- Finding who has certain competence in the company (Well of Experience)
- Resource allocation (Skills Manager)
- Finding projects and external marketing (Skills Manager)
- Competence development (Skills Manager)
- Getting tips and advice in project start-up and execution (Project guide)

If we describe these forms of usage in relation to the theories about learning in Alpha, people who had the same position in the company would sometimes use different tools. Some preferred to use the Skills Manager to find experts in order to solve a technical problem, while others would search in the knowledge repository WoX. This might be an indication that the expected knowledge gain is not the only factor that affects the choice of tool since there is also an interest in how the knowledge is presented.

3.7 Conclusion, and Further Work

We found a variety of specialized knowledge management tools at Alpha. One contained knowledge that was unstructured, the Well of Experience, and one contained packaged knowledge, the Project Guide. We found two knowledge cartography tools, the Skills Manager and the Competence Blocks. From the interviews and the usage logs, we see that the use of these tools varied. From this we conclude that there are many different knowledge management tools in a medium-sized software company, and the tools were used to varying degrees.

In terms of tool usage, it seems that the repositories that present more "packaged" knowledge are used less often than the tools with unstructured knowledge. If we take into account the different groups of employees, it also seems that project managers prefer tools with more abstracted knowledge, while the developers prefer tools with more specific knowledge.

Further, usage of tools varied between people in the same group. Some developers preferred oral communication to written, and tended to make more use of the personalization tools. Others preferred written communication, and some of these preferred to have it on paper while others preferred to have it electronically. Others again were skeptical to the use of tools in general, because it was hard to find relevant information. Overall, we can conclude that the use of knowledge management tools varies both between developers, project managers and managers, and after the employee's personal preferences.

We found 12 different types of usage of the knowledge management tools, some relying on personalization and some on codification. From this we can conclude knowledge management tools are used for a variety of purposes. The practitioners in the company will adapt and use tools to suit their normal work situations.

Knowledge repositories can function as a personalization strategy as well as a codification strategy. For companies that want to develop knowledge management tools, this shows that different groups of users in software companies, such as developers, project managers, and management benefit from different types of tools. Developers require more detailed knowledge, while the other groups seem to benefit more from abstract knowledge in their tool use.

This also shows that a medium-sized software company can gain from being effective at knowledge transfer through both personalization and codification, and that it does not have to select a single knowledge management strategy.

Acknowledgement

We are grateful to contact persons and interviewees at Alpha Consulting who shared their experience on knowledge management. We are further grateful to the Norwegian Research Council for funding the work through the Process Improvement for IT industry (PROFIT) project, and to all colleagues working in the project for providing a stimulating research environment. Finally, we would like to thank the anonymous reviewers for their helpful input.

References

1. Borghoff U.M., Pareschi R. (1998) Information technology for knowledge management. Springer, Berlin Heidelberg New York, ISBN 3-540-63764-8
2. Dingsøyr T. (2002) Knowledge management in medium-sized software consulting companies. Doctoral thesis, Department of computer and information science, Norwegian University of science and technology, Trondheim, ISBN 82-7477-107-9
3. Dingsøyr T., Conradi R. (2002) A survey of case studies of the use of knowledge management in software engineering. International journal of software engineering and knowledge engineering, 12: 391-414
4. Dingsøyr T., Røyrvik E. (2001) Skills management as knowledge technology in a software consultancy company. In: Althoff K.-D., Feldmann, R.L., Müller W. (Eds.), Lecture Notes in Computer Science, Springer, Berlin Heidelberg New York, Kaiserslautern, Germany, 2176: 96-107
5. Fetterman D.M. (1998) Ethnography: step by step. Sage Publications, London, UK, ISBN 0-7619-1384-X
6. Gunnar A.S., Coll J., Dehli E., Tangen K. (1999) Knowledge sharing in distributed Organizations. In: Proceedings of the workshop on knowledge management and organizational Memories, Stockholm, Sweden
7. Hansen M.T., Nohria N., Tierney T. (1999) What is your strategy for managing knowledge? Harvard business review, 77: 106-116
8. Jørgensen M., Sjøberg D. (2000) The importance of NOT learning from experience. In: Proceedings of the EuroSPI conference, Coppenhagen, Denmark
9. Mathiassen L., Pries-Heje J., Ngwenyama O. (2002) Improving software organizations: from principles to practice. Addison Wesley, Boston, ISBN 0-201-75820-2
10. Ruggles R.L. (1997) Knowledge management tools. Resources for the knowledge-based economy, Butterworth-Heinemann, Boston, USA
11. Ruppel C.P. Harrington S.J. (2001) Sharing knowledge through intranets: a study of organizational culture and intranet implementation. IEEE transactions on professional communication, 44: 37-52
12. Srauss A. Corbin J. (1998) Basics of qualitative research: grounded theory procedure and techniques. Sage publications, Newbury Park, CA, ISBN 0-8039-5939-7

Author Biography

Torgeir Dingsøyr wrote his doctoral thesis on *Knowledge Management in Medium-Sizes Software Consulting Companies* at the department of computer and information science at the Norwegian University of Science and Technology in Trondheim. He is currently working as a research scientist on software process improvement at SINTEF Telecom and Informatics in Trondheim, Norway.

Reidar Conradi is a professor in the department of computer and information science at the Norwegian University of Science and Technology in Trondheim. His interests are process modeling, software process improvement, software engineering databases, versioning, object orientation, component-based development, and programming languages.

Part 2
Supporting Structures for Managing Software Engineering Knowledge

Aybüke Aurum

> *No man's knowledge here can go beyond his experience*
> — John Locke

Software engineering knowledge is dynamic and evolves with technology, organizational culture and the changing needs of the organization's software development practices. Software development processes rely heavily on knowledge and creativity of both individuals and teams in software development. The basic principle in software engineering is that the overall quality of software can be improved when knowledge is made available and used proficiently. Furthermore, the need for further development of software engineering practices within organizations adds to the demand for systematic knowledge and skill management at all stages of the software lifecycle. Thus, developing effective ways of managing software knowledge is of interest to software developers.

Three enabling factors support the knowledge management process in software organizations. The first is technology that links developers to one another and creates an organizational memory bank that is accessible to the entire organization; second is leadership that encourages knowledge management in software product development, services and work processes within the organization. The final factor is organizational culture that supports the sharing of knowledge, experiences, and technology and innovation.

There is a need to support the systematic storage of evolving knowledge, and to capture and share emerging knowledge in software organizations [5]. The challenge is twofold. First, software organizations need to capture, share, coordinate and manage implicit and explicit knowledge as well as find complete solutions to problems in the project and organizational level. Second they need to find and integrate partial solutions for continuous improvement, and hence, organizational learning [4]. Once organizations recognize this need, it is essential for them to identify their present position to serve as a baseline. In addition to considering project size and product application domains, software development processes adopted by organizations must be aligned with the expectations of their customers, managerial practices, organizational culture, social dynamics and the knowledge and skills of the developers. Furthermore, these issues have to be integrated to a coherent guidance for performing theses processes.

Making personal knowledge available to other team members is one of the objectives of knowledge management, because maximizing access to knowledge across the development team increases productivity and efficiency. Furthermore, knowledge assets related to the production process can generate significant value within the organization.

In order to build organization-specific software know-how, organizations need to learn from their past software projects. An organizational learning approach to software development involves development of experienced-based knowledge repositories [2]. Hence, knowledge management applications must be embedded within the organizational structure to support organizational learning.

Reuse is one example of transferring existing knowledge to team members. There are several questions that need to be considered when applying reuse approaches, e.g. is it economical to spend time and money to store the knowledge? How frequently do the developers use the knowledge? What is the content of the data and the metadata that describes the structure of the data? What is the best way to forecast the future changes in knowledge?

Another example of a knowledge management application in software organizations is change management. This refers to one of the fundamental aspects of overall project management, i.e. change requests must be documented and the impact of each change on development artifacts must be tracked and retested after the change is realized. There are significant long-term project costs associated with not managing these issues.

Effective knowledge support in software development requires support from both management and technical levels in software organizations [1, 3]. This can be accomplished in three major directions as follows:

- *Supporting software process*: Support is needed for techniques and technology for the software development process. Examples of this type of support emerge in the form of improving software process models, activities within processes, process results or communication between developers.
- *Supporting software product*: Software development is a creative problem solving activity. Support is needed in design, engineering and modeling with appropriate technology to deliver innovative solutions to clients.
- *Supporting people*: Software development processes consist of a number of different kinds of activities and tasks. These require a considerable amount of knowledge and experience. Software developers need support and guidance to perform activities such as adapting a workflow to support knowledge-intensive tasks.

Several potential questions are still waiting to be explored in the field of software engineering, e.g. how do we get the relevant knowledge, and how do we make it available to developers? How do we improve the communication between developers across various projects? How do we store and reuse the best practices, knowledge and experience in different projects? How do we support knowledge sharing? There are few suggested models and frameworks that provide answers from a knowledge management perspective in order to provide support for software engineering to improve the software development process, software products or software team dynamics.

The objective of this section is to highlight existing problems of managing software engineering knowledge and to examine knowledge management frameworks, and to focus on those that may be potentially helpful in managing software engineering knowledge.

There are five chapters in this part. The first of these is written by Mikael Lindvall and Ioana Rus. The authors examine the existing problems that can be addressed by knowledge management in software organizations. The authors provide a comprehensive and self-contained overview of knowledge management and a description of opportunities for software development organizations.

Software engineering knowledge creation is a social collaborative activity, albeit some knowledge management activities are more effective than others. In Chap. 5 Tore Dybå introduces a dynamic model, which illustrates how software teams acquire and use knowledge in an organizational setting in order to improve their software processes. This article provides a model that illustrates communication, coordination, and collaboration between software teams.

Knowledge has limited value to developers if it is not shared. Although we have the technology that allows knowledge workers to communicate their knowledge, e.g. by using e-mail and intranet, the technology has a limited effect in communication unless there is an explicit strategy to create, integrate, and share the knowledge within the organization. Gary Oliver, John D'Ambra and Christine Van Toorn explore software engineering repositories from a knowledge management perspective in Chap. 6. They propose a framework for capturing and sharing knowledge to facilitate learning in software engineering from the experience of others within the same organizational context.

Requirements engineering lies at the heart of software development, which covers activities such as discovering, documenting, and maintaining requirements for software systems. Requirements engineering is a complex problem-solving activity on its own, because the context of requirements changes as more is learned about the system being built, and as the competitive environment changes. Requirements engineering activities engage many stakeholders with varied knowledge, skills, experiences and viewpoints. It is important to provide a support structure to facilitate the communication and interpretation of requirements between stakeholders so that they can better monitor and manage the requirements engineering activities efficiently and effectively. In Chap. 7, Allen Dutoit and Barbara Paech focus on the importance of change in requirements and knowledge, and how to manage this in requirements engineering activities. The article provides a novel and comprehensive methodological development by capturing not only standard explicit knowledge, but also the unique experiences from past projects, the discussion between stakeholders, assumptions, the rationale, or chain of reasoning in their decisions, as well as instances of the problem domain structure and limitations.

Another example of knowledge management application is in the area of the development of applications for the World Wide Web. Whilst there has been an increasing focus on Web-supported knowledge management, particularly in terms of facilitating learning, knowledge sharing and providing open resources and open communication to software developers, little consideration has been given to understanding the nature of how the knowledge itself emerges during the development of Web systems and how this relates to the peculiarities of Web development practices and processes. In Chap. 8, David Lowe focuses on knowledge underpinning the Web development process, examines the differences between Web systems and conventional software systems, and explores the implications of these differences for system modeling, development practices and techniques, and overall development processes. The article introduces specific problems in Web development and provides a good overview of Web characteristics and impacts.

Reference

1. Aurum A., Handzic M., Land L.P.W. (2001) Knowledge management for disaster planning: a case study. In: Proceedings of 2nd European conference on knowledge management, Bled, Slovenia pp. 19-30
2. Basili V.R., Caldiera G.R., Rombach H.D. (1994) Experience Factory. In: Marciniak J.J. (Ed.). Encyclopedia of software engineering, John Wiley and Sons, pp. 469-476
3. Henninger S. (1997) Case-based knowledge management tools for software development. Automated software engineering 4:319-340
4. King W.R., Marks P.V., McCoy S. (2002) The most important issues in knowledge management. Communications of the ACM 45:93-97
5. Land P.W.L., Aurum A., Handzic M. (2001) Capturing implicit software engineering knowledge. In: Proceedings of the Australian software engineering conference, Canberra, Australia, pp. 108-114

Editor Biography

Dr. Aybüke Aurum is a senior lecturer at the School of Information Systems, Technology and Management, University of New South Wales, Australia. She received her B.Sc. and M.Sc. in geological engineering, and M.E. and Ph.D. in computer science. She is the deputy director of the Center for Advanced Empirical Software Engineering Research Group (CAESER). She is also the founder and group leader of the Requirements Engineering Research Group (ReqEng) at the University of New South Wales. Dr. Aurum is an editorial board member of the *Asian Academy of Management Journal*. She is also a member of IEEE and ACM. Dr. Aurum has published various papers in books, journals and international conference proceedings. Her research interests include management of the software development process, software inspections, requirements engineering, decision making and knowledge management.

4 Knowledge Management for Software Organizations

Mikael Lindvall and Ioana Rus

Abstract: This chapter presents an introduction to the topic of knowledge management (KM) in software engineering. It identifies the need for knowledge, knowledge items and sources, and discusses the importance of knowledge capture, organization, retrieval, access, and evolution in software development organizations. KM activities and supporting tools for software development and inter- and intra-organization learning are presented. The state of the implementation of KM in software organizations is examined, together with benefits, challenges, and lessons learned.

Keywords: Knowledge management, Software engineering, Software development organizations, Individual and organizational learning

4.1 Introduction

Software engineering is a fast-paced, changing and knowledge-intensive business, involving many people working in different phases and activities. Since individuals are the ones developing software, the ultimate goal is for them to have access to the right knowledge at the right time. Thus, new knowledge might be acquired, and existing individual knowledge must be leveraged to the organizational level and then distributed back to the individuals who need it. This has to be done in an organized manner because software knowledge is diverse and its proportions immense and steadily growing. At the same time, knowledge is crucial for success. From a business perspective, knowledge is needed, for example, to improve the process and facilitate better decisions. From an operational perspective, the knowledge is needed to master new technologies and problem domains, and to understand and apply local procedures and policies. There is also a need to reuse existing assets and find local expertise.

In this chapter, we identify and analyze knowledge needs in software organizations, identify knowledge objects and sources, and examine how software organizations could manage this knowledge to retain and enhance their intellectual assets, thereby increasing their competitiveness. We also discuss what some organizations are already doing and present their results and the lessons learned. This chapter provides an overview of several areas related to knowledge management (KM) that are covered in more detail in other chapters of this book.

4.2 Business and Knowledge Needs

A software organization has many different needs related to knowledge. These needs can be viewed from a business and from a skills and practice perspective. From a business perspective, the main needs are to produce better, faster, and cheaper software and to make better decisions. Software organizations have and require vast amounts of knowledge to support the business objectives for which technology, process, project, product, and domain knowledge are the most critical areas.

4.2.1 The Need to Decrease Development Time and Cost and Increase Quality

Besides the overall needs of acquiring new business, keeping customers satisfied, and protecting organizational resources in software organizations, there is a constant need to decrease development time and cost in software projects. At the same time, product quality must increase. Reusing previous work and avoiding mistakes would reduce the amount of rework. Repeating successful processes would increase productivity, quality and the likelihood of further success. In order to avoid repeating mistakes but to actively repeat successes, knowledge gained in previous projects could be used to guide and improve future projects. In reality, development teams do not take full advantage of existing experience, but repeat mistakes over and over again [8]. Valuable individual experience is acquired with each project, and much more could be gained if there were a systematic way to efficiently share this diverse knowledge.

4.2.2 The Need for Making Better Decisions

Software development is a process where every person involved constantly makes decisions, either technical or managerial. Most of the time, decisions are based on personal knowledge and experience or on knowledge gained using informal contacts. This is feasible in small and localized organizations, but as organizations grow larger and/or become distributed, more and more people and information must be handled, often over a distance. Large organizations are suboptimizing if they only rely on informally shared personal knowledge. Individual knowledge should be shared and leveraged at project and organization levels, and formal ways of sharing knowledge must be defined to complement informal sharing so that correct decisions can be made throughout the organization.

4.2.2.1   Need for Knowledge about New Technologies

Software engineers learn basic software methods and technologies in school, but new ones are constantly developed. A software engineer who does not keep up with the latest technology developments quickly becomes out of date. The emergence of new technologies makes software more powerful, but at the same time, new technologies could be "the project manager's worst nightmare" [8]. It takes time to become proficient with a new technology, understand its impact, and estimate the cost of applying it. When developers or project managers use a technology that is new to the project's team members, the engineers frequently resort to the "learning by doing" approach that often results in serious delays. There is thus a need to acquire and master knowledge about new technologies.

4.2.2.2 Need for Problem Domain Knowledge

Software development requires knowledge not only about its own domain and software technologies, but also about the domain for which software is being developed. "Writing code is not the problem, understanding the problem is the problem" [10]. When a new project in a new domain is launched, considerable amounts of time are spent on understanding the problem domain. Thus, there is a need to manage problem domain knowledge better.

4.2.2.3 Need for Knowledge about Local Policies, Practices, and Past Projects

Every organization has its own specific culture, policies, and practices, not only technical but also managerial and administrative. In order to perform well at the workplace, each employee must know and practice local rules and policies. New developers especially need knowledge concerning the existing software base and local programming conventions. This type of knowledge might exist only as folklore and is often disseminated to inexperienced developers through ad hoc informal meetings; consequently, not everyone has access to the knowledge they need [32]. Passing knowledge informally is an important aspect of a knowledge-sharing culture that must be encouraged. Nonetheless, formal knowledge capturing and sharing is necessary to ensure its availability to all employees. There is thus a need to formalize knowledge sharing of local policies and practices while also supporting informal and ad hoc knowledge sharing.

4.2.2.4 Need to Locate Sources of Knowledge

Some of the organizational knowledge is captured on different media (paper, electronic files, tapes, and so on). Individuals search for such knowledge in order to learn from it and reuse it, but in order to do so they must know where to search. There is thus a need to efficiently locate and access captured knowledge. At the same time, not all knowledge is captured, and software organizations are heavily dependent on knowledge that lies within knowledgeable people [33]. These people are important for the success of projects, but it can be difficult to identify and access them. One study found that software developers apply just as much effort and attention to determining whom to contact in the organization as to getting the job done [23]. If a person with critical knowledge leaves, severe knowledge gaps are created [8]. The problem is that often no one in the organization is even aware of what knowledge was lost. [4]. Knowing what employees know is a necessity in order to create a strategy for preventing knowledge from disappearing. Knowing who has what knowledge is a requirement for efficiently staffing projects, identifying training needs, and matching employees with training offers.

4.2.2.5   Need to Share Knowledge in a Distributed Manner

Software development is a group activity. Group members are often spread out geographically and work in different time zones and need to communicate, collaborate, and coordinate. Communication is often related to the transfer of knowledge. Collaboration is related to mutual sharing of knowledge. Coordination independent of time and space is facilitated if work artifacts are easily accessible. There is thus a need to collaborate and share knowledge independent of time and space.

4.3   Knowledge Management in Software Engineering

In software engineering, different approaches have been proposed for achieving business and knowledge needs. These approaches address factors such as process improvement, introduction of new technologies, and "peopleware." Knowledge management (KM) mainly addresses peopleware in that it focuses on how to facilitate individuals' access to the right knowledge at the right time. Software engineering has actually engaged for years in KM-related activities aimed at learning, capturing, and reusing experience, although not using the phrase "knowledge management." Examples of such activities are *process improvement, best practices,* and the *experience factory* [2]. What makes KM unique is its focus on the *individual* as a consumer of knowledge and as bearer and provider of important knowledge that could systematically be shared throughout the organization. The scope of KM is organization-wide, as the knowledge and the knowledge needs within an organization can be managed in a more organized way than knowledge outside the organization. KM does not disagree with the value of — or the need for — addressing other aspects of software development, such as process and technology, nor does it seek to replace them. KM is rather an approach to achieve software process improvement and to facilitate adoption of new technologies. KM does this by explicitly and systematically addressing the management of the organizational knowledge from the point of view of its acquisition, storage, organization, evolution, and accessibility. Software process improvement approaches, for example CMM [22], often suggest that knowledge be managed, but do not bring it down to an operational level. KM, on the other hand, explicitly states what knowledge needs to be managed, how, when, where, by whom, and for whom. KM is the "glue" that ties together the daily production activities to improvement initiatives and business goals, supporting the evolution of learning organizations.

In software organizations, knowledge is very diverse and exists in multiple forms. Some of the technical, product and project knowledge is already captured in the documents produced by projects such as project plans, and requirements, design, and testing specifications. In addition to the software product itself, the documents capture some of the knowledge that emerged from solving problems encountered in the project. This documented knowledge can be leveraged by a KM initiative that systematically organizes and makes knowledge available to employees who need it. An optional but highly recommended task the organization can conduct is ensuring that knowledge gained during the project is not lost. This task can be conducted during the project and shortly after its completion. It addresses the acquisition of knowledge that was not documented as part of the core activities as well as the analysis of documents in order to create new knowledge. Included here are all forms of lessons learned and post mortem analyses, as presented for example in [6], that identify what went right or wrong in the project related to both software product and process. Tasks in this category collect and create knowledge about *one* particular project and can be performed by any organization. The results are useful by themselves but also can be the basis for further learning. They can be stored in repositories and experience bases. Once captured, the knowledge becomes *explicit* [21] and can be reused by subsequent projects, for example, by analyzing solutions to different problems. The benefit of explicit knowledge and experience is that it can be stored, organized, and disseminated to a third party without the involvement of the originator. One drawback, however, is that considerable effort is required to produce explicit knowledge. Knowledge that was not explicitly captured (that is, *tacit* knowledge [21]) is still owned by individuals and can only be accessed and leveraged if the organization can identify these individuals, and if they chose to share their knowledge.

4.4 KM Activities and Tools

As a result of a study of the current KM activities and tools, we identified two classes: basic KM not specific to software organizations that can support any type of organization, and KM that specifically support software development. We grouped the latter in three categories by the scope of their inputs (i.e., one or multiple projects); by the purpose of their outcome (i.e., to support core SE activities, to support project improvement, or organizational improvement); and by the level of effort required for processing the inputs in order to serve SE needs. For more extensive discussions of tools and case studies, we refer to [19, 29].

4.4.1 Basic KM

In this category we include KM activities that can be applied to any type of organization, especially to knowledge-intensive industries (e.g., legal services, consulting, or advertising). We emphasize, however, how these activities and tools (*asset reuse, document management, competence management,* and *expert networks*) serve the needs of software organizations.

4.4.1.1   Asset Reuse

One of the approaches in the software engineering community that is related to KM is software reuse. There are endless stories about programmers who reimplement the same solutions over and over again and in slightly different ways. Software reuse aims to reduce this rework by establishing a reuse repository to which programmers submit software assets they believe would be useful to others. The software development process is changed so that instead of developing all software from scratch, the employee first searches the repository for reusable artifacts. Only if nothing useful were found would the software be written from scratch. The same concept can be applied to all software engineering artifacts, such as requirements documents, design, and test specifications. Many of the activities and tools discussed below support asset reuse in one form or another.

4.4.1.2   Document Management

A variety of processes and activities are performed during a software development project [7], many of which are document-driven. Work is many times focused on authoring, reviewing, editing, and using these documents. These documents become the assets of the organization in capturing explicit knowledge. Document management systems help organizations manage these invaluable assets, enable knowledge transferal from experts to novices, and support the location, organization, and reuse of documented knowledge. Common needs that arise in a document-sharing environment are related to identifying the latest version of a document, accessing documents remotely, and sharing the documents in workgroups. Document management systems offer features that include storing and uploading of documents and files; version control, organization of documents in different ways, search and retrieval based on indexing techniques and advanced searching mechanisms, and access from any Internet-connected workstation. Most document management systems also provide some kind of search for experts based on authorship. Document management systems can aid learning software organizations that need to capture and share process and product knowledge.

4.4.1.3 Collaboration

Collaboration is increasingly required by software organizations. Software projects often have many members that need to collaborate. Because of globalization, software development working groups are often spread out geographically and work in different time zones. Collaboration tools help people communicate, collaborate, and coordinate, often independently of time and place. Tools in this category connect employees by providing a computer-based communication channel. This communication can be synchronous or asynchronous. Collaboration using a chat tool or a messenger tool are examples of synchronous tools, while e-mail, bulletin boards, and newsgroups are examples of asynchronous tools. Some tools are designed to capture communication and work results for further use and refinement, for example, a tool that supports electronic workshops (*e-workshops*) in on-line moderated meetings between expert participants [5]. The results of such e-workshops are captured and analyzed in order to generate new knowledge in a particular area. This illustrates that technology and process can be used to bring people together and generate new knowledge. Features for collaboration and communication, both synchronous and asynchronous, are part of many other tools discussed in Sect. 4.5.

4.4.1.4 Competence Management

Far from all the tacit knowledge in an organization can be made explicit, and far from all explicit knowledge can be documented. In order to utilize undocumented knowledge, the organization needs to keep track of who knows what. A solution to this problem is *competence management*, also called *skills* management, which can be based on expert identification. While document management deals with explicit knowledge assets, competence management keeps track of tacit knowledge. Organizations need to develop *knowledge maps* and identify sources of knowledge in terms of *know-who* and *know-where*. Once such a knowledge map is in place it can be used to identify appointed and de facto experts, staff new projects based on skills and experience required, and identify knowledge gaps that indicate the need to hire new people or to develop training programs. Tools that support competence management can be helpful, especially for large organizations, where people do not know each other. Their necessity also becomes obvious in any distributed, decentralized, and mobile organization. A typical feature of these tools is *profiling* or expert identification. Profiles of employees, customers, subcontractors, vendors, partners, projects, and positions can be generated, which also leads to identification of and searches for experts. Some tools automatically create competence profiles by mining various sources of information. Profiling mechanisms extract terms and phrases from e-mail communications and documents produced or shared by individuals. Each user profile provides a detailed index of an individual's knowledge, experience, and work focus. A set of profiles, therefore, represents a composite snapshot of the expertise within an organization.

4.4.1.5   Expert Networks

Expert networks provide a forum for people who need to establish knowledge sharing focused on solving a problem. Expert networks are typically based on peer-to-peer support and can reduce the time spent by software engineers in looking for specific domain knowledge. They can also be used to efficiently transfer knowledge regarding local policies and new technologies. These kinds of systems help geographically distributed organizations communicate and collaborate. Common features of tools supporting expert networks are expertise brokerage, expert identification, communication and collaboration between people, and capture of questions and answers. These tools typically track and rate expertise, customer satisfaction, and rewards that are given to people who contribute to the success of the system.

4.4.2   KM in Software Organizations

With each project, software developers and managers acquire invaluable experience. Learning from experience requires a memory or experience base that captures process-, product- and project-related events. The environment in which software engineers conduct their daily work often supports creating such a memory, which could be leveraged in order to implement KM and learn more about the organization. Version control, change management, documenting design decisions, and requirements traceability are software engineering practices that help build such memories as a direct or side effect of using these tools in software development. Other tools, such as document management tools, defect tracking tools, and competence management tools also build memories in similar ways.

4.4.2.1   Configuration Management and Version Control

Configuration management (CM) keeps track of a project documents and relates them to each other. Version control systems such as the *Source Code Control System* (SCCS) [27] represent a class of tools that indirectly create a project memory. Each version of the documents has a record attached with information about *who* made the change and *when* it was made, together with a comment stating *why* the change was made. This "memory" indicates the software evolution. This information has been used for advanced analysis of software products and processes, [13, 18]. Software engineers can use the information stored in these memories, for example, to look at who made a certain change in order to identify experts for solving the related problem.

4.4.2.2 Design Rationale

Design rationale [24] is an example of an approach that explicitly captures design decisions in order to create a product memory. During design, different technical solutions are tested and decisions are made based on the results of these tests. Unfortunately, these decisions are rarely captured, making it very hard for someone else to understand the reasons behind the solutions. Design rationale captures this information as well as information about solutions that were considered and tested but not implemented. This process can be helpful for making better decisions and avoiding repetition of mistakes in future maintenance and evolution of the software system.

4.4.2.3 Traceability

Software requirements drive the development of software systems, but the connection between the final system and its requirements is often fuzzy [31]. Traceability is an approach that makes the connection between requirements and the final software system explicit [20, 26]. Traceability indirectly contributes to "product memory" and helps answer questions such as "What requirements led to a particular piece of source code?" and "What code was developed in order to satisfy this particular requirement?" This is crucial information for developers adding new capabilities to the software.

4.4.2.4 Trouble Reports and Defect Tracking

Trouble reports and systems for defect tracking are good sources of negative knowledge that can be turned into positive knowledge. They contain knowledge about product features and properties with which users have difficulties as well as knowledge regarding the organization's management of past complaints. By analyzing this knowledge, the organization can learn from past experience and design their products and process better in order to increase both customer satisfaction as well as the efficiency of their processes. Common needs that arise in this environment are registering trouble reports, describing the nature of the issue and how it occurred so it can be reproduced, and if possible, identifying its likely cause. Systems in this category offer features that support searching for a specific trouble report, and report generation for a certain version of a product during a certain period of time.

4.4.2.5 CASE Tools and Software Development Environments

Computer-aided software engineering (CASE) tools and environments for software development primarily support the design, generation, implementation, and debugging of software, but they also support the creation of product and process knowledge in terms of the artifacts that are created. By explicitly capturing design, for example, the organization enables knowledge sharing across time and space. By using a CASE tool, the design is not only documented and thereby memorized, but also captured in a formal way, ensuring that its semantic meaning is well defined. By analyzing the knowledge captured in these systems, the organization can improve product and process design in order to increase their quality and efficiency, respectively. Common needs that arise in this environment are to share design environments among members of a team that might not be physically co-located. These development environments often offer features that support: version management of artifacts, design verification based on design rules, generation of source code based on design, and debugging.

For more information on these technologies we refer to the following chapters in this book: Chap. 7 on knowledge for requirements evolution, Chap. 11 on quality assurance, and Chap. 5 on knowledge creation.

4.4.3 KM to Support Organization and Industry Learning and Decision Making

Many different technologies create knowledge based on results from previous projects. Examples are prediction models, lessons learned and best practices, case-based reasoning, and data and knowledge discovery.

4.4.3.1 Prediction Models

Project managers need to make decisions, both at the beginning as well as during projects. Typically, they use their personal experience and their "gut feelings" to guide decisions. But since software development is such a complex and diverse process, "gut feelings" may be insufficient, and not all managers have extensive experience. For these reasons, prediction models that transform data into knowledge can guide decision making for future projects based on past projects. This requires implementing a metrics program, collecting data from multiple projects with a well-defined goal, and then analyzing and processing the data to generate *predictive models* [3]. The inputs and outputs of these models can be quantitative or qualitative. Input data are analyzed, synthesized, and processed using different methods, depending on the purpose of the model and the type of inputs and outputs. For example, analytical models take numerical data (or qualitative data converted into quantitative levels) from a large number of projects and try to find formulae to correlate inputs and outputs. By using these formulae for the data that characterize a new project, one can make estimations for cost, effort, defects, reliability, and other product and project parameters. Building, using, and improving these models become a natural part of the KM strategy. The drawback is that the quality of the predictions offered by these models depends on the quality of the collected data.

4.4.3.2 Lessons Learned and Best Practices

Information collected from projects can also be in a qualitative form, such as *cases* and *lessons learned,* success and failure *stories*, and problems and corresponding solutions as well as defect tracking, and decisions histories captured by design rationale. This information is usually in textual format such as rules, indexed cases, or semantic networks. By applying generalization and abstraction, new knowledge can be generated (manually, or automatically by applying Artificial Intelligence (AI) techniques) that can be later applied to similar problems, in similar contexts. This is how patterns, best-practice guidelines, handbooks, and standards can be derived.

4.4.3.3 Case-based Systems

For example, in *case-based* systems, project experiences are captured in the form of "cases" in order to accommodate software development process diversity while retaining a level of discipline and standard [15]. These experiences are disseminated to developers to provide knowledge of previous development issues in the organization. Deviations from the standard process are opportunities to improve the process itself. Apart from refining the process, the deviations also work as *cases* in the experience base. As more and more experience is acquired in the form of cases, the development process becomes iteratively more refined. For more information on case-based reasoning we refer to Chap. 9 in this book.

4.4.3.4 Data and Knowledge Discovery

To automatically generate new knowledge from existing data, information, and knowledge bases, there are tools that include visualization and data mining, as well as analysis and synthesis. Data mining tools try to reveal patterns and relationships between data and generate new knowledge about the data and what it represents. Such tools can be used to identify patterns related to both the content and the usage of knowledge. Knowledge discovery also identifies groups of users and their profiles, as well as de facto experts. Thus, more complex knowledge items are generated, for example, through deriving best practices based on lessons learned and frequently asked questions. Tools in this category often provide data visualization. Features for statistical analysis are also common, along with decision support features. These features are sometimes based on AI techniques that can help in the discovery process. Another group of tools analyze multimedia content and transcribe it into text, identify and rank the main concepts within it, and automatically personalize and deliver that information to those who need it.

4.4.4 KM at a Corporate Level

In addition to the KM activities directly related to software development presented above, an organization must also perform additional tasks that support development, such as customer relationship management, intellectual property management, and training and education.

4.4.4.1 Customer Relationship Management

Customer support can help keep customers satisfied and help the organization get new business. There are mainly two forms of customer support tools: tools that enable customers to self-help and tools that help customer support personnel (help-desk). In some cases, vendors set up areas for customers to help each other, i.e., to share knowledge about products and services (peer-to-peer). There are many cases where high repeatability in the support process can be leveraged by reusing answers to the most common questions. Over time, support personnel acquire a vast amount of knowledge about the products and services the organization offers, as well as information about customers and their behavior. This knowledge is a resource for the organization as a whole and should be captured and spread. Systems that support help desks typically have features that direct customer requests to representatives based on customer profiles and the representatives' expertise. Knowledge bases typically provide an interface to capture knowledge about products, services, and their use so that new cases, new incidents, and new lessons learned can be captured and shared.

4.4.4.2 Intellectual Property Management

Software organizations need to protect their intellectual property (IP) in the form of patents, copyrights, trademarks, and service marks. Organizations that own intellectual property need ways to automate workflow and support the management and analysis of inventions, patents, and related matters. It often takes a long time to file and obtain approved rights to intellectual property, and organizations need support to track this process. Intellectual property regulations require owners of copyrights, trademarks, and service marks to pay legal fees at specific points in time, otherwise the rights can be lost. For licensing issues, it is also important to track licensees and royalties. Another aspect of intellectual property is the protection of digital content covered by copyright. IP tools can help software organizations better manage their intellectual property. Typical IP tools include searching for patents capabilities, support filing for patents, searchable knowledge bases with rules and regulations and support for legal help, as well as accessing collections of forms and standard letters. Other related issues that these tools support are licensing of patents and tracking of licenses, as well as calculation of fees.

4.4.4.3 Knowledge Portals

A study found that people in software organizations spent 40% of their time searching for different types of information related to their projects [14]. Employees make decisions every day, but not all of them are based on complete and correct information. When critical data is hard to find, or takes too long to locate, it will not be available when it is needed to make a decision. Making the best decision requires current and relevant information, which is what portals deliver. Portals help organizations provide information to employees in a simple, user-friendly and consistent way, thereby reducing the time spent looking for information. In the search for knowledge, workers use many different computer-based information sources that need to be integrated and accessed through a common interface. Portals create a customized single gateway to a wide and heterogeneous collection of data, information, and knowledge. They also provide different kinds of personalization so that content is presented in a manner that suits the individual's role within the organization and reflects personal preferences. Both the organization and the user can control what information is made available and how it is displayed.

4.5 KM in Support of Learning

New employees must learn about their organization in order to get up to speed in their new job, and existing employees must learn in order to perform their tasks better. From an individual's perspective, learning involves acquisition, assimilation, and application of knowledge. Once an individual has knowledge, it must be shared with peers within a working group or organization in order to increase collective knowledge and performance. We examine how individuals learn and how the knowledge is leveraged at an organizational level. This is intracompany learning, but there is also interorganizational learning. We look at both these processes and also discuss e-learning as a means of using available technology to enable self- and distance learning.

Individuals can acquire knowledge and expertise through organized training or by learning-by-doing as needed. Each of these approaches has strengths and weaknesses. For both, KM helps reduce some drawbacks. For example, organized training is often both time-consuming and expensive and, if done externally to the organization, does not cover local knowledge. KM, by capturing, storing, and organizing knowledge, makes it possible to provide the basis for internal training courses. Learning by doing might be risky due to the fact that mistakes are often made until people find the right solution, and learning occurs in limited amounts because only the knowledge needed to solve the current task is being acquired. In support of this type of learning, KM provides knowledge or pointers to knowledge sources, when and where they are needed.

4.5.1 Intraorganizational Learning (Internal)

Knowledge transfer between individuals can take various forms. Most models that support experience reuse and KM make the assumption that all relevant experience can be collected and recorded, but this does not hold true in practice [34]. There are a variety of more or less automated solutions to KM, addressing different aspects and tasks, and they address both tacit and explicit knowledge.

For example, Ericsson Software Technology AB has implemented a version of the *Experience Factory* called the *Experience Engine* [16]. Instead of relying on experience stored in experience bases, the Experience Engine relies on tacit knowledge. Two roles were created in order to make the tacit knowledge accessible to a larger group of employees. The *experience communicator* is a person who has in-depth knowledge on one or more topics. The *experience broker* connects the experience communicator with the person owning the problem. The communicator should not solve the problem, but educate the problem owner in how to solve it. A similar approach has been implemented at sd&m AG (Germany) [8]. The idea of relying on tacit rather than explicit knowledge is appealing because it relaxes the requirement to document knowledge extensively. Although it utilizes knowledge, this approach still does not solve the problem of the organization being dependent on its employees. We refer to Chap. 13 in this book for more information on this topic.

Knowledge sharing occurs informally at coffee tables, in the lounge, and around the water cooler. When an employee tells a colleague how a particular problem was solved, knowledge is shared. Some development practices, such as pair programming, facilitate knowledge sharing between peers, while pair rotation helps its spread throughout the project or organization [35]. Software organizations should encourage these habits in order to create a knowledge sharing culture. To reach maximum knowledge sharing, employees should also be encouraged to document and store their knowledge in a KM repository. They should be encouraged to deposit information into the knowledge base of the organization whenever they help somebody. By doing so, they ensure that the information is recorded and will help other employees as well, since what is a problem for one can also be a problem for others [32].

4.5.2 Interorganizational Learning (External)

An important part of learning is learning from sources outside the organization. Such learning can occur by sharing knowledge with outside peers, by sharing knowledge with vendors and customers, and by sharing knowledge with the industry as a whole, through industry-wide communities.

Software organizations have formed numerous useful communities. Examples of communities are the Software Program Managers Network[1] (SPMN) for project

---

[1] http://www.spmn.com/ (accessed on 14th April 2003)

managers, the Software Experience Consortium[2] (SEC) for companies seeking to share experience, Sun's community for Java programmers,[3] the Software Process Improvement Network,[4] (SPIN) and the special interest groups of IEEE or ACM.[5]

Organizations may learn from external sources, typically vendors of technology. In support of this, several software vendors provide Web-based knowledge bases. Examples are Microsoft's Knowledge Base[6], Oracle's Support Center[7], and Perl's Frequently Asked Questions[8]. Such knowledge bases are often open to the public and enable software engineers to search for knowledge themselves. These knowledge bases result from capturing product knowledge owned by representatives at the vendor organizations that is then made available to the customers.

At the software industry level, committees or groups of experts identify patterns (e.g., software design patterns) and generate handbooks and standards (e.g. IEEE, ISO) generally applicable to software development in order to leverage the experience and knowledge of all software development organizations. This is not something any individual or organization can perform, as it takes much effort and requires considerable amounts of knowledge about software engineering as well as access to project data. The *Software Engineering Body of Knowledge*[9] (SWEBOK) defines the knowledge that a practicing software engineer needs to master on a daily basis. Other examples of comprehensive collections of software engineering (SE) knowledge are ISO 15504 (SPICE), describes "all" processes related to SE, and the Capability Maturity Model CMM [22]. The Center for Empirically Based Software Engineering (CeBASE) and ViSEK[10] are examples of projects whose goal is to build software engineering knowledge bases. They accumulate empirical models in order to provide validated guidelines for selecting techniques and models, supporting technology transfer, recommending areas for research, and supporting software engineering education.

4.5.3 E-Learning

KM aims to help people acquire new knowledge, as well as package and deliver existing knowledge through teaching. *e-learning* can help software organizations organize their knowledge transfer and conduct it more effectively by using information technology. It is a relatively new area that includes computer-based and on-line training tools. E-learning is appealing because it offers flexibility in

---

[2] http://fc-md.umd.edu/ (accessed on 14th April 2003)
[3] http://developer.java.sun.com/developer/community/ (accessed on 14th April 2003)
[4] http://www.sei.cmu.edu/collaborating/spins/ (accessed on 14th April 2003)
[5] http://www.acm.org/sigs/guide98.html (accessed on 14th April 2003)
[6] http://search.support.microsoft.com/kb/ (accessed on 14th April 2003)
[7] http://www.oracle.com/support/index.html?content.html (accessed on 14th April 2003)
[8] http://www.perl.com/pub/q/faqs (accessed on 14th April 2003)
[9] http://www.swebok.org/ (accessed on 14th April 2003)
[10] http://www.iese.fhg.de/Projects/ViSEK/ (accessed on 14th April 2003)

time and space, as well as collaboration between students and tutors. Many of the collaboration and communication tools mentioned before can be used to support this activity. Common features include reusable learning object libraries; adaptive Web-based course delivery; component-based authoring, scheduling, and reporting tools; student evaluation and progress tracking; and building of skills inventories. E-learning systems often include collaboration tools and support for different types of content, i.e., video, audio, documents and so on.

4.6 Challenges and Obstacles

Implementing KM involves many challenges and obstacles. Some of the most important issues identified by [17] are:

- *Technology issues*: KM is supported by software technology, but it is not always possible to integrate all the different subsystems and tools to achieve the desired level of knowledge access and delivery.
- *Organizational issues*: It is a mistake to focus only on technology and not on methodology. It is easy to fall into the technology trap and devote all resources to technology development, without planning for a KM strategy and implementation process.
- *Individual issues*: Employees do not have time to input or search for knowledge, do not want to give away their knowledge, or do not want to reuse someone else's knowledge.

We discuss some of these issues in terms of KM as a commitment and investment that requires a good strategy and appropriate resources. It takes time to see the benefits from KM activities, and a "champion" is required, who constantly "guards" the KM initiative. Employees need to be rewarded for contributing to the KM effort and a general cultural change might be needed.

4.6.1 KM as an Investment

Planning, implementing, and sustaining KM is challenging because resources, time, and effort are required before benefits become visible. KM is simply an investment. Often this is considered a burden to project managers, who focus on completing the current project on time, not on helping the next project succeed. In KM systems that have been implemented so far, KM activities are often performed by a different set of people, other than developers, e.g., the chief knowledge officer (CKO) and his staff, the experience factory (EF) group, the software engineering process group (SEPG), or the software process improvement (SPI) group. This is to support the developers in their daily work instead of requiring additional effort.

4.6.2 Lightweight Approaches to Knowledge Management

For knowledge bases, it generally takes too long to build a critical mass of knowledge before users perceive it to be useful. Lightweight approaches to knowledge capturing and sharing address this issue, allowing for quick and easy implementation. They have the potential to pay off quickly [30], while at the same time enabling long-term goals. An example of a lightweight approach is the Knowledge Dust Collector [19], which that supports peer-to-peer knowledge sharing. It captures and makes available knowledge that employees exchange and use every day. The knowledge "dust" evolves over time into well-packaged experience in the form of knowledge "pearls," a refined form of knowledge. An example is captured dialogues regarding technical problems (knowledge dust) that are analyzed and turned into frequently asked questions (FAQ, knowledge pearls). These FAQs are further analyzed and turned into best practices (extended knowledge pearls).

4.6.3 The Importance of a Champion

Earlier KM initiatives recognized that any KM initiative requires an evangelist or a champion. This person needs to encourage employees to contribute and use the system, and must always be its proponent. As was noted by the champion of one of the KM initiatives at Hewlett-Packard, "the participation numbers are still creeping up, but this would have failed without an evangelist. Even at this advanced stage, if I got run over by a beer truck, this [knowledge] database would be in trouble", [11]. Many companies realized that such a job requires a lot of effort and they created specialized positions such as KM officer or chief knowledge officer (CKO).

4.6.4 Creating a Culture of Sharing

Although new technology has made it easier than ever to share knowledge, organizational cultures might not promote sharing. Some cultures even encourage individualism and ban cooperative work. Lack of a "knowledge culture" was frequently cited as a critical obstacle to a successful KM [1]. Cultural obstacle occurs, for example, when employees feel possessive about their knowledge and may not be forthcoming in sharing it. Their knowledge is why they are valuable to the organization; they may fear that they will be considered redundant and disposable as soon as the employer has captured their knowledge. Employees might not be willing to share negative experiences and lessons learned based on failures because of their negative connotation. So although the purpose is to avoid similar mistakes, employees might fear that such information could be used against them. Another hurdle is the "not invented here" syndrome. There are beliefs that the SE community has more fun reinventing solutions rather than reusing existing experience. Although change is hard, such beliefs have to be revisited and replaced by a positive attitude, oriented toward a sharing culture.

4.6.5 Implicit-to-Explicit Knowledge Conversion

Another obstacle is that most of the knowledge in software organizations is not explicit. There is little time to make knowledge explicit, there are very few approaches and tools for turning tacit into explicit knowledge, and most of the tacit knowledge is tacit in the most extreme way, being even difficult to be expressed and made explicit. Quick changes in technology often discourage software engineers from reflecting on the knowledge they gained during a project, believing that it will not be useful to share this knowledge in the future.

4.6.6 Reward Systems

It is important that the organization not only encourages but also rewards employees who are willing to share their knowledge, to search for knowledge, and to reuse their peers' knowledge. To encourage sharing and reusing of knowledge, Xerox recommends the creation of a "hall of fame" for those people whose contributions have solved real business problems. Xerox rewards staff that regularly share useful information and identifies them as key contributors to the program. At Hewlett Packard, the main evangelist of the KM initiative gave out free Lotus Notes licenses to prospective users, as well as free airline miles [11]. Infosys rewards contribution and usage of knowledge with "knowledge currency units," eventually converted into a cash equivalent [25]. Another type of reward system is the "points system" used by ExpertExchange,[11] where experts are rewarded with points for answering questions. The experts with the highest numbers of points have answered the most questions and are often recognized on the front page of the Web site.

4.7 State of the Practice

Many organizations have experiences from implementing KM. One of the more interesting case studies is British Petroleum's story on how they implemented KM [9]. A limited, but increasing, number of software organizations report from their KM efforts. Software development companies have realized the importance and potential of implementing KM systems for years. There are reports published in the 1990s regarding KM case studies in large companies such as Microsoft [12]

---

[11] www.expertexchange.com

and Hewlett-Packard [11]. Some of the KM activities that they implemented were document management, expert networks, competence management (linked with training and education), and product development. More recently, software organizations from around the world (USA, Europe, and Asia) are actively reporting on their KM activities, results, and lessons learned [28]. These are commercial and government organizations, developing software for diverse domains such as satellites, cars, electronics, telecommunications, and for the Internet. The growing number of publications and events on this topic indicates an increasing interest from practitioners, consultants, and researchers in applying KM at different levels from project-level knowledge to organization-wide initiatives. Various activities are implemented, from local project analysis and traceability to expert networks, to complex and highly automated knowledge and experience repositories. Companies reported that the introduction of KM activities allowed them to achieve business goals by decreasing the number of defects, increasing productivity, and decreasing cost (mainly by reducing mistakes and rework), as well as reducing the frequency of delayed responses to customer inquiries or complaints. These improvements were due to increased understanding and experience sharing, increased knowledge availability, and reduced production interruptions caused by lack of knowledge, enhanced collaboration and communication, new knowledge creation, and knowledge retention. Learning has become part of daily routine, leading to process improvements, better teamwork, and increased job satisfaction.

4.8 Conclusions

We have analyzed the need for knowledge in software organizations and how leveraging existing knowledge as well as implementing additional KM practices and tools could accommodate those needs. We have discussed different approaches to implementing KM and what organizations have experienced from that work.

There are some lessons learned from implementing KM, useful for organizations that are embarking in such activities. Although technology support is important and must exist, human and social factors are of utmost importance. Some key factors for a successful implementation of KM in software development companies are the acquisition of knowledge performed during projects, not after their completion; the existence of a good atmosphere for discussing issues within the project team; the understanding that KM (similarly to process improvement, for example) implies change and is difficult unless integrated smoothly with the daily activities; and finally the recognition that improvement takes time and results might not be immediately visible, therefore the need for upper management long-term commitment. KM is not a "one size fits all" approach. KM requires an implementation strategy that must address local needs, goals, problems, and specific contexts. KM should start by being focused, evaluate the results of its implementation in order to see what works in a specific environment, and then identify the next steps. KM results must convince developers to use it and prove to them that it is really supporting their daily work. It also must convince management and financial decision makers that it is worth the investment and the effort.

Despite the challenges faced by the introduction of KM initiatives, there are good reasons to believe that KM for software organizations will succeed if appropriately focused and implemented. One of the main arguments is that KM systems must be supported by appropriate information technology [8]. IT might be intimidating to many people, but not to software engineers [30]. Instead, it can be expected that they benefit even more from advanced technology. Another supporting fact is that all software-related artifacts are already in electronic form and thus can easily be distributed and shared. Also, knowledge sharing between software engineers already occurs to a large degree in some environments. A good example is Google Groups [12] (former Usenet discussion groups), where software engineers actively share knowledge by answering questions and helping solve problems that other software engineers post, without any form of compensation. This instance shows that software engineers are willing to share their knowledge with other people, even outside their company, and that it is worth the effort to capture knowledge. Any organization that can adopt and adapt such a knowledge-sharing philosophy should be successful in implementing KM.

Acknowledgements

We would like to thank Jennifer Dix for proofreading.

References

1. Agresti W., (2000) Knowledge management. Advances in computers, 53: 171-283
2. Basili V.R., Caldiera G., Rombach D.H. (1994) The experience factory. Encyclopedia of software engineering, John Wiley and Sons, UK, pp. 469-476
3. Basili V.R., Caldiera G., Rombach D.H. (1994) The goal question metric approach. Encyclopedia of software engineering, John Wiley and Sons, UK, pp. 528-532
4. Basili V.R., Lindvall M., Costa P. (2001) Implementing the experience factory concepts as a set of experience bases. Knowledge systems institute. In: Proceedings of the 13th International conference on software engineering and knowledge engineering, Buenos Aires, Argentina, pp. 102-109
5. Basili V.R., Tesoriero R., Costa P., Lindvall M., Rus I., Shull F., Zelkowitz M.V. (2001) Building an experience base for software engineering: a report on the first CeBASE eWorkshop. In: Bomarius F., Komi-Sirviö S. (Eds.). Proceedings of PROFES 2001, Kaiserslautern, Germany, pp. 110-125
6. Birk A., Dingsoyr T., Stalhane T. (2002) Postmortem: never leave a project without it. IEEE Software, 19:43-45

---

[12] www.google.com

7. Birk A., Surmann D., Althoff K.-D. (1999) Applications of knowledge acquisition in experimental software engineering. In: Proceedings of the 11th European workshop on knowledge acquisition, modeling, and management, Dagstuhl, Germany, pp. 67-84

8. Brössler P. (1999) Knowledge management at a software engineering company - an experience report. In: Proceedings of the workshop on learning software organizations, Kaiserslautern, Germany, pp. 163-170

9. Collison C., Parcell G. (2001) Learning to fly. Capstone publishing, Milford, USA

10. Curtis B., Krasner H., Iscoe N. (1988) A field study of the software design process for large systems. Communications of the ACM, 31:1268-1289

11. Davenport T. (1996) Knowledge management at Hewlett-Packard. Knowledge Management Case Study, http://www.bus.utexas.edu/kman/hpcase.htm (accessed 17th April, 2003)

12. Davenport T. (1997) Knowledge management at Microsoft. Knowledge management case study. http://www.bus.utexas.edu/kman/microsoft.htm (accessed 17th April, 2003)

13. Eick S.G., Graves T.L., Karr A.F., Marron J.S., Mockus A. (2000) Does code decay? Assessing the evidence from change management data. IEEE transactions on software engineering, 27: 1-12

14. Henninger S. (1997) Case-base knowledge management tools for software development. Automated software engineering, 4: 319-340

15. Henninger S. (2000) Using software process to support learning software organizations. In: Proceedings of the 25th Annual NASA Goddard software engineering workshop, Greenbelt, MD, USA

16. Johansson C., Hall P.C.M. (1999) Talk to Paula and Peter-they are experienced, In: the Proceedings of the workshop on learning software organizations, Kaiserslautern, Germany, pp. 171-185

17. Lawton G. (2001) Knowledge management: ready for prime time? IEEE Computer, 34: 12-14

18. Lindvall M. (1998) Are large C++ classes change-prone? An empirical investigation. Software practice and experience, 28:1551-1558

19. Lindvall M., Rus I., Jammalamadaka R., Thakker R. (2001) Software tools for knowledge management. In: Data and analysis center for software (DACS): state-of-the-art-report, Fraunhofer Center for experimental software engineering, University of Maryland, Maryland, USA. Prepared for Air force research laboratory, Information directorate, Rome, NY 13441-4505

20. Lindvall M., Sandahl K. (1996): Practical implications of traceability. Software practice and experience, 26:1161-1180

21. Nonaka I., Takeuchi H. (1995) The knowledge creating company, Oxford university press, USA

22. Paulk M.C. (1993) Key practices of the capability maturity model, Version 1.1. In: SEI, Carnegie Mellon University, technical report, CMU/SEI-93-TR-25

23. Perry D.E., Staudenmayer N., Votta L. (1994) People, organizations, and process improvement. IEEE Software, 11: 36-45

24. Potts C., Bruns G. (1988) Recording the reasons for design decisions. In: Proceedings of the 10th International conference on software engineering, pp. 418-427

25. Ramasubramanian S., Jagadeesan G. (2002) Knowledge management at Infosys. IEEE Software, 19: 53-55

26. Ramesh B. (2002) Process knowledge management with traceability. IEEE Software, 19: 50-52
27. Rochkind M.J. (1975) The source code control system. IEEE transactions on software engineering, 1: 364-370
28. Rus I., Lindvall M. (2002) Knowledge management in software engineering. IEEE Software, 19: 26-38
29. Rus I., Lindvall M., Sinha S. (2001) Knowledge management in software engineering. Data and analysis center for software (DACS) State-of-the-art-report, Fraunhofer center for experimental software engineering, University of Maryland, USA. Prepared for Air Force research laboratory, Information directorate, Rome, NY 13441-4505
30. Schneider K.(2001) Experience magnets - attracting experiences, not just storing them. In: Proceedings of the product focused software process improvement, Kaiserslautern, Germany, pp. 126-140
31. Soloway E. (1987) I can't tell what in the code implements what in the specs. In: Proceedings of the 2nd international conference on human-computer interaction, Honolulu, Hawaii, USA, pp. 317-328
32. Terveen L.G., Sefridge P.G., Long M.D. (1993) From "folklore" to "living design memory". In: Proceedings of the ACM conference on human factors in computing systems, Amsterdam, The Netherlands, pp. 15-22
33. Tiwana A. (2000) The knowledge management toolkit: practical techniques for building a knowledge management system, Prentice Hall PTR, Upper Saddle River, NJ, USA
34. Wieser E., Houdek F., Schneider K. (1999) Systematic experience transfer - three cases from the cognitive point of view. International conference on product focused software process improvement, Oulu, Finland, pp. 323-344
35. Williams L., Kessler R.R., Cunningham W., Jeffries R. (2000) Strengthening the case for pair programming. IEEE Software, 17:19-25

Author Biography

Mikael Lindvall is a scientist at the Fraunhofer Center for Experimental Software Engineering Maryland. Dr. Lindvall specializes in work on experience and knowledge management in software engineering. He is currently working on ways of building experience bases to attract users to both contribute and use experience bases. Dr. Lindvall received his Ph.D. in computer science from Linköpings University, Sweden in 1997. Lindvall's Ph.D. work focused on the evolution of object-oriented systems and was based on a commercial development project at Ericsson Radio in Sweden.

Ioana Rus is a scientist for the Fraunhofer Center for Experimental Software Engineering, Maryland. She graduated from Arizona State University with a Ph.D. in computer science and engineering. Her research interests include software process improvement, knowledge management, process modeling and simulation, measurement and experimentation in software engineering, and artificial intelligence.

5 A Dynamic Model of Software Engineering Knowledge Creation

Tore Dybå

Abstract: Software-intensive organizations that intend to excel in the twenty-first century must learn to manage change in dynamic situations. Rather than seeking stability, they should focus on creating software engineering knowledge and mind sets that embrace environmental change. The model developed in this chapter supports this shift by directing attention to the need for *communication*, *coordination*, and *collaboration*. The key to successful knowledge creation is continuous and simultaneous dialectic interplay between the knowledge that the organization has established over time, and the knowing of the organization's members in their respective contexts.

Keywords: Software engineering, Knowledge management, Knowledge creation, Organizational learning, Software process improvement.

5.1 Introduction

Current models of change, which are founded on the old "unfreeze move refreeze" paradigm [35], provide insufficient guidance in a constantly changing and increasingly unpredictable environment. Rather than seeking an unachievable stability, software organizations should focus on creating software engineering (SE) knowledge and mind-sets that embrace environmental change.

The model developed in this chapter supports this shift by directing attention to the needs for *communication, coordination*, and *collaboration* within and between software teams. The model is about how software teams acquire and use knowledge in an organizational setting in order to improve their software processes. Verbs like "knowing" or "learning" are used to emphasize action-oriented and dynamic properties, while the noun "knowledge" is used to describe static properties.

In developing the model, we have emphasized *the fundamental principle of the hermeneutic circle* [29] in which knowledge is gained dialectically by proceeding from the whole to its parts and then back again. This is also what happens in practice; each time incongruence occurs between part and whole, a reconceptualization takes place. The frequency of such reconceptualizations decreases as the match improves between the conceptualization of the organization and that held by the organization's members.

Another important principle behind the model is the focus on *context-specific needs*. The knowledge that the software organization creates, its methods for creating it, and the criteria by which these methods are considered valid are all based on the organization's prior experience for dealing with "problematic situations" [16]. As situations that the organization considers problematic, change, so may its methods for dealing with them and the criteria for judging them as valid. The uncertainty about situations or what actions to take in them is what makes them problematic. This is the point from which SE knowledge creation begins and is very different from current models in which improvement is seen as starting with the implementation of "best practices" according to a predetermined scheme, independent of the organization's experience of problematic situations.

A critical element in our model, therefore, is the integration of knowledge-creating activities with the "real work" of software development. This way, we consider software teams and their projects as the baseline for knowledge creation and software process improvement (SPI) and as primarily responsible for keeping the organization's processes on the leading edge of technology.

Figure 5.1 presents an overview of the dynamic model of software engineering knowledge creation. The model contains the following four major elements:

- *Organizational context*: This is the general environment that imposes constraints and opportunities about what the organization can and cannot do. Furthermore, since we perceive the organization as an open system, the reality experienced by the various software teams contains elements from outside the organization as well as from the organization itself.

- *Learning cycle*: The organization's learning cycle is a dialectical process that integrates local experience and organizational concepts. All members and groups of members in the organization contribute in the social construction of the software organization's knowledge. At the same time, the organization's memory limits the range of the possible actions for its members.

- *Organizational performance*: This is the performance or results of the organization's improvement activities. It is the dependent variable that is used to measure whether gains have in fact been made with respect to organizational behavior and performance, and not merely at the cognitive level.

- *Facilitating factors*: These are the conditions that facilitate or enable knowledge creation and SPI. They are the key factors for success that the software organization must put in place in order to facilitate the organization's learning cycle and improve its development process.

According to this model, SE knowledge creation is defined as a dynamic interplay between two primary dialectics. The first is that between the local and organizational level. The other is that between generating and interpreting organizational knowledge. These dialectics represent the interplay between the knowing of the organization's members in their respective contexts and the knowledge that the organization has established over time. This interplay is a dynamic and simultaneous two-way relationship between the organization and its members that combines local transformation with the evolution of the organization. This is similar to Piaget's [43] description of the learning process as a dialectic between *assimilating* experience into concepts and *accommodating* concepts to experience. In our model, knowledge is created from the balanced tension between these two processes. Our emphasis is thus on knowledge creation as a dialectic process that integrates local experience and organizational concepts.

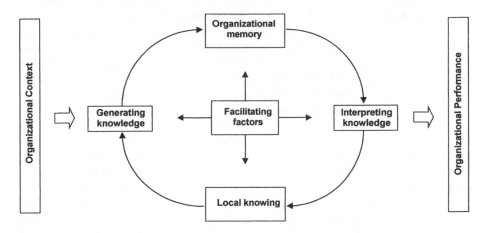

Fig. 5.1. A dynamic model of software engineering knowledge creation

The model presented in this chapter has several advantages compared with current best-practice models. First, it should be clear that organizational knowledge is not being created to mirror a reality that is independent of human action, but to deal with it. Second, starting SPI from problematic situations in software teams reduces the risk that SE knowledge creation will be detached from action, and undertaken to build knowledge for its own sake. Third, it increases the likelihood that knowledge intended for application to practical problems will ultimately serve its purpose, given that knowledge gained from concrete situations is more likely to remain applicable to future concrete situations.

5.2 Organizational Context

Generally, quality management literature supports the proposition that ideal quality management should not be affected by contextual variables. Juran and Godfrey [27], for example, stated that ideal quality management is "universal" and suggested that the expectations regarding quality management should be the same regardless of the context "no matter what is the industry, function, culture, or whatever" [25, p. 2.5]. Crosby [10, 11], Deming [15], and Feigenbaum [22] also support this context-free view of quality management. However, empirical studies have indicated that nevertheless, organizational context influence managers' perceptions of both ideal and actual quality management, and that contextual variables are useful for explaining and predicting quality management practices [5].

Like most of the quality management approaches, a context-free view of process improvement is at the heart of the best-practice paradigm and models like CMM, ISO/IEC 15504, Trillium, and Bootstrap. In contrast to the best-practice or model-based approach to SPI, the analytic approach [9] is more concerned with the contingent characteristics of individual organizations. For example, the importance of context is made explicit in the different steps of quantum information processing (QIP) [2] and also in the various templates and guidelines for the use of goals question metrics (GQM) [3, 55].

However, despite important differences, both the model-based and analytical approach to SPI seem to be most concerned with solving the needs of *large organizations* operating in highly *stable environments* with long-term contracts (e.g., the US Department of Defense and NASA). This is further confirmed by famous cases of successful SPI such as Alcatel [14], Hewlett-Packard [24], Hughes [26], Motorola [13], Philips [44], Raytheon [18], and Siemens [39], which are veritable giants compared to small and medium-sized enterprises (SMEs).

Most SMEs face two challenges: an ever-changing environment, and few projects running at any given point in time. As a result, they have few data that they can analyze and use to build up an experience base. In addition, collected data soon becomes outdated and left irrelevant or— in the best case— uncertain. Taken together, this implies that SMEs cannot base their improvement actions on collecting long time series or amass large amounts of data needed for a tradition statistical improvement approach.

Thus, two contextual variables are included in the model to capture the most influential sources of variation in software organizations: *environmental turbulence* and *organizational size*.

5.2.1 Environmental Turbulence

The software organization's environment refers to various characteristics outside the control of the organization that are important to its performance. These characteristics include the nature of the market, political climate, economic conditions, and the kind of technologies on which the organization depends.

The environment of a particular software organization may range from stable to dynamic, that is from predictable to unpredictable. In a stable environment the software organization can predict its future conditions and rely on standardization for coordination [40]. Certainly, a stable environment may change over time, but the variations are still predictable. But when the conditions become dynamic, i.e., when the market is unstable, the need for product change is frequent and turnover is high. Such change is highly unpredictable, and the software organization cannot rely on standardization. Instead, it must remain flexible through the use of direct supervision or mutual adjustment for coordination, calling for the use of a more *organic* structure. Therefore, the effectiveness of a software organization's structure depends on the environment of the organization.

5.2.2 Organizational Size

Organizational literature suggests that large organizations are less likely to change in response to environmental changes than small organizations. Tushman and Romanelli [51], for example, argued that increased size leads to increased complexity, increased convergence, and thus, increased inertia. Likewise, Mintzberg [40] postulated that the larger an organization, the more formalized its behavior. So, while small organizations can remain organic, large organizations develop bureaucracies with job specialization and sharp divisions of labor, emphasizing stability, order, and control. As a consequence, they often have great difficulties in adapting to changing circumstances because they are designed to achieve predetermined goals— they are not designed for innovation.

From a learning perspective, however, inertia develops as a result of the organization's performance history [33]. Large organizations tend to be successful since an organization grows larger with repeated success. However, since success reduces the probability of change in a target-oriented organization [12], large software organizations less likely to change when the environment changes.

5.3 Learning Cycle

As we have already argued, SE knowledge creation is defined as a dynamic interplay between two primary dialectics. The first is that between the local and organizational level. The other is that between generating and interpreting organizational knowledge. In this section, we make a detailed description of each of these four elements of the learning cycle.

5.3.1 Local Knowing

The primary context within which meaning is constructed, new knowledge created, and improved courses of action are taken, is the shared practice within local software development teams. Software developers do not work in isolation; they work together to develop products that they could not develop by working as individuals. This focus on teams and their collaborative processes is important because no single developer embodies the breadth and depth of knowledge necessary to comprehend large and complex software systems. Also, it is important because codified or explicit organizational knowledge is seldom sufficient to solve a particular problem. Thus, just as a single soccer player cannot play a game of soccer by himself or herself, only a group of software developers, working as a team, can develop software of a certain size and complexity.

The software teams' way of grasping the world and forming local realities is by apprehension, in the present movement of "here-and-now" [30]. They are concerned with concrete situations as experienced in all their complexity during software development. They act in a specific context in which reality is constantly being created and recreated. Local knowledge is therefore not an explicated and static model of causal relationships for software development. Rather, it shows up in the local actions taken by the developers in the team and can, thus, better be characterized as "knowing."

Therefore, by *local knowing* we refer to the knowledge-in-action associated with participating in the collective practice of software development in a specific context. It is important to stress this, since a software organization's primary concern is the actual *practice* of developing software, and not merely the creation of knowledge on how to do it. Local knowing is, therefore, about how the software organization works, or its theories-in-use, as seen from the local teams or work groups in the organization. Participating in software teams is consequently not only a matter of developing software, but also of changing the organization's knowledge about software development and to generate improvement.

The context in which software developers interact contributes to the knowledge-creating process in several ways. First, each software team or work group operates in a particular setting with a particular mix of people, tools, and techniques to define and solve a particular software development problem. Also, the way in which software developers use prior experience and available tools and techniques varies with the particular, concrete circumstances. That is, software developers will approach a certain problem depending on the actual setting because each setting tends to evoke certain kinds of "appropriate" modes of thought and action [52]. Moreover, software developers often take advantage of the setting itself to help them define a problem or to discover solutions.

Also, software developers incorporate codified organizational routines into local informal practices, freely adapting the routines as they work on solving actual problems in their particular circumstances. Local knowing draws on both the organizational members' individual understandings of the situation and their ability to use the relevant parts of organizational memory that is available in a given context. Therefore, the context in which software development takes place partly determines what the organization's members can do, what they know, and what they can learn. Moreover, since different local settings provide different opportunities for learning, any SE knowledge creation activity will also be a *situated* process.

Therefore, all software development and SE knowledge creation have an ad hoc adroitness akin to *improvisation* because they mix together the contingency of the present situation with lessons learned from prior experience [20]. Ryle described this mixture as "paying heed" [45], to be thinking at what one is up against here and now by adjusting oneself to the present situation, while at the same time applying the lessons already learned. In other words, local knowing is affected by the current setting as well as by the organization's memory of its past experience.

Such an improvisational theory of local knowing has its roots in pragmatists' notion that knowledge is not absolute, but rather can only be defined in relation to a specific situation or context [17]. Questions about what is "true" are answered in relation to what works in a given setting. Consequently, local knowing is *pragmatic* and produces actions that are oriented toward established goals, directed at doing whatever is necessary to reach the objective.

Thus, *SE knowledge creation occurs through people interacting in context* or, more precisely, in multiple contexts. This situated and pragmatic characteristic of knowledge creation has important implications for how problem framing, problem solving, and SPI take place in software organizations. Most importantly, this perspective suggests that traditional decontextualized theories of SPI cannot completely account for learning in software organizations. Rather, since learning is an interactive social process, contextual factors affect both how and what organizational members learn.

There are several social groups within a software organization that share knowledge and that may be identified as having a distinct local reality. Examples of such groups are formal project teams and informal groups of software developers and managers. A group's local reality can be seen as a way of acting in relationship to the rest of the organization. However, *shared practice by its very nature creates boundaries* [61].

There are two basic conditions for establishing connections across such boundaries and making communications between the groups effective. First, each group must respect the expertise of the other and must acknowledge the relevance of that expertise to their own problems. Second, each group must have sufficient knowledge and understanding of the other groups' problems to be able to communicate effectively with them. However, experience shows that these conditions are unlikely to be satisfied unless a sufficient number of members of each group have had actual experience with the activities and responsibilities of the other groups [50].

Mutual adjustment [40], which largely depends on face-to-face contact, is the richest communication channel we have and is by far the most effective form of transferring and exchanging knowledge and experience in local teams. Also, face-to-face experience and interaction are the keys to creating and diffusing tacit knowledge. Therefore, people working together with frequent, easy contact will more easily exchange knowledge and experience with each other than people that are separated by time and space. This has important implications for SE knowledge creation, since local software development teams can utilize the flexibility of face-to-face communication and shed bureaucracy.

However, communication capacity rapidly becomes saturated as the group grows. Without compromises, it is impossible to extend mutual adjustment in its pure form to organizations larger than the small group. Nevertheless, with the support of proper technology, considerable extension of the coordination of work by mutual adjustment is possible if the adjustment is mediated by indirect communication through a repository of externalized organizational memory. Such *implicit coordination* [25] of software developers working from a common experience base greatly reduces the need for extra communication and direct supervising efforts in the organizational learning process. Contrary to efforts to provide better tools for handling the increased communication, such as groupware solutions or efforts at standardizing the work process, the attack point in our model is to *reduce the volume of communication needed for coordination*.

In the next section, we describe the process of generating new explicit knowledge based on local knowing so that lessons learned can be incorporated in organizational memory and shared outside the team.

5.3.2 Generating Knowledge

Generating new explicit knowledge is a *collective* process where a group of software developers attempts to externalize their local knowing. This means, for example, that a software team must take time to express its shared practice in a form that can meaningfully be understood and exploited by other organizational members. This process involves the articulation of tacit knowledge into such explicit knowledge as concepts, models, and routines through the use of words, metaphors, analogies, narratives, or visuals. The result of this process is new organizational knowledge and an extended range of explicit organizational memory.

In practice, dialogue [7] and collective reflection [47], or reflective observation to use Kolb's terminology [30], triggers the articulation of explicit knowledge. This process of generating new explicit knowledge brings some of what the software team apprehends into what the team comprehends.

Dialogue is an important way of collectively grasping experience through comprehension such that the software team is able to articulate and build models of their experience and thereby communicate it to others. The team allows others to predict and recreate knowledge to the extent that such experience models are accurately constructed from the team's local knowing.

Collective reflection and dialogue facilitate a greater coverage of past experience, since individual developers can prompt each other to help remember the past. In this sense, multiple and even conflicting individual experience enables a more comprehensive recollection of past events. Such diversity in local knowing between software teams should not be seen as a problem, but rather as a valuable source for SE knowledge creation. It is the differences, not the agreements that are the possibilities for learning and change.

One of the most effective ways of externalizing local knowledge in software organizations is through the use of models, tools, and techniques. When constructing models or systems, however, only parts of the local reality will be externalized since "The program is forever limited to working within the world determined by the programmer's explicit articulation of possible objects, properties, and relations among them." [62, p. 97]. Such modeling creates a blindness that limits it to what can be expressed in the terms that the organization has adopted. Although this is an unavoidable property of models and technology, the software organization should, nevertheless, be aware of the limitations that are imposed.

We have used several knowledge-creation techniques to externalize, evaluate, and organize new knowledge. Among the most widely used have been the GQM approach [3, 55], the KJ Method [48], and Mind Maps [8]. Common to these techniques is that they help a group of developers to create ideas and articulate their knowledge through two phases. During the *divergent thinking phase*, the participants articulate key words, phrases, goals, questions, or metrics that they think are relevant for the dialogue. In GQM, these concepts are documented in GQM abstraction sheets, while the KJ method uses less structured Post-it Notes, and Mind Maps uses a picture of words.

During the *convergent thinking phase*, groups using GQM combine their abstraction sheets into one sheet per goal and jointly try to resolve any conflicts and inconsistencies. With the KJ method, the participants organize their Post-it Notes into logical groups, which are then related into a diagram of concepts and ideas as the conclusion. In a similar way, Mind Maps are used to organize concepts by placing each idea next to the concept to which it is related.

This dialectic of divergent and convergent inquiry facilitates the surfacing of hidden assumptions. The collaborative nature of these processes and the utilization of figurative language for concept creation are what, in our experience, make these techniques such powerful tools for collectively externalizing the tacit knowledge of a group of software developers and, thus, generating new organizational knowledge.

Articulating tacit knowledge and creating new explicit concepts is not enough. For new knowledge to be useful for others outside the team, it must also be packaged. Knowledge gained locally should be consolidated and globalized in the form of *experience packages* and stored in an Organizational Memory Information System, or Experience Base [4], so it is available for future projects. In principle, most kinds of experience can be externalized, packaged, and made available in the organization's experience base.

Still, each organization must decide for itself what knowledge needs to be packaged based on its business values and needs. Furthermore, since face-to-face interactions need to be high when transferring new concepts to a different location, each experience package should be indexed with local areas of expertise and references to groups or individuals who can help the receiving unit. Moreover, the organization should decide how its experience packages should be stored in organizational memory.

However useful the techniques a software organization might use for the articulation of explicit knowledge and experience packaging, the local knowing can never be fully represented in organizational memory. Contextual information is inevitably lost in this process, and what is stored in organizational memory is a decontextualized subset of local knowledge. Therefore, proper consideration of how memory objects will be decontextualized and then recontextualized in future use is necessary. In other words, we must be able to consider the present through the lens of future activity [1].

In the next section, we describe the process of incorporating experience packages into organizational memory together with examples of typical memory categories.

5.3.3 Organizational Memory

Organizational memory is a generic concept used to describe an organization's capability for adoption, representation, and sharing of new beliefs, knowledge, or patterns for action. It is essential for SE knowledge creation to occur by embedding organizational members' discoveries, inventions, and evaluations. Sometimes this may require official action and issuing revised regulations or operating guidelines. However, since each local group within an organization has its own culture, it also requires informal acceptance by enough opinion leaders and rank and file members for it to be disseminated as valid and valued knowledge.

In other words, that which is accepted in one part of an organization may or may not be passed on to other units or parts of the organization— one unit's knowing could be another unit's rubbish or heresy. Thus, lessons learned cannot easily be transferred from one setting to another. Also, higher levels of the power structure can destroy the learning of lower levels as a matter of policy, or even as a matter of neglect or indifference— except sometimes in the case of a strong counter-culture arising out of long conflict and shared grievance. Thus, memories are cooperatively created and used throughout the organization. In turn, they influence the learning and subsequent actions that are taken by the local groups in the organization.

Each time a software organization restructures itself, the contents of its memory are affected. Since much of the organization's memory is stored in human heads, and little is put down on paper or held in computer memories, *turnover of personnel is a great threat to long-term organizational memory*. When experts leave, the costs to the organization are even greater because it takes years of education, training, and experience to become an expert [50]. Loss of such knowledge can undermine the competence and competitiveness of the organization, and can also have a serious impact on cultural norms and values. However, we should be careful not to assume that the availability of organizational memory necessarily leads to organizations that are effective; it can also lead to lower levels of effectiveness and inflexibility [59].

Based on Walsh and Ungson's definition [58], we focus on organizational memory as *the means by which a software organization's knowledge from the past is brought to bear on present activities*. This definition makes no assumptions regarding the impact of organizational memory on organizational effectiveness, since this depends on the ways in which the memory is brought to use. For example, when organizational knowledge is consistent with the goals of the organization, organizational memory can be said to contribute to organizational effectiveness. At the other extreme, organizational memory can be seen as a structure that objectivates a fixed response to standard problems that constrains and threatens the viability of organizations operating in turbulent environments.

Therefore, the members of the software organization must themselves determine what to do with the knowledge they acquire in order to meet the incompatible demands of change and stability. Organizational memory can be viewed as a structure that both enables action within the software organization by providing a framework for common orientation and, at the same time, limits the range of action by constraining the possible ways of developing software. Thus, just as organizational memory provides stability, it can also serve to block change.

To be useful for the software organization as a whole, newly created concepts have to be communicated and explained to others who have not shared the concrete experience. This makes *justification* an essential process since the organization must decide whether new concepts and beliefs are worthy of further attention and investment [56]. There is an inherent dialectic here that the justification process tries to balance. On the one hand, newly generated knowledge has to be related to existing organizational knowledge in order to be acceptable and understandable. On the other hand, new knowledge challenges the organization's existing understanding of the world through its novelty, provoking complex processes of argumentation and justification, to be decided in favor of the existing or the newly emerging views.

Justification processes are therefore important for the software organization's memory since they decide whether new knowledge is *rejected* as irrelevant or uninteresting, *returned* to the local team for further elaboration, or *appropriated* as justified true belief and therefore integrated into organizational memory.

However, for a software development team to be able to reuse a memory object like an experience package (see Table 5.1 for typical examples), it must be recontextualized and made relevant for the new situation. That is, the memory object must be reunderstood for the developers' current purpose. A proper understanding of how local knowing is first decontextualized and adopted as organizational memory and then recontextualized into new local knowing is of critical importance for the utilization of organizational memory. This problem has largely been unnoticed in contemporary debates on experience bases within SPI, which is often limited to the technical challenges of implementing a database. However, if we do not address the problems of recontextualization, the whole concept of organizational memory and experience bases will be more or less useless.

The next section describes how the organization's memory can be put back into use and become part of local knowing through a process of collective interpretation.

5.3.4 Interpreting Knowledge

The collective interpretation of knowledge is the process of making organizational memory an integral part of local knowing by making sense out of the actions, systems, structures, plans, models, and routines in the organization. Through this process, the organization's memory is recontextualized and taken up into the practice of local software development teams. It is a process of "re-experiencing" [42] other teams' experiences.

Table 5.1. Memory categories and examples of typical elements

Memory Category	Typical Elements
Worldview	Culture, beliefs, assumptions, values, norms, strategies, power relations, symbols, habits, expectations
Structure	Task structure, roles, behavior formalization, coordinating mechanisms, unit grouping, workplace ecology
Plans and models	Life cycle models, assessment models, project plans, milestone plans, quality plans, improvement plans, measurement plans, action plans
Systems	Information systems, tools and techniques, quality control systems, training systems, social systems
Routines	Rules, standard operating procedures, development processes
Lessons learned	Experience reports, articles, memos, newsletters, stories, feedback sessions, peer reviews, post mortem reviews

A major confusion in much of the thinking in contemporary knowledge management and SPI is equating easy access of information with learning. However, there is an important difference between passively receiving information and actively interpreting and making sense of it. When an individual software developer receives information, he or she relates that information to past moments of experience in order to make sense of it. It is the differences from what is expected, and not the agreements, that provide the possibilities for SE knowledge creation. Therefore, we attend to that which is different from our current understandings and from our expectations in order to compare it with already extracted cues. Learning can only be said to have taken place when the individual has formed new networks of meaning and new reference points for future sense-making processes from the information encountered.

Collective interpretation processes are still more complex. Not only must each software developer engage in an individual process of sense-making, he or she must do so while simultaneously interacting with other developers. By engaging in *collective interpretation*, each developer is influenced by the meanings held by others, and in turn influences the meanings of others. This way, each developer can better understand the experiences and reasoning the other developers are using in their interpretations and by comparison understand each other's meanings more fully. Based on these interactions, the developers are in a position to form a collective interpretation of the organizational knowledge that is available to them.

Therefore, collectively interpreting organizational knowledge involves *active construction of knowledge* in the form of active formulation and solution to problems with the help of explicit models, guiding routines, and feedback. This highlights an important aspect of SE knowledge creation: collective interpretation is effective not necessarily as a function of simple internalization, with modeled information being transferred across a barrier from the organization to the inside of a team, or with information being transmitted. Rather, these interpretations are effective through peripheral and active participation [34], whereby the members of a team collectively transform their understandings and skills in framing and solving a problem. According to this view, it is the active construction through first-hand experience that is so crucial to SE knowledge creation, not some distant guidance or universal rule.

Rather than being transmitted or internalized, *knowledge becomes jointly constructed in the sense that it is neither handed down ready-made from the organization, nor something a team constructs purely on its own.* Knowledge, understandings, and meanings gradually emerge through interaction and become distributed among those interacting rather than individually constructed or possessed. Furthermore, since knowledge is distributed among participants in a specific activity context it is necessarily situated as well. That is, intimately welded to the context and the activity in which and by means of which it is constructed. Therefore it is important that *participation* becomes the key concept here, as contrasted with acquisition, with conceptual change serving as both the process and the goal of learning.

In the process of forming collective interpretations, it is important that we distinguish between reducing *ambiguity* and reducing *uncertainty*. Ambiguity is the lack of clarity about the technologies and processes of software development when the environment is difficult to interpret, and when cause and effect are disconnected so that the organization is unable to link its actions to their consequences. It has more to do with the confusion of multiple meanings than with the absence of sufficient quantities of information. The lack of meaning drives sense-making, while the lack of certainty drives data collection and information gathering: "In the case of ambiguity, people engage in sense-making because they are confused by too many interpretations, whereas in the case of uncertainty, they do so because they are ignorant of any interpretations" [60, p. 91]. Thus, approaches to measurement-driven SPI can support the reduction of uncertainty, but they don't necessarily assist the software organization in reducing the ambiguity that is essential for SE knowledge creation.

The process of "re-experiencing" other teams' experiences involves experimenting with organizational knowledge in local contexts by "giving it a try." Based on the concepts of ambiguity and uncertainty, we can distinguish between two types of such experiments that are crucial for SE knowledge creation: hypothesis-testing experiments and exploratory experiments. *Hypothesis-testing experiments* are field experiments designed to reduce the organization's uncertainty by discriminating among alternative explanations or solutions from many possibilities. This is the usual way of conducting process improvement experiments according to the experimental approach. Of special concern to us here, therefore, is conducting exploratory experiments to reduce ambiguity.

Exploratory experiments involve learning through discovery, encouraging the flexibility and resilience needed to cope with the situation at hand. When ambiguity is high, the knowledge represented by the organization's memory provides little support. So, during this phase of the learning cycle the focus shifts from justification and exploitation of existing knowledge to skepticism and exploration of new opportunities.

Such exploration or "learning by doing" is of utmost importance in unfamiliar and ambiguous situations and only works when a team receives rapid and unambiguous feedback on its actions. However, in the complex reality experienced by most software teams, the consequences of their actions are neither immediate nor unambiguous. Nevertheless, in these situations, effective learning can be achieved by the use of simulated environments, what Nonaka and Konno termed "exercising *ba*" [41], or "microworlds" to use Senge's terminology [49]. In such microworlds, it becomes possible for software teams to learn about future and distant consequences of their actions by experimenting in environments that "compress time and space" [49].

Prototypes are examples of microworlds that enable the collective interpretation of knowledge. Developing a prototype is an experimental activity mainly concerned with reducing the inherent uncertainty and ambiguity of specifications [38], thus facilitating a shared understanding of the system to be developed.

There are two main approaches to exploration in which prototypes serve an important role: probing and learning, and pilot projects. In *probing and learning* the software organization constructs "quick-and-dirty" mock-ups. To be useful for the learning process, these prototypes still have to be close enough approximations of the final product or development process. Otherwise, such experimentation will be of little value since generalizations will be virtually impossible. Furthermore, the probing and learning process should be designed as an iterative process, since it is hardly possible to "get it right the first time" in an ambiguous environment.

Pilot projects are projects aimed at on-line experimentation in real software projects or large-scale simulations in separate demonstration projects (see [21]). Typically, they are the first projects to embody principles and approaches that the organization hopes to adopt later on a larger scale. They implicitly establish policy guidelines and decision rules for later projects. They often encounter severe tests of commitment from employees who wish to see whether the rules and practices have, in fact, changed. They are normally developed by strong multifunctional teams reporting directly to senior management. Finally, they tend to have only limited impact on the rest of the organization if they are not accompanied by explicit strategies for the diffusion of knowledge gained from the pilot projects [23].

The context-dependent inferences of prior experience and memory objects can only be carried over from one organizational situation to another through "seeing-as" [47]. When a software team makes sense of a situation it perceives to be unique, it sees it as something already present in the repertoire represented by organizational memory. Therefore, "Seeing *this* situation as *that* one, one may also *do* in this situation *as* in that one" [47, p. 139, italics in original].

Consequently, in order to learn and improve their software processes, software teams can sometimes figure out how to solve unique problems or make sense of puzzling phenomena by modeling the unfamiliar on the familiar. Depending on the initial proximity or distance of the two things perceived as similar, the familiar may serve as an "exemplar" or as a "generative metaphor" for the unfamiliar [47]. In both cases, the software team arrives at a new interpretation of the phenomena before it by "reflecting-in-action" on an earlier perception of similarity.

The utility of an experience package lies in its ability to generate explanation and experimentation in a new situation. When the experience package is carried over to the new situation, its validity must be established there by a new round of experimentation through which it is very likely to be modified. The modified experience package that results from this new round of experimentation may, in turn, serve as a basis for transfer and recreation to a new situation.

So, for SE knowledge creation to happen, organizational members must act on the collective interpretations they have made, starting a new cycle of organizational learning. Thus, purposeful action at the local level is a means for the interpretation of organizational knowledge as well as for the generation of new knowledge. Consequently, it is essential for organizational learning and SPI.

5.4 Organizational Performance

Organizational performance is the ultimate criterion for SE knowledge creation. Performance is a complex construct, however, reflecting the criteria and standards used by decision-makers to assess the functioning of a software organization. That is, performance is a value judgment on the results desired from an organization [53].

Traditionally, the assessment of organizational performance has focused on long-term profitability and financial measures. However, in today's technologically and customer-driven global competition, financial measures often provide incomplete guides to performance, i.e., they are insufficient to predict future competitiveness in the software business.

As a fundamental part of our model, therefore, we need a dynamic concept of success that represents a software organization's competitiveness. Performance, which is something an organization does (process) or achieves (outcome), is a concept that can better serve as an operational tool for improvement of competitiveness than pure financial measures.

Furthermore, having satisfied customers is an important asset for a software organization, it is the cornerstone of any TQM program, and it is the most important principle in the recent revision of ISO 9000:2000. Therefore, the customer perspective should be a central part in any model of a software organization's performance.

Lynch and Cross [36] defined customer satisfaction as the difference between the customers' perceived performance and their needs and expectations:

Customer satisfaction = Perceived performance – Expectations

A classic problem, however, is that both performance and expectations are subjective terms, and that performance as seen from the software organization can be viewed differently than performance as seen from the customer. Typically, the customer focuses on *external performance measures* such as price and delivery time, while the software organization focuses on *internal performance measures* such as cost and lead time. Therefore, the relationships between such external and internal performance measures are critical for the integration of customer satisfaction in any model that purports to measure success. However, improved profitability is not an automatic outcome of organizational programs to improve customer satisfaction.

All software processes are expected to deliver a quality product on schedule and on budget in order to achieve customer satisfaction and thereby to ensure long-term profitability for the software organization. Moreover, these fundamental characteristics have importance to both customers and the software organization. Therefore, they are important for the understanding and definition of organizational performance. In other words, SE knowledge creation should lead to "better, faster, [and] cheaper software development" [46]. This is also clear in Krasner's [32] model of the challenges in software development projects, which focuses on the dynamic relationships between software processes and the three outcome factors: cost, schedule, and quality (Fig. 5.2).

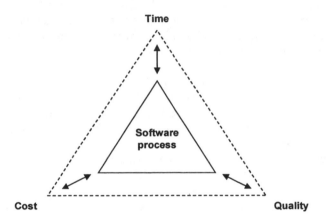

Fig. 5.2. The organizational performance dimension of SPI success [32]

From the preceding discussion we have identified organizational performance as an important dimension in the measurement of successful SE knowledge creation. Furthermore, we have identified the following three elements as central constituents of organizational performance as seen from a customer satisfaction perspective:

- *Time*: Time to market has become a critical measure for software organizations in today's turbulent markets. Being able to respond rapidly and reliably to customer requests and changing market conditions is often critical for a software organization's competitiveness. Including time-based metrics as part of the organizational performance measure, therefore, signals the importance of achieving and continually reducing lead times for meeting targeted customers' expectations. Yet, other customers may be more concerned with the reliability of lead times than with just obtaining the shortest possible lead-time. In addition to lead-time or cycle-time reductions, therefore, measures of on-time delivery rate improvements and schedule slippage rate reductions can also be useful time-based indicators of customer satisfaction and retention.

- *Cost*: Customers will always be concerned with the price they pay for products and services. Long-term profitability, therefore, requires that there is a healthy relationship between price and cost and, consequently, that we include process cost metrics as part of the organizational performance measure. Process cost includes the cost of primary activities (marketing and sales, inbound logistics, operations, outbound logistics, and service) and support activities (infrastructure, human resource management, technology development, and procurement) in the software development value chain [6]. Although the major source of software costs is the operations component, virtually all components are still highly labor-intensive. Thus, effort is frequently the predominant cost driver for most software processes. Examples of potentially useful cost metrics are: ratio of actual versus planned cost of work effort, development hours saved, productivity increases, rework cost reduction, and reuse increases.

- *Quality*: Using the Kano model as the frame of reference [28], we have witnessed a tendency among large customer groups that quality is not always expressed as an explicit requirement— it is so obvious that it is often not even mentioned. Nevertheless, the customers' expectations consist of both the explicitly stated *functional* and *nonfunctional*, requirements and the obvious implicit, or tacit, requirements. However, in certain parts of the software industry, the situation is such that excellent quality may still offer opportunities for companies to distinguish themselves from their competitors. In any case, customer-perceived quality is always relevant for inclusion as an organizational performance measure. Examples of such quality metrics are defect density reductions and customer satisfaction increases. An important part of this picture, however, is that the software organization may not even be aware of the unsatisfied customers; they simply cease to use the organization's products or services. Interestingly, an American study revealed that 96% of unhappy customers never tell the company [31].

To summarize, if our goal is to assess the improvement of software development processes, the ability to answer the following three questions should be regarded as a central concern for the measurement of organizational performance:

1. Are software projects delivered on time?
2. Are software projects delivered on budget?
3. Are customers satisfied with the delivered software?

Using organizational performance as the only dimension of success can entail some adverse complications. These complications include the instabilities of performance advantages, the causal complexity surrounding performance, and the limitations of using data based on retrospective recall of informants [37]. Furthermore, the extent to which organizational members' perceptions of SPI success reflect organizational performance is unclear, as is the extent to which perceptions are influenced by the software organizations' standards. Besides, research on both individual and organizational learning indicates that items that are perceived to be important by the persons concerned will be paid more attention to than items perceived as tangential to these persons [54].

If organizational members' perceptions do not reflect organizational performance, then increases (or decreases) in performance will not necessarily be translated into increased (or decreased) levels of perceived success. A decrease in the perceived level of success, for example, may occur either because the software organization's performance has decreased, or because the organization has not adequately managed the perceptions of its members. Assessment of success is a question of both organizational performance and the perceptions of the organization's members in the absence of data about the relationships between actual performance, perceived performance, and customer satisfaction.

5.5 Facilitating Factors

SE knowledge creation cannot simply be managed like any other project. This is due to the simple fact that the term "manage" typically implies control, while the nature of the learning process is typically uncontrollable or, at the least, stifled by heavy-handed direction [57]. From our perspective, therefore, software organizations need to acknowledge that *SE knowledge creation needs to be enabled rather than controlled*. We have identified six facilitating factors during our investigations [19].

- *Business orientation*: The extent to which SE knowledge creation goals and actions are aligned with explicit and implicit business goals and strategies
- *Involved leadership*: The extent to which leaders at all levels in the organization are genuinely committed to and actively participate in SE knowledge creation
- *Employee participation*: The extent to which employees use their knowledge and experience to decide, act, and take responsibility for SE knowledge creation
- *Concern for measurement*: The extent to which the software organization collects and utilizes quality data to guide and assess the effects of SE knowledge creation
- *Exploitation*: The extent to which the software organization is engaged in the exploitation of existing knowledge
- *Exploration*: The extent to which the software organization is engaged in the exploration of new knowledge

The links between the knowledge creating processes and the facilitating factors that, according to our experience, are the most important are revealed by the 6*4 grid in Table 5.2.

A clear *business orientation* legitimizes the knowledge-creating initiative throughout the software organization. It has a relatively low impact on local knowing but may, nevertheless, help software teams articulate the knowledge created in local groups. Business orientation is especially important in justifying concepts for inclusion in the organization's memory, since concepts must be selected that help the organization achieve its business goals. Therefore, a clear business orientation also encourages better utilization of organizational knowledge and facilitate the collective interpretation of knowledge.

Involved leadership is important for any organizational learning initiative. By involving themselves in the challenges of software development and allowing software teams to act autonomously, the organization's leadership facilitates local knowing. Furthermore, they have an important role in facilitating the generation of new knowledge by creating a context that prioritizes and encourages dialogue and collective reflection. Also, the degree of leadership involvement influences what is considered important for inclusion in organizational memory.

Employee participation is the cornerstone of our model. It is important for all the knowledge-creating activities in the learning cycle. It is the basis for local knowing, since it is only through participation that collective action can be taken and tacit knowledge can be shared. Dialogue and collective reflection are meaningless concepts without participation, and it is therefore an important facilitator for the generation of valid organizational knowledge. Likewise, it is through collective processes of sense-making and active participation through, e.g., personnel rotation programs, that organizational knowledge is diffused and brought to use in new situations.

In addition to personal and collective experience, a *concern for measurement* is important in order to validate the newly created knowledge and to ensure that gains have in fact been made. Most important, a concern for measurement facilitates local knowing by acting as a foundation for the collection, analysis, and feedback of data. Ongoing feedback as a group process is particularly important, since it can be an effective tool for bringing about changes in the way work is done as well as in establishing causal relationships and generating new knowledge.

The exploitation of existing knowledge is closely tied to all the knowledge-creating activities in the learning cycle. It facilitates local knowing by presenting a set of previously learned lessons that can be used in exploring the contingencies of the current setting. It is particularly important in facilitating the generation of new organizational knowledge, since this involves the articulation and packaging of local knowledge and experience. Furthermore, before locally created knowledge is appropriated as part of the organization's memory, it must be related to the existing knowledge. Also, the interpretation of knowledge necessarily involves a relation between new and existing knowledge.

Exploration of new knowledge is particularly important in facilitating the collective interpretation of knowledge through exploratory experiments and prototyping. It is also the basis for local knowing by mixing together the contingency of the present situation with the lessons learned from prior experience [20].

Table 5.2. Links between knowledge creating processes and facilitating factors[1]

Facilitating factors	Local knowing	Generating knowledge	Organizational memory	Interpreting knowledge
Business orientation		✓	✓✓	✓
Involved leadership	✓	✓✓	✓	
Employee participation	✓✓	✓✓	✓	✓✓
Concern for measurement	✓✓	✓		
Exploitation of existing knowledge	✓	✓✓	✓	✓
Exploration of new knowledge	✓✓			✓✓

[1] ✓ denotes an important link, ✓✓ denotes a very important link

5.6 Summary

In this chapter, we have developed a dynamic model of SE knowledge creation. A critical element for developing the model was the integration of SPI activities with the real, situated nature of software development, and focusing on the role of certain facilitating factors in the diffusion of knowledge and experience within and between groups of software developers.

First, organizational context was described as an important element that imposes constraints and opportunities about what and how the organization can learn. Two contextual variables were included in the model to capture the most influential sources of variation: environmental turbulence and organizational size. Then, we emphasized the importance of acknowledging that the learning process is a dynamic interplay between two primary dialectics: one between the local and organizational level, the other between generating and interpreting knowledge. Next, the success of an organization's knowledge creation was described in terms of organizational performance and the software organization's perceived level of success. Finally, we described the key factors of success in SE knowledge creation and their links with the learning processes in the model.

References

1. Ackerman M.S., Halverson C.A. (2000) Reexamining organizational memory Communications of the ACM, 43:58-64
2. Basili V.R., Caldiera G. (1995) Improve software quality by reusing knowledge and experience. Sloan management review, 37: 55-64
3. Basili V.R., Weiss D. (1984) A methodology for collecting valid software engineering data. IEEE transactions on software engineering, 10: 728-738
4. Basili V.R., Caldiera G., Rombach H.D. (1994) Experience factory. In: Marciniak J.J. (Ed.), Encyclopedia of Software Engineering, John Wiley and Sons, UK, pp. 469-476

5. Benson P.G., Saraph J. V., Schroeder R.G. (1991) The effects of organizational context on quality management: an empirical investigation. Management science, 37: 1107-1124

6. Boehm B.W., Papaccio P.N. (1988) Understanding and controlling software costs. IEEE transactions on software engineering, 4: 1462-1477

7. Bohm, D., Peat, F.D. (2000) Science, order, and creativity. Routledge London, UK

8. Buzan T., Buzan B. (2000) The mind map book. Millenium edition, BBC books, London, UK

9. Card D. (1991) Understanding process improvement. IEEE Software, 8: 102-103

10. Crosby P.B. (1979) Quality is free: the art of making quality certain. McGraw-Hill New York

11. Crosby P.B. (1996) Quality is still free: making quality certain in uncertain times. McGraw-Hill New York

12. Cyert R.M., March J.G. (1992) A behavioral theory of the firm. Blackwell, Oxford, UK

13. Daskalantonakis M.K. (1992) A practical view of software measurement and implementation experiences within Motorola. IEEE transactions on software engineering, 18: 998-1010.

14. Debou C., Courtel D., Lambert H.-B., Fuchs N., Haux M. (1999) Alcatel's experience with process improvement. In: Messnarz R., Tully C. (Eds.), Better software practice for business benefit: principles and experience, IEEE computer society press, Los Alamitos, California, US, pp. 281-301

15. Deming W.E. (1986) Out of the crisis. MIT center for advanced engineering study, Cambridge, MA

16. Dewey J. (1929) The quest for certainty. Lame Duck books, New York, Balch, Minton

17. Dewey J. (1938) Logic: the theory of inquiry. Holt and Company New York

18. Dion R. (1993) Process improvement and the corporate balance sheet. IEEE Software, 10: 28-35

19. Dybå T. (2000a) An instrument for measuring the key factors of success in software process improvement. Empirical software engineering, 5: 357-390

20. Dybå T. (2000b) Improvisation in small software organizations. IEEE Software, 17: 82-87

21. Dybå T. (Ed.) (2000c) SPIQ - Software process improvement for better quality. Methodology handbook (in Norwegian), IDI report 2/2000, Norwegian University of Science and Technology Trondheim, Norway

22. Feigenbaum A.V. (1991) Total quality control. McGraw-Hill, New York, USA

23. Garvin D.A. (2000) Learning in action: A guide to putting the learning organization to work. Harvard business school press, Boston, MA

24. Grady R.B. (1997) Successful software process improvement. Prentice-Hall New Jersey, USA

25. Groth L. (1999) Future organizational design: the scope for the IT-based enterprise, John Wiley and Sons, Chichester, UK

26. Humphrey W.S., Snyder T., Willis R. (1991) Software process improvement at Hughes Aircraft. IEEE Software, 8:11-23

27. Juran J..M., Godfrey A.B. (Eds.) (1999) Juran's quality handbook. McGraw-Hill, New York, USA

28. Kano N., Nobuhiro S., Takahashi F., Tsuji S. (1984) Attractive quality and must be quality. Quality magazine, 14: 39-48

29. Klein H.K., Myers M.D. (1999) A set of principles for conducting and evaluating: interpretive field studies in information systems. MIS quarterly, 23: 67-93
30. Kolb D.A. (1984) Experiential learning: experience as the source of learning and development. Prentice-Hall, Englewood Cliffs, New Jersey USA
31. Kotler P. (1988) Marketing management: analysis, planning, implementation, and control. Prentice-Hall, Englewood Cliffs, New Jersey, USA
32. Krasner H. (1999) The payoff for software process improvement: what it is and how to get it. In: El Emam, K., Madhavji, N.H. (Eds.), Elements of software process assessment and improvement, IEEE computer society press, Los Alamitos, CA, USA, pp. 151-176
33. Lant T.K., Mezias S.J. (1992) An organizational learning model of convergence and reorientation. Organization science, 3: 47-71
34. Lave J., Wenger E. (1991) Situated learning: legitimate peripheral participation. Cambridge University Press, Cambridge, UK
35. Lewin K. (1951) Field theory in social sciences. Harper and Row, New York, USA
36. Lynch R.L., Cross K.C. (1991) Measure up! Yardstick for continuous improvement. Blackwell Business, Cambridge, MA, USA
37. March J.G., Sutton R.I. (1997) Organizational performance as a dependent variable. Organization science, 8: 698-706
38. Mathiassen L., Stage J. (1992) The principle of limited reduction in software design. Information technology and people, 6: 171-185
39. Mehner T. (1999) Siemens process assessment approach In: Messnarz R., Tully C. (Eds.), Better software practice for business benefit: principles and experience, IEEE Computer society press, Los Alamitos, CA, USA, pp. 199-212
40. Mintzberg H. (1989) Mintzberg on management: inside our strange world of organizations. The free press, New York, USA
41. Nonaka I., Konno N. (1998) The concept of "Ba": building a foundation for knowledge creation. California management review, 40: 40-54
42. Nonaka I., Takeuchi H. (1995) The knowledge-creating company: how Japanese companies create the dynamics of innovation. Oxford university press, New York, USA
43. Piaget J. (1970) Genetic epistemology. Columbia university press New York, USA
44. Rooijmans J., Aerts H., van Genuchten M. (1996) Software quality in consumer electronics products. IEEE Software, 13: 55-64
45. Ryle G. (1979) Improvisation. In: Ryle G. (Ed.), On thinking, Blackwell, London, UK, pp. 121-130
46. Sanders M. (Ed.) (1998) The SPIRE handbook: better, faster, cheaper software development in small organizations. Centre for Software Engineering Ltd., Dublin, Ireland
47. Schön D.A. (1983) The reflective practitioner: how professionals. Think in action, Basic Books, New York, USA
48. Scupin R. (1997) The KJ method: a technique for analyzing data derived from Japanese ethnology. Human organization, 56: 233-237
49. Senge P.M. (1990) The fifth discipline: the art and practice of the learning organization, Doubleday, New York, USA
50. Simon H.A. (1991) Bounded rationality and organizational learning. Organization science, 2: 125-134

51. Tushman M.L., Romanelli E. (1985) Organizational evolution: a metamorphosis model of convergence and reorientation. In: Cummings L.L., Staw B.M. (Eds.), Research in organizational behavior, JAI Press, Greenwich, Connecticut, 7: 171-222

52. Tyre M.J., von Hippel E. (1997) The situated nature of adaptive learning in organizations. Organization science, 8: 71-83

53. van de Ven A.H., Ferry D.L. (1980) Measuring and assessing organization, John Wiley and Sons, New York, USA

54. van der Bent J., Paauwe J., Williams R. (1999) Organizational learning: an exploration of organizational memory and its role in organizational change processes. Journal of organizational change management, 12: 377-404

55. van Solingen R., Berghout E. (1999) The Goal/Question/Metric method: a practical guide for quality improvement of software development. McGraw-Hill, London, UK

56. von Krogh G., Grand S. (2000) Justification in knowledge creation: dominant logic in management discourses. In von Krogh G., Nonaka I., Nishiguchi, T. (Eds.), Knowledge creation: a source of value, MacMillan, London, UK, pp. 13-35

57. von Krogh G., Ichijo K., Nonaka I. (2000) Enabling knowledge creation: how to unlock the mystery of tacit knowledge and release the power of innovation. Oxford university press, New York, USA

58. Walsh J.P., Ungson G.D. (1991) Organizational memory. Academy of management review, 16: 57-91

59. Weick K.E. (1979) The social psychology of organizing. Addison-Wesley, Reading, MA, USA

60. Weick K.E. (1995) Sense-making in organizations. Sage Publications, California, USA

61. Wenger E. (1998) Communities of practice: learning, meaning, and identity. Cambridge university press, Cambridge, UK

62. Winograd T.A., Flores F. (1986) Understanding computers and cognition: a new foundation for design, reading. Addison-Wesley, MA, USA

Author Biography

Dr. Tore Dybå is a senior scientist at Department of Computer Science at SINTEF and a visiting research scientist at the SIMULA Research Laboratory. He received his M.Sc. degree in computer science and telematics from the Norwegian Institute of Technology in 1986 and his Ph.D. in computer science from the Norwegian University of Science and Technology in 2001. Dr. Dybå worked as a consultant for eight years both in Norway and in Saudi Arabia before he joined SINTEF in 1994. He has been responsible for and worked in several large national and international projects concerning software and business process improvement, organizational learning and knowledge management, software quality assurance and measurement, and empirical software engineering. Dr. Dybå is the author of several publications appearing in international journals and conference proceedings in the field of software engineering.

6 Evaluating an Approach to Sharing Software Engineering Knowledge to Facilitate Learning

Gary R. Oliver, John D'Ambra and Christine Van Toorn

Abstract: This chapter explores learning from repositories of software engineering knowledge— stores of practice created through knowledge sharing over time. Knowledge sharing is acknowledged as one of the most important processes to enhance organizational knowledge. A general model describing how the unique aspects of a software engineering environment shape knowledge sharing is introduced; this framework is known as software engineering knowledge sharing. In addition, CORONET, a system that provides functionality for knowledge sharing and for lifelong learning of software engineers in an organizational context, is briefly addressed. CORONET is a Web-based environment and incorporates knowledge management as an integral component. This chapter seeks to associate the two by fitting CORONET into the software engineering knowledge-sharing framework. We believe that the proposed model is useful for small projects, even those with different characteristics, and has the potential to be extended and refined by other researchers and practitioners.

Keywords: CORONET system, Intellectual capital, Knowledge sharing, Organizational learning, SEKS, Software engineering

6.1 Introduction

The Corporate Software Engineering Knowledge Network for Improved Training of the Workforce (CORONET), is designed to support life long learning of software engineers in an organizational context via the World Wide Web. The European research project is the focus in this paper for learning in software engineering (SE). Learning occurs through sharing and utilization of knowledge accessed from software engineering repositories. Readers seeking details of the CORONET approach to knowledge management (KM) are directed to Part 3 of this volume, where a full description is provided.

In this chapter we demonstrate that a knowledge-sharing perspective highlights important relationships between individuals and team members concerning software engineering and organizational learning, which has many overlooked dimensions. We discuss the general relationship between software engineering and KM with reference to the knowledge economy in this section, thereby establishing the importance of knowledge sharing. In Sect. 6.2, a model is proposed with the dual capability for knowledge sharing and organizational learning. This model is then tested against the CORONET system in Sect. 6.3. The paper concludes with a discussion of the fit between the software engineering knowledge sharing (SEKS) model and CORONET. Finally, some limitations of the paper and opportunities for further research in KM are presented.

6.1.1 Theoretical Foundations of Knowledge Management in Software Engineering

In order to maximize organizational performance, KM embraces activities aimed at capturing and reusing experience. In a knowledge economy [17] "the only thing that increasingly will matter in national as well as international economics is management's performance in making knowledge productive" [13]. Software engineering and KM are related [27] through their common recognition that competencies to enable organizational capabilities are "scarce resources" [29]. In an environment where strategy is likely to amalgamate intentions and eventualities [21], KM has the capability of contributing to organizational success. This will be attained via maximizing learning opportunities by individuals and within teams through a sharing perspective. Thus KM is the catalyst allowing connections to be made between the experiences and perspectives of software engineers with events requiring an innovative or creative response.

6.1.2 Knowledge and the Potential of Knowledge Management in Software Engineering Processes

From the theoretical foundations of KM, applications supporting organizations and the individuals within them are now emerging. Typically these applications serve to store and retrieve knowledge, codify knowledge and encourage and ensure knowledge sharing in an organizational context. It is through the use of such applications that organizations compete to ensure their position and success in the marketplace. SE has long recognized such initiatives, the Software Experience Factory [4] being one example of making experience available to other individuals in an organizational context [16]. Recent initiatives include project post mortems [5] to assist experience sharing for improvement. Traditional KM activities supporting SE include document management, identification of expertise and reuse of software or components [28]. Both organizational and external standards form an important element of the SE knowledge repository. Thus KM provides an implicit guide for determining whether or not software needs to be developed from scratch and how available technology can be harnessed.

6.1.3 Knowledge Management Applications in Software Engineering

The need for evaluation of knowledge management systems is more salient on considering the expected roles and outcomes of knowledge management applications within organizational contexts. All new information technologies change human behavior within both the organizational and individual domains [7].

These changes in behavior should realize outcomes that justify investment in new information technologies. Therefore the measurement and evaluation of these changes and the match between these changes and expected outcomes must be undertaken. Evaluation of knowledge management systems should be undertaken on two levels: the efficacy of technologies implementing knowledge management theories and principles, and the evaluation of technologies in the implementation context.

6.1.4 Software Engineering, Knowledge Assets and People

Among the most important knowledge assets are the stored repositories of experience and knowledge available to an organization, usually after capture and codification. According to Wiig, the components include "experience, expertise, proficiency, competency, skills, capabilities and embedded knowledge of all kinds" [35]. People are an essential component of the software engineering discipline, making a significant contribution to the organization. This is the intellectual capital view advocated by Edvinsson [15] and Sveiby [31]. Through emphasis on competence and knowledge, distinctive capabilities emerge from learning since it creates value from the intangible assets of an organization. Thus learning and knowledge sharing are often closely intertwined.

6.1.5 Reframing Knowledge Sharing

Many discussions concerning knowledge sharing depend upon definitional distinctions between knowledge and information. A distinction must therefore be drawn between KM and information management. Information management is characterized by the use of preplanned responses or techniques to generate new insights. Knowledge creation and flow are factors in codification and abstraction. The two reinforce each other with both functional and dynamic relationships. This view is an elaboration of the distinction between explicit and tacit knowledge as drawn by Polanyi [26]. Influential thinkers in KM, notably Nonaka [22], argue for knowledge conversion (socialization, externalization, combination and internalization) overlaid with the knowledge spiral to emphasize that knowledge creation may begin at any of the four modes. However, it is purported that "organizational knowledge creation usually starts with sharing tacit knowledge, which roughly corresponds to socialization [so] the key is to develop methods for sharing it and amplifying it" [23]. Challenges are offered by the resource view and the organizational learning view. Knowledge possessed by individuals may be transformed into routine practices through initiatives of individuals themselves. Forms of organization learning (single-loop, double-loop and deutero-loop) [2] are associated with cognitive and behavioral change. While imperfect performance may occur, learning still takes place and thus an asset evolves [10, 11]. In turn, this asset is capable of being shared and is of value to the organization.

6.2 Knowledge-Sharing Models

While there is no generic agreement on the form of the knowledge cycle, the essential components comprise capture, dissemination and use, with the common underlying aspect being the sharing of knowledge. The direct impact is upon processes by which knowledge is mobilized, conserved, leveraged and embraced within organizations. More research is required in the areas of knowledge creation, diffusion and use within and across organizations and cultures, and in identifying the nature of relationships with customers, suppliers and other stakeholders. In this section the visual model is first presented, then the constructs within the model are discussed and the operation of the overall model is examined.

6.2.1 Software Engineering Knowledge Sharing Model

The SEKS model of knowledge sharing demonstrates how the unique aspects of a software engineering environment shape knowledge sharing. In essence, the model recognizes the interaction between individuals and within teams. It is the product of three factors: motivation to discover knowledge, supportive culture and prior experience. Associated with these factors is the desire and opportunity to learn. The model depicted in Fig. 6.1 can be read as a series of processes with inputs and outputs, which are discussed in the following subsections.

6.2.1.1 Desire and Opportunity to Learn

Desire and opportunity to learn is an overarching factor in SEKS; generally, individuals learn by themselves or together. A number of recent initiatives in software development (pair programming and extreme programming) affirm the value of situating learning between solo effort and large teams. Traditional organizational learning theory [2] confirms the benefit of cognitive change, combined with behavioral change. Disseminating knowledge is insufficient for ensuring that it can be used productively. Much knowledge is fragmented [9], therefore integration or contextualization contributes to understanding. Traditional organizational methods for providing opportunities to learn, such as job rotation and frequent meetings, are potentially disruptive to both the organization and the individual. KM approaches include knowledge sponsors and pinpointing knowledge advisors.

In the knowledge economy it is inevitable that the tacit knowledge possessed by employees can be lost through career-based shifts in employment. While controls may be introduced to protect the loss of strategic knowledge to competitors, a KM approach seeks active sharing. Employees conscious of their value may be assisted by cultural support, perhaps together with emphasis on personal transfer rather than computer-mediated [19, 32] transfer.

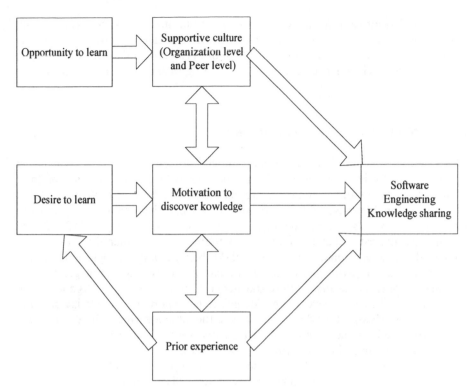

Fig. 6.1. Software engineering knowledge-sharing (SEKS) model

6.2.1.2 Supportive Culture

A supportive culture may emanate from a number of sources, the organizational culture, peer culture and the recipient's environment. Within an organizational context, the first two factors are crucial and may vary even in different geographic locations. There is considerable theoretical and empirical research that places culture ahead of structures and systems [33]. By viewing culture as the context, a connection is made with the informal, fluid aspects of interpersonal relationships. Some studies [3, 30, 33] identify the benefit of using a community to structure knowledge and thus introduce a vertical dimension to the organizational levels. Information-seeking behavior [8], together with affective responses, is one characteristic of a community of practice. There is an expectation that while some information will be redundant, it may still have value in building confidence [23]. The use of best practices is regarded as a related form of learning [1, 20]. This may unfortunately be inhibited through the ignorance of better practices and the difficulty in transferring perceived best practices to a new operating environment [30]. For this reason, the informal grouping of people into networks where practice can be shared is an important facilitator of learning and is less likely to encounter disruptive influences [19]. In addition, there is a connection with competencies, that is, in "learning how to learn" one accepts uncertainty in the organizational environment. This view of culture is significantly different from the culture-as-tools view since it avoids privileging technology as a knowledge discovery motivator.

6.2.1.3   Motivation to Discover Knowledge

Motivation to discover knowledge is an impetus to selectively form cooperative arrangements. Individuals make decisions about knowledge sharing based on their view of their own motives and those around them. One form of motivation is that of organizational learning, although reward is also significant. Knowledge transfer has several rewards for the recipient when it can be leveraged [18]. Social psychology indicates that the motivations themselves are manifold, including: enhanced personal reputation, direct task benefit and recognition of the contribution as a performance factor. Managing knowledge strategically can enhance organizational capabilities and generate new processes. Organizational recognition and reward systems provide positive support for knowledge sharing. Paradoxically, sharing knowledge may create the situation where the employee is both recognized for the worth of their tacit knowledge, while being targeted by competitors. Organizations in partnership or alliance may be able to overcome this effect through moving toward similar structures and processes. On the other hand, wholly technological solutions may be perceived as disembodied asset repositories and left impoverished. Of course, it must be remembered that there is a close relationship with culture and prior experience.

Table 6.1. Examples of artifacts demonstrating prior relationships

Source	Category	Example
Organization documentation (Formal or informal)	Explicit	Guidelines, handbooks, procedure manuals
Results of empirical work	Explicit	Metrics for estimation
Published evaluations of experience	Explicit	Lessons learned
Publicly available information	Explicit	IEEE standards
Specialist information	Explicit	Software engineering textbooks

6.2.1.4 Prior Experience

Prior experience in SEKS concerns the extent to which the prior relationship in knowledge sharing facilitates cooperation by reducing uncertainty and accelerating productivity. The lessons learnt from knowledge sharing may well affect future knowledge sharing. In such circumstances, the experience itself is transformed into useful knowledge, the existence of prior artifacts and demonstrates the existence of prior relationships. Examples of these artifacts are included in Table 6.1.

6.2.2 Sharing Software Engineering Knowledge

The result of this software engineering knowledge-sharing process is the ability to share knowledge without being totally conscious of the existence of the process. By internalizing the principles associated with the activity or event, it reinforces awareness of knowledge and can contribute to the desire to learn, thus reopening the cycle [6]. Our discussion now moves from the theoretical foundations of the knowledge-sharing model to assessing its usefulness in the context of the CORONET software engineering system.

6.3 Applying SEKS to CORONET

In this section, the characteristics of CORONET are outlined and an evaluation of the efficacy of CORONET is presented. CORONET components are analyzed and mapped to the SEKS model as presented in Sect. 6.2. In addition, some propositions for the evaluation of CORONET in an implementation context are provided. The impetus for applying SEKS to CORONET originated from its reliance on learning through knowledge, which has been contributed to and distributed in a computer-mediated environment.

6.3.1 An Overview of CORONET

CORONET is a collaboration between a consortium of member nations of the EC and one non-European partner [12, 24, 25]. It was funded under the European Community's Fifth Framework Program (FFP), a structure to implement the EC's research and development policy.

One approach to understanding the development and implementation of CORONET-Train, is to view it as a strategic tool. Using the framework of knowledge with strategic value suggested by Earl [14], it fulfils all four aspects of strategic knowledge:

- *Knowledge system*: A hypermedia learning environment incorporating knowledge sharing to support the training/learning needs of software engineers in an organizational context.
- *Knowledge network*: A corporate knowledge network, provides multiple learning environments and utilizes an infrastructure connecting experts and novices to support on-demand, career-long training in the domain of software engineering with group interaction.
- *Learning organizations*: A common reference model is developed, including the process of courseware development, collaborative training with group interaction and knowledge sharing via corporate knowledge networks. Different industrial environments validate the new training approach, and organizational and individual learning are integrated in the one platform. The benefits are demonstrated based on empirical data gathered during industrial validation.
- *Knowledge workers*: The target group is software engineers. Addressing training and learning needs as they occur in the workplace— learning on demand — across all organizational levels.

These four dimensions support the main objective of the CORONET system, to improve the efficiency of Web-based training of employees in the area of software engineering, and to ensure knowledge sharing.

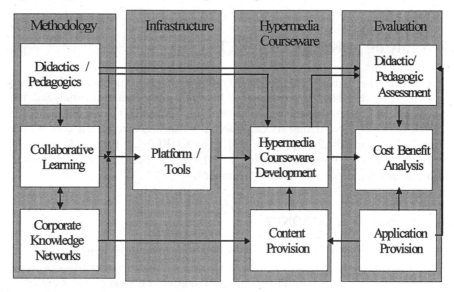

Fig. 6.2. Interrelationship of key components of CORONET [24]

CORONET-Train encourages knowledge sharing in two main capabilities. First, by harnessing the expertise on software quality within corporate networks. This is achieved by integrating all the hard and soft knowledge stored within the corporate knowledge network within an integrated learning environment. Second, CORONET allows users to contribute to the corporate knowledge base. Not only does CORONET retrieve knowledge from the corporate knowledge base, it also maintains this knowledge base. The components of this integrated learning environment are illustrated in Fig. 6.2.

These components of CORONET can be mapped to Earl's four components [14]:

- *Methodology supports the learning organization*: The approach relies on identifying roles within the organization's software engineering domain. Based on these roles, scenarios of learning have been developed. These range from highly structured learning tasks to highly unstructured learning tasks. These scenarios represent learning needs that participants will encounter within their work-based context. CORONET will then support each one of these scenarios (learning needs/tasks) by connecting users to corporate knowledge networks via pedagogically sound learning processes.
- *Infrastructure connects users to the system*: The infrastructure will provide the multi-media learning environment to support on-the-job learning needs. This environment will support the integration of human networks and tacit knowledge in the corporate knowledge networks and will support knowledge usage by new forms of individual knowledge visualization. Fig. 6.3 provides an overview of the CORONET infrastructure, showing the relationship between the knowledge base and the courseware from which training is selected.

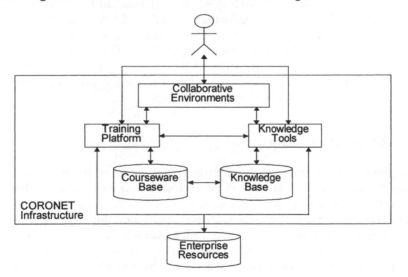

Fig. 6.3. Infrastructure of CORONET [24]

- *Hypermedia courseware facilitates involvement of knowledge employees*: Collaboration is one-to-one, one-to-many and many-to-many didactics through communication media.

- *Evaluation is on-going to assess learning within a corporate environment*: In order to measure the outcome of this objective, on-going evaluation is required. This evaluation will take place within the context of the learning scenarios and the processes used. The generic processes are resource retrieval, the value of the resource in the learning context, facilitating communication and contributing to corporate knowledge.

In summary, knowledge sharing within CORONET is facilitated by features of the system and reinforced by the learning gains of the participants.

6.3.2 Evaluation of CORONET

This section evaluates the CORONET approach to KM outlined in Sect. 6.3.1, with the SEKS model outlined in Sect. 6.2. Previously illustrated in Fig. 6.1, the SEKS model recognizes the unique processes of a software engineering environment and the requirements for knowledge sharing. In essence, the model recognizes that the interaction between individuals and within teams is the product of three factors: motivation to discover knowledge, a supportive culture and prior experience. Associated with these factors is the desire and opportunity to learn. We will now explore how well these requirements are reflected in CORONET. The methodology for this exploration considers the level-of-fit of each of the components of CORONET to the SEKS model. This is achieved by considering the components of KM within the implementation platform of CORONET-Train (and associated software, including WBT-Master), and the efficacy of each of these components to the referential model, SEKS. For consistency, the material on CORONET is sourced from Part 3 in this book.

6.3.2.1   Desire to Learn

Desire to learn is very much an intrinsic motivation of the individual, although there is no clear view on the role of external inducements and whether they will return a positive or negative value. However, as software engineering undergoes continuous change in terms of tools and application domains, there is a need to provide opportunities for learning and relearning in many different contexts. CORONET will not only connect individuals with formal learning resources, but will also support mentoring of individuals by experts with given domains of knowledge. The innovative characteristics of CORONET-Train can be summarized as follows:

- Offers a long-term approach to learning by providing a career-path to subject matter expertise (systematic development of competencies)
- Focuses on Web-based collaboration between learners on different competence levels, and uses corporate knowledge

In terms of the model, the greatest strength of CORONET is that the desire to learn is itself encouraged by having a system that is capable of satisfying and further igniting the desire (provided there is access to the Web-based learning environment).

6.3.2.2 Opportunities to Learn

Learning is provided on-demand as software engineers become aware of their own learning needs, recognizing the different contexts in which learning should take place and the modes of interaction that can take place to satisfy that learning need. These include:

- Interaction with formal resources (self-learning)
- Interaction with a learning process supported by a tutor (dyadic learning)
- A supported network approach to learning in which individuals can contact content experts with specific domain expertise (collaborative learning)

A comprehensive suite of methods is available:

- Five learning methods (case-based learning, theme-based learning, knowledge sharing, Web-based learning and Web-based tutoring)
- Three knowledge transfer methods (training, tutoring and mentoring)
- Two knowledge-based engineering methods (authoring courseware and structuring knowledge)

It is important to note that these opportunities exist across all organizational levels (from operational staff to senior management).

6.3.2.3 Prior Experience in Knowledge Sharing

Prior experience in using CORONET is captured, stored and made available as required. Individuals with prior experience are also made available to learners through the infrastructure supporting dyadic and collaborative learning. The knowledge card is used to track this information.

The knowledge card is more than a means of indexing knowledge for storage and retrieval in the repository. It does more than just serve to provide an algorithm for the codification of knowledge its primary and major role is to facilitate the sharing of knowledge. This is achieved by the provision of "learning maps" to link a wide variety of learning resources, tutors and experts. For example, a "Relational Data Model" learning course may be associated with the "Relational Data Model" knowledge card. In turn, this knowledge card could also be associated with other learning units, learning goals, discussion forums, documents, and so on, thereby establishing a learning map. In addition, WBT-Master regards users as learning resources or peer helpers - which may also be associated with a knowledge card, thus adding a further dimension and value to the learning map.

The creation of the learning map and the accumulation and addition of resources of value enables the use of knowledge cards to support the three modes of learning: self-learning, dyadic and collaborative learning.

Research has shown that capturing prior experience is integral to knowledge sharing, since all relevant resources can be made available to the learner. By providing road maps of knowledge domains, connecting learners with peers and experts, and consolidating all related resources through the one entity, knowledge cards are an integral component in the sharing of knowledge.

6.3.2.4 Supportive Culture

Being supported in learning and being provided with adequate and quality resources are fundamental to learning outcomes. The CORONET infrastructure aims to support the "networked organization", connecting all software engineers without regard to their role or level of expertise.

The learning methodology CORONET-Train promotes the integration of Web-based training with collaborative learning in the workplace (work-based learning), and provides a link to KM. It introduces the idea of reciprocal learning into software organizations, since both of these events having implications for organizational culture. They signal the value placed on learning through software engineering knowledge sharing by management.

6.3.3 Software Engineering Knowledge Sharing

Knowledge sharing is facilitated via the learning methodology supported by CORONET. On considering the artifacts used in Sect. 6.3 to demonstrate prior experience, (organizational documentation, results of empirical work, published evaluation of experience, publicly available information and specialist information), it may be argued that CORONET goes beyond these boundaries. Not only does it seek to link these artifacts, but also to link the tacit knowledge of domain experts within its scope of functionality. CORONET recognizes the many artifacts that contain and represent knowledge from previous relationships. Essentially, these artifacts are managed through a hierarchical structure of definition, and relationships. These are defined by the content-structuring model, and superimposed by the logical and semantic structures of the WBT-Master. Access to these artifacts can be via a variety of tools. These may be either system tools, for logical and semantic access, or content management tools, to allow browsing locally or by means of an FTP client.

In summary, the SEKS model of knowledge sharing presented in Sect. 6.2, can be seen as useful in its own right. It can also be applied to an independently developed knowledge-sharing tool.

6.4 Conclusion and Implications for Further Research

This chapter has established a relationship between KM and knowledge sharing, using the SEKS model as the framework to evaluate CORONET. This system is both innovative and extensive in meeting the learning needs of professionals working in the software engineering domain. From the analysis presented here, the KM components map well to the constructs of the SEKS model, knowledge representing a good fit. Through a comparison and analysis of the CORONET components to the SEKS model, it appears that CORONET more than adequately implements the theoretical foundations of KM.

The introduction of any new technology in the work place causes changes in human behavior. According to the SEKS model, software engineering knowledge sharing occurs in the context of individual and organizational learning. Although this is a complex user task, the twin factors of a supportive culture and motivation will produce a learning behavior. The detailed discussion of CORONET demonstrates that in this case, learning and knowledge sharing occurred. This ranged from short-term problem solving to long-term competency improvement. Collaborative problem solving was also encouraged. Since CORONET is a relatively small project, this suggests that SEKS is useful for small projects and can be used, extended and refined by other researchers and practitioners in projects with different characteristics.

In order to determine how well the CORONET system supports knowledge sharing and learning in the workplace, it needs to be further evaluated in its implementation environment. From a research perspective, it is important to know how well the SEKS model fits CORONET, so that specific improvement areas can be identified in the model or changes in the scope of the system can be suggested. From a utility point of view, it is important to know how effective the SEKS model is in supporting organizational learning. However, this evaluation goal can only be realized by observing and evaluating the learning process in the implementation environment. This falls outside the scope of this paper and is an avenue of future investigation.

Software engineering knowledge sharing can be judged against the two prerequisites:

- The learners accept and use CORONET-Train
- The competence level of the learners increases through the use of CORONET

Adult learning is a process that is embedded in individuals' behavior within their various life contexts. As a tool, CORONET aims to support the learning of software professionals within their work environments. Sufficient time must be allowed for users to integrate the CORONET tool within their learning and information seeking behavior. The SEKS model is unbounded by time and thus lacks an empirical base. On the other hand, as a training course, the duration and sequence is integral to its own learning programme. This has been demonstrated in the detailed discussion of CORONET in Part 3 of this book.

The approach to KM taken in this chapter requires direct connection be made between people and the benefits to be gained from the organizational learning that occurs. From the detailed discussion in Sect. 6.3 it can be concluded that:

- Learners apply the knowledge they acquired through CORONET usage in their work.
- CORONET supports Web-based collaborative learning.
- Web-based training with CORONET is at least as effective as classroom training.

A knowledge-sharing approach to CORONET using the SEKS model should be useful to practitioners who are concerned with the efficacy of KM approaches as implemented in software systems. In addition, it should also provide some insight on how these software systems may be evaluated post-implementation.

Acknowledgements

The participation of The University of New South Wales in the CORONET project (EU-Project CORONET/Grant IST-1999-11634) was made possible by a grant from the Australian Federal Government Department of Industry, Science and Resources. We also wish to thank the three referees for their comments and suggestions, which guided the reformulation of the paper in its current version.

References

1.   Ahmed P.K, Kok L.K., Loh A.Y.E. (2002) Learning through knowledge management. Butterworth-Heinemann Boston, USA
2.   Argyris C., Schon D. (1978) Organizational learning: a theory of action perspective. Addison-Wesley, MA, USA
3.   Baird L., Henderson J.C. (2001) The knowledge engine: how to create fast cycles of knowledge-to-performance and performance-to-knowledge. Berret-Koehler, San Francisco, CA, USA
4.   Basili V.R., Caldiera G. (1995) Improve software quality by reusing knowledge and experience. Sloan management review, 37: 56-64
5.   Birk A; Torgeir D., Stalhane T. (2002) Postmortem: never leave a project without it. IEEE Software, 19: 43-45
6.   Boisot M. (1998) Knowledge assets. Oxford university press, New York, USA
7.   Buckland M. (1994) Information as thing. In: Buckland M., (Ed.) Information and information systems. Praeger Westport, Connecticut, USA, pp. 43-54
8.   Choo C.W. (1998) The knowing organization: how organizations use information to construct meaning, create knowledge and make decisions. Oxford university press, New York, USA
9.   Crossan M.M., Inkpen A.C. (1992) Believing is seeing: an explanation of the organizational learning concept and evidence from the case of joint venture learning. Working paper, Western Business School, University of Western Ontario, Canada

10. DiBella A.J., Nevis E.C. (1998) How organizations learn: an integrated strategy for building learning capability. Jossey-Bass, San Francisco, USA
11. Dixon N. (1994) The organizational learning cycle: how we can learn collectively. McGraw-Hill, London, UK
12. D'Ambra J., Jeffery R. (2001) CORONET: An Australian software engineering experience in collaborative research with the European community. In: Proceedings of the Australian software engineering conference, Canberra, Australia, pp. 255-261
13. Drucker P. (1998) From capitalism to knowledge society. In: Neef D. (Ed.) The knowledge economy. Butterworth-Heinemann, Boston, pp. 15-34
14. Earl M. (1994) Knowledge as strategy: reflections on Skandia International and Shorko films. In: Ciborra C., Jelassi T. (Eds.), Strategic information systems: A European perspective. John Wiley and Sons, UK
15. Edvinsson L., Malone M.S (1997) Intellectual capital: the proven way to establish your company's real value by measuring its hidden brainpower. Piatkus, London, UK
16. Feldmann R.L., Tautz C. (1998) Improving best practices through explicit documentation of experience about software engineering technologies. In: Proceedings of the international software process improvement conference in education and research, UK, pp. 10-11
17. Grant R. M (2000) Shifts in the world economy: the drivers of knowledge management. In: Despres C., Chauvel D. (Eds.), Knowledge horizons: the present and promise of knowledge management. Butterworth-Heinemann, London, UK, pp. 27-53
18. Hamel G. (1991) Competition for competence and interpartner learning within international alliances. Strategic management journal, 12: 83-103
19. Kollock P., Smith M. (1996) Managing the virtual commons: cooperation and conflict in computer communities. In: Herring S. (Ed.), Computer-mediated communication: linguistic, social and cross-cultural perspectives. John Benjamins Publishing Company, Amsterdam, The Netherlands, pp. 109-128
20. Marquardt M.J (1996) Building the learning organization. McGraw-Hill, New York
21. Mintzberg H. 1994) The rise and fall of strategic planning. Prentice Hall, London, UK
22. Nonaka I., Takeuchi H. (1995) The knowledge creating company: how Japanese companies create the dynamics of innovation. Oxford university press, UK
23. Nonaka I. (1998) The knowledge-creating company. Harvard business review: Knowledge management. Harvard business school press, Boston, MA, USA, pp 25-40.
24. Pfahl D., Ankasaputra N., Differding C., Ruhe G. (2001) CORONET-Train: a methodology for Web-based collaborative learning in software organizations. In: Lecture notes in computer science, Springer, Berlin Heidelberg London, 2176: 37-51
25. Pfahl D., Trapp S., de Teresa J., Stupperich M., Rathert N., Molu R., Sherbakov N., D'Ambra J., (2002) CORONET Final report. Fraunhofer IESE, technical report no. 045.02/E.
26. Polanyi K. (1958) Personal knowledge. University of Chicago press, Chicago, USA
27. Robillard P.N. (1999) The role of knowledge in software development. Communications of the ACM, 42: 87-92
28. Rus I. Lindvall M. (2002) Knowledge management in software engineering. IEEE Software, 19: 26-38
29. Schneider K.; Hunnis J-Pe von, Basili V. R (2002) Experience in implementing a learning software organization. IEEE Software: 19: 46-49
30. Szulanski G. (1996) Exploring internal stickiness: impediments to the transfer of best practice within the firm. Strategic management journal, 17: 27-43

31. Sveiby K.-E. (1997) The new organizational wealth: Managing and measuring knowledge-based assets. Berrett-Koehler publishers, San Francisco, CA, USA
32. Weick K. (1997) Cosmos versus Chaos: sense and nonsense in electronic contexts. In: Prusak, L. (Ed) Knowledge in organizations. Butterworth-Heinemann, Boston, USA, pp. 213-226.
33. Wenger E (1996) Communities of practice: the social fabric of a learning organization. Healthcare forum journal, 39: 20-26
34. Wiig K. (1993) Knowledge management: foundations. Schema press, Arlington, Texas, USA

Author Biography

Gary R. Oliver is the Chief Information Officer at the Australian Graduate School of Management, which is a school of both The University of New South Wales and the University of Sydney. Prior to joining the school in 2002, he completed over 20 years managing all aspects of computing, in private enterprise and government, at state and international levels, including as a chief information officer. Mr. Oliver's current research focus concerns both practice and theory: the behavior of people when faced with situations where knowledge sharing is opportune and necessary for effective performance, and the part played by knowledge frameworks in understanding and quantifying all the dimensions of knowledge sharing.

Dr. John D'Ambra is a senior lecturer in the School of Information Systems, Technology and Management at UNSW, Australia. Dr. D'Ambra has considerable commercial experience in the area of information technology. His research interests include the study of computer-mediated communication within organizations and evaluation of the World Wide Web as an information resource. Dr. D'Ambra is also a member of the Centre for Advanced Software Engineering Research (CAESER) where he has worked on several projects, including the CORONET project.

Christine Van Toorn is a lecturer at the School of Information Systems, Technology and Management, University of New South Wales, Australia. She has extensive industry experience in the fields of information systems and information technology. Her research interests lie in the areas of knowledge management and decision support, with particular emphasis in relation to human computer interaction. Ms. Van Toorn's commercial background is diverse, and she has considerable experience across a wide variety of industries. She is the Director of the Business Information Technology and Information Systems and Management Co-op Scholarship Programs at UNSW.

7 Eliciting and Maintaining Knowledge for Requirements Evolution

Allen H. Dutoit and Barbara Paech

Abstract: Two of the biggest challenges in knowledge management are making tacit knowledge explicit and keeping explicit knowledge up-to-date. In this chapter, we focus on how to manage knowledge about a software system with respect to change, so that changes can be evaluated and realized with less effort and without reducing quality. We use a rationale-based approach for making explicit change knowledge and the knowledge activities that need to occur during requirements specification and evolution. The knowledge activities keep the requirements and the change knowledge up-to-date. While these issues have been examined to some extent independently in the requirements, change, and knowledge management communities, we focus on the integration of methods from all three communities. The goal of the chapter is to illustrate the synergy effects and resulting benefits that occur when interleaving knowledge and requirements activities.

Keywords: Requirements evolution, Knowledge management, Rationale, Traceability, QOC, Use case

7.1 Introduction

Knowledge management (KM) in software engineering aims at decreasing time and cost and increasing quality by supporting decision making [25]. There are many different kinds of knowledge and many different knowledge activities that could be useful for this purpose. All of them face two major challenges, one well known from knowledge management, the other from software development:

- *Making tacit knowledge explicit*: KM "focuses on the individual as a customer of knowledge and as the bearer and provider of important knowledge that could systematically be shared throughout an organization" [25]. Some of this knowledge is made explicit during every day development activities, for example, in the form of process and system models, templates, and documents. Some of this knowledge, however, remains tacit, as it is difficult to express and often depends much on beliefs, perspectives, and values. Examples of tacit knowledge include crafts and skills, which can take years of apprenticeship to transmit, knowledge about an organizations culture and procedures, necessary for individuals to effectively collaborate with their colleagues, and knowledge distributed among many individuals and geographical locations and not owned by any specific individual. Tacit knowledge that is not made explicit is lost when individuals leave the organization.

- *Keeping explicit knowledge up-to-date*: Over 50% of the software developers' effort is dedicated to maintenance [34, 2]. As exemplified by the European Space Agency's Ariane 5 flight 501 incident (1996) poor change management lead to the reuse of an older software component without sufficient validation against new requirements, resulting in the loss of a launcher with its payload and severe economic losses [26]. Thus, any activity during development must be assessed against two important criteria: how to cope with changes of the created artifacts and how much additional effort is necessary to keep the artifacts up-to-date.

Requirements engineering is a specific area of software engineering in which these two challenges are especially difficult. First, requirements engineering features the collaboration of a variety of individuals with different technical backgrounds and in different locations. Second, requirements engineering occurs over the entire life cycle of the system, as requirements are updated and changed. Examples of tacit knowledge in requirements engineering include:

- *Application domain knowledge not accessible to developers*: For example, this knowledge is required to understand why specific requirements are included or excluded from the system specification.
- *Solution domain knowledge not accessible to the client*: For example, this knowledge is required to estimate the trade-offs in cost and functionality when considering a new requirement.
- *Relationships between the requirements and the design of existing system*: For example, this knowledge is required to understand the impact of a requirements change on the performance of the system.

In practice, however, making the above knowledge explicit and up-to-date is costly and difficult. Not all knowledge about the application domain or the solution domain is required to understand the system. Making all of it explicit would be wasteful. Identifying the relevant parts that are critical to requirements decisions, however, is not trivial. Also, generating and maintaining more documentation represents an overhead for clients and developers, who may not see a short term incentive for accurately capturing this knowledge [16]. Finally, capturing relationships among the requirements and the design may be difficult in the absence of sufficient application- and solution-domain knowledge.

Developers and clients deal with tacit knowledge through close collaboration. Informal communication among developers, through hallway conversations, apprenticeships, or peer exchanges, ensures that at least some of this knowledge is transmitted to the right developers. However, projects increase in duration and in the number of locations where they are conducted. Thus, such informal exchange of knowledge is not sufficient. To ensure a coherent and cost-effective approach, a formal framework is needed, allowing developers to classify different pieces of knowledge, make them explicit, relate them to the requirements and the system, and finally, trace dependencies as changes are considered, and keep the knowledge up-to-date.

In this chapter, we focus on such a knowledge framework for requirements evolution. We first sketch the different change activities that occur in the context of requirements evolution (Sect. 7.2). We then identify the types of knowledge required to support requirements changes and emphasize the central role of rationale for making this knowledge explicit and coherent (Sect. 7.3). Next, describe an example for capturing, using, and preserving change knowledge in the context of use-case based requirements specification (Sect. 7.4). We conclude this chapter with a summary and a discussion of the open issues in dealing with requirements change knowledge (Sect. 7.5).

7.2 Requirements Change

Software systems typically have an extended life cycle. The US air route traffic control system includes hardware and software components that are more than 30 years old [14]. Operating systems such as Unix or Windows XP include code that is several decades old. Even application software and custom software developed for a single client see many years of operation before being replaced. Such an extended life time results in the incorporation of many changes into the system. Some changes result from changes in the environment or in the way clients accomplish their work. Other changes repair requirements errors and improve the system for the client. Yet other changes increase the scale or the quality of the system as a result of increased workload or reliability requirements. In order to discuss the types of knowledge and knowledge activities needed to support requirements change, we first need to characterize the system knowledge gathered during development that is relevant for requirements change, as well as the activities for changing this knowledge.

Figure 7.1 gives an overview of the activities involved in requirements change. Fig. 7.2 illustrates a meta model of system and change knowledge in which the system knowledge consists of requirements and design elements. We do not distinguish between different levels of requirements, e.g., user and developer requirements. For the purpose of this paper it is sufficient to distinguish *functional requirements* (FR) (i.e., tasks that the clients accomplish and the system functions for supporting them) and *non-functional requirements* (NFR) (i.e., properties of the application domain and quality criteria that the system must meet). Design models describe the system from the developers' perspective. Design models consist of *design elements*, each representing decisions about how to realize the functional and nonfunctional requirements. In this paper, we use the phrase *system model elements* to generally refer to both requirements and design elements. System elements constitute the *system knowledge* necessary to understand and describe the system.

For the purpose of this chapter we do not go into detail of the requirements activities. We just stipulate an activity for the creation of the requirements from some problem statement, where the latter may just be in the client's head.

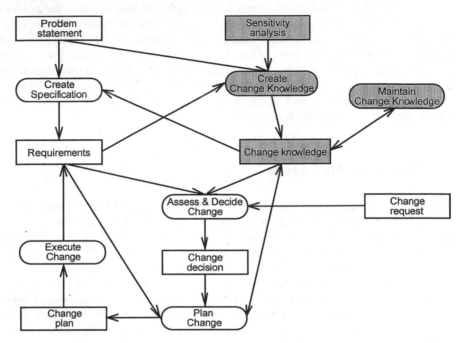

Fig. 7.1. Change process overview (UML activity diagram, additional knowledge management activities shown in *gray*)

A change is initiated by a *change request*. The change request represents a formal step in which the client asks the development organization to amend the requirements specification and, as a result, to modify the system. The change request may include examples or alternatives of how the requirements specification could be changed, but remains a high-level description. As a result of a change request, the development organization needs accomplish the following activities (see elements in white in Fig. 7.1):

- *Assess change*: During this activity, the developers try to understand the change request. They generate a list of *change impacts*, i.e., the system model elements that would need to change. This is used to estimate the cost of the change. Developers identify possible conflicts with other requirements that this change would introduce. The client may also provide additional information with the change request to denote how critical the realization of this change is with respect to other changes or requirements.
- *Decide on* change: During this activity, the client and developers decide whether to proceed with the change or not, based on the assessment knowledge. If they decide to realize the change, they proceed to the next two activities.

- *Plan change*: During this activity, the developers refine the change assessment so that the work related to the change realization can be divided and assigned to individual developers. In particular, any remaining conflicts are resolved, and a detailed description of how the change impacts need to be revised is written.
- *Execute change*: During this activity, the change plan is executed and the changes are validated.

As described in IEEE Standard 1219-1998 [16, 17], a full maintenance process is more complex than the activities sketched above. The above activities are sufficient, however, to study the knowledge involved in requirements changes. In particular, we do not go into details of changing design elements or other artifacts. We only study how relationships between requirements and design elements influence requirements change.

In practice, the main issue during the assessment, planning, and execution of the change is to ensure that only the intended FR and NFR of the system change and no more. Changes are difficult to localize, assess, and realize, as the system under consideration has usually been developed by different sets of individuals whose assumptions are not captured in the requirements specification or the design documentation. Hence, changes are expensive and constitute the main source of software defects [24], degrade the architecture of the system [13], and eventually lead to the retirement of the current system and its replacement by a completely reengineered system. Mäkäräinen [28] describes further change management problems having to do with the effectiveness, communication, analysis and location, traceability, decision processes, and tools for change management.

In the following section, we discuss how additional knowledge can be captured *before* the change request to support the change activities. These additional knowledge management products and their related activities are depicted in gray in Fig. 7.1.

7.3 Knowledge for Requirements Evolution

There are five main types of knowledge that usually remain tacit in a development project and that can be used for supporting a change (see Fig. 7.2):

- *Sensitivity characterization* [32]: This knowledge includes a list of changes that are most likely in the future. Such knowledge can be extracted with sensitivity analysis by studying the history of similar systems, identifying worst case scenarios, and market research. Sensitivity analysis enables developers to focus their resources, for example, when capturing additional knowledge (rationale, traces).
- *Rationale* [11]: This knowledge consists of the reasons *why* developers have made the decisions they have. Rationale (represented as *Questions*, *Options*, *Arguments*, and *Decisions* in Fig. 7.2) helps to retain the original concept as much as possible and reduces the effort needed by developers to re-assess

different options using a new set of requirements. Often, errors can be avoided by not re-evaluating an option that has already been discarded. In other cases, a change can be realized by selecting a previously discarded option that has become more relevant.

- *Pre-traceability* [18]: This knowledge consists of *Contributor Links* between system model elements and the stakeholders that originated them. Such dependencies make it easier to trace the human source of each requirement, the reasons for including (or excluding) the requirement from the specification, and to identify conflicts among stakeholders.
- *Post traceability* [18]: This knowledge consists of *Trace Links* among requirements elements, and design elements. Such dependencies make it easier to identify the elements impacted by the change.
- *Change impacts* [4]: This knowledge includes, for a given change, *its impact and cost*. Impact analysis is often only performed as a result of a change request. Here, however, we stipulate this activity during the initial development of the system for a set of likely future changes to assess the modifiability of the system.

Similar knowledge types and their related activities are described in [22] and [6]. The latter focuses more on code changes and thus also includes program understanding and truth maintenance. The former discusses the activities in the context of the knowledge framework that helps to gather experiences from and for change processes.

As depicted in Fig. 7.2, *options* are a central element of change knowledge. Options briefly describe alternative requirements that can answer a change request or a question raised by the client. Options, hence, can also be treated as potential changes generated by the sensitivity analysis and can have attached change impacts and argumentation knowledge. Options are usually left tacit in most development processes. They are discussed, refined, and evaluated in the scope of meetings and face-to-face negotiations, but are not documented or systematically captured. By making options explicit and maintaining their dependencies to the rest of the change and system knowledge, all other change activities become much simpler as they leverage off existing knowledge and minimize the additional effort needed to keep this knowledge up to date.

In the following, we examine in detail these five types of knowledge: sensitivity characterization (Sect. 7.3.1), requirements rationale (Sect. 7.3.2), pretraceability (Sect. 7.3.3), post-traceability (Sect. 7.3.4), and impact analysis (Sect. 7.3.5). In particular, we discuss the obstacles in making this knowledge explicit.

7.3.1 Sensitivity Characterization

Minimally, sensitivity characterization, the result of sensitivity analysis, is a list of high-level requirements that are unstable or likely to change [35]. In most cases, however, sensitivity analysis not only captures which requirements are likely to change, but also *how* they are anticipated to change. We can represent this type of knowledge the same way as we represent requirements: Future changes are represented as different options. As options are high-level descriptions, it costs minimal effort from the part of the developers to document this knowledge. Sensitivity analysis can be viewed as a simpler form of product line scoping [33]. The latter not only captures variabilities, but also commonalities.

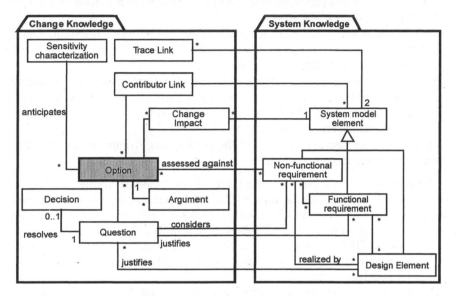

Fig. 7.2. Change knowledge and its relationship to system knowledge

As the goal of sensitivity analysis is to focus resources on the most likely changes, a detailed sensitivity characterization also captures the likelihood and the time frame of each possible change. For example, developers focus first on changes that are very likely or changes that are likely to occur in the short term, as opposed to changes that are unlikely or changes that will occur in the long term.

The main obstacle today for making sensitivity characterization explicit is that there are no standard methods for this. Recently, risk management methods [20] have become more popular which give some guidance on how to systematically deal with expectations on system evolution. Even if developers and clients only use personal heuristics, it is important to make this explicit so that the heuristics can be improved.

7.3.2 Requirements Rationale

Rationale captures the options that were considered, the criteria used to evaluate them, and the reasons for preferring the current options to the discarded options. This can be represented in several different ways [36], including natural language, rules in a knowledge-based system, or arguments structured in rhetorical steps.

The latter case, called argumentation-based rationale, represents rationale as a graph of nodes and edges, each node representing a decision-making element or rhetorical step and each edge representing a relationship between two elements. For example, the questions, options, criteria (QOC) notation [27] uses the following rhetorical steps:

- *Questions* represent problems to be solved, such as a requirements issue, a need for clarification, or a disagreement.
- *Options* represent considered alternatives for answering a question. Options include requirements, changes to a document, or clarifications. If a question is closed, the chosen option is called *decision*.
- *Criteria* represent qualities that are used to evaluate options in a certain context. Criteria are NFRs (e.g., reliability, cheapness, performance). The assessment of an option against a set of criteria is represented with assessment links between the option and the criteria nodes.
- *Arguments* represent the opinions of the participants. Arguments can support or oppose another rhetorical node.

Developers first capture bits and pieces of rationale during review and negotiation. These can take the form of lists of defects, change requests, proposed alternatives, and argumentation that takes place electronically via e-mail or within a tool-supporting rationale. Developers then consolidate these bits and pieces into well-structured QOC models during revisions to the specification. The output of rationale capture is a QOC model that can be used to organize the rest of the change knowledge.

Argumentation-based representations are widely used in rationale management [21, 27, 29]. One of the early drivers to capture rationale has been traceability, e.g., in the REMAP approach [31].

Major problems for rationale capture involve cost (in particular, since the rationale providers are often different from the rationale users), completeness (because it is lost, if not captured early), and complexity (since rationale models are larger than system models). In [11] we discuss process and tool integration as a means to overcome these obstacles.

7.3.3 Pretraceability

Pretraceability enables a developer to follow a requirement back to its human source and the context in which it was captured. Pretraceability is needed during change assessment to identify conflicts between proposed requirements and original stakeholder criteria, especially when some of the stakeholders are not available for comment.

Capturing and representing pretraceability is a particularly difficult problem, as requirements elicitation is a process driven by negotiation, brainstorming, informal contacts, and creativity. Given any specific requirements, there may be many invisible individuals that contributed to it to various degrees. There are several approaches to this problem.

Using *WinWin* [3], stakeholders initiate the elicitation process by posting win conditions, which represent the stakeholders' success criteria. Win conditions are high-level NFR or FR, which, if not met, result in a system that fails to support the stakeholder. During the elicitation, win conditions are refined into actual requirements that are then organized in the requirements specification document. Conflicting win conditions are detected and resolved through negotiation. The options and their assessment are captured with an issue model similar to QOC, discussed in Sect. 7.3.2. As a groupware tool supports the complete process, the traceability from a specific requirement to a win condition is also captured. This approach, however, assumes that the client that posts win conditions in the tool is the stakeholder. In many situations, this is not the case, as stakeholder requirements are elicited during face-to-face meetings or during task observation, after which the analyst documents these requirements.

Using *contribution structures* [15], stakeholders indicate the different types of contributions for different artifacts. The contribution structures framework distinguishes three capacities:

- The *principal* motivates the requirement and is responsible for its effects and consequences.
- The *author* develops the requirements structure and content and is responsible for its form and semantics.
- The *documentor* records or transcribes the requirements content and is responsible for its appearance.

Recording the role of a contributor with respect to a requirement provides a simple way to document the commitment and responsibility of the contributor. This enables change requests to be directed to the right contributor, based on the nature of the change and the requirements being changed. Contribution structures can also take advantage of relations between requirements. For example, if one requirement is a specialization of another, more general, requirement, the contributor for the general requirement retains some responsibility for the specializations.

Recording traceability to human sources remains a difficult task because of acceptance issues. Such knowledge reveals more detail about the social network in the organization and the rate and quality of contribution of each participant. This can only be alleviated through organizational measures as discussed in [25].

7.3.4 Post-traceability

Post-traceability enables a developer to follow a requirement to its corresponding architecture, design, source code, and test elements. Given a requirement, a developer can deduce which design elements realize the requirement and which test cases check its realization. Similarly, given a test case, a developer can deduce which set requirements are checked and which are not. Post-traceability is needed during impact analysis to identify the change impacts.

Capturing and representing post-traceability is a better-understood problem, as the ability to explain and document the results of development activities has been forced on industries in life-critical businesses, such as aerospace, pharmaceutical, and medical application domains, for addressing liability and accountability issues. However, the challenges of post-traceability are also not technical (i.e., post-traceability is essentially a link between two elements), but rather, related to social and methodological factors. That is capturing all traceability links introduces a large bureaucratic overhead on developers, traceability links need to be related with other knowledge, such as rationale, to provide sufficient information. This results in proposed methods that generate traceability links as a side effect of developer activity or rationale [30, 31]. In [19], von Knethen describes in detail a traceability approach for embedded systems and its empirical evaluation.

7.3.5 Impact Analysis

Given a possible change, impact analysis results in the list of system elements that could be affected by the change and an estimation of the cost required to revise these elements. The input to impact analysis is typically a list of likely changes from the sensitivity analysis, rationale, and post-traceability links generated during development. For each change, developers follow traceability links from the impacted requirement to other elements and use rationale and their experience to assess how the target element is likely to be impacted. If the developer assesses the target element as likely to change, the impact analysis is repeated recursively [35]. Impact analysis provides initial cost estimates for changes. Since the impact analysis knowledge was generated during development, the cost estimates are more accurate than if performed during change assessment.

In the last few years, a number of approaches for impact analysis have been developed; for an early overview see [4]. One major problem is that impact analysis is an activity that requires much judgment from the developer. Simply following all post-traceability links only yields all the elements that are potentially impacted, hence, yielding cost estimates that overestimate the actual cost of change. Moreover, in the event some post-traceability links have not been captured, an automated approach could also yield an underestimate of the actual cost. Similar to sensitivity analysis, it is important to make the personal heuristics of experts explicit in order to improve them.

7.3.6 Summary

Table 7.1 summarizes the activities capturing the five types of knowledge discussed in this section. Typically, capturing rationale and traceability occurs during development. Sensitivity analysis occurs after a first stable version of the requirements is completed, while impact analysis occurs once the software architecture is defined. To ensure that the change knowledge remains up-to-date, all five types of knowledge need to be revisited during requirements and design change.

Table 7.1. Knowledge activities for supporting change

	Sensitivity analysis	Capturing rationale	Capturing pre-traceability	Capturing post-traceability	Impact analysis
Who	Specialist	Requirements engineers, reviewers, knowledge consolidator	Requirements engineers	Developers	Specialist
When	After first stable version of requirements	During requirements review and requirements changes	During requirements elicitation	During design	After first stable version of architecture.
Inputs	Domain model, history of similar systems	NFRs	Stakeholders	FRs and NFRs, architecture rationale	Sensitivity characteriz ation
Outputs	Unstable or likely to change requirements	Questions, options, criteria, arguments, and decisions	Contributor links to human sources	Trace links between requirements and design elements	Cost estimate, list of impacted elements

To reduce the cost of capturing this knowledge and make it easier to keep it up to date, we organize these five types of knowledge around options (Fig. 7.2):

- Likely changes in sensitivity characterization are represented as *options*.
- Pretraceability is represented as a *contributor link* between each option and the corresponding system model, including the contributing stakeholder. The contributor link also includes the role the stakeholder had in the contribution.
- The links between the rationale elements and the system elements represent dependencies between the change knowledge and the system knowledge. If a system model element is changed, the corresponding change knowledge that needs to be updated can be found by identifying the corresponding option.
- Traceability is not directly interconnected to options. Instead, *trace links* connect two related system model elements. Note, however, that trace links can be used to find indirect relationships between two options responding to different questions.
- The result of impact analysis is represented as a *change impact* object linking the option with the impacted elements.

In the next section, we describe an example for capturing and maintaining requirements change knowledge in the context of use case-based requirements specification.

7.4 Using Options for Dealing with Evolving Requirements

This section illustrates the change knowledge and the change activities identified in the previous sections with a specific approach for capturing and evolving change knowledge and requirements. The method and the REQuest tool used to create the requirements documents and the options are described in detail in [12]. In the following, we first describe the representation and use of FR and NFR in REQuest. Then, we sketch the process for changing the options and the requirements. The latter is illustrated with the meeting scheduler example [23].

7.4.1 Rationale-based Use Case Specification with REQuest

In REQuest, we describe the functional aspects of a requirements specification with *user tasks*, *use cases*, and *system services*. This is similar to other use case-based approaches. User tasks are similar to Cockburn's Summary Goal Use Cases [8]. We use the term user task because we rely on techniques from task analysis for their identification [10]. Only by knowing the user tasks in detail can a system with maximal support to the client be designed. The use cases correspond to Cockburn's *user goal use case,* and the system services to Cockburn's *subfunction goal use cases* [8]. Table 7.2 depicts as an example the user task "manage interaction among participants".

Table 7.2. User task: manage interactions among participants

User task name	Manage interaction among participants
Initiating actor	Meeting facilitator (MF)
Participating actors	Meeting participant (MP)
Task description	The MF is responsible for getting replies from MPs who have not reacted promptly, for notifying MPs of changes of date or location, and for keeping MPs aware of current unresolved conflicts or delays in the scheduling process
Realized in use cases	Handle replies, remind participant, react to replan request
Referenced NFR	None

Table 7.3 shows as an example the "handle replies" use case. We use the essential use case style of [9], where each use case step has a number, and actor and system steps are explicitly distinguished.

Table 7.3. Use case: handle replies

Name	Handle replies	
Realized user task	Manage interaction among participants	
Initiating actor	Meeting facilitator (MF)	
Participating actors	Meeting participant (MP)	
Flow of events	Actors	System
	1. The MP selects "Handle Replies" for a meeting and a question	
		2. The system checks if all MP replied (Exception: slow participant)
		3. The system starts the "close question service" and notifies the MF accordingly
Exceptions	(Slow participant) The MF decides whether to remind the MPs or to close the question and possibly disqualify the MP. In the first case they remind the MP. In the second case they disqualify the MP. Then they enter the disqualification into the system through the "disqualify participant" service and then selects the "close question service"	
Precondition	The meeting initiator has initiated the meeting and asked some question	
Postcondition	The MPs have been reminded or the question is closed	
Includes use cases	None	
Used services	Check participant replies, remind participant, close question, disqualify participant	
Referenced NFRs	Response time, minimize amount of messages, flexibility	

In contrast to goal-oriented approaches to requirements engineering (e.g., GBRAM [1] or KAOS [23]), where NFRs are used to drive the requirements elicitation, we use user tasks to drive the elicitation. NFRs are only used as criteria for the evaluation of the adequacy of use case or service design with respect to user tasks and use cases, respectively.

In REQuest, we use the QOC model to represent the rationale for a specific requirements element [12]. As criteria we use NFRs. In addition, we use a special kind of question type, called *justifications*. These are used to summarize the arguments as to why a specific use case or system service is preferred against its alternatives. For example, Table 7.4 depicts the justification of the handle replies use case of Table 7.3.

Typically, REQuest specifications are created in two ways:

- Either different options are first created and assessed, and then one of these options is chosen and refined into a full-fledged use case. During refinement new insights might be gained that lead to changes on the options.

- Alternatively, a use case is first created and then justified. During the justification other options are made explicit and evaluated. This might lead to an adaptation of the use case.

Table 7.4. QOC model: justification for the handle replies use case

Justification	What is the best option for the system boundary within in the "handle replies use case" satisfying the NFRs?		
Criteria:	Response time	Minimize amount of messages	Flexibility
Option 1 (fully automatic): The system collects replies and reminds slow MPs automatically during a given time within a given interval. The system then closes the question, disqualifies all MPs who did not respond from the meeting, and informs the MF	+	–	–
Decision (fully manual): The MF chooses when to handle replies, checks status accordingly, and decides whether to remind MPs personally, or to close the question and disqualify MPs personally	–	+	+
Legend: + Option complies with criterion, – Option fails to meet criterion			

7.4.2 Change Management in REQuest

In REQuest, rationale and trace links are captured to support change. This is facilitated through the tool. For example, glossary terms are identified in the text and linked automatically. When creating or editing an element a template is provided that includes references to the other elements. As soon as a link in one direction is created (e.g., between user task and a use case), the other direction is automatically also created.

These links can then be used for impact analysis. REQuest recommends carrying this out early for likely changes. This information can then be used as arguments in the evaluation of different design options. REQuest does not give particular support for sensitivity analysis.

To reduce the effort for creating the change knowledge for the developers, we introduce the role of a *change knowledge consolidator*. The task of this role is to identify missing knowledge (such as missing decisions or missing links) and to consolidate the knowledge (e.g., unifying similar options).

This role can also carry out the impact analysis for likely changes identified during sensitivity analysis. However, typically requirements engineers or developers carry out impact analysis, since it not only provides input necessary to plan and execute changes. Its main contribution is to the design activity, because it enables design for change. In the following we give an example how a change request is handled in REQuest, in particular how options support this step.

Table 7.5. Change request

Change request: new quality constraint minimize facilitator effort	
Objective	Improve use cases from the viewpoint of the meeting facilitator
Originator	Meeting facilitator
Current system behavior	In the current system the meeting facilitator has to spend too much time on interaction with the meeting participants
Desired system behavior	New quality constraint on the user task and therefore on all use cases: minimize the time the meeting facilitator has to be spend on interacting with meeting participants
Needed change	Find a new solution so that the new quality constraint and all existing constraints are satisfied

Table 7.5 shows an example change request to the use cases of the meeting scheduler. It mainly impacts the existing use case handle replies (see Table 7.3). This use case realizes the fully manual (FM) option, since the fully automatic (FA) option severely restricts the user flexibility criterion. The reason is that it is not tolerable for the users to be disqualified by the system. The change request basically consists of adding a new quality constraint. In the following we explain how this change request is processed.

The requirements engineer proposes different options to implement a change request. One possibility that is always available is the status quo, that is, not to change the specification. Other possibilities arise from reevaluating existing options in the context of the change. If neither of these is satisfying, then new options have to be devised. In the example, a new option for the handle replies use case has to be created, because neither of the given ones satisfies all constraints. The FA option invalidates the user flexibility, and the FM option invalidates the new constraint minimal facilitator effort. Therefore new options have to be generated. Table 7.6 shows the option informed and manual (IM) that satisfies all the constraints. For each option proposed, the requirements engineers need to evaluate it and refine it to satisfy the NFRs. The evaluation of the new option is also shown in Table 7.6.

In addition, requirements engineers create arguments supporting and opposing options. This helps to validate the evaluations and to prioritize criteria. Once requirements engineers have evaluated and refined (most or) all options, they create a decision by selecting an option. This can result in minor or substantial change in the requirements specification. The decision to realize the change with a given option is not only based on the rationale (that makes explicit which option best satisfies all the criteria), but is also based on effort and cost considerations (which have to be validated later with the change plans). In particular, an impact analysis for the options is carried out. The impacts are documented as a list of elements to be changed according to the chosen option. In particular, this includes elements arising from trace links indicating dependencies that have to be assured in spite of the change. The cost and effort considerations are recorded elsewhere, e.g., in a system or project planning document.

Table 7.6. New justification for use case handle replies

Justification:	What is the best option for the system boundary within in the "handle replies use case" satisfying the NFRs?				
Criteria		Response time	Minimize amount of messages	User flexibility	Minimize facilitator
Option 1 (fully automatic): The system collects replies and reminds slow participants automatically within a given interval. The system then closes the question, disqualifies all participants who did not respond from the meeting and informs the meeting facilitator		+	−	−	+
Option 2 (informed and manual): The system collects replies and automatically reminds the participants. After a given interval it informs the meeting facilitator about the status. The meeting facilitator closes the question and decides whether to disqualify the participants who did not respond		+	−	+	+
Decision (fully manual): The Meeting Facilitator chooses when to handle replies and accordingly checks the status and decides whether to remind participants personally, close the question, or disqualify participants personally		−	+	+	−

Legend: + Option complies with criterion,
            − Option fails to meet criterion

Based on this, detailed change plans are created that list the change steps necessary to implement the options. Table 7.7 shows the change plan of the new option (IM). It requires only few changes to the handle replies use case and the corresponding rationale. In addition to the direct impact, the impact on related use cases also has to be treated. In the example, the handle replies is included in the schedule meeting use case. Thus, the latter has to be reconsidered. In this case the use case itself need not be changed, but the evaluation of the new constraint has to be added to its rationale. Note that not all use cases are evaluated against all criteria, because not all criteria are relevant. The traces capture the knowledge necessary to propagate the relevance of criteria. Based on the change plans, the cost and effort estimates are also reconsidered. Finally, the change plans are executed. In addition, the changes have to be validated, e.g., through inspections.

Table 7.7. Change plan for option IM

Change Impact	Facet	Type	Description
UC handle replies	1	Del	The meeting facilitator does not need to initiate the check
UC handle replies	2	Mod	The system checks according to a given interval
UC handle replies	2	Mod	If a participant did not reply, they are reminded by the system
UC handle replies	3	Add	After another given interval the system checks again. It informs the meeting facilitator about the status
UC handle replies	3	Add	The meeting facilitator closes the question and decides whether to disqualify participants who did not respond
UC handle replies	Exception	Mod	The meeting facilitator does not remind the participant again
UC handle replies	Post-condition	Mod	The question is closed
Justification handle replies	Option and evaluation	Add	New option: informed and manual, Evaluation for the new option +,–,+,+ Evaluation for the new criteria –,+,+
Justification schedule meeting	Evaluation	Add	Evaluation for the new criteria :

Legend: Del = delete, Mod = modify, Add = add

7.4.3 Discussions of the REQuest Process

As discussed in [12], we have developed and refined the REQuest process and tool for capturing change knowledge and requirements in a series of students' experiments during projects, lectures, and seminars. These experiments have enabled us to develop detailed guidance. This guidance improved the quality of the use cases and the rationale written by the students. We have started experiments with guidance for using change knowledge to process change requests as described in the process above. Again, the feedback of the students is positive in that they were able to define new options, assess and plan them, and execute the change. They felt very positive about having detailed guidance for change processing as they had not had such guidelines available to them before. Of course, they also indicated many possibilities for improvement such as a graphical representation of traceability links (similar to requirements management tools like DOORS or RequistePro). Another idea is to standardize and improve the structure of options. This would help to compare options and to identify the detailed changes necessary to implement the option.

Several processes for changing requirements have been proposed, e.g., the NFR Framework [7] or REMAP [31] or COMANCHE [5]. The main features of the REQuest process are:

- NFR are used as criteria to compare different options for functionality. Typically, NFR are only used to assess architectural decisions. We take the view of the NFR framework that NFR should be refined in parallel with the refinement of functional requirements.
- High-level options for use cases are created and maintained as change knowledge. In contrast to the NFR-framework we do not focus on the decomposition, but on the compact description of options and their evaluations. Thus, we use the notion of user task and use case to cluster user-relevant functionality. In the goal-graphs of the NFR framework several issues relevant for one use case may be scattered around. The drawback of our approach is that changing the use case structure impacts on many places. However, in our experience the use case structure is typically quite stable (at least in cases where the system has to support existing user tasks).
- In case of change the rationale is updated, but the old versions are not kept. The reason is that the change knowledge always includes all options identified at a specific point in time and the evaluations of these options. If the evaluations change, then the old evaluations are outdated (or incorrect). If the options change, then similarly, previous versions are outdated. Again this is a difference from the NFR framework, which makes the changes explicit in the goal graphs. This supports the detailed comparison of the impacts of different changes, but after several changes the graphs will be overwhelmed with details.

7.5 Open Issues and Future Directions

In this chapter we discussed different kinds of knowledge necessary to support change. We argued for the central role of options in making this knowledge explicit. We also sketched a process for creating and using this knowledge during use case based requirements engineering. First experiences indicate that this process is feasible and supports making tacit knowledge explicit. Furthermore, this explicit knowledge helps to keep the requirements up-to-date in that it provides a basis for systematically assessing and planning change. With the role of the change knowledge consolidator we propose to keep the effort for the requirements engineers as small as possible. We see three challenges that require further studies:

- *Reliably predicting changes*: An important factor in minimizing cost and effort is to concentrate the change knowledge activities only on these parts of the system that are most likely to change. The solution to drive the complete change knowledge process by the sensitivity analysis is conceptually simple, however, reliable methods for sensitivity analysis are still an issue for further research.
- *Presenting change knowledge*: An open question, in our opinion, is how to structure and present the change knowledge so that it is of the highest benefit in different change activities. This requires a detailed analysis of further change types, like changes of user tasks, of use cases, and of system services as well as

changes of different kinds of quality criteria. Only after detailed guidance for carrying out these different changes has been developed, the cost of the change knowledge can be evaluated against its benefits. In particular, this is a prerequisite for further studies in an industrial setting.

- *Recording invalid decisions*: Capturing change knowledge makes explicit the organization's learning processes. Options that were prematurely discarded can be revisited, actual costs can be compared with inaccurate change impact estimates, overly cautious arguments can be contradicted, and invalid decisions reopened. As the changes and rationale behind such improvements are captured, the organization can learn and make better decisions in the future. However, an individual's view of this process can be that mistakes are documented and never forgotten, hence reducing the individual's incentive for making tacit knowledge explicit.

Similar to [25], we are convinced that in spite of these challenges, the benefit of making software engineering knowledge explicit exceeds its cost. Since change is a particularly prevalent problem during software development, it seems especially important to further explore the benefits and costs of change knowledge management.

References

1. Anton A., Potts C. (1998) The use of goals to surface requirements for evolving systems. In: Proceedings of international conference on software engineering, Kyoto, Japan, pp. 157-166
2. Bennett K.H., Rajlich V.T. (2000) Software maintenance and evolution: a roadmap. In: Proceedings of international conference on software engineering, Limerick, Ireland pp. 75-87
3. Boehm B., Egyed A., Kwan J., Port D., Shah A., Madachy R. (1998) Using the winwin spiral model: a case study. IEEE Computer, 31: 33-44
4. Bohner S.A., Arnold R.S. (1996) Software change impact analysis. IEEE computer science press, Los Alamitos, CA, USA
5. Canfora G., Casazza G., de Lucia A. (2000) A design rationale based environment for cooperative maintenance. International journal of software engineering and knowledge engineering, 10: 627-245
6. Chandra C., Ramamoorthy C.V. (1996) An evaluation of knowledge engineering approaches to the maintenance of evolutionary software. In: Proceedings of the international conference on software engineering and knowledge engineering, Lake Tahoe, Nevada, USA, pp. 181-188
7. Chung L., Nixon B.A., Yu E. (1996) Dealing with change: an approach using non-functional requirements. Requirements engineering journal, 1: 238-260
8. Cockburn A. (2001) Writing effective use cases. Addison Wesley, Reading, MA, USA
9. Constantine L.L., Lockwood L.A.D. (2001) Structure and style in use cases for user interface design. In: van Harmelen (Ed.) Object-oriented user interface design, Addison Wesley, Reading, MA, USA
10. Diaper D. (1989) Task analysis for human-computer interaction. Ellies, Horwood.

11. Dutoit A.H., Paech B. (2001) Rationale management in software engineering. In Chang S.K. (Ed.) Handbook of software engineering and knowledge engineering, Vol. 1, World scientific publishing, Singapore
12. Dutoit A.H., Paech B. (2002) Rationale-based use case specification. Requirements engineering journal, 7: 3-19
13. Eick S.G., Graves T.L., Karr A.F., Marron J.S., Mockus A. (2001) Does code decay? Assessing the evidence from change management data. IEEE transactions on software engineering 27: 1-12
14. FAA (1999) NAS architecture version 4.0, Blueprint for NAS modernization
15. Gotel O., Finkelstein A. (1995) Contribution structures. In: Proceedings of IEEE, 2nd international symposium on requirements engineering, York, UK, pp. 100-107
16. Grudin J. (1996) Evaluating opportunities for design capture. In: [29]
17. IEEE (1998) IEEE Standard for software maintenance, 1219-1998, IEEE
18. Jarke M. (1998) Requirements tracing. Communication of the ACM, 41: 32-36
19. von Knethen A. (2001) Change-oriented requirements traceability. Support for evolution of embedded system. PhD thesis in experimental software engineering, Fraunhofer IRB Verlag, Germany
20. Kontio J. (1997) The riskit method for software risk management. Version 1.00, CS-TR-3782, Computer science technical reports, University of Maryland, USA
21. Kunz W., Rittel H. (1970) Issues as elements of information systems. In: working paper No. 131, Institut für Grundlagen der Planung, Universität Stuttgart, Germany
22. Lam W., Shankararaman V. (1998) Managing change during software development: an incremental, knowledge-based approach. In: Proceedings of the international conference on software engineering and knowledge engineering, pp. 124-127
23. van Lamsweerde A., Darimont R., Massonet P. (1998) Goal-directed elaboration of requirements for a meeting scheduler: problems and lessons learned. In: Proceedings of the international symposium on requirements engineering, pp. 194-203
24. Lindvall M., Sandahl K. (1998) How well do experienced software developers predict software change? Journal of systems and software 43: 19-27
25. Lindvall M., Rus I. (2003) Knowledge management in software organizations. Chap. 4 in this book
26. Lions J.-L. (1996) ARIANE 5 Flight 501 Failure: Report by the Inquiry Board," http://ravel.esrin.esa.it/docs/esa-x-1819eng.pdf (accessed 5th May 2002)
27. MacLean A., Young R.M., Bellotti V., Moran T. (1991) Questions, options, and criteria: elements of design space analysis. Human-computer interaction, 6: 201-250
28. Mäkäräinen M. (2000) Software change management processes in the development of embedded software. Espoo 2000, Technical research center of Finland, VTT Publications, Turku, Finland
29. Moran T.P., Carroll J.M. (1996): Design rationale: concepts, techniques, and use. Lawrence Erlbaum Associates, Mahwah, NJ, USA
30. Pohl, K. (1996): Process-centered requirements engineering. John Wiley and Sons, New York, NY
31. Ramesh B., Dhar V. (1994) Representing and maintaining process: knowledge for large scale system development. IEEE Expert 9: 54-59
32. Savolainen J., Kuusela J. (2001) Volatility analysis framework for product lines. In: Proceedings of symposium on software reusability, Toronto, Canada

33. Schmid K. (2002) A comprehensive product line scoping approach and its validation. In: Proceedings of international conference on software engineering, Orlando, FL, USA, pp. 593-603
34. Sharon D. (1996) Meeting the challenge of software maintenance. IEEE Software, 13: 122-125
35. Strens M.R., Sugden R.C. (1996) Change analysis: a step towards meeting the challenge of changing requirements. In: IEEE symposium and workshop on engineering of computer based systems, Friedrichshafen, Germany, pp. 278-283
36. Shipman III F.M., McCall R.J. (1997) Integrating different perspectives on design rationale: supporting the emergence of design rationale from design communication. Artificial intelligence in engineering design, analysis, and manufacturing, 11: 141-154

Author Biography

Allen H. Dutoit is a research scientist in the Informatics Department of Technische Universitaet Muenchen. His research interests include rationale management, requirements engineering, tool support for distributed projects, and empirical software engineering. He has been involved since 1993 with Prof. Bruegge in teaching software engineering project courses in Carnegie Mellon University and Technische Universitaet Muenchen. Allen Dutoit was previously affiliated with the software engineering institute, where he investigated natural language techniques for risk management. In the institute for complex engineered systems at Carnegie Mellon University, he researched the use of communication metrics as a diagnostic tool for software projects. During his stay at Carnegie Mellon University, he also contributed to the development of several complex information systems in collaboration with industry. Allen Dutoit received an Engineering Diploma in Computer Science from the Swiss Federal Institute of Technology and an M.S. and a Ph.D. in computer engineering at Carnegie Mellon University.

Dr. habil Barbara Paech heads the Quality Software Development department at the Fraunhofer Institute for Experimental Software Engineering (Fh IESE). Her research interests include requirements engineering and management, rationale and knowledge management, component-based software development, and validation and verification through inspection and testing. She has studied computer science at the TU München, University of Edinburgh (GB), and University of Pennsylvania (US). She received her Ph.D. from the LMU München. In 1998 she received the Habilitation in Computer Science from the TU München. She heads research and transfer projects in cooperation with industry and regularly holds seminars and lectures in both academic and industrial settings.

8 Emergent Knowledge in Web Development

David Lowe

Abstract: Although Web development can be considered a derivative of software engineering, it exemplifies a class of development projects with some unique characteristics that lead to changes in the development approach. Among other factors, there is substantial volatility in clients' articulation of their requirements, particularly as their understanding evolves of the way in which the systems under development might affect their client and stakeholder interactions, business processes, and ultimately their business model. We discuss these differences and the impact that they have on the development processes that are adopted for commercial Web systems. Specifically, we look at the ways in which client knowledge (and understanding) emerges progressively during the development process, often as a consequence of the design process, and the ways in which this results in a design-driven requirements process.

Keywords: Web development, Process, Design, Requirements

8.1 Introduction

Web systems were originally (i.e. in the early to mid 1990s) characterized by a strong emphasis on content and information provision. As such, they were often viewed not as software systems but as information systems. This characterization was evidenced in the focus of most of the early Web design methods, such as relationship management methodology (RMM) [24] and object-oriented hypermedia design model (OOHDM) [41] that emerged out of the hypertext community and emphasized content modeling and information structuring.

As Web technologies matured and became more sophisticated, the systems being developed exhibited increasingly complex functionality and consequently more complex underlying software. Again, this was typified by the emergence of Web design methods that aligned more closely with mainstream software design approaches (such as a plethora of approaches based on unified modeling language (UML)— see [2, 8, 22, 25, 30] for examples) and an increasing debate over whether "Web engineering" can be viewed as a particular class of software engineering (see [38, Chap. 29] for a discussion of this issue).

Whilst it is true to a limited extent that Web system development is primarily the creation of software systems, there is a growing recognition that Web systems — or rather that category of applications for which Web systems are an exemplar — have various unique characteristics that are only poorly addressed by conventional development practices [31]. Among other factors, there is substantial uncertainty in clients' understanding of the ways in which the systems under development might affect their client and stakeholder interactions, business processes, and ultimately their business model. This, in turn, has some major implications for the ways in which, and particularly when, clients' are able to articulate their requirements during the development process.

Development practices from related domains (software engineering, graphic design, marketing, etc.) do not typically address these differences particularly well. Despite this, there has been little consideration within the research literature of the implications of these characteristics on the development process. This is in spite of the obvious growth in importance of these systems to business success.

In this chapter we begin by investigating some of main differences between Web systems and other software systems. We then move on to explore the implications of the key differences for the ways in which client's knowledge evolves during the development process and how this should be addressed. We will, in particular, look at the role that the design process plays in this evolving understanding.

Before starting to look at Web systems in more detail, one point of clarification is worth raising. Whilst we use the term *Web system* in this paper for simplicity, we see these systems (i.e. those that have an architecture based on the utilization of Web technologies and protocols) as being exemplars of a much broader category of applications. This broader category can be understood by looking at the characteristics discussed in the next section, but can probably be best defined by one key characteristic—that the system under development changes the nature of the interaction with external stakeholders (such as clients, customers, and business partners). Hence, it potentially triggers changes in business processes and ultimately business models. In other words, the solution under development inherently changes the nature of the problem that it was addressing. This can be described as the *problem domain and the solution domain being mutually constituted*—a concept that is well understood in the social informatics literature! We will discuss this is much more in Sect. 8.3, but at this point it is simply worth noting that where we refer to *Web systems*, this broader interpretation will often be applicable.

8.2 Web System Characteristics and Implications

There is a growing body of research [5, 13, 35] that is attempting to understand the differences between Web systems and more conventional software systems. That is given the above comments at the end of the introduction, we describe as conventional systems those that have minimal impact on the fundamental nature of the interactions with external stakeholders and/or the nature of the problem being addressed. In general, we can draw a distinction between the unique characteristics of Web systems that are technical (that is, related to the specific technologies that are used and how these impact on the structure of the application) and those that are organizational (that is, related to the ways in which organizations make use of these systems).

It is also worth noting that although Web systems can be viewed as software systems, this does not automatically imply that existing representations of various aspects of these systems will be able to be directly applied. Indeed, to blindly apply existing models to the representation of Web systems would encourage developers to overlook the peculiarities of these Web systems, and hence not address these peculiarities, leading to inappropriate solutions. This is not to say that existing models should not be utilized — simply that we need to do so with an awareness of their limitations with respect to the aspects of Web systems that we wish to understand and document. We also need to understand how these limitations may be circumvented by appropriately supplementing (or replacing, where necessary) the models.

Further, improving the modeling support for the unique characteristics of Web systems is a useful first step, but on its own, it is not sufficient. We also need to consider how we actually carry out the development. This includes both the specific activities and tasks that are desirable, as well as broader process issues related to how we organize this work. We shall look at the various unique characteristics of Web systems and investigate the impacts on both what we may wish to represent and potential changes to the development process.

8.2.1 Technical Differences

There are obvious technical differences between Web systems and more conventional software and IT systems. The most significant of these are as follows:

8.2.1.1 Link Between Business Model and Technical Architecture

Possibly the most obvious difference between Web and traditional software development is seen in regard to the specific technologies that are used and the ways in which these are interconnected. For example, the technical structure of Web systems merges a sophisticated business architecture (which usually implies significant changes to the business model of the client) with both a complex information architecture and a highly component-based technical architecture [39]. The linkage between the business architecture and the technical design of the system is much tighter than for conventional software systems (i.e. the technology is more visible to users and influences an organizations interaction with its stakeholders very significantly). Similarly, the information architecture (which covers aspects such as the content viewpoints, interface metaphors and navigational structures) is substantially more sophisticated than conventional software systems.

The impact that Web systems have on business models implies that there is a need to be able to understand (and document) the link between business models and system architectures. This has typically been only implicitly addressed in traditional development as the business models are well established and understood. This is less true for Web projects and, as a result we see a growing body of work — largely emerging from large technology vendors such as IBM, Sun and Microsoft — that considers how to represent supported business functions and the technical architectures required to support these. The most mature of these approaches is the patterns for e-Business work being developed by IBM (see http://www.ibm.com/framework/patterns/). This work provides a framework for identifying common patterns of business models. As stated in [28]:

> The paths to creating e-businesses are repeatable. Many companies assume that they are unique and that therefore every creation of an e-business has to be learned as you go. In fact, there are lessons and architectural paths or patterns that can be discerned from all these engagements.

For each business pattern, a number of logical architectures (or topologies) are defined. These topologies provide a mechanism for fulfilling a particular business need. In effect, these models provide a direct link between the business models that underpin the systems being developed and the technical architecture that supports these business models. One problem with these current approaches is that the architectural models tend to emphasize functionality, with little consideration of how to represent the information architecture. In particular, aspects such as content modeling, information viewpoints and so on are not addressed.

Although the relationship between the business model and the system architecture is beginning to be addressed at a notational level, there is little work in this area in terms of processes that support the interpretation of business requirements and the relationship that these have to the architecture. Even more significantly, there is little understanding of the impact of a given architecture on the business processes and models. The work that does exist tends to focus on the design of architectures (see Sect. 8.2.1.2). One of the few exceptions is the IBM work on patterns mentioned above. Although it does not provide a formal process, it does suggest an implicit process whereby the broad business needs are used to select a suitable business pattern, which is then used to guide the selection of suitable architectures.

8.2.1.2   Open Modularized Architectures

Related to the above point is the emphasis that is typically placed on open and modularized architectures for Web systems. Although this is not unique to Web systems, it is often more pronounced. Web systems are often constructed from multiple commercial off-the-shelf (COTS) components that are adapted and integrated together, particularly for the system back-end middleware layers. This implies that strong integration skills become much more critical in most Web projects.

Although there is significant attention on modeling of open and component-based systems, little attention has yet been applied to considering the modeling of these systems or the associated development processes in the context of the Web.

Given this component-based development, strong integration skills become much more critical in most Web projects. The importance of a strong architectural design is also increased. Indeed, many see creating a solid architecture as the most crucial component of a successful Web systems development. One aspect that is yet to be effectively addressed is appropriate support (either as tasks or suitable techniques) for the linking of the various disparate elements of the architecture (i.e. informational and technical to the business architecture) [19].

8.2.1.3   Rapidly Changing Technologies

The technology that underpins most Web systems is changing very rapidly. This has several consequences. First, it increases the importance of creating flexible solutions that can be updated and migrated to new technologies with minimal effort. For example, the need for reusable data formats (such as XML) increases substantially. A second consequence is that developers' understanding of these technologies is often restricted, thus increasing project risks.

The work on detailed design notations for representing certain aspects of Web systems may actually create problems in terms of the portability of designs into new technologies. Alternatively, work on architectures and, more broadly, on information models tends to create designs that are less dependent on specific technologies, and hence more likely to be able to be adapted to changes.

8.2.1.4   Content is King

Of notable significance is the importance of content. Irrespective of the sophistication of the functionality and the creativity of the interface, a site is likely to fail without appropriate, substantial, and up-to-date content. This implies both an effective information design as well as suitable content management. This importance of content within Web sites also implies a need to at least consider how we understand and represent the informational elements of a Web system. It is not surprising therefore that that much of the earliest work on Web development models focused on information modeling and structuring.

Early approaches in this area evolved out of work on data modeling (such as entity-relationship models) and applied this to modeling the information domain associated with applications. Indeed, much of this work predate the Web and focused on hypermedia design. For example, RMM [24] claims to provide a structured design model for hypermedia applications. In reality, the focus is very much on modeling the underlying content, the user viewpoints onto this content and the navigational structures that interlink the content. OOHDM [42] is a similar approach, though somewhat richer in terms of the information representations and based on object-oriented software modeling approaches. Other similar examples include EORM [26] and work by Lee [27]. WSDM [11] attempts to model slightly different characteristics beginning more explicitly from user requirements, but these are only addressed in a very rudimentary fashion. In general, these notations were either developed explicitly for modeling information in the context of the Web, or have been adapted to this domain.

More recently, work on both Web modeling Language (WebML) [6] and the adaptation of UML [34], an emerging industry standard for modeling object-oriented systems, (see for example [3]) has begun to amalgamate these concepts into a richer modeling language for describing Web applications. However, despite aims to support comprehensive descriptions, the focus (as with the above techniques) is very much on content modeling rather than describing the functionality that is a key element of most current commercial Web systems. This leads on to the next point.

Even less consideration has been given to process related issues in terms of dealing with content. Approaches such as usage-centered design [9] provide some indications of suitable activities—though typically not as part of a broader framework. The actual authoring of the content itself is also a significant development issue that is often overlooked. With conventional software development the population of the system with data is largely viewed as an operational issue (or at best, part of deployment). With Web development, the generation of "data" (i.e. content authoring) is fundamentally part of the development process [18] which involves significant editing and layout of text, preparation of images and other media, obtaining copyright clearances and so on. The development processes that underpin some of the information management approaches discussed earlier recognize this explicitly.

8.2.1.5   Increased Emphasis on User Interface

With conventional software systems, users must make an often considerable investment in time and effort to install and learn to use an application. With Web applications, however, users can very quickly switch from one Web site to another with minimal effort. As such, it becomes much more critical to engage users and provide much more evident satisfaction of users' needs and achievement of their objectives. The result is an increased emphasis on the user interface and its associated functionality. This is even more significant when it is recognized that many direct users of the systems are external rather than internal stakeholders.

A little more subtly, the emergence of authoring tools has focused on supporting rapid development and on visual design rather than functionality. This in turn has promoted a greater use of designs as a part of a specification, which allows a more interactive process between gathering requirements and building solutions.

A key element of user interfaces is the functionality that they provide. A few attempts have been made to integrate information modeling concepts with system functionality [8, 45], though in general these approaches are still rather simplistic, lack scalability, and focus on low-level design representations. Conallen's [8] work in particular is interesting insofar as it attempt to link a user's view of the system (as seen through the interaction with Web pages) to the back-end processes that support this interaction.

Other researchers have looked at modeling the way in which systems are utilized. For example, Guell et al. [20] extend OOHDM to include tools such as user scenarios and use cases. Vilain et al. [47] adapted UML to represent user interactions. Other researchers have investigated the use of formal methods for representing navigational requirements [17] or timing constraints [36], though these tend to focus on ensuring consistency rather than directly addressing the quality of the user interface. Possibly the most fruitful work in this area is usage-centered design [9], although a rigorous analysis of the application of these techniques to Web development has yet to be carried out.

The development process for user interface also raises numerous issues. Effectively this brings together content authoring and software development or, more precisely, creative design and technical development. It is worth noting that this highlights the difficulties that occur when combining two different cultures together within the same project.

8.2.1.6. Increased Importance of Quality Attributes

Web systems represent an increase in mission-critical applications that are often, as mentioned above, directly accessible to external users and customers. Flaws in applications (be they usability, performance, or robustness) are therefore typically more visible and hence are more problematic.

As with some other aspects, this has not been directly addressed at a modeling level, except insofar as developing effective architectures that support characteristics such as robustness, scalability, and reliability. These elements have not been effectively woven into the detailed Web requirements or design models.

In terms of development processes, there is a need to address quality assurance (QA) issues. Some work has been carried out looking explicitly at quality assurance issues in Web development, though in general this has been restricted to specific domains such as educational applications [12]. One key element of effective QA is evaluation. Indeed, it has been claimed that the quality of multimedia projects is directly determined by the effort put into evaluation [37]. For effective evaluation we need to establish suitable quality criteria — particularly in terms of how the Web system will be actually tested against client requirements. This also implies the need to actually understand client requirements, an issue that we discuss further shortly.

Another important issue is the establishment of suitable standards in order to ensure consistency, both from a usability perspective and from a development perspective. It is worth noting that considerable attention is beginning to focus on usability standards and, in particular, accessibility standards such as the World Wide Web Consortium's (W3C) Accessibility Initiative [7].

8.2.2 Organizational Differences

In addition to the technical differences, and possibly more important than them, are a number of organizational characteristics that are either unique or heightened in Web systems [5]. One of the key ones is the issue of client uncertainty. This, however, relates strongly to how client and developer knowledge emerges during the project, and so will be discussed in the following section. Various other issues are worth briefly considering.

8.2.2.1   Short Time Frames for Initial Delivery

Web development projects often have delivery schedules that are much shorter than for conventional IT projects — often in the range of 1- 3 months. This is partly a consequence of the rapid pace of technological development and partly related to the rapid uptake of Web systems. This is an issue that has yet to be considered in any substantive way in terms of how it impacts on Web design models and notations.

In terms of processes, the shorter development timeframes increase the importance of incremental development approaches and consequently also increase (as discussed above) the reliance on flexible system architectures, particularly with respect to the user interface and the way in which information is managed within the site.

8.2.2.2   Highly Competitive

Web projects tend to be highly competitive. This is, of course, not new; in fact it is typical of the IT industry in general. The nature of the competitiveness is, however, somewhat different. There is regularly a perception that with simple Web authoring tools anyone can create an effective site. This creates inappropriate expectations from clients, coupled with numerous small start-up companies claiming to be doing effective Web design, but in reality offering little more than HTML skills and rudimentary graphic design. The result is a highly uninformed competitiveness.

8.2.2.3   Fine-Grained Evolution and Maintenance

Web sites typically evolve in a much finer-grained manner than conventional IT applications. The ability to make changes that are immediately accessible to all users without their intervention means that, the nature of the maintenance process changes.   Rather than a conventional product maintenance/release cycle, we typically have an ongoing process of content updating, editorial changes, interface tuning, and so on. The result is a much more organic evolution. It is also useful to note that a consequence of the emphasis on rapid development and fine-grained development is that there can tend to be less thought given to formal evaluation as this is often perceived as interrupting the build process.

As with many other aspects, this has yet to be considered in any substantial detail. It is worth pointing out, however, that one aspect of modeling that actively inhibits effective Web system maintenance is the lack of a cohesive architectural modeling language that actively links the information architecture with the technical architecture [19]. Conversely, the information models, such as OOHDM [42] and WebML [6], actively support a much clearer understanding of the impacts of changes to various aspects of the underlying content, viewpoints, or navigational structures.

One interesting avenue of work is that related to configuration management (CM). Dart [10] argues that, because of the incremental nature of Web projects, and the fine-grained way in which they change, CM is even more important than for conventional projects. Only very rudimentary consideration is, however, given to the way in which CM is integrated into the broader development process.

One unusual area that has been used as an analogy for Web development and may provide some useful insights into maintenance processes is landscape gardening [30]. Web site development is often about creating an infrastructure (laying out the garden) and then "tending" the information that grows and blooms within this garden. Over time the garden (i.e. the Web site) will continue to evolve, change, and grow. A good initial architecture should allow this growth to occur in a controlled and consistent manner. This analogy has been discussed in terms of providing insights into how a site might be maintained.

8.3 Evolving Project Knowledge

The above discussion highlighted various aspects that characterize Web development. Few, if any of these characteristics, are unique to Web projects. When taken as a whole they tend, however, to characterize these projects.

There is a characteristic that was skimmed over, but is much more significant in the overall impact that it is likely to have on the development process. This characteristic is the impact that a developed system has on the nature of the problem being addressed and how this relates to client uncertainty and emerging knowledge. As we stated in Sect. 8.1, the solution being developed inherently changes the nature of the problem that it addresses—i.e. *the problem domain and the solution domain are mutually constituted and interdependent*! This will affect not only the way in which the solution is developed, but more fundamentally the way in which the problem itself is understood (and indeed, how this understanding changes over time).

Whilst there has been substantial work on using the Web to manage knowledge whilst carrying out development projects, there has been very little consideration given to how knowledge *about* Web systems emerges and is managed during development. To understand this a little better, we begin by considering the issue of client uncertainty and requirements volatility.

8.3.1 Client Uncertainty

It is often argued that with Internet and Web-based systems, the technology, development skills, business models, and competing systems are changing so rapidly that the domain is often not only poorly understood, but also constantly evolving [43]. This can lead to a client not understanding their needs. Specifically, clients often have difficulty not only articulating their needs, but also in understanding whether a particular design will satisfy their needs. This is typically a result of a poor understanding of the consequences of the given solution. It is also worth noting that many Web projects are vision-driven rather than needs-driven, leading to an initial lack of clarity.

This interpretation is, however, a little simplistic. More commonly, clients will have sound knowledge about their own (current) business models, contexts, processes, and hence the problem to which they are seeking a solution. Whilst it is true that they may have difficulties in articulating this knowledge, there is a plethora of work in the requirements engineering domain about how this particular challenge can be addressed. A greater challenge arises in the situation where a client does not initially comprehend that a given problem definition will result in a solution that has impacts beyond the confines of the problem as defined, i.e. a possible solution that adequately addresses the problem as defined by the client will change or impact on other elements of the clients business model, processes, or context. In this situation, the client's knowledge of the solution impacts only emerges progressively as possible designs are created by the developer and jointly explored [44].

An alternative way of conceptualizing this is that the underpinning technology that enables the solution implies certain linkages between different aspects of the solution, and so when one of these aspects is addressed by a solution, the other elements are also affected. This can possibly be clarified with a simple example. Consider an existing company that does event promotion by regularly collecting information from event venues and using this to construct promotional posters for distribution, with advertising space available to generate an income stream. Developing a Web-based system to support distribution of the event information may seem like a relatively straightforward extension of existing business models and processes, but the interaction with the customer base (i.e. event patrons) and advertisers is changed by the nature of the Web. Specifically, it is likely that the patrons will have new expectations regarding the ability to dynamically provide feedback on events, which in turn will change the value of this information. Advertisers will perceive differing value in a transient online presence as compared to more permanent hardcopy advertising material. In other words, the solution that is constructed will change the value chains that exist in the business and possibly even ultimately the business model itself. The client's knowledge regarding these changes will only develop once the system itself takes form and can be used to gain feedback.

8.3.2 Addressing Client Uncertainty and Understanding Requirements

So, client uncertainty largely arises from a lack of understanding of the likely broader impact on business problems of addressing a given set of business needs, and client knowledge about their evolving needs emerges progressively during the development. How is this issue addressed by current approaches? A useful place to start in understanding this issue is to look at how requirements are handled in Web projects. Stated rather simplistically, conventional development tends to assume that requirements are known to clients, and they simply need to be elicited and analyzed. Requirements processes usually differentiate (at least conceptually, if not in the way they are represented) between user requirements that capture the user understanding of their needs and the system specification that represents the system that will meet these needs. The user requirements are often elicited and formalized in a user requirements definition (URD) and then analyzed to construct the system requirements which are formalized in a system requirements specification (SRS). In effect, the two documents are different representations of the same concepts.

One significant difficulty with this paradigm is that it presumes that clients either understand their requirements, or at the very least understand the problem that is being addressed and can be led through a process of articulating their needs. Even when clients are not able to articulate their requirements precisely, they are at least able to understand whether a given design will address their needs. In cases such as these, the design may commence prior to full resolution of requirements. The design will then be used to ascertain (from client feedback) whether the proposed solution addresses the identified need.

Given the characteristics of Web projects that have been outlined, this will problematic. A fundamental problem arises out of the evolving client knowledge about the changes to the problem domain and the fact that this evolving knowledge is actually triggered by the system designs, prototypes and implementations.

Turning this around, we can see that it becomes impractical to resolve the requirements (which in essence are an articulation of what needs to be done to address the problem domain) without an understanding of the proposed solution domain. In our research work we refer to this as a design-driven requirements process [32]. An interesting analogy is found in the area of social informatics [40], which encompasses the concept that technology and the use of that technology are mutually constituted, i.e. the desired use defines the desired technological solution, but the actual solution changes the usage. Web systems could be described as an exemplar of that class of systems where the system and the problem domain are mutually constituted.

Whilst there has been little work addressing this specific issue, some of the techniques mentioned above that focus on modeling the way in which systems are utilized [20, 47] may help reduce client uncertainty and allow clients to obtain a clearer view of potential changes to their businesses. One avenue being pursued by the authors is the investigation of a characterization model that represents the key aspects that need to be woven into an evolving specification of a Web system

[29] (see Table 8.1 for an example). The complete form of the model highlights the links between the various characteristics, especially including the link between the business architecture and the technical and information architectures. The intention is that it be used to guide the formulation and evaluation of project acceptance criteria, user requirements, and detailed contractual specifications.

Table 8.1. Acceptance criteria framework

Dimension	Possible Representations	Example Elements
Client/User		
Client problem statement	(Natural language)	
Product vision	(Natural language)	Client needs and business objectives
Users	(Natural language)	User descriptions and models
Application		
Content modeling	Structured language, hypermedia/information modeling languages (OOHDM, HDM, entity modeling, etc.)	Existing content structure, information views, navigational structures, required content
User interaction	Modified TAM	Usability and usefulness metrics
	Structured language, hypermedia modeling, HCI models, etc	Access mechanisms, user control behavior, user orientation, search requirements, security control
Development constraints	Natural language, standards	Adherence to corporate policies, resource availability
Nonfunctional requirements	Natural language, quality metrics, adherence to standards	Reliability of content, copyright constraints
Application evolution		
Evolution directions	(Natural language)	Expected content changes
Client adoption/ integration of Web	Business process reengineering	Information dissemination paths, workflow changes
Maintenance processes	Natural language, process models	Content maintenance responsibility, Web management cycles

8.3.3 Development Processes

So what development approach can be used to address this "design-driven requirements" process and assist clients in constructing knowledge about the impacts of the solutions being developed? We can begin by considering the increasing use of lightweight development processes for software projects [1, 15]. One of the approaches receiving the most attention is the use of eXtreme Programming (XP) [4]. XP is based on the incremental development of partial solutions that address component requirements. These partial solutions are then integrated into the evolving system through refactoring of the current solution to incorporate these components. When used in conventional software development XP has (arguably) proven to be effective for projects that are initially ill-defined — a characteristic of many Web projects. This is possibly because it allows a client to see the emerging solution early in the development when further clarification of the requirements is still possible. As a result, many of the proponents of XP and similar approaches see them as ideal to be adopted for Web development [46]. In effect, the emerging solution will facilitate the development of client knowledge about the impacts of the solutions, and allow the refinement of the system definition early in the development.

It can be argued, however, that there are certain problems that restrict the applicability of approaches such as these to Web projects (see, for example [33]). The first is that a number of studies have shown that approaches such as XP only work effectively for projects that have cohesive development teams. This is often not the case with Web projects, which often lack cohesiveness between the technical development and the creative design as a result of the disparate disciplinary backgrounds of the development team members. XP can also result in a brittle architecture and poor documentation, which makes ongoing evolution of the system difficult — something that is important for Web systems. Finally, and perhaps most fundamentally, XP utilizes partial solutions to resolve uncertainty in requirements, but does not inherently handle subsequent changes in these requirements (i.e. requirements volatility) as the system evolves. In other words, the incremental development implicit in XP can be viewed as a form of prototyping that aims to either consider the applicability of a given design to a known problem, or to assist the developers in ensuring that they have understood the clients' problem. The prototyping in Web development however aims to help a client develop an understanding of how different solutions may impact on the nature of the problem being addressed.

A useful divergence at this point is to consider a comparison with the approach that is often referred to as "Ready - Fire - Aim" [23]. This essentially is referring to approaches where the design is commenced prior to a full understanding of the requirements (or coding commenced prior to a full design, depending on the interpretation) as a way of informing clients in the presence of uncertainty. In contrast, commercial Web development is typically about developing prototype solutions as a way not of resolving initial uncertainty, but rather to understand the impact of a given solution. This is a little bit like saying "Well, if we fire there, then it will have this impact, but if we fire there it will have that impact". Possible solutions are jointly investigated by the developer and client (typically, through a design prototyping approach, but *prior* to committing to a specific solution) in terms of their impact on the problem domain and hence the requirements, with the ultimate result that a solution is identified that matches a problem that has been changed by that solution.

In effect, conventional software engineering processes see requirements as preceding and driving the design process. Even where an incremental approach (such as XP) or an iterative approach (involving multiple feedback loops) is adopted, the design is viewed as a way of assisting in the identification and validation of requirements; yet rarely does it help the client to actually formulate their needs. In Web development, the situation is fundamentally different. The design process not only helps developers and clients articulate their needs, but also helps clients understand the system domain and therefore their needs.

In effect, the design drives the requirements process. We begin with a client's poor understanding of their needs (as well as system capabilities), and during the course of the project this understanding evolves and matures. This has several consequences. First, it increases the importance of creating flexible solutions that can be updated and migrated to new technologies with minimal effort. For example, the need for reusable data formats (such as XML) increases substantially. A second consequence is that developers' understanding of these technologies is often restricted, increasing project risks.

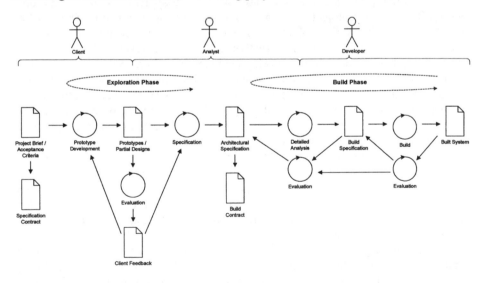

Fig. 8.1 Typical web development process

Figure 8.1 shows a depiction of a development process for Web systems that incorporates this understanding. In this figure, the first cycle iterates around a series of exploratory design prototypes, including elements such as white sites and story-boards. The aim is to move from an initial set of acceptance criteria to a clear specification of the system — but to a specification that includes not only requirements but also the broad architectural design elements of the site [16, 21]. The second cycle covers usually fine-grained, incremental design and build process. In effect, the process (specifically the first of the two key cycles shown in Fig. 8.1) is aimed at developing (or rather evolving) a joint understanding of the combined problem/solution domain.

Finally, it is worth noting that anecdotal evidence indicates that these issues are well understood and accepted within industry. Research has been limited to empirical work using scenario-based redesign of partially developed sites, though this work has at least recognized the importance of designs in assisting clarification of client needs [14].

> We practice a revised method of scenario-based design inferred from a theoretical perspective which treats design as inquiry, inquiry as dialogue and dialogue as the source of all tools, including mental constructs. The result is a set of techniques for using structured dialogue between users and designers to increase designers' understanding of specific domains of users' work.

In commercial Web projects, these concepts, particularly the mutual interdependence of requirements and design are typically reflected in the absence of separate requirements and design documents. Rather, developers tend to create a hybrid *specification* that blends design and requirements (something that is usually viewed as anathema in conventional software engineering).

In other words, system design allows stakeholders to understand technical possibilities and limitations, and hence improve their understanding of the development context. The result is a vehicle for reducing the underlying uncertainty. For this to be effective, however, we need to develop a suitable model of the relationship between system design, client requirements, and uncertainty within these requirements. This *uncertainty* model can then be used to adapt the requirements engineering process, resulting in a design-driven requirements process. This is the focus of our ongoing research.

8.4 Future Trends and Conclusions

So what conclusions can we draw from the above discussions regarding how knowledge is managed in Web projects? The key insight is that the nature of Web projects implies that since the solution changes the nature of the problem we therefore need to acknowledge that a client will be inherently unable to define their problem in the absence of a possible solution. Different solutions (i.e. the Web systems to be developed) will fundamentally lead to differing impacts on the stakeholder interactions and business processes and hence to different problem domains. This in turn means that we need to recognize the importance of exploring a range of possible solutions, and to do so not only to determine the optimal design, but possibly to determine the optimal problem!

Further, it also indicates that client involvement in the design process becomes crucial (something that is often viewed as very dangerous). Without an understanding of the possible system designs, the client is unlikely to develop a clear understanding of the implications of a proposed solution. Thus design knowledge becomes a crucial enabling tool within Web projects.

Ongoing work of the author and others has begun to explore exactly what level and form of design knowledge will best assist clients in developing a clear conceptualization of the impact of possible designs. This work is, however, still too early to have provided concrete outcomes.

Another project that is only just commencing is looking at process modeling and project management tools that track the evolving process that accompanies the evolving product understanding. By monitoring the relationships between these models (often expressed as project plans) and the initial templates from which they were derived it is possible to identify the points at which the process deviated. Once this is identified, the developer can be interrogated as to the cause of the deviation, and this information can then be fed back into the underlying project templates to support future project planning. This approach becomes much more crucial in Web projects where the nature of the process is difficult to determine a priori because of the evolving system.

Ultimately, the insights explored in this paper are not only about Web projects, but rather about those systems where, as we mentioned, the *solution and the problem* are mutually constituted. That is neither can exist without the other, and they need to be jointly understood, developed, and evolved.

Acknowledgements

The author wishes to acknowledge the assistance and insights of numerous people in developing the concepts described in this chapter. In particular the author is grateful to John Eklund, Brian Henderson-Sellers, Ross Jeffery, Didar Zowghi, Aybüke Aurum, Nick Carr, Marcus Carr, Vassiliki Elliott, Norazlin Yusop, Louise Scott, Lucila Carvalho, and John D'Ambra, for their contributions to this research.

The author also wishes to acknowledge the collaborative funding support from the Australian Research Council, Access Online Pty Ltd., and Allette Systems Ltd. under Grant No. C4991-7612.

References

1. Angelique E. (1999) A lightweight development process for implementing business functions on the Web. In: WebNet'99. Honolulu, Hawaii, USA, pp. 262-269
2. Baresi L., Garzotto F., Paolini P. (2001) Extending UML for modeling Web publications. In: Proceedings of 34th Hawaii international conference on system sciences, Hawaii, USA, pp. 1285-1294

3. Baumeister H., Koch N., Mandel L. (1999) Towards a UML extension for hypermedia design. In: <<UML>> 1999: IEEE, the second international conference on the unified modeling language, Fort Collins, Colorado, USA, pp. 614-629

4. Beck K. (1999) Extreme programming explained. Addison-Wesley, Reading, MA

5. Burdman J. (1999) Collaborative Web development. Addison-Wesley, Reading, MA

6. Ceri S., Fraternali P., Bongio A. (2000) Web modeling language (WebML): a modeling language for designing Web sites. In: Proceedings of WWW9 conference. Amsterdam, The Netherlands, pp. 137-157

7. Chisholm W., Vanderheiden G. Jacobs I. (1999) Web content accessibility guidelines 1.0. World Wide Web Consortium, http://www.w3.org.TR/WCAG10 (accessed 16th April)

8 . Conallen J. (1999) Building Web applications with UML. Addison Wesley Object technology series: Addison-Wesley, Reading, MA

9. Constantine L.L., Lockwood L.A.D. (1999) Software for use: Addison-Wesley, MA

10. Dart S. (2000) Configuration management: the missing link in Web engineering: Artech House, Norwood, MA

11. De Troyer O., Leune C. (1997) WSDM: A user-centered design method for Web sites. In: 7th International World Wide Web conference. Brisbane, Australia, pp. 85-94

12. Eklund J., Lowe D. (2000) A quality assurance methodology for technology-delivered education and training. In: WebNet 2000: World Conference on the WWW and Internet. San Antonio, Texas, USA, Association for advancement of computing in education.

13. England E., Finney A. (1999) Managing multimedia: project management for interactive media. Addison Wesley, Reading, MA

14. Erskine L., Carter-Tod D., J., Burton J. (1997) Dialogical techniques for the design of web sites. International Journal of Human-computer studies, 47: 169-195

15. Fournier R. (1999) Methodology for client/server and Web application development. Yourdon Press, Englewood Cliffs, NJ

16. Gates L. (2001) Analysis and design: critical yet complicated. In: Application development trends, 101 Communications, Framingham, MA, pp. 40-42

17. German D.M., Cowan D.D. (1999) Formalizing the specification of Web applications. Lecture Notes in computer science, Springer, Berlin Heidelberg London, 1727: 281–292

18. Ginige A., Lowe D., Robertson J. (1995) Hypermedia authoring. IEEE Multimedia, pp. 24-35

19. Gu A., Lowe D., Henderson-Sellers B. (2002) Linking modeling capabilities and abstraction levels: the key to Web system architectural integrity. In Proceedings of the eleventh international World Wide Web conference, Hawaii, USA: ACM Press, published on CD ROM

20. Guell N., Schwabe D., Vilain P. (2000) Modeling interactions and navigation in Web Applications. In: World Wild Web and conceptual modeling workshop - ER'00 conference. Salt Lake City, USA, pp. 115-127

21. Haggard M. (1998) Survival guide to Web site development: Microsoft press, Redmond, OR, USA

22. Hennicker R., Koch N. (2001) Systematic design of Web applications with UML. In: Siau K., Halpin T. (Eds.), Unified modeling language: systems analysis, design and development issues,. Idea group publishing, USA

23. Holtzman J.K. (1993) Ready, fire!! Aim?. In: Proceedings of the 11th annual international conference on systems documentation. ACM press, Waterloo, Canada

24. Isakowitz T., Stohr E., Balasubramanian P. (1995) RMM: A methodology for structured hypermedia design. Communications of the ACM, 38: 34-44

25. Koch N., Kraus A. (2002) The expressive power of UML-based Web engineering. In: second international workshop on Web-oriented software technology, Malaga, Spain

26. Lange D. (1994) An object-oriented design method for hypermedia information systems. In: Proceedings of the twenty seventh Hawaii international conference on system sciences, Maui, Hawaii

27. Lee S.C. (1997) A structured navigation design method for intranets. In: Proceedings of the third Americas conference on information systems, Association for information systems, Indianapolis, USA

28. Lord J. (2000) Patterns for e-business: Lessons learned from building successful e-business applications. IBM, pp. 4

29. Lowe D. (2000) A framework for defining acceptance criteria for Web development projects. In: Proceedings of the Second ICSE Workshop on Web Engineering. Limerick, Ireland, pp.126-131

30. Lowe D. (2000) Web engineering or Web gardening?. WebNet Journal, Internet technologies, applications and issues, pp. 9-10

31. Lowe D., Henderson-Sellers B. (2001) Web development: addressing process differences. Cutter IT Journal, pp. 11-17

32. Lowe D., Eklund J. (2002) Client needs and the design process in Web projects. Journal of Web engineering, 1: 23-36

33. Martin R. (2000) A case study of XP practices at work. In: Proceedings of XP2000. Cagliari, Italy, pp. 74-77

34. OMG (2000) OMG unified modeling language specification. Version 1.3 (released to the general public as OMG document formal/00-03-01 in March 2000) http://www.omg.org/cgi-bin/doc?formal/00-03-10 (accessed 16th April)

35. Overmyer S. (2000) What's different about requirements engineering for Web sites? Requirements engineering journal, 5: 62-65

36. Paulo F.B., Turine M.A.S., de Oliveira M.C.F., Masiero P.C. (1998) XHMBS: A formal model to support hypermedia specification. In: Proceedings of the ninth ACM conference on hypertext, pp. 161-170

37. Philips R. (1997) The developer's handbook to interactive multimedia: Kogan Page, London, UK

38. Pressman R. (2001) Software engineering: A practitioner's approach. McGraw Hill, New York, USA

39. Russell P. (2000) Infrastructure - make or break your e-business. In Proceedings of the technology of object-oriented languages and systems, Sydney, Australia, (keynote)

40. Sawyer S., Rosenbaum, H. (2000) Social informatics in the information sciences: current (2000). Informing science, 3: 89-96

41. Schwabe D. Rossi, G. (1995) The object-oriented hypermedia design model. Communications of the ACM, 38: 45-46

42. Schwabe D. Rossi, G. (1998) Developing hypermedia applications using OOHDM. In: Workshop on hypermedia development processes, methods and models. Pittsburgh, USA, pp. 207-225

43. Sinha G. (1999) Build a component architecture for e-commerce. E-Business Advisor, http://advisor.com/doc/05328 (accessed on 16th April)

44. Stein L.D. (2000) Profit, the prime directive. Web techniques, 5: 14-17
45. Takahashi K., Liang E. (1997) Analysis and design of Web-based information systems. In: Proceedings of the 7th international World Wide Web conference, Brisbane, Australia,   pp. 367-375
46. Thomas D. (2000) Managing software development in Web time software. In: Proceedings of XP2000. Cagliari, Italy
47. Vilain P., Schwabe D., Souza C.S. (2000) A diagrammatic tool for representing user interaction in UML. In: Proceedings of the IEEE, third international conference on the unified modeling language. York, UK, pp. 133-147

Author Biography

A/Prof. David Lowe is Associate Dean (Teaching and Learning) in the Faculty of Engineering at the University of Technology, Sydney. His research focuses on Web development processes and Web project specification, and information contextualization. He has published widely, including several books focusing on Web development. In the last 7 years, he has published over 50 refereed papers and attracted over 1,300,000 AUD in funding. He is on numerous Web conference committees, is the information management theme editor for the *Journal of Digital Information* and is on the editorial board for the *International Journal of Web Engineering and Technologies*. He has undertaken numerous consultancies related to software evaluation, Web development (especially project planning and evaluation), and Web technologies.

Part 3
Application of Knowledge Management in Software Engineering

Claes Wohlin

Knowledge is power.
— Francis Bacon

Software development is a human intensive activity. It is heavily dependent on the creativity and ingenuity of talented people. This implies that the most important assets in software organizations are the employees [3]. It is well known that software is intangible and that the development of software is a design activity and not a manufacturing activity. These characteristics make a learning organization particularly important for software development. Some of the challenges pinpointed in the knowledge management literature are highlighted below, where it also is emphasized that they are highly relevant in the software engineering field. A software development organization is so heavily dependent on individual software developers that the only way for an organization to avoid becoming too dependent on its personnel is to adopt a learning organization approach. The need for viewing software organizations as learning organizations has been proposed in different forms in the software engineering literature [1, 8]. However, there is still much to learn from knowledge management literature. The chapters in Part 3 illustrate how knowledge management approaches can be applied to software engineering in different ways. Before going into the articles, it is important to appreciate how the "traditional" knowledge management literature relates to the needs in software engineering.

In [6], a selection of knowledge management papers is published by some of the worlds' leading experts on knowledge management. Drucker explains how large organizations will increasingly resemble orchestras, hospitals and universities rather than traditional manufacturing companies [5]. By this he means that the organizations will be knowledge-based and composed mainly of specialists. This is already the situation in software development, with most employees being highly educated individuals. Thus, a challenge in software organizations is to be able to capture the individual's knowledge and turn the organizations into learning organizations.

Nonaka stresses that it is not sufficient to be able to handle explicit or quantifiable knowledge [9]. He emphasizes the need for organizations to learn how to handle tacit knowledge. This is also very important in software organizations, since the software is intangible and not all knowledge is quantifiable. Thus, the challenge is to capture both explicit and tacit knowledge in software development.

Garvin links the learning organization with the need for continuous improvement [7]. He discusses the need for systematic problem solving, experimentation, learning from past experiences and best practices, as well as the need for knowledge transfer to the whole organization. These needs are based on the basic improvement paradigms such as the Plan - Do - Check - Act cycle introduced by Deming [4] and the Quality Improvement Paradigm [2] in software engineering literature. Further, experimentation as a method for evaluation of methods and techniques in software engineering is discussed in [11]. Given the above, one challenge is to master the improvement cycles to become a true learning organization.

Argyris discusses the challenges in getting smart people to learn [1]. He stresses that people are often enthusiastic about improvement, but are often fairly reluctant to change. Given the high educational level in most software organizations, this challenge is highly relevant for most of them. Thus, a challenge is to encourage and manage learning and improvement.

Quinn et al. points to the fact that a company's success lies more in intellectual capital than in other assets [10]. This raises questions with respect to different types of knowledge. The authors divide the knowledge into four levels with an increasing level of importance: cognitive knowledge (know-what), advanced skills (know-how), system understanding (know-why) and self-motivated creativity (care-why). Quinn et al. argue that organizations that manage to capitalize on the fourth level will be the most successful companies. Thus, a challenge for the software development organizations is to be able to reach and maintain the fourth level of knowledge management.

In summary, knowledge has to be captured, managed and reused with the above in mind. This includes being able to handle both explicit and tacit knowledge. In particular, it is a challenge to manage the mixture of explicit and tacit knowledge. Moreover, this involves being able to capitalize on the intellectual capital of the individuals and turn this into a learning organization that excels in continuous improvement. The ability to manage knowledge in software engineering is likely to be a key success factor for software projects and organizations in the future. Managing knowledge, however, is not an easy task in an environment where there is constant pressure to develop new and better products faster, cheaper and with higher quality than your competitors. Thus, it is clear that supporting methods and ways to manage changing knowledge in software engineering are greatly needed.

The objective of this part is to provide a selection of articles presenting methods and experiences of managing knowledge in software engineering. The chapters provide illustrations of how the challenges depicted in the knowledge management literature may be addressed in software engineering. The authors of the articles share their experiences and insights with the readers. This includes the application of different methods to managing knowledge as well as knowledge management in different areas of software engineering. The chapters in this part illustrate some possible methods to use when working with knowledge management in software engineering.

There are five chapters in this part. In Chap. 9, "Case-based Reasoning and Software Engineering", Martin Shepperd provides an introduction and overview of case-based reasoning and reviews some of the software engineering applications of case-based reasoning. The applications include project effort prediction and reuse of software artifacts, processes and past experiences. The chapter also points out some challenges in this area and some future areas for research. In summary, the chapter illustrates how case-based reasoning can be used as a method to manage knowledge in software engineering.

In Chap. 10, "A Process for Identifying Relevant Information for a Repository: A Case Study for Testing Techniques", Sira Vegas, Natalia Juristo and Victor Basili propose a process to identify the information that a characterization schema should include for the purpose of building an experience base. They provide a case study from software testing of how such a schema may be used. In summary, the chapter illustrates how schemas may be constructed to store experiences that may be used in later projects.

In Chap. 11, "A Knowledge Management Framework to Support Software Inspection Planning", Stefan Biffl and Michael Halling introduce a framework for decision support in software inspections. The framework consists of three levels: inspector level, inspection level and quality management level. The authors discuss how the framework can be used to manage knowledge for software inspections. In summary, the chapter illustrates how a framework can help in structuring questions and knowledge related to a specific development activity, in this case software inspections.

In Chap. 12, "Lessons Learned in Software Quality Assurance", Linda Rosenberg discusses lessons learned during the implementation of software quality assurance. The lessons are documented to support project managers, and hence help the managers increasing the probability of a successful project. The author shares experiences from one environment and hence illustrates the necessity to articulate lessons learned. This is particularly important when lessons learned often are based on tacit knowledge. In summary, the chapter illustrates how tacit knowledge from one environment, although relevant for many other environments, has been documented as lessons learned.

In Chap. 13, "Making Software Engineering Competence Development Sustained through Systematic Experience Management", Klaus-Dieter Althoff and Dietmar Pfahl present how to extend the current state of the art in experience management through integration with e-learning. They present their view on the integration of e-learning and knowledge management and discuss a system that supports this. They continue by presenting some recent advances in experience management and finally discuss how to connect e-learning with experience management.

The intention is that the articles Part 3 should form a source of information and inspiration for those practitioners and researchers who would like to, more effectively, use and manage knowledge in software engineering. This includes, for example, managing knowledge to enable reuse of experiences between software projects and within software organizations.

References

1. Argyris C. (1998) Teaching smart people how to learn. In: Harvard business review on knowledge management, Harvard business school press, USA, pp. 81-108
2. Basili V.R., Caldiera G., Rombach, H.D. (1994) Experience factory. In: Marciniak, J.J (Ed.), Encyclopedia of software engineering, John Wiley and Sons, Hoboken, NJ, USA
3. Boehm B. (1981) Software engineering economics. Prentice-Hall, Englewood Cliffs, NJ, USA
4. Deming E. (1986) Out of the crisis. MIT center for advanced engineering study, MIT Press, Cambridge, MA
5. Drucker P.F. (1998) The coming of the new organization. In: Harvard business review on knowledge management. Harvard business school press, USA, pp. 1-19
6. Drucker P.F., Leonard D., Brown J.S. (1998) Harvard business review on knowledge management. Harvard business school press, USA
7. Garvin D.A. (1998) Building a learning organization. In: Harvard business review on knowledge management, Harvard business school press, USA, pp. 47-80
8. Lennselius B., Wohlin C. (1987) Software metrics: motivation and fault content estimation. Microprocessors and microsystems, 11: 365-375
9. Nonaka I. (1998) The knowledge-creating company. In: Harvard business review on knowledge management, Harvard business school press, USA, pp. 21-45
10. Quinn J.B.P., Anderson P., Finkelstein S. (1998) Managing professional intellect: making the most of the best. In: Harvard business review on knowledge management, Harvard business school press, pp. 181-205
11. Wohlin C., Runeson P., Höst M., Ohlsson M.C., Regnell B., Wesslén A. (1999) Experimentation in software engineering: an introduction. Kluwer Academic, Boston, MA, USA

Editor Biography

Dr. Claes Wohlin is professor of software engineering at the Department of Software Engineering and Computer Science at Blekinge Institute of Technology in Sweden. Prior to this, he held professor chairs in software engineering at Lund University and Linköping University. He has a Ph.D. in communication systems from Lund University. His research interests include empirical methods in software engineering, software metrics, software quality and systematic improvement in software engineering. Dr. Wohlin is the principal author of the book *Experimentation in Software Engineering — An Introduction,* (Kluwer 1999). He is co-editor-in-chief of the *Information and Software Technology journal* (Elsevier). Dr. Wohlin is on the editorial boards of *Empirical Software Engineering: An International Journal* and *Software Quality Journal.*

9 Case-Based Reasoning and Software Engineering

Martin Shepperd

Abstract: Case-based reasoning (CBR) is a technology that is based on the idea of analogy. Solutions from past problems (cases) can be retrieved and deployed, with adaptation where necessary, to solve new problems. It is argued that CBR as a technology has a number of strengths, since it deals well with poorly understood problem domains, does not require explicit knowledge elicitation and supports collaboration with users. This chapter provides some general background information on CBR and then considers how CBR has been deployed to solve problems in the domain of software engineering. These problems fall into two general categories, namely prediction and reuse. The main prediction problems are related to project characteristics such as effort and duration, whilst the chief reuse foci are related to learning from past experiences. The chapter concludes by identifying three research challenges. These are to be able to better adapt retrieved solutions to solve new problems, to explore richer forms of representation for complex problems and, last, to encourage better collaboration between the user and the CBR system.

Keywords: Case-based reasoning, Software engineering, Reuse, Project management

9.1 Introduction

Case-based reasoning (CBR) was first formalized in the 1980s following from the work of Schank and others on memory [41], and is based upon the fundamental premise that similar problems are best solved with similar solutions [36]. The idea is to learn from experience. However, a crucial aspect of CBR lies in the term "similar". The technique does not require an identical problem to have been previously solved. Also CBR differs from many other artificial intelligence techniques in that it is not model based. This means, unlike knowledge-based approaches that use rules, the developer does not have to explicitly define causalities and relationships within the domain of interest. For poorly understood problem domains this is a major benefit.

CBR is a technique for managing and using knowledge that can be organized as discrete abstractions of events or entities that are limited in time and space. Each such abstraction is termed a case. Software engineering examples could be projects, design patterns or software components. Cases are characterized by vectors of features such as file size, number of interfaces or development method. CBR systems typically function by solving the new problem, often termed the target case, through retrieving and then adapting similar cases from a repository of past (and therefore solved) cases. The repository is termed the case-base.

CBR is argued to offer a number of advantages over many other knowledge management techniques, in that it:

- Avoids many of problems associated with knowledge elicitation and codification
- Only needs to address those problems that actually occur, whilst generative (i.e. algorithmic) systems must handle all possible problems
- Handles failed cases, which enable users to identify potentially high risk situations
- Copes with poorly understood domains (for example, many aspects of software engineering) since solutions are based upon what has actually happened as opposed to hypothesized models
- Supports better collaboration with users who are often more willing to accept solutions from analogy-based systems since these are derived from a form of reasoning akin to human problem solving. This final advantage is particularly important if systems are not only to be deployed, but also to have trust placed in them

Since the 1980s CBR has generated significant research interest and has been successfully applied to a wide range of problem domains. Typical applications are diagnostic systems; for instance, CASCADE addressed solving problems with the operating system VMS. More recently, Alstom have deployed CBR technology in conjunction with data mining of past fault data to support diagnosis of system error messages from the on-board computers that control all the train electronics. Another application area has been legal systems, unsurprisingly, since the concept of precedent and case law lie at the heart of many judicial systems such as those of the UK and USA. Design and planning are other problem domains that have also been tackled. For instance, CADET was developed as an assistant for mechanical designers, and ARCHIE provides support for architects. Decision support, classification (e.g. PROTOS was developed to classify hearing disorders) and e-commerce (e.g. a last-minute Web-based travel booking system that uses a CBR engine in order to overcome the problem of not always being able to exactly match client requirements) are other problem domains that have been successfully tackled using CBR. Although a little dated, Watson and Marir [49] provide detailed descriptions of a wide range of CBR applications. Lists of more recent examples of applications may be found in [18, 46].

The remainder of this chapter provides more background on CBR technology (principally from a machine learning viewpoint), reviews some specifically software engineering applications of CBR, namely project effort prediction, defect prediction, retrieval from component repositories and the reuse of successful past experience. It then goes on to consider some of the outstanding challenges (e.g. similarity measures, feature and case subset selection, dimension rescaling and learning adaptation rules) and point to potentially fruitful areas of future work.

9.2 An Overview of Case-Based Reasoning Technology

As previously indicated, case-based reasoning has at its heart the notion of utilizing the memory of past problems solved to tackle new problems.[1] Problems are organized as cases where each case comprises two parts: the description part and a solution part. The description part is normally a vector of features that describe the case state at the point at which the problem is solved. The solution part describes the solution for the specific problem and may vary in complexity from a single value for a classification or prediction system to a set of rules or procedures to derive a solution that might include a range of multimedia objects such as video and sound files.

9.2.1 The Basic CBR Cycle

Aamodt and Plaza [1] helpfully identify four stages of CBR—sometimes referred to as the R^4 model—that combine to make a cyclical process:

- Retrieve similar cases to the target problem
- Reuse past solutions
- Revise or adapt the suggested solutions to better fit the target problem
- Retain the target and solution in the case-base

Figure 9.1 illustrates this cycle diagrammatically. Central is the case-base, which is a repository of completed cases, or in other words the memory. When a new problem arises it must be codified in terms of the feature vector (or problem description) which is then the basis for retrieving similar cases from the case-base. Clearly, the greater the degree of overlap of features, the more effective the similarity measures and case retrieval. Ideally, the feature vectors should be identical since CBR does not deal easily with missing values, although of course there are many data imputation techniques that might be explored [38]. Measuring similarity lies at the heart of CBR and many different measures have been proposed.

Irrespective of the measure, the objective is to rank cases in decreasing order of similarity to the target and utilize the known solutions of the nearest k cases. Choosing a value for k is a matter of some debate, but for a systematic exploration see [30]. Solutions derived from the retrieved cases can then be adapted to better fit the target case either by rules, by a human expert or by a simple statistical procedure such as a weighted mean. In the latter case the system is often referred to as the k-nearest neighbor (k-NN) technique. Once the target case has been completed and the true solution known, it can be retained in the case-base. In this

---

[1] Strictly speaking, some authors such as [37] differentiate between interpretative and problem solving CBR. Interpretative CBR focuses upon classification rather than direct problem solving, although it could always be argued that classification can be viewed as a subgoal to solving another problem. However, this distinction is not pursued in this chapter.

way the case-base grows over time and new knowledge is added. Of course, it is important not to neglect the maintenance of the case-base over time so as to prevent degradation in relevance and consistency.

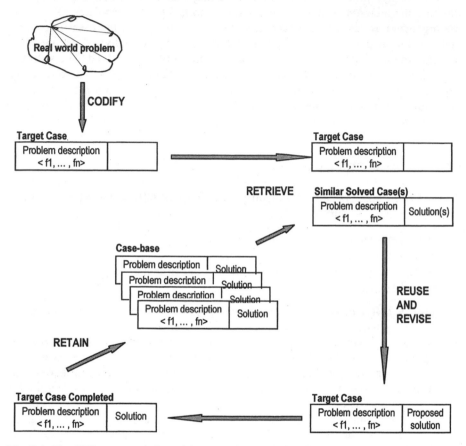

Fig. 9.1. The CBR process (adapted from Aamodt and Plaza [1])

This CBR process is best illustrated by an example. Consider the problem of a project manager predicting how many resources to allocate for the development of different software components. Knowledge or memory of the past is the basis for predicting future effort. Here the case is a software component. Each case will comprise a vector of features to describe each component. Examples of features might include the programming language (categorical), the number of interfaces (discrete) and the time available to develop, since severe schedule compression may adversely affect the development effort (continuous). Notice how the vector can comprise features of different types. This adds some complexity to the way in which distance is measured. The choice of features is arbitrary and may be driven by both pragmatic considerations—what is easily available—and domain considerations—which features best characterize the problem. One constraint is that the values for the features must be knowable at the time the prediction is required, which will usually militate against the use of features such as code length. For effort prediction the solution part of the case is trivial, merely a single value denoting the actual effort consumed.

For our effort prediction problem, the case-base grows as components are completed and the solution, i.e. the actual required amount of effort in person hours or whatever, becomes known. When a new prediction problem arises, the new component must be described in terms of the feature vector so that it can be viewed as the target case. The problem then becomes one of retrieving similar cases from the case base and using the known effort values as a basis of the prediction for the target case. The prediction may be modified by the application of rules, typically obtained from a domain expert such as an experienced project manager, or by a simple procedure such as finding the mean. Once the component has been completed and the true effort value is known, the case can be added to the case-base. In this way the case-base is enlarged over time and can also follow trends or changes in the underlying problem domain, such as the introduction of new technologies and programming languages. For this reason some similarity measures explicitly include a notion of recency so that newer cases are preferred.

9.2.2 Similarity Measures

As mentioned, measuring similarity has generated a range of different ideas. These include

- Nearest neighbor algorithms are the most popular and are based upon straightforward distance measures for each feature. Each feature must be first standardized, so that the choice of unit has no influence. Some variants of this algorithm enable the relative importance of features to be specified, although for poorly understood problem domains this may be very problematic. A common algorithm is given by Aha [2].

$$SIM(C1, C2, P) = \frac{1}{\sqrt{\sum_{j \in P} Feature\_dissimilarity(C_{1j}, C_{2j})}}$$

where P is the set of n features, C_1 and C_2 are cases and

$$Feature\_dissimilarity(C_{1j}, C_{2j}) \begin{cases} (C_{1j} - C_{2j})^2 \\ 0 \\ 1 \end{cases}$$

where (i) the features are numeric, (ii) if the features are categorical and $C_{1j}=C_{2j}$ or (iii) where the features are categorical and $C_{1j}\neq C_{2j}$ respectively.

- *Manually guided induction*: here an expert manually identifies key features, although this reduces some of the advantages of using a CBR system in that an expert is required
- *Template retrieval*: This is similar to query by example database retrieval in that the user supplies values or ranges for a subset of the problem description vector, and all the cases that match are retrieved.
- *Specificity preference*: Here cases are preferred that match features exactly over those that match generally.
- *Frequency preference*: Here preference is given to those cases that have been most frequently retrieved in the past.
- *Recency preference*: This type of algorithm favors more recently matched cases over those that have not been matched for some period of time.
- *Object-oriented similarity*: For complex problem domains it may be necessary to make similarity comparisons between differently structured cases. In the object-oriented approach cases are represented as collections of objects (each object has a set of feature-value pairs) organized in a hierarchy of part-of relationships [14].
- *Fuzzy similarity*: This approach uses concepts such as at-least-as-similar and just-noticeable-difference [42] as opposed to crisp values.

These similarity measures suffer from a number of disadvantages. First, symbolic or categorical features are problematic. Although there are several algorithms that have been proposed to accommodate categorical features, these tend to be fairly crude in that they tend to adopt a Boolean approach: features match or fail to match with no middle ground. Note though that the fuzzy similarity can be an exception since the linguistic concepts of, say, "quite similar" might be applied to some categorical features, for example, comparing a feature programming language containing the values C and C++.

A second criticism of many of these similarity measures is that they fail to take into account information that can be derived from the structure of the data; thus, they are weak for higher-order feature relationships such as one might expect to see exhibited in legal systems. By contrast, the object-oriented similarity measures can still be applied to complex problem domains where it may be necessary to assess similarity between differently structured cases. Here, in order to consider similarity it is necessary to take into account both intra- and interobject similarity. Intraobject similarity is based on common properties. However, the difference between two cases may reside in their differing class structures rather than in their shared features, hence the need for a measure to take into account interobject similarity. An example might be comparing software projects that are differently comprised of staff and staff roles. For instance, project (case) A may comprise management, clerical and technical teams, each characterized by their own set of features, whilst project (case) B might comprise technical and sales teams. A traditional similarity metric can only compare features in common, but cannot compare the differing structures of these two projects or cases. Bergmann and Stahl [14] describe a sophisticated similarity metric based on the product intra- and interobject similarity. The main difficulties for such metrics are validation and encouraging collaboration between the human user and the CBR system since this approach is somewhat less intuitive than a simple Euclidean distance measure.

9.2.3 Feature and Case Subset Selection

Another difficulty for CBR, which is common to all machine learning approaches, is that the similarity measures retrieve more useful cases when extraneous and misleading features are removed. Knowing which features are useful is not always obvious for at least three reasons. First, the features contained in the feature vector are often determined by no more a systematic reason than availability. Second, the application domain may not be well understood: There is no deep theory to guide. Third, the feature standardization used by some similarity measures can substantially complicate any analysis. This is because some features may actually be more important than others, however, the standardization will assign each feature equal influence. In such circumstances colinearity can be usefully exploited. In effect, by using several closely related features, one underlying dimension can be made more important in the search for similar cases. Deciding which features to remove is known as the feature subset selection problem. There is an equivalent problem relating to case removal, known rather unsurprisingly as the case subset selection problem. Here the situation is one of eliminating unhelpful solutions from the case-base. Unfortunately, both are computationally intractable since they are NP-hard search problems. It is interesting to note that in general, the pattern is for smaller, more relevant case-bases to substantially outperform larger, less focused ones.

Approaches to searching for subsets fall into two categories: filters and wrappers [33]. Filters operate independently of the CBR algorithm, reducing the number of features prior to training. By contrast, wrappers use the CBR algorithm itself on some sample of the data set in order to determine the fitness of the subset. This tends to be computationally far more intensive, but generally can find better subsets than the filter methods. Various wrapper methods have been investigated by a number of researchers. Early versions of ANGEL [43] addressed the problem of searching for the optimal feature subset by an exhaustive search using a jack knife[2] on the case base in order to determine fitness. However, as previously stated, the search is NP-hard, so once the number of features exceeds 15 - 20 this becomes computationally intractable. Other approaches have included different variants of hill climbing algorithms [45], sequential feature selection algorithms, both forward and backward [3] and genetic algorithms [51]. These have generally

---

[2] A jack knife is a validation strategy that works by successively holding out each case, one at a time, and using the remainder of cases to generate the prediction for the hold-out case [20]

been reported to lead to good improvements in solution quality without the prohibitive computational cost of an exhaustive search.

Essentially all these methods have a search component to generate candidate subsets from the space of all possible subsets and a fitness function that is a measure of the error derived from the solution proposed by the CBR system using the subset, trained on a sample from the data set and validated on a holdout sample. Typical sampling techniques are the jack knife and n-fold[3] validation. The fitness function is generally a measure of deviation between the proposed and desired solution, and as such is a cost that should be minimized. The exact nature of the measure depends upon the nature of what is being predicted, but is usually either based on the cost of misclassifications or the sum of absolute residuals.

9.2.4 Adaptation

Another important aspect of CBR is adaptation of the solution, particularly when even the most similar cases differ substantially from the target case. This might occur if the case-base is small or heterogeneous. The simplest approach, that of k-NN systems, is to use the solution of the nearest neighbor, or mean (possibly distance weighted so that the nearest solutions are most influential) of several neighbors. Hanney and Keane [24] describe an interesting alternative, which learns how to adapt by comparing feature differences and solution differences. Unfortunately, this structural approach is limited to linear, or near-linear problems. Another widely used adaptation strategy is the use of rules to modify proposed solutions. The difficulty here is that the motivation for using CBR in the first place is often the challenge of performing knowledge elicitation, so where do the rules come from [37]? Whilst Watson and Marir [49] identify a number of additional adaptation strategies, k-NN and rule-based approaches are the most popular.

9.2.5 Unsuited Problem Domains

So far this section has focused on the successful application of CBR technology. It is, however, also important to stress that there are problem domains that are not so well suited to CBR. These can be characterized by one or more of the following:

- Lack of relevant cases, for example, when dealing with an entirely new domain. In truth, such situations are extremely resistant to solution by any technique, though one possibility is a divide-and-conquer strategy so whilst the problem

---

[3] n-fold validation is another common validation procedure within the machine learning community whereby the data set is divided into n approximately equal subsets. Each subset is successively held-out and then returned to the training set. This process is repeated n times so that each case forms part of the hold-out set exactly once. This is a generalization of the jack knife where n is the total number of cases in the case-base.

may be novel in its entirety, it may be that useful analogies may be sought for some, or all, of its constituent parts.

- Few cases are available due to a lack of systematically organized data, typically due to information not being recorded or being primarily in a natural language format. CBR does not deal well with large quantities of unstructured text [4].
- The problem domain can be easily modeled and is well understood, for example, when regression techniques can find simple structural equations that have high explanatory power. In such circumstances it would seem wiser to use the model-based technique.

This overview has been necessarily brief. For more detail, the reader is referred to the classic book by Kolodner [34], more recent works such as Althoff [8], Bergmann [13] and for a comparison of different approaches, to the paper by Finnie and Sun [21].

9.3 Software Engineering Applications of CBR

Having considered case-based reasoning in general we now turn to its application to problems drawn from the domain of software engineering. Broadly speaking, this work falls into two categories: prediction and reuse type applications. We discuss each in turn.

9.3.1 Prediction in Software Engineering

It has long been recognized that a major contribution to successful software engineering is the ability to be able to make effective predictions particularly in the realms of costs and quality. Consequently, there has been significant research activity in this area, much of which has focused on effort and defect prediction. Both these problems are characterized by an absence of theory, inconsistency and uncertainty that make them well suited to CBR approaches.

It was suggested in the early 1980s that analogy might form a good basis for software project effort prediction [16]. However, the earliest work to formalise this process was by Vicinanza and coworkers [27]. They developed a CBR system with rule-based adaptation named Estor. This involved knowledge elicitation from

---

[4] This not to say there has been no research into textual CBR. Much work has focused on the extraction of predetermined features. Where the set of features required for describing each case varies greatly, then an interactive CBR method (see for example, Aha et al., [4, 5]) may be useful for guiding the author through the elicitation process (i.e. through a series of prompted questions whose answers assign values to relevant attributes). One advantage of this method is that it can help avoid some standard problems with information retrieval systems (e.g. how to interpret text expressions that have multiple potential meanings) by clarifying the lesson writer's inputs during elicitation. However, in general, natural language processing (NLP) remains an extremely intractable problem.

a domain expert—an experienced software project manager—to derive adaptation rules. They reported encouraging results based upon a small industrial dataset of 15 projects [31]. Estor was comparable to the expert and significantly more accurate than COCOMO model [16] or function points [7]. However, their approach requires access to an expert in order to derive estimation rules and create a case-base. Also the rules are couched in terms of the particular set of features in Kemerer's data set, which severely limits their applicability as there are wide discrepancies in the range and types of features collected by different software organizations.

Another early project [15] Finding Analogies for Cost Estimation (FACE) also used CBR technology and reported results based upon another publicly available data set, COCOMO [16]. The authors reported accuracy levels of MMRE[5] = 40 - 50%; however, the system was only able to make predictions for 46 out of a total of 63 projects. By contrast, Finnie et al. [22] reported good results using CBR with adaptation rules for a large industrial data set of 299 projects, split into a training set of 249 projects and a validation set of 50 projects. Their CBR approach proved to be significantly more accurate than a regression-based approach and comparable with an artificial neural net (ANN), with the added advantage of better explanatory value than the ANN. As with the Vicinanza [27], the disadvantage of this approach is that new adaptation rules must be derived for new data sets.

At the same time, a simpler approach was being pursued by Shepperd and others [43, 44] based on the idea of a k-NN system named ANGEL. The work was guided by the twin aims of expediency and simplicity so as to make the approach as widely applicable as possible whilst at the same time providing transparency in order to increase trust by project managers. Similarity was defined in terms of Euclidean distance between arbitrary sets of project features, such as number of interfaces, development method, application domain and so forth. The number and type of features chosen could depend upon what data is available to characterize projects. The authors reported having analyzed datasets with as few as 1 feature and as many as 29 features. Features could be either categorical or continuous and are standardized so that each feature has equal influence. The other distinctive characteristic of the ANGEL approach is the implementation of an automated feature subset selection search.

As per Finnie et al., Shepperd and co-workers used stepwise regression analysis as a benchmark for evaluating the predictive performance of ANGEL. Table 9.1 summarizes the results from an empirical evaluation of ANGEL-based upon nine different data sets. It can be seen that for these data sets the k-NN approach consistently outperformed regression-based models. Subsequent studies have reported more mixed experiences. A study of software maintenance effort [29] found similar results. However, other researchers, most notably [17, 28] obtained conflicting results where the regression model generated significantly better

---

[5] MMRE or mean magnitude of relative error is a widely used accuracy indicator by software project cost researchers. It is defined as $1/n \sum abs((act_i-pred_i)/act_i)$ where i is the ith prediction and there are a total of n cases. One disadvantage of MMRE is that it is asymmetric, nevertheless it is widely quoted.

results than the ANGEL based approach. While there are some differences in implementation, in particular [17] used a different procedure to select the best feature subset based on a filter, this does not fully explain differences in the results. Doubtless, the underlying characteristics of the problem data set are likely to exert a strong influence upon the relative effectiveness of different prediction systems. For example, the two datasets [17] used, both appear to contain well-defined hyperplanes such that the regression procedures are able to generate models with good explanatory power as evidenced by the high R-squared values. One would not expect case-based reasoning to perform well since instead of interpolating or extrapolating it endeavors to draw data points to the nearest cluster. Clearly, this is not an effective strategy if the data falls upon, or close to, a hyperplane. In other words, a linear function exists that "explains" the relationship between the dependent variable and the independent variables.

Recent work has shown that the difficulties with feature and case subset selection for large data sets can be overcome using search metaheuristics, for example random mutation hill climbing and forward and backward selection search, drawn from the artificial intelligence community [32]. These techniques resulted in substantial improvements in the performance of ANGEL, typically from an MMRE of in excess of 50% down to 15%.

Table 9.1. Comparison of CBR and regression effort prediction accuracy (adapted from Shepperd and Schofield [44])

Data set	Source	No. of cases	No. of features	ANGEL (MMRE)	Stepwise regression (MMRE)
Albrecht	[7]	24	5	62%	90%
Atkinson	[10]	21	12	39%	45%
Desharnais	[19]	77	9	64%	66%
Finnish	Finnish dataset: dataset made available to the ESPRIT Mermaid project by the TIEKE organization	38	29	41%	101%
Kemerer	[31]	15	2	62%	107%
Mermaid	MM2 Dataset: Dataset made available to the ESPRIT Mermaid project anonymously	28	17	78%	252%
Real-time 1	Not in the public domain	21	3	74%	N/A
Telecom 1	[44]	18	1	39%	86%
Telecom 2	Not in the public domain	33	13	37%	142%

Despite these advances, CBR prediction of effort is still an uncertain process with quite variable levels of accuracy. This should not be too surprising as the pursuit of a "best" or universal prediction technique is unlikely to be a fruitful quest. Probably what is most encouraging is the results of an experiment on professional project managers that found that k-NN (ANGEL) augmented by expert judgment led to the most accurate effort prediction [28].

Another prediction problem that has been tackled with CBR technology is classifying software components into low and high levels of defects [42]. The authors report a success rate in excess of 85% when studying a military command, control, and communications system. One interesting aspect of this work is their use of fuzzy rather than crisp values to describe case features coupled with fuzzy logic to assess similarity. Fuzzy logic is a form of logic used in some systems in which feature set membership can be described in terms of degrees of truthfulness or falsehood represented by a range of values between 1 (true) and 0 (false). For example, a software component might be described as belonging to the set of large components to a degree 0.8, in other words it is believed to be quite large. Note this is quite different from making a probabilistic statement where $p=0.8$ that the component is large. Set membership may also overlap so we might also have the same component with a membership of the set of medium components to the degree 0.3. Since we are not dealing with probabilities, there is no requirement for the degrees of set membership to sum to unity.

9.3.2 Reuse in Software Engineering

The concept of reuse within software engineering has long been acknowledged as an important potential source of productivity gain. Moreover, reuse has been seen in a much broader sense than just software or code artifacts to include designs, patterns, specifications, processes and software project experience in general. Reuse is perceived as a natural application for CBR since exact matching is generally very difficult to achieve because it is precisely the *difference* between software projects that makes software engineering a challenging discipline. Instead, the problem is to retrieve *similar* components.

An early contribution was by Maiden and Sutcliffe [25, 26], who suggested that analogical reasoning techniques might be employed to support the reuse of software specifications. This was achieved by mapping both the target and source (case-base) requirements specification descriptions into more abstract representations to facilitate the measurement of similarity. In this system a domain model of requirements is based on object structural knowledge, actions, object types, pre- and postcondition constraints on state transitions, transformations that lead to state transitions and events that trigger transformations. To determine if two requirements are similar, Maiden and Sutcliffe compare the domains using four different dimensions (semantic, structural, pragmatic and abstract) utilizing a structural coherence algorithm. The target requirement is compared to the requirements in the abstract domain hierarchy to form a set of possible matches. Next a heuristic-based abstraction selector is used to select the best abstract domain from the candidate set. Two domains are considered similar only if they share the same abstract domain class.

Another early application of CBR technology was to support the reuse of software packages within Ada and C program libraries [39]. Ostertag et al. used a distance measure based on a combination of semantic networks (providing conceptual connectivity) and the faceted index approach (which allows the user a view from different perspectives) [40] and demonstrated their ideas with a prototype system and some examples. Interestingly, the authors also noted another potential application in the form of Basili's Goal Question Metric framework [12] together with process reuse.

The most ambitious form of CBR-supported reuse is that of experience reuse, in other words to explicitly learn from past software projects and to make the lessons widely available through sophisticated retrieval mechanisms using similarity metrics. Such metrics are important due to the difficulty of finding exact project matches within the domain of software engineering. Of course the idea of experience reuse, or what is often termed a "lessons learned" (LL) system is not unique to software engineering. For an interesting review of LL systems in commercial, government and military applications see Weber et al. [50].

Much of the motivation for experience reuse within the domain of software engineering stems from Basili's ideas of an Experience Factory [11] although other researchers have reached similar conclusions, for example Grupe et al. [23]. An Experience Factory (EF) is based upon a number of premises:

- A feedback process is required to best support learning and improvement.
- Experience must be viewed as a resource for an organization and therefore stored appropriately in an experience base.
- Experience must be appropriately packaged in order to support appropriate reuse, for example, it might be unwise to reuse the successful experiences of writing game software when developing a protection system for a nuclear reactor.
- Mechanisms must be provided to support the retrieval of experience packages.

These ideas are closely aligned with CBR technology so that it is no surprise that many researchers have seen organizational learning as a natural application, see for example, Tautz and Althoff [47] and von Wangheim et al. [48]. The quality improvement paradigm (QIP)/EF provides a framework for continuous learning about software engineering practices and techniques. In other words it provides "an organizational infrastructure necessary for operationalizing CBR systems in industrial environments" [9].

In order to make a reuse decision it is necessary to characterize the technology, the goal and the context or domain in which the technology will be applied, e.g. developer experience. The context is particularly emphasized because the diversity of software engineering activities and problem domains might otherwise result in appropriate reuse. The context often is assessed subjectively, e.g. on a five-point scale. Typically a project is viewed as a case. This implies the following process:

1. Decide upon the task and goal. This will determine the relevant context features.
2. Characterize the new project (case) in terms of relevant features.

3. Perform a similarity-based retrieval of other projects. The retrieval may be in two stages first, use a clustering or filter approach to find broadly similar projects, and second, use a distance metric.
4. Adaptation of the most relevant retrieved case(s) since it may not be possible to use the retrieved experience directly.
5. Perform the project.
6. Evaluate the project based on empirical evidence collected during the running of the project. Empirical evidence is encouraged in order to promote objectivity.
7. Identify lessons learned that can be added to the experience or case-base.

Two features distinguish the EF from many more general LL systems. First, there is the explicit notion of context. Second, there is the use of empirical evidence in order to evaluate potential new cases. These address some of the reported problems of poor usage rates for deployed LL systems by Weber et al. [50], such as difficulties in retrieving *relevant* cases and validation of experience prior to storing within the LL system.

Maintenance of the EF is another challenge in order to avoid obsolete, inconsistent, invalidated or subjective, irrelevant and redundant cases. Weber et al. report on a number of LL systems that contain in excess of 30,000 cases or lessons. Interestingly, in an example of case-base maintenance they describe how it was possible to reduce from 13,000 cases to 2,000 cases. For further information on the topic of EFs, see Chap. 13 of this book ("Making Software Engineering Competence Development Sustained through Systematic Experience Management").

9.4 Summary and Future Work

In this chapter we have seen how case-based reasoning is a relatively recent technology that has emerged from the artificial intelligence and cognitive science communities. It is based on the idea of memory rather than explicit models. It would also seem to fit closely with how humans often solve problems, that is, by means of analogy [35]. This is important as it can help users to trust CBR systems and, potentially, to better interact with them. We have also seen that CBR approaches do not require a deep understanding of the problem domain, which suggests they are well suited to many software engineering problems. This is because we are dealing with creative processes, complexity, change and uncertainty. There is also a strong sense within software engineering circles that reuse is important. Again CBR is appropriate since it provides a mechanism of organizing, storing and reusing an organization's memory or experiences. Thus it is unsurprising that a major application area is that of implementing experience bases. The other principal area is that of prediction. Here CBR is more seen as another machine learning, or inductive technique, but one that has good explanatory value and with which the user can interact.

Whilst there are undoubtedly exciting opportunities for the deployment of CBR methods there remain many challenges. First is the challenge of adaptation. As seen from the examples discussed in this chapter, there are two main approaches for adaptation. One is rule based, which can embody substantial domain knowledge, but suffers from specificity to a particular case-base, plus there are the difficulties of elicitation. Rule induction techniques may help overcome the latter problem. The other approach is to use simple arithmetic techniques and rely more on feature and case subset selection. This approach can be particularly vulnerable to novel problems.

Second is the challenge of constructing cases from richer sources of data. Many of the software engineering applications described above are restricted to simple numeric information. Even categorical features can be troublesome. There has been a range of work looking at textural CBR. Some researchers, for example Grupe et al. [23] looked at using textural information by means of trigrams. Others deployed a range of other information retrieval techniques. Nevertheless in a recent survey, Weber et al. [50] comment that

> Our survey reinforced that the two most evident problems contributing to the ineffectiveness of LL systems concern text representations for lessons and their standalone design. Text formats are troublesome for computational treatment, and attempts to create structure in records have rarely addressed core issues, such as highlighting the reuse component of a [case].

Perhaps markup languages such as XML may also be a means of dealing with semistructured data. Aha and Wettscherek [6] argue that CBR should move beyond simple vector-based approaches and consider a range of richer forms of case representation, such as directed graphs, preference pairs and Horn clauses. Whatever approach making use of richer sources of information is likely to be extremely fruitful when considering the range of data that is typically available in software engineering projects and is a growing research topic.

The third challenge is that of finding better ways to support collaboration between the human expert and the CBR system. In the past, in some quarters, there has been a tendency to view many of these systems as replacements for the human. For many applications, particularly when dealing with infrequent but high-value problems, such as experience factory-supported decision-making and project prediction, this view may be inappropriate. Therefore we should explicitly address the problem of how to bring about the most effective forms of interaction between the human and the CBR system. Given the findings of Weber et al. [50] of the limited impact of deployed lessons learned systems this final challenge is of great significance to the practical benefits of CBR systems.

References

1. Aamodt, A. Plaza E. (1994) Case-based reasoning: foundational issues, methodical variations and system approaches. AI Communications, 7: 39-59
2. Aha D.W. (1991) Case-based learning algorithms. In: 1991 DARPA Case-based reasoning workshop: Morgan Kaufmann, Washington, DC, USA

3. Aha D.W., Bankert R.L. (1995) A comparative evaluation of sequential feature selection algorithms. In: Proceedings of the Fifth international workshop on artificial intelligence and statistics, Ft. Lauderdale, FL, USA, pp. 1-7
4. Aha D.W., Breslow L.A. (1997) Refining conversational case libraries. In: Leake D., Plaza, E. (Eds.), Case-based reasoning research and development, Springer, Berlin Heidelberg New York, pp. 267-278
5. Aha D.W., Maney T., Breslow L.A. (1998) Supporting dialogue inferencing in conversational case-based reasoning. In: Smyth B., Cunningham P., (Eds.), Advances in case-based reasoning, Springer, Berlin Heidelberg New York, pp. 262-273
6. Aha D.W., Wettscherek D. (1997) Case-based learning: beyond classification of feature vectors. In: Proceedings of 9th European conference on machine learning, Prague, Czech Republic, pp. 329-336
7. Albrecht A.J., Gaffney J.R. (1983) Software function, source lines of code, and development effort prediction: a software science validation. IEEE transactions on software engineering, 9: 639-648
8. Althoff K.-D. (2001) Case-based reasoning. In: Chang S.K. (Ed.) Handbook on software engineering and knowledge engineering. Vol. 1, World Scientific, Singapore, pp. 549-588
9. Althoff K.-D., Birk A., Wangenheim C.G., von Tautz C. (1998) Case-based reasoning for experimental software engineering. In: Lenz M., Bartsch-Spörl B., Burkhard H.-D., Wess S. (Eds.) Case-based reasoning technology–from foundations to applications, Springer, Berlin Heidelberg New York, pp. 235-254
10. Atkinson K., Shepperd M.J. (1994) The use of function points to find cost analogies. In: Proceedings of 5th European software cost modeling meeting, Ivrea, Italy, pp. 170-178
11. Basili V.R., Caldiera G., Rombach H.D. (1994) Experience factory. In: Encyclopedia of software engineering, Marciniak J.J. (Ed.), John Wiley and Sons, New York, USA pp. 469-476
12. Basili V.R., Rombach H.D. (1988) The TAME project: towards improvement-oriented software environments. IEEE transactions on software engineering, 14: pp. 758-771
13. Bergmann R. (2002) Experience management — Foundations, development methodology, and Internet-based applications. Lecture notes in artificial intelligence, Springer, Berlin Heidelberg New York, Vol. 2432
14. Bergmann R., Stahl S. (1998) Similarity measures for object-oriented case representations. In: Lecture notes in computer science, Springer, Berlin Heidelberg London, 1488: 25-36,
15. Bisio R., Malabocchia F. (1995) Cost estimation of software projects through case base reasoning. In: Proceedings 1st International conference on case-based reasoning research and development. Springer, Heidelberg New York, pp. 11-22
16. Boehm B.W. (1981) Software engineering economics. Prentice-Hall, Englewood Cliffs, NJ
17. Briand L., Langley T., Wieczorek I. (2000) Using the European space agency data set: a replicated assessment and comparison of common software cost modeling techniques. In: Proceedings of 22nd IEEE international conference on software engineering, Limerick, Ireland, pp. 337-386
18. Case-Based Reasoning Homepage, University of Kaiserslautern. Available from: www.cbr-web.org (Accessed 4th December, 2002)

19. Desharnais J.M. (1989) Analyse statistique de la productivitie des projets informatique a partie de la technique des point des fonction, Master thesis, University of Montreal, Canada
20. Efron B., Gong G. (1983) A leisurely look at the bootstrap, the jackknife and cross-validation. The American statistician 37: 36-48
21. Finnie G.R., Sun Z. (2002) R^5 model for case-based reasoning. Knowledge-based systems 16: pp. 59-65
22. Finnie G.R., Wittig G.E., Desharnais J.-M. (1997) Estimating software development effort with case-based reasoning. In: Proceedings of 2nd international conference on case-based reasoning, Providence, Rhode Island, pp. 13-22
23. Grupe F.H., Urweiler R., Ramarapu N.K., Owrang M. (1998) The application of case-based reasoning to the software development process. Information and software technology, 40: 493-500
24. Hanney K., Keane M.T. (1997) The adaptation knowledge bottleneck: how to ease it by learning from cases. In: Proceedings of the 2nd international CBR conference, Amsterdam, The Netherlands, pp. 359-370
25. Maiden N.A. (1991) Analogy as a paradigm for specification reuse. Software engineering journal, 6: 3-15
26. Maiden N.A., Sutcliffe A.G. (1992) Exploiting reusable specifications through analogy. Communications of the ACM, 35: 55-64
27. Mukhopadhyay T., Vicinanza S.S., Prietula M.J. (1992) Examining the feasibility of a case-based reasoning model for software effort estimation. MIS quarterly, 16: 155-171
28. Myrtveit I., Stensrud E. (1999) A controlled experiment to assess the benefits of estimating with analogy and regression models. IEEE transactions on software engineering, 25: 510-525
29. Niessink F., van Vliet H. (1997) Predicting maintenance effort with function points. In: Proceedings of international conference on software maintenance, Bari, Italy, pp. 32-39
30. Kadoda G., Cartwright M., Shepperd M.J. (2001) Issues on the effective use of CBR technology for software project prediction. In: Proceedings of the 4th international conference on case based reasoning, Vancouver, Canada, pp. 276-290
31. Kemerer C.F. (1987) An empirical validation of software cost estimation models. Communications of the ACM, 30: 416-429
32. Kirsopp C., Shepperd M.J., Hart J. (2002) Search heuristics, case-based reasoning and software project effort prediction. In: Proceedings of the genetic and evolutionary computation conf., New York, USA, pp. 1367-1374
33. Kohavi R., John G.H. (1997) Wrappers for feature selection for machine learning. Artificial intelligence, 97: 273-324
34. Kolodner J.L. (1993) Case-based reasoning. Morgan-Kaufmann, San Mateo, CA, USA
35. Klein G. (1998) Sources of power: how people make decisions. MIT press, Cambridge, MA, USA
36. Leake D. (1996) Case-based reasoning: experiences, lessons, and future directions. AAAI press, Menlo Park, CA, USA
37. Leake D. (1996) CBR in context: the present and the future. In: Leake D. (Ed.), Case based reasoning: experiences, lessons and future directions, AAAI press, Menlo Park, pp. 1-35
38. Little R.J.A., Rubin D.B. (2002) Statistical analysis with missing data. John Wiley and Sons, New York, USA

39. Ostertag E., Hendler J., Prieto-Díaz R., Braun C. (1992) Computing similarity in a reuse library system: an AI-based approach. ACM transactions on software engineering methodology, 1: 205-228

40. Priéto-Diaz R., Freeman P. (1987) Classifying software for reusability. IEEE Software, 4: 6-16

41. Schank R. (1982) Dynamic memory: A theory of reminding and learning in computers and people. Cambridge university press, Cambridge, UK

42. Schenker D.F., Khoshgoftaar T.M. (1998) The application of fuzzy enhanced case-based reasoning for identifying fault-prone modules. In: Proceedings of the 3rd IEEE international high-assurance systems engineering symposium, Washington, D.C., USA, pp 90-97

43. Shepperd M.J., Schofield C., Kitchenham B.A. (1996) Effort estimation using analogy. In: Proceedings of 18th international conference on software engineering, Berlin, Germany, pp. 170-179

44. Shepperd M.J., Schofield C. (1997) Estimating software project effort using analogies. IEEE transactions on software engineering, 23: 736-743

45. Skalak D.B. (1994) Prototype and feature selection by sampling and random mutation hill climbing algorithms. In: Proceedings of the 11th international machine learning conference, New Brunswick, NJ, USA, pp. 293-301

46. Success stories, INRECA Center, University of Kaiserslautern. Available from: www.inreca.org/data/cbr/success.html (Accessed 4th December, 2002)

47. Tautz C., Althoff K.-D. (1997) Using case-based reasoning for reusing software knowledge. In: Proceedings of the 2nd international conference on case-based reasoning, Springer, Berlin Heidelberg New York, pp. 156-165

48. von Wangenheim C.G., Althoff K.-D., Barcia R.M. (2000) Goal-oriented and similarity-based retrieval of software engineering experienceware. In: Ruhe G., Bomarius, F. (Ed.). Learning software organizations: methodology and applications, Springer, Berlin Heidelberg New York, pp. 118-141

49. Watson I., Marir F. (1994) Case-based reasoning: a review. The knowledge engineering review, 9: 327-354

50. Weber R., Aha D.W., Becerra-Fernandez I. (2001) Intelligent lessons learned systems. Expert systems with applications, 20: 17-34

51. Whitley D., Beveridge J.R., Guerra-Salcedo C., Graves C. (1997) Messy genetic algorithms for subset feature selection. In: Proceedings of the international conference on genetic algorithms, East Lansing, Michigan, USA, pp. 568-575

Author Biography

Martin Shepperd has a chair of software engineering at Bournemouth University, UK. He received his Ph.D. in computer science in 1991 from the Open University, UK. His main research interests are empirical aspects of software engineering and machine learning. He has published more than 75 papers and 3 books. Presently he is co-editor of the journal *Information & Software Technology* and associate editor of *IEEE Transactions on Software Engineering*.

10 A Process for Identifying Relevant Information for a Repository: A Case Study for Testing Techniques

Sira Vegas, Natalie Juristo and Victor R. Basili

Abstract: One major issue in managing software engineering knowledge is the construction of information repositories for software development artifacts (techniques, products, processes, tools, and so on). But how does one package each artifact so that the package contains the appropriate information to understand and use the artifact? What is the appropriate characterization schema? This chapter proposes an empirical and iterative process to identify the information that should be used to characterize a software engineering artifact, using theoretical knowledge, practical experience, and expert opinion to generate a schema. The ultimate goal is to improve the schema and the package contents based upon it experience in their application. The proposed process has been applied to define a characterization schema for testing techniques. Nowadays, there are numerous testing techniques available for generating test cases. However, many of them are never used, while a few are used over and over again. Testers have little (if any) information about the available techniques, their usefulness and, generally, how suited they are to the project at hand. This lack of information means less appropriate decisions on which testing techniques to use. This chapter also shows this characterization schema and discusses the information it contains and why it is included in the schema.

Keywords: Knowledge management, Experience packaging, Software testing, Testing techniques.

10.1 Introduction

The goal of knowledge management (KM) is to take advantage of an organization's intellectual capital [15]. When applied to software development, this discipline deals with knowledge related to the whole range of software engineering *artifacts* (techniques, products, processes, methods, and so on).

To make the best possible use of organizational knowledge, this knowledge must be created, captured, distributed and applied [15]. Information organization, also known as packaging, is a key activity within this process. It is so critical that a poor information structure has led to the failure of many KM initiatives [11]. If the available information is well structured, knowledge will be more widely and better disseminated and applied, as people will be interested in and tend to consult well structured information and will be clearer about when to use it. The knowledge generation and capturing activities will also be more effective, as the format of this knowledge is defined beforehand, specifying which items of knowledge need to be gathered.

One possible means of recording and giving access to the knowledge of an organization is experience bases [4]. Experience bases are composed of experience packages. SE experience packages usually contain knowledge on how to use given artifacts. This knowledge must be associated with information for deciding when and where a given artifact will be useful. Experience packages are described by instantiating characterization schemas. The information reflected by the characterization schema is vital for effectively identifying which artifacts are useful in a given situation. But experience packages should be as compact as possible, meaning that characterization schemas should contain the least possible information; that is, they should include the minimum set of relevant information. Nevertheless, it is not easy to find out which information these characterization schemas should include. On the one hand, the information reflected by a characterization schema is totally dependent on the artifact it characterizes, which means that when characterizing a new artifact, we cannot benefit from the fact that other artifacts have already been characterized. On the other hand, the theoretical foundation of the artifact in question may not be mature enough to be of assistance in deciding which information the characterization schema should include. If we do not know the parameters that may influence the behavior of an artifact, it will be more difficult to develop a characterization schema for it than if these parameters were known.

Here, we propose a process for identifying what information a characterization schema should include for the purpose of building an experience base. The proposed process is empirical and iterative. It is empirical because it is not based purely on how the person who is designing the schema sees the artifact to be characterized, but also takes into account the view of potential experience base users and artifact builders. It is iterative because it begins with a preliminary schema that is refined as different views are incorporated.

The proposed process has been applied to define a characterization schema for testing techniques. Besides the generation process, we also show the resulting characterization schema for testing techniques and discuss the information it contains and why it has been included in the schema.

The chapter has been organized as follows. Sect. 10.2 presents a series of approaches described in the literature for developing characterization schemas for a range of software artifacts. Sect. 10.3 discusses the proposed process for developing characterization schemas. Section 10.4 is an application of the process presented in Sect. 10.3 for a particular artifact: software testing techniques. Section 10.5 presents the evaluation of the proposed process, and finally, Sect. 10.6 provides some conclusions.

10.2 Related Work

Although the activities of which KM is composed are clear, it is not so clear which methods should be applied within each of these activities. Indeed, while it is generally accepted that the acquired knowledge needs to be packaged [2, 15], and several proposals have been made [1, 18, 19], no one has formalized or standardized what these knowledge packages should be like, not to mention how they should be built.

Nonetheless, the use of characterization schemas in SE as an aid for selecting different artifacts is not new. In the field of software reuse, where there is a repository of coded software modules ready for use, there is already an emerging need for characterization schemas. In the case of reuse, characterization schemas summarizes the characteristics of the module and then, by inspecting these characteristics, a decision can be made on which module or modules are best suited. The characteristics encompass the module attributes, its application conditions and the characteristics of the operating environment. Apart from the reuse field, other areas of SE, like software architectures or software technology selection, also use characterization schemas.

Below, we examine a series of characterization schema proposals described in the literature, as we have not found any formalized proposal of how to develop such a schema within KM. For each proposal, we discuss the artifact it aims to characterize, the characterization proposal, the process followed for characterization and the information proposed for inclusion.

Prieto-Díaz [14] was the first researcher to realize the benefits of using characterization schemas for classifying reusable artifacts. In [14], he presents a characterization schema for reusable software modules to aid the identification and later retrieval of such modules (stored in a repository) and find the components that are less costly, in effort terms, to adapt to the current project. The schema was constructed by means of discrimination or examination and later classification of existing reusable modules (what is called *literary warrant*), analyzing the similarities and differences between these modules. This schema contemplates two aspects of the modules: the functionality of the object (which represents *what*), and the environment (which represents *where*).

Based on the idea that anything related to development, and not just software products, is reusable, Basili and Rombach [3] present a characterization metaschema for any software development element: products, processes, techniques, and so on. Owing to the generality of this metaschema, it needs to be adapted to the type of artifact to be characterized before it is used. The process they have followed to design the metaschema, reflection by the schema designers, is based on a reuse model, which is gradually refined through reasoning. Each step of the refinement captures the logic of the resulting schema. The schema contemplates three aspects: it should contain characteristics proper to the artifact (the object), characteristics of the relationships between the artifact and other artifacts (interface) or environment, and characteristics of the environment in which the artifact can be used (the context or problem).

In [10], Henninger proposes a characterization schema together with a support tool to capture and, thus, enable later dissemination of different problems related to software development, alongside their solution. The process followed for creating the schema is not fully explained, from which we infer that it is developed from the reflections of the schema designer. The aspects included in the schema are descriptions of problems, which are associated with resources (or solutions to the problem, possibly tools, development methods, people, process models, technology, etc.), and which constitute the object, and projects or the environment associated with the object. Accordingly, one can start from any of the three aspects to arrive at any of the other two.

Bass et al. [5] provide a catalogue of architectural design styles, which means that the schema is already completely instantiated. The catalogue was designed following a process of discrimination by studying and classifying numerous designs. This means that the different designs were observed, and on this basis, the authors deduced which characteristics differentiate one style from another. The catalogue contemplates not only the characteristics proper to the styles (the object), but also characteristics of the application requirements (the problem) and characteristics of the environment in which the design is to be implemented (the context), which can place restrictions on the developer when using the style.

In [7], Birk proposes a characterization metaschema for characterizing software technologies. This work is based on the fact that methods, techniques and tools are not universally applicable, and the goal is to improve the selection of technologies for use in a software project. The process followed to design the schema is not made explicit, and it is, therefore, assumed to be the result of the reflection of the schema designer. This metaschema focuses primarily on reflecting the application domain (the context) and the problem for which the technology is suited.

Similarly, von Wangenheim proposes a metaschema for characterizing software engineering experiences in [19]. The author recommends asking experts on the artifact to design the schema. Therefore, the author does not discuss the information that the metaschema should contain.

Maiden and Rugg [12] present a schema for characterizing requirements acquisition methods to improve method selection and help developers to prepare an acquisition programme. Apart from the schema, they propose a series of tables, which are actually the instantiation of the schema as a catalogue. With regard to the process followed to produce the schema, the authors speak of research and their own experiences. As the developers of the schema are experts in the area, one can infer that the process was based on observation and discrimination of the existing methods. However, the authors have added a stage where a series of experts validate the work they have done. The aspects reflected in the schema are the object and the problem.

After studying the characterization area, the findings are as follows:

- There is no proposal that sufficiently formalizes the process to be followed for defining or building experience packages for a knowledge base. This process must be defined so that other people attempting to build a knowledge base can follow it.

- The schemas are usually designed either by discriminating existing elements, asking experts (which is at least justified) or, at worst, on the basis of the personal opinions of the schema designers and are not checked against reality. The opinions of other groups, like software developers or other researchers, are never taken into account.
- Only a few proposals take into account the three desirable aspects: object, environment and problem. However, although they propose storing information based on developers' experiences in using the elements, they do not have an aspect that asks developers for their personal (subjective) opinions about the elements.

The process proposed here intends to overcome these problems.

10.3 Proposed Process for Discovering Relevant Information

Having detected the pitfalls of current characterization schema construction processes, we propose a means of determining relevant information about any particular artifact type for inclusion in an experience repository. Sects. 10.3.1 to 10.3.5 justify each stage of the proposed characterization schema construction process. This process can be divided into two parts: schema generation and schema testing.

- *Schema generation.* Schema generation has been divided into four different stages. They explicitly state each source of information used to formulate the schema, and each stage aims to gather different information types. The generation stages are: development of a theoretical schema, development of an empirical schema, synthesis of perspectives and expert peer review.
- *Schema testing.* Schema testing or start up involves having two different population groups examine the schema and assess two different facets: population and use.

Figure 10.1 shows the resulting process for developing the characterization schema.

10.3.1 Know the Artifact: Development of a Theoretical Schema

As discussed in Sect. 10.2, there are two usual ways of developing characterization schemas:

- Starting from the set of artifacts for characterization (or as complete as possible a subset of these artifacts, if this is not feasible), analyze the similarities and differences between the different artifacts to build a schema that contains the parameters that reflect the differences.

- On the basis of the knowledge that the people who are building the characterization schema have of the artifact type, reflect the most prominent features of this artifact type that are likely to vary from one artifact to another.

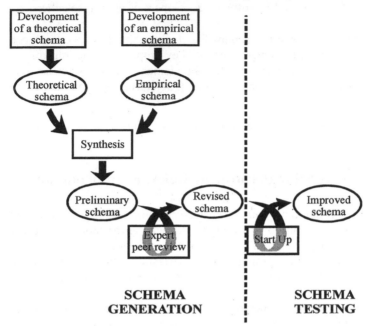

Fig. 10.1. Proposed characterization schema development process

Therefore, the construction of a schema is guided by deductive reasoning concerning available artifacts and what relevant characteristics they all have in common. Here, we propose to use a combination of the two strategies, aiming primarily to develop a first draft of the characterization schema to serve as a starting point that will be added to and improved in later iterations. A secondary goal of this stage is to familiarize the people developing the schema as much as possible with the artifacts they are trying to characterize. This is why this step is done first. This stage is, therefore, a sort of introduction to the development of what will be the final characterization schema.

A strategy of decomposition is followed to build this theoretical schema. First, the high-level information the schema should contain is identified. Then, this information is refined until an adequate level of granularity is reached.

10.3.2 Incorporation of Diverse Viewpoints: Development of an Empirical Schema

Our aim is to facilitate or improve the process of artifact selection in experience bases and thus contribute to the construction of higher-quality software systems. The proposed process can be considered successful if the resulting characterization schema is used; that is, the schema should *be workable*, which means that the process must be aimed at promoting (and even guaranteeing) its use. This focus on schema use is what made us decide to get people related to the artifact area involved.

During characterization schema design, the main decision relates to what information it should contain. This is not an easy task, however, as the schema has to meet the information needs of a variety of people with different goals. More precisely, it must be

- Useful for consumers when selecting the artifacts for their project situation
- Possible for producers to fill in the information asked for in the schema

The schema obtained in the first iteration reflects the opinion of the schema designer on the information that can influence decision-making on which artifacts should be used in a given project. However, this schema does not necessarily respond, at least completely, to the consumers' opinion of selection.

Therefore, the question is *what information does the consumer need to select an artifact from the experience base.* One possibility is to think about what one believes consumers would like to know when deciding on which artifact or artifacts to use and even gather a collection of information that appears to be more or less coherent. But, would this collection of information be the real solution to the selection problem? This problem is far from trivial. If the inclusion of the information that appears in the schema is not justified by a theory (and no such theory exists today for most SE artifacts) or is incomplete with respect to the items required to make the selection, the fitness of the resulting characterization schema, or even its validity, could be questioned. By this reasoning, the schema generated would possibly be of little use, and it would take longer to reach a satisfactory solution.

We need to be pragmatic and have the resulting schema used (in fact, this is the only way of improving artifact selection). So, in the absence of a theory that confirms why some information facilitates or is necessary for selection and other information is not, the schema should reflect the opinion of consumers and producers (future schema users). But, being a matter of opinion, there is a risk of the schema being a mere collection of nonconvergent information. The process is, therefore, subject to two restrictions:

1. The thoughts of the schema designer are used as a basis upon which the opinions of the participants take shape
2. A study is carried out to see if the theoretical and empirical opinions converge, i.e. if there is sufficient common ground between the theoretical and empirical knowledge about the subject to generate an experience base for the artifact type. If this study were to find that the opinions did not converge, it would mean that there is not enough common ground between opinions; that is, there is neither a theory nor empirical knowledge enough about the subject to generate an experience base for this kind of artifacts.

The empirical schema is developed incrementally. A set of opinions (questions or information) about the information required to completely select/define an artifact is gathered for each consumer/producer surveyed. The sets of questions/information obtained are analyzed incrementally. This means that the producers/consumers are gradually incorporated, making it possible to cover the total set of possible producers/consumers according to their characteristics. Therefore, the process is inductive, producing a schema containing the characteristics desired by producers and consumers.

To be more precise, the iteration for running the analysis is as follows. Taking a reference set (originally empty) and the opinions of the producer/consumer, the reference set is updated to include any opinions not included before, and the respective empirical schema is obtained. The reference set can be updated in several ways: either by adding new opinions or reformulating others to make them more generic or more specific (never by deletion). Fig. 10.2 shows the activities to be performed to get "the ith" empirical schema.

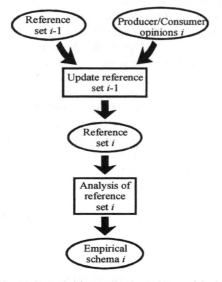

Fig. 10.2. Activities to get the "ith" empirical schema

One interesting point is that the characteristics of the participants should be known, as it is important to be acquainted with what type of producers/consumers are represented in the schema. Another point (not as important as accounting for all producer/consumer types) is the number of people that have to participate in this stage. The number is not essential, as Glaser and Strauss [9] state that the number of data collected during research is relevant for testing and not for generating the hypothesis. So, the number of individuals involved will be important at that point and, as such, will be taken into account later on.

The stopping criterion for this activity is the stability of the characterization schema. It is not possible to stop gathering information from different people until the rate of change of the schema is zero for at least the last 25% of subjects. Therefore, what we are examining at this stage is the evolution and change of the characterization schema as new producers/consumers are incorporated.

10.3.3 Synthesis of Perspectives: Theory and Practice

As we now have two independent sets of information about the object to be characterized, they have to be merged. Accordingly, a synthesis stage is required in which the theoretical and empirical schemas are united to produce a schema that contains the information from both.

In this stage, the two characterization schemas created earlier (the theoretical and the empirical schemas) are taken and synthesized into a single characterization schema to provide a single view of the information that is relevant for selection. Rules should be defined to guide this process and ensure that the schemas are synthesized in an orderly manner and no information is lost. Depending on the environment in which the schema is to operate, the synthesis rules could vary from the collection of all the information that appears in the two schemas to the selection of given types of information if performance or the amount of information handled for selection are critical factors. However, if there is no restriction on the amount of information the preliminary schema should contain, the recommended heuristic is that all information appearing in either the empirical or theoretical schema should appear in the preliminary schema. This can be translated into

- Any information that appears in at least one schema will be directly entered in the preliminary schema.
- If there is similar information or some information is more generic or more specific than others, study the best way of adding it to the schema to assure that no information is lost during synthesis and there is no redundancy.

Once the preliminary schema has been built, it might be of interest to examine the source of the information of which it is composed so as to analyze the different viewpoints of the subject types that have contributed to creating this preliminary schema.

10.3.4 Expert Peer Review

The schema obtained after the synthesis of the theoretical and empirical schemas reflects the viewpoint of the schema designer, consumers and producers concerning the selection problem. However, neither the consumers nor the producers have so far seen the schema (they were asked for their opinion on selection, but they were never shown what information had been input). It would, therefore, appear to be a good idea to get someone else to inspect and give an opinion on the schema. Also, according to the principles of some sciences, for example, medicine, it is advisable to get a second opinion about a complex problem. Therefore, a series of experts in the area to which the artifact belongs to, should be asked to give their verdict on the preliminary schema prior to start up. The goal of this expert peer review is to correct possible schema defects caused by the way in which it was derived. The typical defects of the schema obtained prior to the review by experts are as follows:

- *Defects of form*: Both producers and consumers have given their particular view of the information they believe to be relevant for selecting that particular artifact. However, the schema designer alone created the structure that reflects this information. It would not be amiss to get a second opinion on this structure.
- *Defects of substance*: The information for the preliminary schema is gathered indiscriminately. It may contain errors involuntarily introduced by the schema designer or by the people participating in the research. For example, there may be redundant information (dependencies between information contained in the schema), or missing or unworkable information not detected by the designer.

The preliminary schema will be modified on the basis of the analysis of the opinions of the experts to incorporate their suggestions, giving rise to a new, improved and almost final schema. The ideal number of experts for an expert peer review is as many as possible, and no less than three, so that discrepancies among experts can be handled. However, it is not easy to find experts, and therefore any number would be acceptable.

10.3.5 Start Up

Owing to the risk involved in deploying the characterization schema, a preliminary evaluation must be run in order to detect possible improvements. The best way of examining product validity is to put it into operation and observe how well it fits in with development to determine what problems users come up against and how the product could be improved to make it useful for developers. For this purpose, once the preliminary schema has been built, it will be first instantiated for a range of artifacts, and then potential users of the repository (producers, consumers and librarians) will be asked to use it under several circumstances. The use of the schema will provide feedback to the schema designer, which can be used to improve it.

As mentioned before, the start-up stage consists of two parts: first, a mini-repository is populated with representative artifacts from the whole population; later, this repository is used by people under different circumstances. A refined version of the schema is created on the basis of the results of the data analysis.

1. *Repository Population*: The aim of this part of the start-up stage is to examine basic schema characteristics, namely, its feasibility and flexibility from the producer viewpoint. For this purpose, the characterization schema will be instantiated over again to study these aspects. The ideal situation is to have the future producers, consumers and librarians instantiate the characterization schema for the different artifacts. However, if this is not possible, the people who created the schema are perfectly qualified to do this job. They can act as librarians, getting the necessary information from books, papers and past projects.
2. *Repository Use*: This part of the start up involves running the repository populated during repository population. The primary aim of this part of the

start-up stage is to observe the feasibility and completeness of and user satisfaction with the schema from the consumer viewpoint.

This second part of the start-up stage is again carried out on the preliminary schema. Here, a number of subjects will act as consumers and use the schema to select artifacts. Both quantitative and qualitative data is collected during this stage, which, after analysis, will be used to again modify and improve the schema. Again, it would be desirable to have real consumers perform a pretest of the schema. If no real consumers are available, however, other types of developers could be used (students, for example).

10.4 Case Study: Developing a Characterization Schema for Software Testing Techniques

The process described in Sect. 10.3 has been applied to build a characterization schema for testing techniques. The construction of this schema is described step by step throughout this section as an example for readers who are interested in applying the process for characterizing any SE artifact in order to build an experience base.

10.4.1 Development of a Theoretical Schema

As discussed in Sect. 10.3.1, the schema was developed by gradually refining the information that it is to contain. In this case, the relevant information for selecting testing techniques (schema attributes) is grouped around the elements that are involved in software testing, which are then organized around the levels of which the testing process is composed.

10.4.1.1 Schema Levels

The software system testing process can be divided into the following stages:

1. Selection of the quality attributes that are to be tested, as well as the expected values for each attribute, when they are to be tested, the metrics to be used for the evaluation, and the parts of the system that will be affected by each test.
2. For each of the attributes identified in the previous stage, the tests identified above should be performed, which means: generate and execute the test cases and evaluate the results obtained, always considering the environment where the test took place.

The main difference between points 1 and 2 lies in the fact that the purpose of point 1 is to establish a generic framework within which the testing of the software in question will take place. This stage is necessary because not all software systems are the same, and a decision must therefore be made on which is the best way to evaluate each system. Stage 2 is necessary because not all projects are the same, even if they are building the same software. This means that neither the characteristics of the developer organization nor the team members nor the technologies will be the same, and the tests to be run must therefore be carried out differently.

The characterization schema must capture all this to assure selection of the optimum testing techniques. More formally, we have named these types of information as tactical and operational information, and they correspond to two different levels. The information contained in the *tactical level* is related to the initial or tactical planning that will be followed to run the tests, and reflects information related to the use to which the generated test cases will be put.

As is the case with the industrial manufacturing of some materials, where the characteristics that the material should have are established by analyzing the uses to which the material is to be put, the use to which the generated test cases will be put determines the characteristics they should have for testing purposes. For example, whether a plastic is to be used either to manufacture the inside of a car, to make plastic bags, to fabricate bottles, etc., will determine how flexible, how resistant and how malleable it has to be. Likewise, the fact that a set of test cases is to be used to test the security of a software system or the correctness of an algorithm implementation determines whether the cases should be exhaustively test all sorts of inputs, only the most common inputs or perhaps the inputs that entail anomalous behavior on the part of the user. Finally, we should explain that just as a given material cannot be used on all occasions and some of its properties have to vary depending on its use (leading to variations or versions of the material), when a set of test cases is generated for a given purpose it is very likely that it will not be useful in other circumstances.

The information contained in the *operational level* is related to the optimal conditions of testing techniques suitability, once given characteristics of the environment in which the technique is to be applied have been determined. Just as certain pressure and temperature conditions are required for a chemical reaction to take place, the technique application conditions have to be as conducive for the expected test cases to be generated effectively (in terms of time and resources) and efficiently during software testing. This means that it may or may not be appropriate to apply a given technique depending on the knowledge and experience of the personnel and whether or not the available tools are suitable. This is equivalent to the reaction not taking place or to the products obtained being of poor quality.

In other words, the operational level reflects the characteristics of both the technique and the project environment. These include tools, knowledge of the personnel, characteristics of technique applicability and so on from which it is possible to deduce whether or not the technique in question is the best suited for the project situation in question.

10.4.1.2 Tactical Level

As mentioned above, the aim of this level is to identify the test to which the code will be subjected or to choose the tactic to be followed to test the code. There are two parameters:

1. The *purpose* or *objective* of the test, which defines the software attribute that is to be evaluated and how rigorously this is to be done. The set of cases generated when applying a testing technique cannot be used to test any software quality attribute or to test the same attribute in the same way. For example, a set of test cases generated to test whether an algorithm is correctly implemented is not generally useful for checking whether the implementation of this algorithm is efficient or whether the system is acceptable. Suppose that one wants to check, on the one hand, system security and, on the other, system usability. The best way to test security is to use test cases that represent attacks or unlikely situations rather than the routine use of the system. To test usability, on the other hand, one looks for test cases that represent the usual or common uses of the system. And, again, if one wants to test the correctness of an algorithm, one must use test cases that test both the normal actions of the algorithm and the exceptional cases (whether or not they are erroneous).

   Furthermore, a technique that generates cases to test security in a safety-critical system is of no use for generating cases in a non-safety-critical system. And this is precisely what the purpose of the test reflects the software attribute that is to be evaluated using the test and how rigorously or with what degree of confidence this is to be done.

2. The *scope* of the test, which can be defined by saying what part of the software system is to be tested, when the test is to be run and the components of the software system that are affected by the test.

   Depending on which test is run, are affected different parts of the software, ranging from an algorithm, through an entire module, a group of modules that perform a system function, to a subsystem and even the entire system. Also, depending on how system development has been organized, the test takes place at one time or another within the process. We should also specify the part of the functionality offered by the system that needs to be tested. The scope, then, refers to the part of the system involved in the test.

10.4.1.3 Operational Level

As mentioned earlier, the aim at this level is for the application (or use) of the technique to be as effective as possible, as well as efficient. This involves a series of factors, which are discussed below.

Being a software process, the generation of test cases can be represented generically as shown in Fig. 10.3a. As shown in Fig. 10.3a, a software process generates a software product, where the techniques used, on the one hand, and the resources used, on the other, are the controllers of the process. If this generic view is specified for the case at hand, the process is then the generation of test cases, the input is the software (generally, as each testing technique calls for specific inputs that vary from one technique to another). The output is the generated test cases and the controllers are, on the one hand, the technique or techniques used and, on the other, the tools and personnel, as shown in Fig. 10.3b. In other words, the test case generation technique that is applied to the software outputs a series of test cases within an environment that is determined by the tools available for performing the task and the personnel who carry out the task.

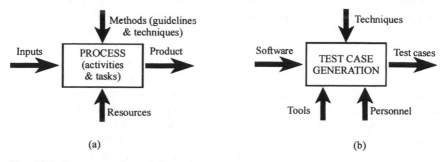

(a)   (b)

Fig. 10.3. Representation of the software process: (a) Generic process, (b) Specific case, generation of test cases

Therefore, according to Fig. 10.3b, it can be said that the information that the operational level of the characterization schema should contain has to refer to:

- The people who are to use the technique or *agents*. The characteristics of these people can lead to one or another technique being chosen. If the testing personnel are not very experienced in one technique and there is no time for training, another is likely to be selected.
- The *tools* that should or could be used. The fact that a company does or does not own a given tool that supports the use of a given technique can lead to the selection of one technique over another.
- The software (code) to be tested or the *object*. The code has certain characteristics that can determine the use or rejection of a technique, for example, the type of programming language used, the code size and so on.
- The *technique*. Depending on the characteristics of the technique, a decision can be made on whether or not to use it at a given time. Characteristics like complexity, effectiveness, maturity, usability, and so forth will be the key for deciding on its use.
- The generated test cases; that is, the *results* (and/or consequences) of using the technique. Some characteristics of the technique are environment dependent, and these are precisely the ones that reflect its behavior. How good a technique is when applied can be ascertained from the generated test cases and not from the technique. Thus, some characteristics of these test cases will be of interest for selection purposes.

10.4.1.4 Attributes of the Theoretical Schema

Table 10.1 shows the composition of the theoretical schema.

Table 10.1. Theoretical schema

LEVEL	ELEMENT	ATTRIBUTE
Tactical	Objective	Quality attribute
		Rigor
	Scope	Phase
		Element
		Aspect
Operational	Agents	Experience
		Knowledge
	Technique	Tools
		Comprehensibility
		Cost of application
		Sources of information
		Dependencies
		Repeatability
		Adequacy criterion
	Results	Completeness
		Cost of execution
		Type of defects
		Effectivencss
		Correctness
		Adequacy degree
	Object	Software architecture
		Software type
		Programming language
		Development method

10.4.2   Development of an Empirical Schema

The tasks to be carried out to get the empirical schema include sending out two different questionnaires to respondents: a questionnaire that asks the consumers what information they believe to be relevant for selection purposes, and another that asks the producer what information they believe to be necessary to define a testing technique. The responses are then analyzed to produce a characterization schema that reflects the opinions of both consumers and producers about the selection problem. The empirical schema is built incrementally, as described in Sect. 10.3.5. That is, the first version of the empirical schema is generated with the information received from the first respondent and the schema version was updated as the information from successive respondents, is analyzed. When working with the empirical schemas, we tried to use the levels and elements of the theoretical schema as far as possible, because the respondents only supplied attributes.

An important issue we had to deal with during this stage was the stability analysis of the empirical schema. This analysis was performed in order to find out when to stop gathering information. Fig. 10.4 shows the accumulated growth speed of the empirical schema. The x-axis shows the different people surveyed ordered according to time (C stands for consumer and P stands for producer), and the y-axis shows the size of the empirical schema as a percentage of its final size. It can be seen that the empirical schema reaches 50% of its final size with the first respondent. This figure increases to 80% with the second respondent, and the schema reaches its final size with the tenth respondent. This means that the last six respondents did not add any new information to the empirical schema, and therefore the empirical schema can be considered as stable at this point.

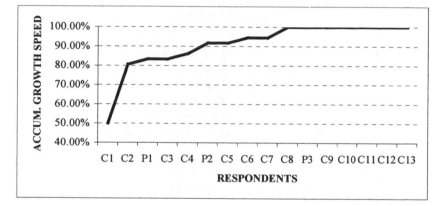

Fig. 10.4. Schema accumulated growth speed

Another of the key tasks for designing the empirical schema was the selection of the respondents. The characteristics of the people involved in the construction of the empirical schema a significant influence on the resulting schema. The people involved should be as heterogeneous as possible to assure that the schema does not reflect a unilateral viewpoint. For this purpose, an attempt was made to include respondents with a wide variety of characteristics: from a range of fields, with varying experience and of different nationalities. As the set of participant subjects had to be as heterogeneous as possible, we looked for people who played different roles in the testing area. Also, when asking for information we started with those respondents who were most likely to give us more useful information.

Table 10.2 shows the contents of the empirical schema. Note that the empirical schema provides us with some information that did not appear in the theoretical schema, since practitioners care about practical issues that are very often overlooked by theoreticians. The main differences of the empirical schema from the theoretical schema are

- *Use level*: It was not possible to associate the information contained in this level with any of the two levels in the theoretical schema. Therefore, a new level was created: the use level. The questions of which this new level is composed refer to the personal experiences of people who have used the technique. This level contains two elements:

Table 10.2. Empirical schema

LEVEL	ELEMENT	ATTRIBUTE
Tactical	Objective	Quality attribute
		Rigor
	Scope	Phase
		Element
		Aspect
Operational	Agents	Experience
		Knowledge
	Tools	Identifier
		Automation
		Cost
		Environment
		Support
	Technique	Comprehensibility
		Maturity level
		Cost of application
		Inputs
		Adequacy criterion
		Test data cost
		Dependencies
		Repeatability
		Sources of information
	Results	Coverage
		Effectiveness
		Type of defects
		Number of generated cases
	Object	Software type
		Software architecture
		Programming language
		Development method
		Size
Use	Project	Reference projects
		Tools used
		Personnel
	Satisfaction	Opinion
		Benefits
		Problems

- *Project*: The information covered in this element refers to the respondents' interest in learning about and characterizing software projects in which the technique has been applied in order to compare these earlier projects with the current situation.
- *Satisfaction*: The information covered in this element complements the above information on earlier projects. The respondents are also interested in

knowing the results of using the technique in the project from the viewpoint of what impression it caused on the person who used the technique.

- *Tools element*: The information covered in the tools element refers to the characteristics of the tools that can be used when applying the technique.

However, the inclusion of too much information can also lead to difficulties. Experts play an essential role during peer review in dealing with this matter.

10.4.3 Synthesis

At this point, we have two characterization schemas, a theoretical and an empirical schema, that reflect different viewpoints or perspectives of the problem of selecting testing techniques in software projects. These are theory, represented by the schema designer, and practice, represented by testing technique producers and consumers. The next step is to synthesize these two perspectives into one.

The heuristic to be followed for the synthesis is based on the preservation of information: all information appearing in either the theoretical or empirical schema will appear in the synthesized schema. In no case has the possibility of removing information from the characterization schema been considered at this stage. The fact that the schema designer has not been able to deduce any attribute mentioned by any respondent from the theory (or vice versa) does not necessarily mean that this attribute is not important or necessary. The omission may be due to a mistake or oversight. Likewise, as there is no way of knowing which attributes are not necessary for selection (this information was never solicited), it is better to play it safe and include all information.

Before defining the rules of synthesis, two fundamental concepts related to these rules must be defined:

- *Equality*: Two attributes are considered equal if they bear the same name and belong to the same element and level.
- *Similarity*: Two attributes are considered similar if they do not bear the same name or do not belong to the same element or same level, although they represent the same or similar concepts.

Accordingly, the following rules are defined for synthesis:

1. The levels and elements of the synthesized schema are the union of the levels and elements of the original two schemas.
2. Any attributes that appear in just one of the characterization schemas appears unchanged in the synthesized schema.
3. Any attributes that appear in both schemas and are equal appear unchanged in the synthesized schema.
4. Any attributes that appear in the two schemas and are similar are studied to decide whether they are used to generate one or several attributes.
5. In no case is information deleted from the characterization schema.

Table 10.3. Preliminary schema

LEVEL	ELEMENT	ATTRIBUTE	THEOR. SCHEMA	EMPIR. SCHEMA
Tactical	Objective	Quality attribute	•	•
		Rigor	•	•
	Scope	Phase	•	•
		Element	•	•
		Aspect	•	•
Operational	Agents	Experience	•	•
		Knowledge	•	•
	Tools	Identifier	•	•
		Automation		•
		Cost		•
		Environment		•
		Support		•
	Technique	Comprehensibility	•	•
		Maturity level		•
		Cost of application	•	•
		Inputs		•
		Adequacy criterion	•	•
		Test data cost		•
		Dependencies	•	•
		Repeatability	•	•
		Sources of information	•	•
	Results	Completeness	•	•
		Correctness	•	
		Effectiveness	•	•
		Type of defects	•	•
		Number of generated cases	•	•
		Adequacy degree	•	
	Object	Software type	•	•
		Software architecture	•	•
		Programming language	•	•
		Development method	•	•
		Size		•
Use	Project	Reference projects		•
		Tools used	•	•
		Personnel		•
	Satisfaction	Opinion		•
		Benefits		•
		Problems		•

On the basis of the above rules, the two original characterization schemas are synthesized into what termed hereinafter the preliminary schema which is shown in Table 10.3. Table 10.3 also shows the source of the attributes of the preliminary characterization schema. Columns 1 to 3 show the schema itself (levels, elements and attributes). The next two columns indicate whether the information represented by an attribute is present in either of the two schemas: theoretical and empirical. Accordingly, the original composition of the two schemas can be traced back from Table 10.3.

It is interesting to note that 14 of the attributes present in the preliminary schema do not appear in the theoretical schema. On the other hand, there are only two attributes that are present in the preliminary schema and not in the empirical schema. This means that, except for two attributes, the empirical and the preliminary schema are practically identical. In other words, 58% of the attributes of the preliminary schema are common to the two original schemas, 5% are supplied by the theoretical schema, and 37% by the empirical schema. This is an interesting point that is worth analyzing in more detail. The major omissions of the theoretical schema are the *use* level and the *tools* element. As regards the *use* level, one reason why it is not present is possibly that it was assumed during the investigation that the information provided by the producers with respect to a testing technique is complete enough for consumers not to have to look for other sources of information. As regards the *tools* element, they were considered important, but details like their *automation* (part of the technique automated by the tool), their *cost*, the *support* provided by the tool vendor, or the *platform* (hardware and software) and programming language (*environment*) that support the tools were not taken into account. This could be due to the fact that pragmatic aspects of the techniques were overlooked. The minor omissions of the theoretical schema are some attributes of the *technique* element (*maturity level*, *inputs* and *test data cost*) and the object attribute (*size*), which corroborate the above supposition that pragmatic aspects of the testing techniques were overlooked when building the theoretical schema.

The empirical schema, on the other hand, has only minor omissions, as the respondents failed to detect only two attributes of the final schema: *adequacy degree* and *correctness*, both belonging to the *results* element. The absence of these concepts in the empirical schema is likely due to the fact that not enough people were interviewed or that the set of possible respondents was not satisfactorily covered.

10.4.4 Expert Peer Review

Taking into account that the experts use open-ended questionnaires, in which their response is a description rather than a quantification, the opinions are analyzed critically. This means that the opinions of all the experts on a particular subject are read and understood. Then, the schema designer checks whether the opinions are contradictory or coincident and, finally, makes a decision on whether or not to accept the suggestion and, when accepted, how it can be included. The decision on whether or not to accept the experts' suggestions is made according to a series of rules, which are now presented. Table 10.4 shows the results of this stage.

1. If the experts disagree, the majority view is respected.
2. If more than one expert recommends a given change, the recommendation is taken into account.

3. If only one expert recommends a change, this change is accepted, provided the proposed change is not due to a misinterpretation of the schema, its logic or its contents. When only one expert recommends a given change, this change is not always as evident as when it is recommended by several experts. In this case, it is the expert's versus the schema designer's opinion. It is sometimes impossible to reconcile the two viewpoints, and it was decided that the opinion of the schema designer should take precedence. One such case is the suggestion to replace the attribute *cost of application* (technique) by *complexity*, as the schema designer is of the opinion that a technique can be easy and still take a long time to use. It is contradictory to make modifications in which the schema designers do not believe or about which they are not sure.
4. If the solution of the problem stated by the expert goes beyond structural changes to the schema (for example, build a tool to improve schema use), the suggestion is accepted, but the solution will be left for future research.

The changes the four experts involved in the expert peer review made to the preliminary schema can be briefly summarized as follows:

- Five attributes have been deleted: three from the *tactical* level (*quality attribute*, *rigor* and *phase*) and two from the *operational* level (*maturity level* and *adequacy degree*). This was done because the experts pointed out dependencies or redundancies with respect to other attributes.
- The *correctness* attribute of the *operational* level was replaced by another named *precision*.
- Two attributes were moved from the *operational* level to the *tactical* level (*effectiveness* and *defect type*).
- A new attribute, termed *purpose*, was created and placed in the *objective* element, as the experts noted that it was missing and justified its need.
- The *results* element was renamed as *test cases*.
- The *use* level was renamed as *historical* level.

10.4.5 Start Up

The reviewed characterization schema has been put into practice according to the process described in Sect. 10.3, for a university environment, using final-year (sixth grade) students as consumers. The results are presented below.

10.4.5.1 Repository Population

The first thing to do before starting to populate the repository is to decide which techniques will be used to check both schema feasibility from the producer viewpoint and schema flexibility. For this purpose, it was decided to select a number of technique families, which cover the variation between techniques of different families, and a number of techniques within each family, which cover the variation between techniques of the same family. Additionally, we resolved to choose well-known techniques, as this gives a better understanding of how the schema is instantiated.

Table 10.4. Final schema (1 of 2)

LEVEL	ELEMENT	ATTRIBUTE	DESCRIPTION
Tactical	Objective	Purpose	Type of evaluation and quality attribute to be tested in the system
		Defect type	Defect types detected in the system
		Effectiveness	Percentage of defects detected by the technique out of the total number of defects detected
	Scope	Element	Elements of the system on which the test acts
		Aspect	Functionality of the system to be tested
Operational	Agents	Knowledge	Knowledge required to be able to apply the technique
		Experience	Experience required to be able to apply the technique
	Tools	Identifier	Name of the tool and the manufacturer
		Automation	Part of the technique automated by the tool
		Cost	Cost of tool purchase and maintenance
		Environment	Platform (SW and HW) and programming language with which the tool operates
		Support	Support provided by the tool manufacturer
	Technique	Comprehensibility	Whether or not the technique is easy to understand
		Cost of application	How much effort it takes to apply the technique
		Inputs	Inputs required to apply the technique
		Adequacy criterion	Test case generation and stopping rule
		Test data cost	Cost of identifying the test data
		Dependencies	Relationships of one technique with another
		Repeatability	Whether two people generate the same test cases
		Sources of information	Where to find information about the technique

Table 10.4 (*cont.*). Final schema (2 of 2).

LEVEL	ELEMENT	ATTRIBUTE	DESCRIPTION
Operational	Test cases	Completeness	Coverage provided by the set of cases
		Precision	How many repeated test cases the technique generates
		Number of generated cases	Number of cases generated per software size unit
	Object	Software type	Type of software that can be tested using the technique
		Software architecture	Development paradigm to which it is linked
		Programming language	Programming language with which it can be used
		Development method	Development method or life cycle to which it is linked
		Size	Size that the software should have to be able to use the technique
Historical	Project	Reference projects	Earlier projects in which the technique has been used
		Tools used	Tools used in earlier projects
		Personnel	Personnel who worked on earlier projects
	Satisfaction	Opinion	General opinion about the technique after having used it
		Benefits	Benefits of using the technique
		Problems	Problems with using the technique

Accordingly, the chosen techniques were:

- *Functional testing techniques:* Boundary value analysis and random testing
- *Control flow testing techniques*: Sentence coverage, decision coverage, path coverage and thread coverage
- *Data flow testing techniques:* All-c-uses, all-p-uses, all-uses, all-du-paths, and all-possible-rendezvous
- *Mutation testing techniques:* Mutation and selective mutation

The authors of this chapter were responsible for instantiating the above-mentioned techniques. Table 10.5 shows the results of instantiating the chosen technique for feasibility purposes: *decision coverage*. The findings of the *schema feasibility* check were:

- There is information that is difficult to find, especially information related to reference projects. This is due to the fact that companies do not like to see

their confidential data published. A cultural change has to take place at
companies for it to be possible to get reliable information about the past uses
of a testing technique. Also, companies have to get used to doing *postmortem*
analyses of projects to weigh up the results of using the techniques.

Table 10.5. Decision coverage technique

LEVEL	ELEMENT	ATTRIBUTE	VALUE
Tactical	Objective	Purpose	Find defects
		Defect type	Control
		Effectiveness	48%
	Scope	Element	Units
		Aspect	Any
Operational	Agents	Knowledge	Flow graphs
		Experience	None
	Tools	Identifier	LOGISCOPE
		Automation	Obtain paths
		Cost	€3,000 - 6,000
		Environment	Windows; C/C++
		Support	24-hour hotline
	Technique	Comprehensibility	High
		Cost of application	Low
		Inputs	Source code
		Adequacy criterion	Control flow
		Test data cost	Medium
		Dependencies	Supplemented with techniques that find processing errors
		Repeatability	No
		Sources of information	Sommerville
	Test cases	Completeness	–
		Precision	–
		Number of generated cases	Exponential # decisions
	Object	Software type	Any
		Software architecture	Any
		Programming language	Any
		Development method	Any
		Size	Medium
Historical	Project	Reference projects	–
		Tools used	–
		Personnel	–
	Satisfaction	Opinion	OK, but should be complemented with others
		Benefits	It is easy to apply
		Problems	Dynamic analyzer should be avoided when used with real time and concurrent systems due to code instrumentation

- There were also two schema attributes (*precision* and *completeness*) whose value was not found anywhere. This casts doubts upon the advisability of these two attributes appearing in the schema. However, they are found in both the theoretical and empirical schemas and the experts did not consider them unsuitable. This appears to be relevant information that is not available in the literature on testing techniques. So, it is an omission of the testing literature, not of the schema, as this information is considered relevant from all viewpoints (note that there are not many attributes in the schema of which this can be said), but is, however, not easy to locate.

- Contradictory information is often found about the testing techniques. This is inevitable, because as long as the parameters that affect the use of a testing technique are not perfectly defined, some may not be studied. The studies carried out on testing techniques should be as rigorous as possible and, thus, reflect the information more correctly in order to output noncontradictory information.

- The metrics used to fill in some attributes are not easy to interpret. For example, for technique effectiveness, one often finds *probability of finding a given fault* as the associated metric. However, this attribute should really reflect the *percentage of faults that the technique can detect*. Can both metrics really be considered to reflect the same information? Or, contrariwise, do they reflect different things? This problem has to do with what developers would like to know and what can be easily collected [8]. This problem could be solved if the metrics expressly asked for by the schema were used every time studies were carried out on testing techniques.

However, it is important to stress that the potential of the schema, which is now limited by the existing theory on testing techniques, is much greater. The schema can be very useful as an aid for looking for information on testing techniques. This includes information that is at present very dispersed and information that is not now disseminated, like the opinions of other people who have used the technique.

As regards *schema flexibility*, it was possible to satisfactorily instantiate all the testing techniques that were originally selected. This means that we were able to instantiate the schema for thirteen testing techniques from four different families. Of course, this does not mean that the schema is totally flexible. It would be necessary to instantiate the schema for *all* existing testing techniques to make such a claim. However, the fact that a series of techniques that are representative of existing techniques have been able to be instantiated without any problem indicates that the schema is flexible enough to be able to instantiate the huge majority of, if not all, testing techniques.

10.4.5.2 Repository Use

Repository use aims to assess schema feasibility, completeness and user satisfaction from the consumer viewpoint. The following project was used to check schema feasibility.

A system is to be built to manage a car park (concurrent system). At this stage of the project, the quality assurance team has identified the key quality attributes of this software system. These were deduced by examining the characteristics of the software to be developed, as well as its application domain. In this particular case, the essential attributes are correctness, security and timing.

Having examined the quality attributes of interest, the question is to decide which techniques would be best suited to evaluate the correctness of the above-mentioned software system, bearing in mind the following project situation. The system is to be coded in ADA, the development team is quite experienced in developing similar systems and it has also been found that almost all the errors that the developers make are proper to concurrent programs. The testing team is also experienced in testing this type of systems.

When illustrating how the problem is solved, the process defined is also shown:

- *Determine bounded variables* (attributes of the schema whose value is determined by the software project and cannot be changed): According to the problem statement, correctness is to be evaluated, which means that the *purpose* would be to detect faults in any type of element. The system is to be developed in Ada, which is a *language* for real-time systems. The development team is experienced in developing this type of systems, which means that they are unlikely to make many errors. Table 10.6 shows the associated variables for the example.
- *Preselect an initial set of techniques*: Given the associated variables in Table 10.6, their value was compared with those of the technique contained in the repository. The techniques selected are: *boundary value analysis, random, path coverage, all-possible-rendezvous, all-c-uses, all-p-uses, all-uses, all-du-paths, standard mutation* and *selective mutation*. The techniques *sentence coverage* and *decision coverage* are rejected because their effectiveness is low, and the technique *threads coverage* is discarded because it is for object-oriented software.

Table 10.6. Bounded variables

LEVEL	ELEMENT	ATTRIBUTE	VALUE
Tactical	Objective	Purpose	Find faults
		Defect type	ANY
		Effectiveness	>50%
	Scope	Element	ANY
		Aspect	ANY
Operational	Object	Software type	Real time
		Software architecture	Concurrent
		Programming language	Ada
		Development method	ANY
		Size	Medium

- *Identify the best-suited techniques for selection*: Of the preselected techniques, there is one that is specific for Ada-style programming languages (concurrency implementation using *rendezvous*). Although there are general-purpose techniques (for all software types) that are more effective, it appears that the technique that is specific for concurrent software detects the faults proper to concurrency better than the other techniques. Furthermore, the technique *path coverage* states that when used with concurrent and real-time systems, a dynamic analyzer cannot be used as a tool. Additionally, the techniques *all-c-uses, all-p-uses, all-uses, all-du-paths, standard mutation* and *selective mutation* cannot be used without a tool (which is not available). Therefore, the *all-possible-rendezvous* techniques will be selected. However, the dependency attribute states that the technique should be supplemented with a black-box technique. Observing the black-box techniques in the preselected set (*boundary value analysis* and *random*), it is found that the *random testing* technique is useful for people with experience in the type of tests to be run and is therefore, also selected.

The finding for *schema feasibility* is, therefore, that it is possible to make at least one selection using the characterization schema.

The study of *schema completeness* addressed both the information the subjects used during selection and the missing information. The main finding of this study is that it is important for the characterization schema to be completely instantiated for users to be able to take full advantage of the schema and for them to consider it useful (this can pose a threat to its utility). Another interesting point observed is that subjects are not always able to ascertain the value of variables that do not appear in the schema, but whose values can be easily deduced from the schema. This is the case of the time it will take to apply the technique. If the cost of application of the technique, the knowledge of the people who are to use the technique, whether or not tools are to going to be used and the size of the software are known, it is easy to find out how long it takes to apply the technique.

To assess *satisfaction* with the schema, the subjects are asked by means of open questions to subjectively summarize their perceptions of the selection process. These questions are related to the advantages and disadvantages the subjects have seen with the schema, whether they would use it in their work if available, the improvements they would make to the schema, what they liked and did not like about the schema, whether their view of the selection problem has changed after using the schema, what have they learned and the suitability of the names in the schema. Generally, the subjects like the schema. However, they do stress the fact that there are uninstantiated attributes. They also think that the schema contains too much information. This again suggests the need to build a tool to make the information the schema contains easier to handle. All the subjects would be prepared to use the schema, provided they do not have to instantiate it. They miss some information, although, interestingly, the information they do not find either refers to things that they can deduce from the schema (like the time it will take to apply a technique, for example) or information that they should extract from their project context for comparison with a schema attribute (as is the case of the experience of the development team, where what they are really looking for are the defect types to be detected). As regards the suitability of the names, the names that they allege not to be very intuitive are precisely the ones that refer to non-intuitive concepts about the techniques (adequacy criterion, precision, etc.), which suggests that the schema names are suitable.

10.5 Process Evaluation

Additionally, we wanted to check whether the process followed output a suitable schema and whether repository use really improves selection. For this purpose, we ran an experiment with the repository built with 87 students. For details about the experiment, see [17]. The experiment compared characterization schema use with books used for selecting testing techniques [6, 13, 16]. The findings are reported below.

As regards *schema efficiency*, the total time required to solve the selection problem is the sum of the study time plus the selection time and consultation time (which is zero if books were used for selection). This experiment found that the schema helps to reduce both the study and the selection time as compared with books, and that the time spent consulting the schema can be considered negligible with respect to the other two. Accordingly, it can be concluded that one of the objectives of this research has been achieved, which is the construction of a characterization schema that makes selection more efficient. However, the results are subject to the following conditions: non-English-speaking and inexperienced subjects.

After studying *schema effectiveness*, it was found that the number of original techniques is lower for books than with the schema and varies from subject to subject. It was also found that the number of selected techniques is lower for the schema than for books, and the subjects select either families of techniques, things that are not techniques or techniques with which they are very familiar.

Combining these results, the conclusion is that the subjects using books are unable to distinguish between a technique and a family or something that is not a technique even though they were given an explanation as to what a technique is. This is indicated by the fact that the set of original techniques is different for the subjects who made the selection using books and who select things that are not techniques. As none of the subjects is *incompetent* for performing the task (they would also have failed in the selection using the schema), this could be explained by saying that books are confusing as regards the information they provide. This could also be the reason why the subjects tend to select more techniques, gaining more assurance that the tests will turn out right, and why they choose techniques with which they are very familiar. Finally, it should be stressed that the schema leads to more precise selections.

With respect to *schema completeness*, it was observed that the schema contains more useful information for selection purposes than books. Books focus on explaining how a technique works rather than when to use it.

As regards *schema usability*, the number of problems found during selection, the sort of problems, the number of schema attributes that are problematic for selection purposes and the sort of attributes were taken into account to evaluate schema usability. The first two variables provide relative results on schema behavior as compared with books, whereas the latter two provide absolute results, irrespective of books.

From the relative comparison of the schema against books, it was found that the subjects have fewer problems using the schema than books. It was also discovered that the frequency of appearance of each problem lower. In addition the main problems encountered by the subjects using the schema are the result of there being attributes that are not instantiated in the schema, as well as there being too much information (a problem that was predicted by an expert and which could be solved by building a tool). On the other hand, the problems concerning the selection with books are well known: poor organization of the available information, as well as missing information of interest and the existence of information that is unnecessary for selection purposes.

From the absolute comparison, it was found that the frequency with which the meaning of attributes is consulted is low. It was also found that the most often consulted attributes appear to be the attributes that represent concepts that are not intuitive or are difficult for the subjects to interpret. Finally, it can be said that characterization schema usability is acceptable, although there is room for improvement. It is acceptable insofar as the frequencies of appearance of problems are lower than for books, and the frequency with which the meaning of the attributes is consulted is also low. However, schema usability could be improved, for example, by building a tool to make the information easier to handle. It could also be improved by assuring that, every time a technique is added, the entry contains as much information as possible.

From all this, it can be concluded that the use of characterization schemas improves selection and also that the proposed process helps in the construction of characterization schemas, since it defines a systematic way of identifying relevant information.

10.6 Conclusions

Throughout this chapter, we presented a process for developing characterization schemas. As discussed in Sect. 10.2, the generation of characterization schemas is one of the most important activities for creating an experience base. We also found that no process has yet been defined for their development.

The proposed process was applied to a particular artifact type: software testing techniques. The existence of a large group of testing techniques, the lack of pragmatic information about these techniques and the lack of a theoretical foundation makes them a paradigmatic example of the difficulties involved in building experience bases. Thanks to the practical application of the proposed process, we demonstrate first, the adequacy of the characterization schema output by following the process and, second, the soundness of the process. We operated a mini-repository containing thirteen testing techniques to test the adequacy of the resulting schema. By setting up and using the repository, we were able to detect some of the possible schema defects (in this case, none).

Additionally, we ran an experiment to check the soundness of the proposed process, which compared the use of the mini repository developed from the schema with the use of testing books. From this experiment, we were able to find that the schema generated with the process proposed here contains more complete information than testing books, is easier to use, is more efficient and leads to better selections than books. Thanks to this experiment, we were also able to confirm the generic hypothesis that artifact selection improves with the use of characterization schemas.

Going back to the more generic problem of using characterization schemas in software engineering, it is important to note that the areas that can benefit most from these conceptual tools are the ones that have a wide variety of elements to be characterized and knowledge to be stored.

While the first point represents an essential issue, the second one represents an issue that can be somehow overcome by having researchers perform more research into the issues that are relevant for the characterization schema (for example, inspections where there is not much knowledge). At the moment there would be no point in developing a characterization schema for selecting development paradigms, since there are only two paradigms i.e. structured and OO. However, some knowledge must always be available about the element that is to be characterized.

References

1. Althoff K.D., Birk A., Hartkopf S., Müller W., Nick M., Surmann D., Tautz C. (1999) Systematic population, utilization and maintenance of a repository for comprehensive reuse. In: Proceedings of the 11th international conference on software engineering and knowledge engineering, Springer, Berlin Heidelberg New York, pp. 25-50
2. Basili V.R., Lindvall M. Costa P. (2001) Implementing the experience factory concepts as a set of experience bases. In: Proceedings of the 13th international conference on software engineering and knowledge engineering. Buenos Aires, Argentina, pp. 13-15
3. Basili V.R., Rombach H.D. (1991) Support for comprehensive reuse. IEEE software engineering journal, 6: 303-316
4. Basili V.R., Rombach H.D., Caldiera G. (1994) The experience factory. Encyclopedia of Software Engineering, John Wiley and Sons, UK, pp. 469-476
5. Bass L., Clements P., Kazman R. Bass K. (1998) Software architecture in practice. SEI series in software engineering. Addison-Wesley, Readings, MA, USA
6. Beizer B.. (1990) Software testing techniques. International Thomson computer press, London, UK
7. Birk A. (1997) Modeling the application domains of software engineering technologies. In: Proceedings of the 12th international conference on automated software engineering, Lake Tahoe, California, 291-292

8. Fenton N, Krause P. Neil M. (2002) Software measurement: uncertainty and causal modeling. IEEE Software, 19: 116-122
9. Glaser B., Strauss A. (1967) The discovery of grounded theory: strategies for qualitative research. Aldine publishing, Chicago, USA
10. Henninger S. (1996) Accelerating the successful reuse of problem solving knowledge through the domain lifecycle. In: Proceedings of the 4th international conference on software reuse, Orlando, Florida, USA, pp. 124-133
11. Komi-Sirvio S., Mäntyniemi A., Seppänen V. (2002) Toward a practical solution for capturing knowledge for software projects. IEEE Software, 19: 60-62
12. Maiden N., Rugg G. (1996) ACRE: Selecting methods for requirements acquisition. Software engineering journal, 11: 183-192
13. Pfleeger S. L. (1999) Software engineering: theory and practice. Mc-Graw Hill, New Jersey, NY, USA
14. Prieto-Díaz R. (1989) Classification of reusable modules. In: Biggerstaff T., Perlis A. (Eds.), Software reusability, ACM Press, New York, NY, USA, pp. 99-124
15. Rus I., Lindvall M. (2002) Knowledge management in software engineering. IEEE Software, 19: 26-38
16. Sommerville I. (1998) Software engineering. Pearson Education, Harlow, UK
17. Vegas S. (2002) A Characterization schema for selecting software testing techniques. PhD thesis, Facultad de Informática, Universidad Politécnica de Madrid, Spain
18. von Wangenheim C.G. (1999) REMEX- A case-based approach for reusing software measurement experienceware. In: Althoff, K.-D., Bergmann R., Branting L.K. (Eds.), Case-based reasoning research and development, Springer, Berlin Heidelberg London, pp. 173-187
19. von Wangenheim C.G., Althoff K.-D., Barcia R.M. (2000): Goal-oriented and similarity-based retrieval of software engineering experienceware. In Ruhe, G., Bomarius, F., (Eds.), Learning software organizations: methodology and applications, Springer, Berlin Heidelberg New York, pp. 118-141

Author Biography

Dr. Sira Vegas is assistant professor of computer science at the Universidad Politécnica de Madrid in Spain. She had a summer student grant at the European Center for Nuclear Research (Geneva) in 1995. In 1997, she worked at GMV (Madrid) in the ENVISAT project for the European Space Agency. She has been a regular visiting scholar at the University of Maryland from 1998 to 2000. Dr. Vegas has a Ph.D. in computer science from the Universidad Politécnica de Madrid. She is a member of the IEEE Computer Society and ACM.

Dr. Natalia Juristo is professor in computer science at the Universidad Politécnica de Madrid in Spain. She is the Head of the Politecnica Master of Software Engineering degree program. Dr. Juristo has worked at the European Center for Nuclear Research (Geneva), and at the European Space Agency (Rome). In 1992 she was Resident Affiliate at the Software Engineering Institute (Pittsburgh) on a NATO Fellowship. Dr. Juristo has a Ph.D. in computer science from the Universidad Politécnica de Madrid. She has served as Member of the editorial board of the *IEEE Software Magazine* from 1997 to 2001. She is a senior member of IEEE Computer Society and member of ACM, AAAS and NYAS.

Dr. Victor Basili is professor of computer science at the University of Maryland, College Park, the executive director of the Fraunhofer Center Maryland and one of the founders and principals in the Software Engineering Laboratory (SEL) at NASA/GSFC. He works on measuring, evaluating and improving the software development process and product. Dr. Basili is the recipient of the 2000 Outstanding Research Award from ACM SIGSOFT, has authored over 160 journal and refereed conference papers, and has served as editor-in-chief of the *IEEE Transactions of Software Engineering*. He is co-editor-in-chief of the *International Journal of Empirical Software Engineering*, and is an IEEE and ACM Fellow.

11 A Knowledge Management Framework to Support Software Inspection Planning

Stefan Biffl and Michael Halling

Abstract: Software inspection requires customization to each development context and guidelines for planning for optimal results. In this work we present a role-oriented knowledge management framework for key decisions in software inspection planning and focus on how to use available knowledge from literature, which may vary considerably in different contexts, with local empirical data. We identify three decision levels, which differ by knowledge requirements and the level of uncertainty for decision inputs: the *quality management level*, the *project planning level*, and the *inspection level*. On each inspection planning level we provide scenarios with key decisions that outline the decision-making process and show how available inspection knowledge based on measurement in a particular context can be used for decision support. The conceptual framework is a first step to make inspection planning more explicit and procedural in order to be able to further improve this process.

Keywords: Quality management, Project management, Software inspection, Decision support, Knowledge management framework, Empirical software engineering.

11.1 Introduction

Software inspection is a full-life-cycle and economic quality assurance (QA) approach to detect defects [1]. For best results inspection requires customization to each development context, because for each development context there is a large variety of goals, process variants, and context factors to consider [14]. Inspection in general is cost intensive and often shows big performance variations in different contexts [43]. In the past 25 years a considerable amount of inspection data has been collected in many contexts, but little universally applicable inspection knowledge was created. Especially regarding knowledge in support of inspection planning, very little progress has been documented so far. However, appropriate knowledge management (KM) that generates inspection knowledge promises to further enhance software inspection performance in many contexts.

Knowledge management is the systematic sharing of documented knowledge [33]. This knowledge can consist of quite heterogeneous items, for example, simple performance measures collected in the past; process models with varying levels of detail and complexity; or unstructured experience from past applications of a technology [12]. Key components of knowledge are data and information [33] available to organizations data includes measures collected during events, and information represents data organized to make it useful for end users.

The term knowledge has multiple definitions (see Kakabadse et al. [22] for a summary of the most popular ones). We refer to knowledge as information that has been organized and analyzed to make it understandable and applicable to problem solving or decision making. A further distinction of knowledge includes factual and procedural knowledge. According to Kahneman et al. [23], factual knowledge implies having long-term memory and an extensive database, while procedural knowledge is represented as a repertoire of mental procedures or heuristics used to select, order, and manipulate information in the database and is used for purposes of decision making and action planning.

In Sect. 11.2 we provide a brief overview of existing factual knowledge in software inspection. We refer to software inspection knowledge as, for example, knowledge [33] in the following areas: software inspection process variants, defect detection techniques, and role definitions (e.g., expertise and training as inspector, moderator, or inspection manager). The most important and challenging aspect of inspection KM is to link context parameters like characteristics of the inspection object, expected or targeted classes of defects, available inspectors, and time budget available to inspection process design parameters.

In Sect. 11.3 we outline an inspection framework to help move factual knowledge to create procedural knowledge. This framework incorporates traditional inspection activities, but also provides an insight into managerial and knowledge-oriented dimensions of the inspection process as a first step to applied knowledge management in software inspection. We identify decisions on three levels according to the different users/customers of the inspection process and present examples for key decisions on these levels:

1. The *quality management level* concerns the selection of the set of quality assurance techniques applied during software development, which may include some form of review or inspection.
2. On the *inspection level*, the detailed inspection planning, conduct, and analysis influences the determination of the team composition, i.e., team size and defect detection techniques, for the execution of specific inspections.
3. On the *inspector level*, the inspector follows the inspection process description and has to decide for when to stop and whether an issue is really a defect.

Furthermore, these levels of inspection planning differ by decision-making role (quality manager, inspection manager, and inspector), context (environment factors influencing the decisions), uncertainty, and knowledge requirements for these decisions. Thus they need separate treatments in a KM framework/system.

In Sect. 11.4 we summarize important decisions and knowledge items in the inspection process, discuss the knowledge generation potential of inspection, and derive requirements for a knowledge management system. Sect. 11.5 summarizes and concludes the chapter.

11.2   Knowledge in Software Inspection

In the past 25 years a considerable number of empirical studies have been published (for surveys refer to [8, 19, 24, 31]). Overall, inspection research shows potential for improvement regarding general validity, as available studies usually focus on individual problems. In this section we provide a brief review of the existing inspection information and discuss the current level of knowledge in key inspection areas.

11.2.1   The Software Inspection Process

The core inspection process was developed by Fagan [16] nearly 30 years ago and consists of defect detection defect collection and defect correction. However, we focus particularly on defect detection in the remainder of this paper, as it is the most important and challenging inspection activity. Gilb and Graham [17] offer a practical introduction into the software inspection field while Laitenberger and DeBaud [24] provide a detailed overview of inspection-related research over the past decade. Different alternative inspection process designs have been proposed, like N-fold inspection, active design reviews, and phased inspection (for more details refer to [24]). However, very little empirical evidence is available on the performance of these inspection techniques in comparison to the traditional inspection approach.

As far as the traditional inspection process is concerned, empirical studies clearly document that defects are detected on average with satisfying effectiveness and efficiency [24]. However, inspection performance shows large variations in individual defect detection effectiveness [4, 18, 25, 30]. The origin of this variation is not fully understood so far the possible explanations include inspection process parameters, the inspection environment, or the inspectors involved. In our opinion a major potential for improving software inspection lies in reducing performance variability and making the process more predictable.

Therefore, inspection planning is a particularly important preliminary step of inspection as it customizes the inspection process to the development context. In Sect. 11.3 we mainly focus on inspection planning. A structured approach towards inspection planning is important as it lowers the risk to select incompatible inspection ingredients, such as products incompatible with the chosen inspection technique or defect detection techniques with inspectors who lack the expertise for these techniques. An experience factory [33] can support the analysis, packaging, and communication of inspection knowledge on several levels: use of inspection as a black-box quality assurance process, tailoring of inspection process steps and roles, and detailed techniques for inspection conduct.

11.2.2   Team Defect Detection

A very fundamental general question is whether defect detection is a group activity (i.e., defect detection during a meeting) or an individual activity. While early inspection designs emphasized the importance of inspection meetings [16], later research encouraged individual defect detection and instead used meetings for defect collection [3, 21]. Consequently, different empirical results exist which in some case emphasize the benefits and in other cases the costs of inspection meetings.

For a detailed overview of the information on the difference between individual and group defect detection, see [3, 21]. Related behavioral studies have found no evidence of synergy as a source of group advantage [45]. In general, a widely accepted opinion proposes that synergy only justifies meeting costs in few, specific situations and that other aspects like, for example, the removal of false positives encourages group activity. However, no consolidated inspection knowledge on group defect detection is available so far.

11.2.3   Individual Defect Detection

As far as individual defect detection is concerned, reading is the key activity in individual defect detection to understand a given software artifact and to compare it to a set of expectations regarding structure, content, and desired qualities. The recognition of differences between expectations and the artifact helps readers to spot defects. Reading of software artifacts has been identified as a process for scientific study lately, resulting in quite a comprehensive set of related theories [2, 35].

Inspectors often have to learn how to read and analyze documents for particular purposes. Most inspection related research in the past has focused on the development of reading techniques (RTs), which assist the reader in extracting, gathering, and understanding the information necessary to assess certain quality requirements [2]. In an ad hoc inspection no RT is applied, and therefore inspection performance depends completely on the capability of the inspector and not on a repeatable process. Examples of more systematic reading techniques include checklist-based reading [13, 17], scenario-based reading [2, 15, 31, 35, 36], usage-based reading [37, 38], and traceability-based reading [39].

There are many studies that provide empirical data on individual defect detection: A very good survey on the available data is presented in [31]. They come to the conclusion that it is not clear whether more sophisticated reading techniques like scenario-based reading really outperform the simpler defect detection approaches.

11.2.4   Inspection Team Size and Inspector Characteristics

Other important inspection process parameters related to defect detection are team size and inspector expertise. However, these areas are even less evaluated and documented than the area of reading techniques. Sauer et al. [34] propose that the effectiveness of both individual preparation and the team meeting depend on the level of inspector task expertise for defect detection and defect discrimination, i.e., the ability of an inspector to discern a defect, to distinguish among defect types, and to detect certain defect types. Inspector task expertise may vary with several parameters of the inspection object (e.g., type and notation) and detection aids used (none, checklist, or specific procedures). A recent study on inspector selection shows little influence of inspector experience and software development skills on inspection performance [10].

As far as the influence of team size on defect detection performance is concerned, some preliminary inspection data indicate that increasing team size has decreasing marginal benefits, and that comparatively large team sizes up to ten inspectors may make sense in some situations [5, 11]. Petersson [27] determines the contribution of individual inspectors to the performance of teams with different sizes and finds that, on average, the individual reviewer contribution to the inspection team effectiveness is limited and decreases with team size. In general, the limited number of studies and inspection environments considerably limits the general applicability of available inspection knowledge in this area.

11.3   A Conceptual Knowledge Management Framework for Software Inspection Planning

This section introduces a decision- and knowledge-oriented framework of the inspection process. In the previous section we saw that some inspection knowledge is clear but some is very ambiguous. Therefore it is important to emphasize research in the area of procedural knowledge to support planning and decision-making. The presented framework (see Fig. 11.1) is a first step in this direction and extends existing inspection research by adding two managerial levels to the traditional technical inspection process. The framework is hierarchical to distinguish different types of knowledge and levels of uncertainty. It is also role-oriented to support a clear definition of responsibilities and competencies and is decision-oriented to help take the most important decisions in the process.

Figure 11.1 consists of three levels (large surrounding boxes): quality management in a software development project as context for a possible inspection; inspection management, if an inspection is actually conducted; and the technical inspection process. The small boxes represent activities on the different levels. Arrows between the boxes indicate a flow of information. The left column of process boxes (especially on the top two levels) deals with KM for inspection planning, while the right column describes processes, which extract information out of past inspections and therefore generate knowledge from inspection analysis.

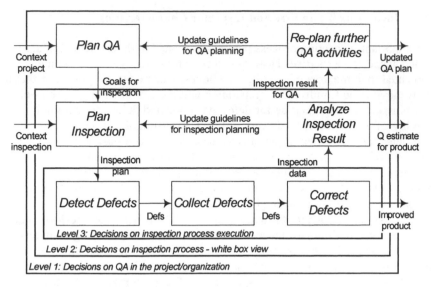

Fig. 11.1. Process steps and associated decisions

In the following subsections we focus on the inspection planning side and provide a detailed level-oriented description of the framework, including a selection of key planning decisions (see Table 11.1 for an overview). For each decision we discuss the level of knowledge, both theoretical and empirical, available. However, we do not provide general strategies for decision making. We view this work as a first step towards gathering procedural knowledge for inspection planning. A further step in the future is to extend the existing level with explicit decision support techniques, like economic valuation approaches [40] and multi-criteria decision aid [41].

11.3.1   Level 1: Quality Manager

At the quality manager level, inspection is one of several approaches to defect reduction. The challenge for quality managers is to appropriately determine the mix and timing of different QA techniques while facing a high degree of uncertainty combined with limited data. Usually decisions on this level require a less detailed but more extensive set of knowledge (e.g., a quality manager needs to have some but not detailed knowledge on a large variety of QA techniques) compared to lower levels in the framework. The combination of these characteristics makes decisions on this level especially difficult: Little knowledge is available on the interpretation of data items, and little theoretical support exists. Therefore an organization could, in our opinion, profit most from a comprehensive KM system on this level.

Table 11.1. Overview on roles, decisions, and decision input information

Scope	Decision	Decision input information
Quality manager	1.1 To what extent and at what time should inspections be used for defect reduction? [9, 29]	*Project context* defect density and defect impact defect reduction potential
	1.2 Is it worthwhile to conduct a reinspection? [4, 6]	Same knowledge items as before plus inspection performance data from first inspection, product quality estimates after first inspection.
Inspection manager	2.1 Which defect detection techniques are to be applied? [2][15]	*Inspection context* Effectiveness of different individual reading techniques; effectiveness of individual and group defect detection
	2.2 What is the optimal team structure, i.e., team size and assignment of defect detection techniques? [5]	*Detailed inspection context* Defect detection redundancy defect overlap.
	2.3 Who are the most suitable inspectors to perform this type of inspection? [10][34]	*Detailed inspection context* Inspector qualification, theory on important inspector characteristics for selection.
Inspector	3.1 Is a defect a true defect? [2]	Inspection material.
	3.2 When to stop inspection?	Inspection material, opportunity costs

Decision 1.1: To what extent and at what point should inspections be used for defect reduction in a certain project (in competition to development and other QA approaches)? Inspections should be used in a project whenever it is likely to be the most effective or efficient way to find important defect classes. We map this decision to an allocation problem of limited resources (staff hours) to QA activities rather than on a selection problem of exclusive QA activities. With regard to the defect reduction, there are several alternatives to inspection that should be assessed and compared to each other, for example:

- Rework defects later can be reasonable if the impact on development effort, duration, and product quality is bearable in the context, e.g., in a prototyping activity or the extreme programming process [26].
- Rigid/uniform development processes in organization; defect-focused development process, e.g., pair programming or iterative development, which result in products of sufficient quality [26].
- Testing on several levels of intensity.

One specific technique to take this decision whether to use inspection as defect reduction approach or not is to apply an economic model considering both the costs and benefits of inspection. Detailed information on inspection benefits and costs can be found in [9]. The main advantage of an economic model is that it allows estimation of a functional relationship between all decision variables. Using appropriate information on the benefits and costs of other quality assurance techniques, an economic model can be used to determine a close-to-optimal mix and timing of activities. Important knowledge items for this decision are (a) the likely impact of defects in the project context, (b) an estimate of the likely defect density and severity in key products, and (c) the likely effectiveness and cost of defect reduction candidates.

Project context: Usually the quality manager knows the project context, e.g., time and cost schedule, and quality requirements. However, only little public knowledge is available on the influence of project context parameters on software inspection (see [14] for an analysis of a limited variety of scenarios) or on optimal QA planning in order to satisfy project guidelines. This requires historic company data to create a company-specific database and a KM framework to support the quality manager in using these data items.

Defect density and defect impact: These items are very dependent on the project context, e.g., time pressure and staff quality. Some theories exist on defect introduction and defect spreading. Combining these theories with historic company data can provide reasonable estimates.

Defect reduction potential: The only public empirical information available at this level deals with the defect reduction potential and associated costs of quality assurance approaches. Detailed overviews of inspection are presented in [3, 4, 24]. Although this information has, of course, some uncertainty, it enables quality managers to roughly assess the defect reduction potential to be expected. As far as comparing effort of inspection and other defect reduction techniques is concerned, Laitenberger and DeBaud [24] summarize that most of the available literature presents solid data supporting the claim that the costs for detecting and removing defects during inspections is much lower than detecting and removing the same defects in later phases.

Decision 1.2: Is it worthwhile to conduct a reinspection (several inspection cycles)? If an inspected product is suspected to still contain a substantial number of defects, a second inspection cycle, called reinspection, can be conducted to find more defects [6]. The decision whether or not to conduct such a reinspection is similar to the decision whether to conduct an inspection, with the valuable additional information on the product and defects from the recent inspection. Benefits of a reinspection are fewer defects in the product and improved accuracy of measuring the number of defects remaining in the product [4, 6, 7]. Note that data from the first inspection cycle resolves a considerable amount of uncertainty, e.g., better estimates for the remaining defect density and the defect reduction potential of inspection given the specific context. So far, there are very few reports on empirical data on reinspections [4, 6, 8]. These reports, however, document that a reinspection can be a reasonable option after an inspection.

11.3.2   Level 2: Inspection Manager

Under the assumption that the quality manager decides to use inspection at some point in the project, the inspection manager is responsible for planning and conducting an inspection for a given context in order to reach the quality goals. Therefore inspection managers operate in a less uncertain world as they receive certain guidelines from quality managers as inputs to the planning process. While the quality manager only requires aggregated knowledge of the inspection process, the inspection manager has to determine the specific inspection design to be executed within a given inspection context.

This planning involves a sequence of decisions regarding different inspection process parameters, like the individual defect detection techniques or the inspection team. In practice, the sequence of steps may vary and follow several iterations until a stable concept has been found. Before we discuss a selection of the most important decisions on this level (for a detailed survey see [19]), we want to emphasize that our analysis is based on the traditional inspection process defined by [16] and that we do not deal with different inspection process designs and their implications on the following decisions. For an overview on inspection process variants see [24].

Inspection context: While a key knowledge item on the quality management level has been project context, we identify the inspection context partly given by the quality manager, partly determined by the project context as an important knowledge item on this level. Basically, the inspection context including inspection goals, schedules, and resources is given. However, the interrelationship between inspection context and inspection design is uncertain.

Decision 2.1: Which defect detection techniques are to be applied? The most important inspection goal is usually to detect defects in the inspection object. Therefore, a main inspection planning decision is to determine the defect detection techniques optimally used during inspection.

Individual versus team defect detection effectiveness: As far as defect detection in inspection meetings is concerned, so far no systematic or theoretically motivated support exists. Existing knowledge on group defect detection is very heterogeneous and therefore provides little support. However, recent work [3, 21] concludes that synergy effects hardly take place. However, meetings can still be useful to remove false positives, provide training for novice team members, and to discuss unclear issues on the work product or the inspection process. Votta [42] presents different types of meetings for these purposes.

Because of the lack of explicit group defect detection theories, group defect detection performance depends to a large degree on inspector ability and tacit knowledge, i.e., on group interaction knowledge, which is personal to inspectors, not easily visible or easy to formulate [28]. If the project and inspection contexts justify inspection meetings, a KM framework should focus on collecting data from the meeting process and on making this tacit knowledge more explicit.

Reading Techniques Effectiveness: A large variety of inspection data exists on individual defect detection (Sect. 11.2). However little generally applicable knowledge has been created from this data. Therefore the selection of defect detection techniques is a difficult and uncertain activity. From a theoretical point of view, a set of concepts exists that are potentially helpful for this decision. For example, reading techniques can be classified according to the following characteristics [24]: the *usability* regarding the guidance of the reader, the *adaptability* to a range of different document notations and typical sets of defects, the person-independent *repeatability* of results, the *coverage* of important quality aspects, and the *focus* it assigns to the inspectors in a team on different aspects of the document and target defects. These characteristics strongly influence the feasibility of reading techniques in different project situations and enable the inspection manager to better identify the best set of reading techniques for a given inspection context. Unfortunately, ambiguous empirical evidence with little general applicability exists on the performance of different reading techniques. Nevertheless, structured reading techniques like scenario-based reading reduce the amount of tacit inspector knowledge required for inspection. If ad hoc and checklist-based reading are applied, little information is gained on how inspectors identify defects. Structured reading techniques combined with knowledge generation techniques like feedback questionnaires and interviews enable organizations to transform tacit defect detection knowledge into explicit defect detection techniques.

Decision 2.2: What is the optimal team structure, i.e., team size and assignment of defect detection techniques? The team structure describes the combination of defect detection techniques and the number of inspectors applying a specific defect detection technique. An important aspect of this planning step is to estimate the trade-off between defect detection:redundancy and defect overlap.

Defect detection redundancy: The term defect detection redundancy is used to indicate that several inspectors apply the same defect detection technique, which usually increases the defect overlap. Defect detection redundancy increases costs because inspectors are added but decreases the risk of undetected defects. Therefore some redundancy might be reasonable and advantageous.

Defect overlap: The term defect overlap denotes the number of defects that are detected by more than one inspector. Usually the inspection manager aims at reducing both defect detection redundancy and defect overlap.

Most empirical reports contain data on inspections with team sizes of two to six [24] and yield contradicting results concerning the influence of team structure on their results. See [5] and [11] for a first step to a more systematic analysis of team structure based on synthetic nominal teams, where we confirm the theoretical expectations that defect overlap increases and the marginal number of newly detected defects decreases with an increase in team size. However, in some situations detecting another individual but important defect might justify the increased effort. Therefore the inspection manager's target is to determine the optimal team size to increase the variety of expertise available while avoiding process loss from too large groups [34].

Decision 2.3: Which inspectors are most suitable to perform this type of inspection? As reported in Sect. 11.2, empirically documented inspection performance shows large variation, which can only partly be explained through process variation: the remaining part seems to stem from individual inspector variation [34]. In general, Sauer et al. [34] report that the implications of behavioral theory for software inspection are that interventions, which significantly increase the available defect detection expertise, should have the largest impact on performance. If processes are poor, expertise may be lost. But, when expertise is poor, an excellent process does not increase the available expertise and, hence, does not improve performance. Therefore selecting the right inspector for a particular inspection job is very important.

Inspector qualification: Key criteria for inspector selection are certainly the knowledge of the inspectors with respect to the inspected artifact and with respect to the inspection process and defect detection techniques used. However, these knowledge items are often only implicitly given since it is difficult to objectively measure qualification. A KM system should provide a variety of inspector-related information, including performance measures on past inspections, in order to enable inspection managers to select those inspectors who fit the selected inspection design best.

In general, the issue of identifying a good inspector is a topic of current research. Although different papers argue that inspector qualification is an important aspect, only little systematic empirical evidence on this issue is available [10]. In practice, the best approach seems to use data from past inspections in the target context to evaluate the qualification of potential inspectors, as the general influence of development skills and experience on inspection performance is unclear.

11.3.3   Level 3: Inspector

While the previous two levels describe real management activities, the third level is an executing level, where the inspection is, in fact, conducted. Inspectors' decisions neither face a large amount of uncertainty (dependent on the inspection design) nor require detailed expert knowledge of the inspection process. Furthermore, inspectors receive detailed information compared to quality and inspection managers in the form of inspection material from inspection managers.

Nevertheless, inspectors' decisions are of crucial importance for software inspection performance and have so far received very little attention. Most of the knowledge required to make the decisions on the inspector level is tacit knowledge, i.e., remains to the inspector's judgment. However, using a KM framework and appropriate inspection designs can make parts of this tacit knowledge explicit by collecting inspection measures and providing explicit guidelines to inspectors.

Decision 3.1. Is an issue really a defect? The inspectors follow the procedures to detect and collect defects and have to decide quickly for each issue that they observe whether this issue is a noteworthy defect. This is actually the most frequent key decision in the process, as lost defects lower the effectiveness of the process, while many false positives create nonproductive extra work. Although detailed inspection material should usually be available, including a defect classification and characterization, this decision is not trivial and still involves uncertainty.

Structured defect detection techniques aim at providing explicit decision support to inspectors. Empirical studies show some success using aggregated measures concerning inspection performance. However, so far, research has devoted little effort to explicitly model and document the decision processes of inspectors. Especially in this context, knowledge provided usually through inspection material but potentially also through a KM framework is of key interest.

Decision 3.2. When to stop the inspection step? A decision of the inspection manager, which has not been discussed in detail in the preceding section, is to determine and plan inspection duration by setting a deadline. However, in the end it is the inspectors who decide upon their real inspection effort. From an objective point of view, when to stop depends on the coverage of the document, the duration/number of sessions, and process conformance for specific RTs. From a subjective point of view, it depends on the inspector's personal opportunity costs.

Opportunity costs: these costs measure the inspectors' benefits if they invests their time into inspection compared to the benefits they can create if not inspecting. If opportunity costs of inspection are high, inspectors may try to finish inspection as fast as possible, jeopardizing the success of the inspection. However, these opportunity costs are to a large extent implicit. Therefore a comprehensive KM system should try to make these opportunity costs explicit as a key knowledge item for inspection planning.

Similar to the first inspector decision there is very little information on the time issue of inspections, as most inspection experiments make sure that all inspectors can and do finish their tasks in the allotted time frame. Furthermore, experiments are unable to capture the influence of personal opportunity costs. For this purpose, real-life company data is needed.

11.4   Discussion

KM supports software development and inspection by helping the people involved — quality managers, inspection managers, and inspectors — to learn effectively and efficiently from the existing knowledge in the community and their organization. The scope and usefulness of the KM approach with software inspection depends on the possibility to make the existing published knowledge available to prospective users and to help in eliciting further knowledge, which in turn depends on a functioning measurement program and the ability to create context descriptions to structure the available knowledge. In this section we summarize important decisions and knowledge items in the inspection process, discuss the knowledge generation potential of inspection, and derive requirements for a KM system.

11.4.1   Inspection Knowledge in Theory and Practice

Decisions on each level require very different types of knowledge. Quality managers face a strategic decision problem with a large amount of uncertainty in planning general QA activities. Therefore they need broad overview knowledge but only little understanding of details. Furthermore, they require decision models, which allow for comparison of different quality assurance techniques and are capable of dealing with uncertainty. So far, very little theoretical and empirical knowledge is available on this topic. An initial step is described in [29].

In contrast to this decision, the reinspection decision is a tactical decision, as it responds to detailed feedback on the first inspection cycle and the resulting product quality, which must be provided by the inspection manager. However, as a reinspection represents an alternative to passing the document on or redoing the document, there is also a large strategic part in this decision.

As far as inspection manager decisions are concerned, they require a very detailed understanding of the inspection process and the impact of context variables and design parameters on the likely performance. As pointed out in Sect. 11.3 there is a large amount of both theoretical and empirical knowledge available for the selection of defect detection techniques and comparatively little on the determination of team structure and inspector selection. In general, the main challenge associated with available empirical data is to transfer it to specific project situations, which might differ considerably from the context of the empirical study. Therefore current research activities like CeBase (www.cebase.org) and Visek (www.visek.de) aim at characterizing the usefulness of defect reduction approaches in different project contexts based on empirical data. Their goal is to combine results from individual empirical studies and to derive generally applicable knowledge. Wohlin et al. in [44] present a benchmark-oriented approach that combines various empirical data sources in order to derive comparatively general results on inspection effectiveness for different inspection objects and group sizes.

However, even these approaches cannot fully substitute for a data collection framework within an organization. Data collection is a necessary requirement for a KM system. Some tool support is currently discussed in order to support the inspection process and the data gathering [18, 20]. Finally, inspectors have to make decisions on a very frequent basis, whenever they identify potential issues and have to decide whether to report them or not. However, appropriate inspection material should support inspectors in making these decisions. So far, little theoretical and empirical material is available on the behavior of inspectors.

11.4.2   Knowledge Generation from Inspection

For knowledge generation from inspection data, there are three main additional activities: process elicitation and improvement, defect content estimation, and defect matching. Note that data from a good inspection can be very useful, while a sloppy inspection yields very often unreliable data, which should be viewed with proper caution. As pointed out in Sect. 11.3, appropriate inspection analysis not only creates new knowledge, but it also enables corporations to make implicit knowledge explicit (e.g., by improving reading techniques to inspector characteristics).

Process elicitation and improvement gathers data on the actually conducted inspection process and on suggestions to increase inspection performance. The development team and quality engineers can apply "defect cause analysis" to find out which development activity introduced defects to the product. Consequently, weak development processes can be improved, and project management can adjust their assumptions on likely results of these development processes for project planning. If feedback suggests faulty development or inspection processes, then they can report to QM for further monitoring and possibly improving these processes. Long-term benefits can be improved development and QA processes based on information on weak points.

Defect content estimation determines the likely number of defects in the inspected product after inspection to help evaluate the quality of the product and the inspection process. There are objective defect content estimation techniques, such as capture - recapture and the detection profile method [7, 8]. Another defect content estimation technique is based upon interviewing the inspectors and collecting subjective estimates for the defect content of the inspected document [8]. Reports on these measures show that they perform comparably to objective methods [8] in experimental environments. The main argument for subjective estimates is that inspectors have achieved expert knowledge on the quality of the document during inspection and therefore they qualify for subjective estimation.

Matching reported defects to true defects to eliminate false positives is either performed by the author individually or in a team meeting. Further, it can be useful to match the defects from several inspectors to find out how often a certain defect was found, which enables the analyzer to calculate defect overlap in a team and prepares the defect data for use with objective defect content estimation models. Matching the defects in a long list from several inspectors can be a major effort. Tool support can considerably accelerate the collation of defects, e.g., by sorting defects according to location or keywords in the description. In addition, voting on the severity of each defect can help to uncover differences in the opinions of team members on the severity rating, which can be valuable input to a discussion on the views of defect importance in the project context.

11.4.3   Requirements for a Knowledge Management System

A KM system should support the following main functions: knowledge generation, capture, transfer, and sharing. While this sounds straightforward, the implementation of a useful system needs to fit the process domain, in our case software inspection. The framework presented in Sect. 11.3 supports feedback and learning as a part of software inspection on several levels according to the views of the main roles involved. The use of the framework encourages context-specific measurement and analysis on the levels of a single inspection, along a project, and on company level.

A KM system building on the framework and supporting the most important decisions should have the following functions:

- Systematic context description.
- Store, evaluate, and retrieve reports from theory and practice: e.g., guidelines and data.
- Help to establish relationships between reported data and local data from ongoing inspections within the organization.
- Provide feedback to quality manager, inspection manager and inspectors. An important aspect of a KM system is to document the impact of decisions on different levels on inspection and project success. This feedback enables participating roles to adjust their behavior and optimize the decision-making process.

In addition to these functional requirements for a knowledge management system, we identify the following quality requirements: the knowledge must be provided in time (e.g., especially the feedback cycle must be quick enough to allow for correcting actions during inspection); the collected data must be accurate because wrong knowledge is potentially more dangerous than no knowledge; data must be sufficiently complete enough in order to support the decisions [32].

There are two key components for the successful usage of a KM system in practice: for a practitioner to find out whether a KM system is worth the extra effort to improve the current process; and whether it is possible to lower the threshold of effort for using such a KM system to make it easy to share and use the available knowledge.

Current research activities in the academic inspection community focus on the following areas which are important from a knowledge-oriented perspective:

- Databases for available empirical and theoretical data e.g., from CeBase (www.cebase.org), Visek (www.visek.de), ISERN (www.iese.fhg.de/ISERN).
- Tool support for inspection management and data collection, which must be further integrated with a more general knowledge management system.
- Simulation and decision-making model to provide techniques to quality managers, inspection managers and inspector to make their decisions.

11.5   Conclusion

In this chapter we present a framework that adds two managerial levels to the technical inspection process and represents a first step to make inspection planning more explicit and procedural in order to be able to further improve the inspection process. The framework adds important insight since it is role oriented to support a clear definition of responsibilities and competencies, and decision oriented to help take the most important decisions in the process. Decisions on the various levels differ by knowledge requirements and the level of uncertainty. This systematic approach helps to identify data for taking planning decisions, enables process- and role-oriented reasoning, and proposes KM requirements to turn public and company-specific information into procedural knowledge.

Using our KM framework for software inspection we identify the following implications for KM in the inspection context:

- Inspection planning needs a variety of different know how for different roles, which should be systematically managed.
- Available academic inspection knowledge can yield some important input to inspection planning in practice, as it outlines a variety of alternatives and offers empirical data in several application domains.
- Inspection analysis, i.e., the systematic collection and evaluation of measures during software inspection; is a central component of knowledge management in inspection.
- Combined with a process improvement approach, such as an experience factory, the framework can integrate knowledge aspects of all roles involved, which helps to transfer proven inspection know-how.

To conclude this work, we would like to emphasize that significant progress has been made in the area of software inspection in the past years, but that existing inspection knowledge is often ambiguous and merits further research.

References

1. Aurum A., Petersson H. Wohlin C. (2002) State-of-the-art: software inspections after 25 years. Software testing, verification and reliability, 12: 133-154
2. Basili V.R., Green S., Laitenberger O., Lanubile F., Shull F., Soerumgaard S., Zelkowitz M. (1996) The empirical investigation of perspective-based reading. Empirical software engineering: an international journal, 1: 133-164
3. Bianchi A. Lanubile F., Visaggio, G. (2001) A controlled experiment to assess the effectiveness of inspection meetings. In: Proceedings of IEEE Metrics'01, London, UK, pp. 42-50
4. Biffl St., Halling M., Köhle, M. (2000) Investigating the effect of a second software inspection cycle. In: Proceedings of the IEEE Asia-Pacific conference on quality software, Hong Kong, pp. 155-164
5. Biffl S., Gutjahr W. (2001) Influence of team size and defect detection methods on inspection effectiveness. In: Proceedings of IEEE Metrics'01, London, UK, pp. 63-75
6. Biffl S., Freimut B., Laitenberger O. (2001) Investigating the cost-effectiveness of reinspections in software development. In: Proceeding of ACM/IEEE international conference on Software Engineering, Toronto, Canada, pp. 155-164
7. Biffl St., Grossmann W. (2001) Evaluating the accuracy of objective estimation models based on inspection data from multiple inspection cycles. In: Proceedings of ACM/IEEE international conference on software engineering, Toronto, Canada, pp. 145-154
8. Biffl S. (2001) Software inspection techniques to support project and quality management. Habilitation thesis, Shaker Verlag, Aachen, Germany

9. Biffl S., Halling M. (2001) A value-based framework for the cost-benefit evaluation of software inspection processes. In: Proceedings of the workshop on inspection in software engineering, Paris, France http://www.cas.mcmaster.ca/wise/ (date accessed 22nd April, 2003)

10. Biffl S., Halling M. (2002) Investigating the influence of inspector capability factors with four inspection techniques on inspection performance. In: Proceedings of 8th IEEE Metrics'02, Toronto, Canada, pp. 115-121

11. Biffl S., Halling M. (2003) Investigating the defect detection effectiveness and cost-benefit of nominal inspection teams. To appear in the IEEE transactions on software engineering

12. Birk A., Dingsoyr T., Stalhane T. (2002) Postmortem: never leave a project without it. IEEE Software, 19: 43-45

13. Chernak Y. (1996) A statistical approach to the inspection checklist formal synthesis and improvement. IEEE transactions on software engineering, 22: 866-874

14. Ciolkowski M., Shull F., Biffl S. (2002) A concerted family of experiments to investigate the influence of context on the effect of inspection techniques. In: IEE Proceedings of the EASE conference, Keele University, UK

15. Dunsmore A., Roper M., Wood M. (2002) Further investigations into the development and evaluation of reading techniques for object-oriented code inspection. In: Proceedings of the 24th international conference on software engineering, Orlando, Florida, pp. 47-57

16. Fagan M.E. (1976) Design and code inspections to reduce errors in program development. IBM systems journal, 15: 182-211

17. Gilb T., Graham D. (1993) Software inspection. Addison-Wesley, Reading, MA, USA

18. Halling M., Grünbacher P., Biffl S. (2001) Tailoring a COTS group support system for software requirements inspection. In: Proceedings of 16th IEEE international conference on automated software engineering, San Diego, California, pp. 201-208

19. Halling M. (2002) Supporting management decisions in software inspection process. PhD thesis, Vienna University of Technology, Austria

20. Halling M., Biffl S., Grünbacher P. (2002) A groupware-supported inspection process for active inspection management. In: IEEE Proceedings of 28th Euromicro conference, track on software product and process improvement, Dortmund, Germany, pp. 251-258

21. Halling M., Biffl S. (2002) Investigating the influence of software inspection process parameters on inspection meeting the performance. In: IEE Proceedings - Software engineering, 149: 115-122

22. Kakabadse N.K., Kouzmin A., Kakabadse A. (2001) From tacit knowledge to knowledge management: Leveraging invisible assets. Knowledge and process management, 8: 137-154

23. Kahneman D., Slovic P., Tversky A. (1984) Judgment under uncertainty: heuristics and biases. Cambridge university press, Cambridge, UK

24. Laitenberger O., DeBaud J.M. (2000) An encompassing life-cycle centric survey of software inspection. Journal of systems and software 50: 5-31

25. Laitenberger O., El-Emam K; Harbich T.G. (2001) An internally replicated quasi-experimental comparison of checklist and perspective-based reading of code documents. IEEE transactions on software engineering, 27: 387-421

26. Marchesi M., Succi G., Wells D., Williams L. (eds.) (2002) Extreme programming perspectives. Addison-Wesley professional series, Boston, MA, USA

27. Petersson H. (2001) Individual reviewer contribution to the effectiveness of software inspection teams. In: Proceeding of IEEE Australian software engineering conference, Canberra, Australia, pp. 160-168
28. Polanyi M. (1966) The tacit dimension. Routledge and Kegan Paul, London, UK
29. Port D., Halling M., Kazman R., Biffl S. (2002) Strategic quality assurance planning. In: Proceedings of the 4th international workshop on economics driven software engineering research (EDSER-4) at the international conference on software engineering, Orlando, Florida, USA
30. Porter, A.A., Johnson P.M. (1997) Assessing software review meetings: results of a comparative analysis of two experimental studies. IEEE transactions on software engineering, 23: 129-145
31. Regnell B., Runeson P., Thelin T. (2000) Are the perspectives really different? Further experimentation on scenario-based reading of requirements. Empirical software engineering, 5: 331-356
32. Reifer D.A. (2002) A little bit of knowledge is a dangerous thing. IEEE Software, 19: 14-15
33. Rus I., Lindvall M. (2002) Knowledge management in software engineering. IEEE Software, 19: 26-38
34. Sauer C., Jeffery R., Land L., Yetton P. (2000) The effectiveness of software development technical reviews: A behaviorally motivated program of research. IEEE transactions on software engineering, 26: 11-14
35. Shull F.J. (1998) Developing techniques for using software documents: A series of empirical studies. PhD thesis, University of Maryland, College Park, USA
36. Shull F., Ioana R. Basili V.R. (2000) How perspective-based reading can improve requirements inspections. IEEE Computer, 33:73-79
37. Thelin T., Runeson P. Regnell B. (2001) Usage-based reading - An experiment to guide reviewers with use cases. Information and software technology, 43: 925-938.
38. Thelin T., Runeson P. Wohlin C. (2002) An experimental comparison of usage-based and checklist-based reading. Submitted to IEEE transactions on software engineering
39. Travassos G., Shull F., Fredericks M. Basili V. (1999) Detecting defects in object-oriented designs: using reading techniques to increase software quality. In: Proceedings conference on object-oriented programming systems, languages and applications, Denver, Colarado, USA, ACM Sigplan notices, 34: 47-56
40. Trigeorgis L. (1996) Real options. MIT Press, Boston, MA, USA
41. Vincke P. (1992) Multicriteria decision-aid. John Wiley and Sons, New York, NY
42. Votta L. (1993) Does every Inspection need a meeting? ACM software engineering notes, 18: 107-114
43. Weller E.F. (1993) Lessons from three years of inspection data. IEEE Software 10: 38-45
44. Wohlin C., Aurum A., Petersson H., Shull F., Ciolkowski M. (2002): Software inspection benchmarking - a qualitative and quantitative comparative opportunity. In: Proceedings of 8th IEEE Metrics'02, Toronto, Canada, pp. 118-127
45. Yetton P.W., Bottger P.C. (1982) Individual versus group problem solving: an empirical test of a best-member strategy. Organizational behavior and human performance, 29: 307-321

Author Biography

Prof. Stefan Biffl is professor of software engineering at the Vienna University of Technology. His main research interests include project and quality management in software engineering: software quality, economic software engineering models, software inspections, risk management, and know-how transfer between research and engineering practice.

Dr. Michael Halling is a researcher at the Johannes Kepler University Linz and the University of Vienna. His main research interests include the empirical evaluation of software quality techniques and software engineering processes, the integration of economic concepts in the software engineering field, and the development of simulation models for decision-making support.

12 Lessons Learned in Software Quality Assurance

Linda H. Rosenberg

Abstract: Software quality assurance (SQA) is a vital aspect of software engineering — one that is honed by experience rather than coming straight from a book. SQA is comprised of many areas of software engineering, e.g., life-cycle development, metrics, safety, and reliability. Extensive research has been conducted in each of these areas resulting in several theories, yet the actual practice of SQA and its supporting activities must be grounded in practical experience. This chapter discusses lessons learned by the NASA community as it dealt with day-to-day issues of software quality, reliability and safety. Lessons are written broadly so as to be applicable to almost any software assurance activity; these should then be tailored to an organization's needs.

Key words: Software quality assurance, Process assurance, Product assurance, Safety, Reliability, IV&V, Metrics

12.1 Introduction

Over the years, National Aeronautics and Space Administration (NASA), along with all large enterprises, has become increasingly reliant on software to provide the complex functionality of its systems. The effectiveness of software directly impacts projects' success. NASA long ago recognized the importance of improving development processes. Thus, the activities of software quality assurance (SQA) are critical to the success of every project, and yet the roles and responsibilities are often misunderstood. SQA plays a vital role in all phases of the software development process including safety, reliability, independent verification and validation (IV&V), and metrics. However, it is often difficult for those involved in projects to understand either the interrelationships or how to apply appropriate quality assurance practices at a cost that is also affordable.

All federal agencies are under pressure to downsize, while, at the same time, the workforce within NASA is aging. As the most experienced people retire, the valuable lessons learned about the implementation and practice of software quality assurance are being lost. Each of NASA's ten space flight centers is making an effort to capture this knowledge so that it can continue to be utilized and applied into the future. The purpose of this chapter is to identify some of the knowledge nuggets gleaned about software quality assurance so that we can continue to improve NASA's missions without having to rediscover what we already know.

This chapter discusses lessons learned during the implementation of an SAQ program on projects at NASA in the hope that project managers will be able to increase the probability of a successful mission. These lessons were distilled primarily during the author's ten years of working in the quality assurance directorate at NASA's Goddard Space Flight Center (GSFC), in Greenbelt, MD. This is a relatively small office, and the lessons are a compilation of the author's experience and those of the approximately 50 SAQ engineers who have worked at GSFC over the past decade.

The chapter starts with a general discussion on the meaning of SAQ, those tasks that comprise quality, and their interdependencies. The discussion also covers the processes and products of SQA as well as the activities called for by quality assurance (QA) planning documentation as systems progress through the software development life cycle. There is also an exploration of issues relating to the requirements phase, testing activities, and the importance of metrics. Lessons learned when implementing three specific areas, safety, reliability and IV&V, are then discussed since these areas are critical for NASA's approach to software assurance. The chapter concludes by exploring the importance of risk management to SQA.

12.2   Lessons Learned

The concepts of knowledge management (KM) are neither generally nor consistently applied; thus, the lessons that are captured become even more valuable. The lessons presented here were chosen because they are generally applicable for most software development projects. Quality assurance tends not to be a major topic of software engineering courses, and although it is not a new activity, it is generally not very visible to the end user. If, however, quality assurance is not made an integral part of the project development life cycle, the end result, in extreme cases, can be the loss of a mission — the ultimate catastrophic failure. It is, therefore, of vital importance that NASA captures this knowledge accurately and ensures this information is passed on to future practitioners.

12.2.1   Lesson 1: Project Managers and Software Developers Need To Understand What "Software Quality Assurance" is, and How Their Project Can Benefit by Its Application

Shortly after a project is conceived, a budget is developed. At this point in time, funds should be earmarked for QA activities, and, of course, this includes software. Yet, history shows that funds are generally *not* carefully designated for software quality assurance. Rather, they are later squeezed from some other part of a strained budget. The result is a minimization of quality assurance. Why this happens time and time again is ascribable to an incomplete understanding what SQA entails as well as the real benefits to be gained. Hence, the first lesson is a statement of the need for increasing the awareness and general understanding of the value that software quality assurance truly adds to a project's success. Software quality assurance is actually a combination of three concepts: quality,

QA, and SQA. While these terms are often used interchangeably, we need to understand the basics of quality before we can understand the components and problems of software quality assurance.

Before defining the term "software quality," it is important to understand the broader concept of "quality." NASA, as well as many other federal agencies, has adopted standards from externally recognized sources; thus, the agency has chosen to use the IEEE Standard Glossary of Software Engineering Terminology to define this term. Quality is "the degree to which a system, component, or process meets (1) specified requirements, and (2) customer or user needs or expectations" [5]. The International Standards Organization (ISO) defines quality as the totality of features and characteristics of a product or service that bear on its ability to satisfy specified or implied needs [8]. IEEE and ISO definitions associate quality with the ability of the product or service to fulfill its function. Thus, quality is the net result of a product's features and characteristics.

While this definition would seem to be clear and unambiguous, the concept of quality really is not. Kitchenham states that quality is "hard to define, impossible to measure, easy to recognize" [9]. Gilles states, "Quality is generally transparent when present, but easily recognized in its absence" [2]. Therefore, while we can define quality in theory, in practice, and in use, an absolute definition is elusive. Although fundamental, this is the kind of abstract knowledge that NASA strives to capture, preserve, and most important, apply to real systems. Software quality is defined in the Handbook of Software Quality Assurance in multiple ways but concludes with the definition: "Software quality is the fitness for use of the software product" [16]. This definition implies the evaluation of software quality related to the specification and application of software quality. There are, however, criteria that help in the evaluation of software quality. For each NASA project, the appropriate criteria need to be identified within the context of both the application and the intended operating environment, which frequently means the harsh conditions of space.

McCall and Boehm recognized that in order to develop models of quality, criteria are needed [2]. As a starting point, GSFC developed the following list of quality criteria for software:

- Correctness: Extent to which a program fulfills its specifications
- Efficiency: Use of resources execution and storage
- Flexibility: Ease of making changes required by changes in the operating environment
- Integrity: Protection of the program from unauthorized access
- Interoperability: Effort required to couple the system to another system
- Maintainability: Effort required to locate and fix a fault in the program within its operating environment
- Portability: Effort required to transfer a program from one environment to another
- Reliability: Ability not to fail
- Reusability: Ease of re-using software in a different context

- Testability: Ease of testing the program to ensure that it is error-free and meets its specification
- Usability: Ease of use of the software

In a perfect world, all criteria would be met, but software is not developed or run in such a world, and trade-offs are a part of all development projects. This may be a software developer's first real-world lesson learned, and the companion lesson is learning how to choose the appropriate evaluation criteria. Often the most efficient software is not portable, as portability would require either general or additional code, which would decrease the level of efficiency. Another difficulty is the subjective nature of several attributes. For example, degrees of usability vary not only from developer to developer but also among the end users of a system.

When using any of the above criteria to define assurance objectives for a software system, the ultimate purpose and use of the system must be taken into account. In the real world of software development, criteria for quality are identified and applied to differing extents as a result of trade-off decisions, which often have little to do with technological considerations and more to do with programmatic and management motivations.

IEEE defines the QA as "a planned and systematic pattern of all actions necessary to provide adequate confidence that an item or product conforms to established technical requirements" [5]. This definition needs to be adapted to software since, unlike hardware systems software is not subject to the physical laws of nature and does not wear out or break in the traditional sense. Consequently, its usefulness over time remains unchanged from its original state at the time of delivery. Thus, the goal of software quality assurance is to establish a systematic effort to improve the delivery condition.

In the SQA Handbook, the following definition is given: "Software quality assurance is the set of systematic activities providing evidence of the ability of the software process to produce a software product that is fit to use" [16]. Within NASA, we strive to achieve a systematic approach to SQA, and we rely heavily on the knowledge from previous successes and failures. The criteria chosen are evaluated in part against the above criteria and measured as described in a later section of this chapter.

12.2.2   Lesson 2: Software Quality Assurance Implementation is a Balancing Activity That Must Be Tailored as Project Appropriate

No project in the history of software development at NASA has ever had "enough" money, especially when it comes to implementing SQA programs. In the quality attributes listed above, it is not possible to achieve all aspects of quality because of the interrelationships. SQA engineers must determine which trades are to be made based on accumulated experience as well as on specific knowledge of the current project. Some of the interrelationships between the QA criteria were stated by Gilles [2]. In order to make the most reasonable trade-off decisions, we need to understand these relationships and use experience to anticipate the impact.

In reading the remainder of this chapter, keep in mind that the lessons presented are shared not to produce a one-size-fits-all QA program, but rather to impart knowledge compiled from multiple development projects. SQA should always be tailored to meet each project's specific needs — good tailoring is essential to the success of SQA.

While SQA must be embedded into and merged with the project's other business practices, it must also fit seamlessly and appropriately with the level and criticality of the development project. Not all aspects presented here are appropriate for every project; not all projects have safety as an aspect, for example. To achieve all criteria to the level of 100% would be an "ideal" set of SQA activities on a project, but perfect projects do not happen in the real world. Furthermore, no project has sufficient time or resources even to attempt such a feat. Most projects, therefore, define the amount of SQA activity based on mission objectives, degree of overall risk, and available funding. Finding just the right balance between attributes and tradeoffs is critical to the ultimate success of all SQA programs. The obvious lesson in this case is to tailor with care. Good managers know how to factor into these decisions the relevant experiences from previous projects and missions, and to ensure that the degree of SQA to be applied is appropriate to achieve characteristics of quality, while not negatively impacting others to an unacceptable level.

12.2.3   Lesson 3: Software Quality Assurance Must Evaluate the Process as well as the Products

Historically, software quality assurance at NASA tended to focus on the final products, i.e., deliverables, such as the requirements documents, designs, code listings and test plans. A more effective approach to SQA, however, is to monitor activities continuously throughout the software development life cycle to ensure the quality of the delivered product and to avoid any "surprises" later in the schedule. This requires monitoring both the processes and the products. In process assurance, SQA provides management with objective feedback regarding compliance to approved plans, procedures, standards, and analyses. Product assurance activities focus on the changing — and, it is to be hoped increasing — level of product quality within each phase of the life cycle. The objective is to identify and eliminate defects as early as possible throughout the course of the life cycle, thereby reducing test and maintenance costs.

12.2.3.1   Process Assurance

It has been proven that the use of standards and process models has a positive impact on the quality of delivered software. Standardization of SAQ activities ensures that there is discipline and control in the software development process via independent evaluation [16]. ISO 9001 and subsequent versions provide a way to gain external accreditation for a quality management system. The application of ISO for developing software has been used by many organizations, but the complaint is that rigid adherence tends to fossilize procedures rather than encourage process improvement [8]. A range of standards and models has been developed that seek to realize the intended benefits of quality standards while recognizing the different stages of development. All NASA Centers are ISO certified including quality assurance.

The Software Engineering Institute (SEI) at Carnegie Mellon University developed one of the most common software development models. The original Capability Maturity Model (CMM) has recently evolved into Capability Maturity Model Integrated (CMMI). The fundamental premise of both the CMM and CMMI is that the quality of the software product is largely determined by the quality of the software development and maintenance processes used to build it. The CMM/CMMI is defined as a five-level framework assessing the maturity of an organization's software processes, based on specific key process areas [17].

In addition to ISO, NASA centers have adopted either the CMM or CMMI as the baseline for their software development activities. The implementation of a development model is the responsibility of the quality assurance area at the NASA Centers, including GSFC [15].

Software process improvement and capability determination (SPICE) is a major international initiative focused in Europe and Australia to develop a Standard for Software Process Assessment. This project is carried out under the auspices of the International Committee on Software Engineering Standards, ISO JTC1. The SPICE standards cover software process assessment, improvement, and capabilities [4]. Many of NASA's international partners utilize SPICE instead of CMM/CMMI, thus, the quality assurance engineers must be familiar with multiple models.

Many commercial standards are also followed in the development of software. Some of the more common ones are the US Department of Defense (DOD) issued MIL-STD-498, Software Development and Documentation; IEEE-STD1074, IEEE Standard for Developing Software Life Cycle processes; and EIA/IEEE 12207, Information Technology — Software Life Cycle Processes [16]. Many organizations, including NASA, have in the past developed their own standards for software development. Current thinking recognizes both the value and efficiency gained by adopting commercial standards rather than creating them. It is now NASA's policy to use commercial standards whenever possible; the result is to encourage more standardization not only across NASA but also within the international aerospace industry.

SQA is an ongoing process that attempts to ensure that software development is carried out according to procedures set forth by a standard or model. SQA's other role is to measure the effectiveness of the procedures on product quality.

12.2.3.2 Product Assurance

Product assurance includes activities that focus on the quality of the products with the objective of identifying and eliminating defects early in order to reduce testing and maintenance costs. Many different methods are applied to achieve these goals, such as traceability of requirements, software development folders, configuration audits, formal inspections, reviews, and testing. Software products follow a development process, and many plans are developed that define details of the processes. For each of the documents listed in the following sections, the SQA function is to ensure that procedures are followed as well as that final products are accurate.

At GSFC, the depth and breadth of coverage depends on the mission's criticality, risk and funding. SQA engineers depend on guidance and collaboration with more experienced engineers, developers, and test teams but especially on project managers to determine appropriate evaluation criteria for individual projects.

12.2.4 Lesson 4: There Must Be a Software Assurance Plan

Most project managers feel there are too many plans, and suggesting another one that specifically lays out SQA might be the proverbial straw that breaks the camel's back! The ultimate success of any undertaking is tightly coupled with knowing exactly what you are trying to achieve and how you expect to accomplish it. Therefore, a plan for software quality assurance can be critical to successful development projects. A good plan clearly specifies project goals, what is to be performed, standards against which the development work is to be measured, and all relevant procedures. In addition, the organizational structure of the quality assurance group in relation to the other parts of the project should be carefully and clearly specified. At NASA, a software assurance plan is required.

The software assurance plan serves another function. It is an agreement between the project and the quality assurance engineers stating what the scope of responsibility is in order to ensure no misunderstandings. It should start by stating which standards, guidelines, processes, and procedures the quality engineers are to use to monitor and evaluate the project. It is, furthermore, a statement by management regarding accountability: all reviews, analyses, audits, tools, techniques, and methodologies that are going to be used should be spelled out in advance.

A comprehensive software assurance plan also includes a baselined schedule (we say "baselined" since schedules change and evolve during the course of a project to reflect real-world events). A timetable of when critical milestones are planned should also be included. The document should state what the SQA expects from the project teams in order to complete their work as well as their possible needs for technical support.

The extent and nature of participation in project- and software-specific reviews, inspections, configuration management, testing, problem reporting, corrective action processes, and so on needs to be clearly specified. Since software is often developed by teams, roles and responsibilities need to be stated unambiguously, e.g., how SQA will work with IV&V, contractors, subcontractors, system safety, operations, and so forth. Finally, the project team has both the right and need to know what, when, and how SQA will deliver its products, services, reports, and findings to the project team and what the appropriate communication paths will be. A software assurance plan should spell out the steps to resolve any disagreements or conflicts that may arise in completing the defined activities.

NASA has developed many standards and guidelines over the years. However, the trend is to rely on those developed by organizations recognized as experts in the field of software engineering. An example of this is the use of IEEE Standard 730, which specifies the constituent elements of a SQA Plan [6]. The sections of the plan have been very useful at NASA in achieving the objects discussed above.

12.2.5   Lesson 5: Software Quality Assurance Must Span the Entire Software Development Life Cycle

At NASA's Goddard Space Flight Center (GSFC), SQA is carried out by an independent group of people whose function is solely to monitor the implementation of quality. In this context "independence" means not being part of the development organization, which avoids any conflicts of interest. At GSFC, responsibility for SQA is assigned to the Office of Systems Safety and Mission Assurance. In an effort to help project managers and less-experienced software quality engineers, the Assurance Management Office at GSFC recently created a list of tasks that SQA should perform at each phase of the software development life cycle [13]. Below is a partial list of activities associated with the various life cycle development phases. This information is not in any book or standard, rather it was gleaned from the experiences of countless quality assurance engineers at GSFC over 25 years of developing software applications.

12.2.5.1   Concept Phase Activities

- Attend concept reviews and facilitate tracking and resolution of issues, concerns, risks, and so on.
- Generate or assist in the identification of program and project risks, and mitigation strategies and techniques.

12.2.5.2   Requirements Phase Activities

- Review and analyze requirements for industry — acceptable and required characteristics (testability, traceability, consistency, clarity, and so on. See IEEE Standards.
- Review and provide guidance on program and project metrics including strengths, weaknesses, limitations, and so forth.

- Observe witness and participate in prototyping efforts. Provide feedback as applicable on prototyping efforts and results.

12.2.5.3 Design Phase Activities

- Attend and participate in design reviews, and track and maintain any issues or resolution tracking logs, tools, and so on.
- Observe witness and participate in prototyping efforts. Provide feedback as applicable on prototyping efforts and results.

12.2.5.4 Implementation Phase Activities

- Attend code walkthroughs and peer reviews. Participate in the tracking and resolution of any issues, and so forth.
- Review and assess code per organization's coding standards.
- Review unit test plans and procedures.
- Test Phase Activities.
- Witness, observe and assist in testing activities (integration, system acceptance, operational readiness and launch readiness).
- Attend change control and defect review board meetings and participate in the assessment of changes and defects.

12.2.5.5 Operations and Maintenance Phase Activities

- Support launch range activities in an oversight capacity.

This list represents an "ideal" set of SQA activities on a project, but projects rarely have sufficient funds or need to perform them all. For most projects, the amount of SQA to be applied is negotiated based on the purpose, degree of mission risk, and the funding level of the project. As stated previously, experience guides these decisions.

12.2.6   Lesson 6: Requirements, the Birthplace of Successful Projects

Although SQA is performed across the entire life cycle, success of a project can often be determined by the attention paid to requirements. It is generally accepted that the earlier in the life cycle potential risks are identified, the easier it is to eliminate or at least manage the conditions that introduce that risk. Problems that are not found until the testing phase are as much as 14 times more costly to fix than they would have been if they were found early in the requirements phase [2, 3]. The requirements specification document is the first tangible representation of the functional and performance capabilities to be produced, whether they are system, hardware, software, or operational requirements. The document also serves to establish the basis for all of the project's engineering management and assurance functions. If the quality of the requirements specification is poor, the project is at risk even before work begins [18]. Therefore, a specific lesson in SQA is on the importance of high quality requirements [14].

Requirements are the basis for software development, but if they are neither complete nor understandable, the final product cannot be either. Effort must be invested in the development of requirements, as well as their verification and validation. There are specific attributes that can be used as guidelines when evaluating the quality of the requirements; in addition, tools are currently available to assist in this area.

It is critical that the requirements be written in such a way that no misunderstanding between the developer and the client is possible. For successful projects, requirements must be structured, complete, and easy to implement (design and code). A set of complete requirements is both stable, that is, not subject to significant modifications, and thorough in specifying the functional expectations. Furthermore, they must be sufficiently detailed to be translatable into a design without being so specific that they force design decisions onto the developer. Requirement specifications should not contain placeholders or phrases such as to be determined (TBD), or to be added (TBA) since vagueness only leads to a disjointed architecture, low functional integrity, or completely missing system capabilities.

To increase the ease of capturing requirements, they are usually written in ordinary language (as opposed to symbolic notation such as "Z"). The result of using everyday language is a level of ambiguity due to the inherent richness of meanings, terms, and implications. In order to develop reliable software of high quality, the requirements must never contain ambiguous terms, nor should a requirement statement be interpretable as an option. Ambiguous requirements are those that may have multiple meanings; optional ones leave the choice of inclusion or omission up to the development organization. Requirements are not choices or options.

The importance of correctly documenting requirements has spurred the software industry to produce a significant number of tools that aid in the creation and management of the requirements specification documents as well as the individual statements themselves. Very few tools, however, are capable of addressing the inherent quality of either the requirements document or the individual specification statements.

The Software Assurance Technology Center (SATC) at GSFC developed a tool to parse requirement documents. The Automated Requirements Measurement (ARM)[1] software was developed to scan a file that contains the text of the requirement specification. During this scan process, it searches each line of text for specific words and phrases. SATC studies have found these search arguments (specific words and phrases) to be indicators of a document's quality, which are useful to the QA engineers [12]. The evaluation of the quality of the requirements should be one of the primary emphases of QA, assessing both the process of iteratively developing them and the final requirements themselves.

---

[1] ARM is available from the SATC homepage: http://satc.gsfc.nasa.gov.

12.2.7 Lesson 7: Software Quality Assurance ≠ Testing

All too often project managers assume they have adequate quality assurance coverage simply by planning for significant software testing. Alternatively, they might even believe that no software quality assurance activities are needed prior to a formal testing phase, but unfortunately these assumptions are incorrect. IEEE defines testing as

the process of operating a system or component under specified conditions, observing or recording the results, and making an evaluation of some aspect of the system or component. The process of analyzing a software item to detect the differences between existing and required conditions (that is, bugs) and to evaluate the features of the software items.

Simply stated, testing is way of demonstrating that the system performs according to expectations, i.e., the requirements are met. It is important to note in the IEEE definition there is no reference to quality assurance; nor should there be, since the activities and purposes are different.

From the perspective of quality assurance, the purpose of testing is to

- Assure problems are documented, corrected, and used for process improvement
- Assure problem reports are valid, accurate, and complete
- Ensure all reported problems and their associated corrective actions are implemented in accordance with customer-approved solutions
- Provide feedback to the developer and the user of problem status
- Provide data for measuring and predicting software quality and reliability

Note, the above list does not include the responsibility to identify problems. That is the job of the test team. Too often, however, there is a common misperception that the job of software quality assurance is the same as that of the tester. This is emphatically not the case. Whenever this incorrect assumption is made, others follow.

Another managerial mistake is to assume that developers test their own programs sufficiently; however, programmers are motivated to show that a program works, not that it fails. A third fallacy is the one that assumes software needs to be tested only once, i.e., at the end of the development phase. In reality, testing, which is to say defect prevention, must be done throughout the development process. Finally, there is the philosophical mistake that assumes testing should focus solely on the *product* rather than on the *process* by which the product was built. Yet we clearly know the most significant improvements in quality and productivity come from process improvements, not more rigorous product testing.

As stated in an earlier lesson learned, software quality assurance is most effective when implemented across the entire life cycle, not just at the end of the development activity. The lesson to be learned here is clear: You cannot test quality into a product; you have to build it in from the start.

12.2.8   Lesson 8: The Necessity of Metrics

Software metrics are often overlooked during the early phases of the software development life cycle and are not an activity generally associated with SQA; however, they should be! Given the broad responsibility of SAQ practitioners for assessing both the processes and products of software development, have a critical need to establish procedures for measurement. Metrics, when relevant and accurate, have proven invaluable in the evaluation of the quality.

At GSFC and throughout NASA, many SQA professionals have become cognizant of, and to differing degrees proficient in, the use of relevant metrics to aid their assurance efforts. When projects establish software metrics as a constituent part of their development processes, the SQA team needs only to validate the metrics and ensure the correct interpretation of the data. If a project, for any reason, is not routinely employing metrics in its feedback loops, the job of SQA becomes more difficult. One of the first tasks of an SQA organization, then, is to encourage and perhaps facilitate the development of an independent metrics program as a means of managerial insight into all development activities.

The US Department of Defense founded the Practical Software Measurement (PSM) program in 1996 with the intention of capturing experiences of metrics applications throughout industry and government. The purpose was to develop a generic but commonly usable metrics program. One of their first products was a set of seven principles for successful development of a metrics program. These have been adapted and applied throughout many companies, industries, and government agencies, including GSFC [1].

1. The goals and objectives of the project should drive the metrics program.
2. The software developer's process defines how the software is actually measured.
3. Collect and analyze data at a level of detail sufficient to identify and isolate the software problems.
4. Implement an independent analysis capability.
5. Use a structured analysis process to trace the measures to decisions.
6. Interpret the measurement results in the context of other program parameters.
7. Integrate software measurement into the management process throughout the entire software life cycle.

It is the responsibility of the SQA organization to be cognizant of available and relevant metrics that help evaluate and assure products. For each development phase, metrics should be chosen to help guide the developers, designers and testers, as well as to help managers become more effective. When projects use software metrics consistently as part of their development, the SQA team needs only to validate the metrics and ensure correct interpretation of the data. When a project fails to implement metrics gathering or, worse yet, utilize the metrics it gathers, the challenge rests on the SQA organization to find ways to make metrics an effective reality.

12.2.9   Lesson 9: Safety and Reliability are Critical Aspects of Software Quality Assurance

12.2.9.1 Safety

Safety is both a collective effort and everyone's responsibility. Software within NASA is a vital part of the system, and therefore has a role in system safety. Project managers, systems engineers, software leads, and engineers, both software assurance or QA, and system safety personnel must all contribute to the creation of a safe system. Safety-critical software is defined by the NASA Software Safety Standard as "software that directly, or indirectly, contributes to the occurrence of a hazardous system state, controls or monitors safety-critical functions, runs on the same system as safety-critical software or impacts systems which run safety critical software, or handles safety critical data" [11]. The goal is for quality assurance teams to ensure that software contributes to the safety and functionality of the whole system.

When a device or system could possibly lead to injury, death, or the loss of vital (and expensive) equipment, system safety is always involved at NASA. Often hardware devices are used to mitigate the hazard potential or to provide a "fail - safe" mechanism. As software becomes a more pervasive part of electromechanical systems, hardware hazard controls are being replaced, or backed up, by software controls. Software has the ability not only to detect certain types of error conditions more quickly than hardware but also to respond more intelligently, thereby avoiding a potentially hazardous state. The increased reliance on software means that the safety and reliability of the software become vital components in a safe system [11].

The system safety program plan should adequately describe interfaces within the assurance disciplines as well as the other project disciplines. It is the responsibility of the SQA organization not only to identify the safety critical software components but also to ensure the appropriate processes are correctly followed. All analyses and tasks should be complementary and supportive regardless of which group (development or assurance) has the responsibility. The analyses and tasks may be shared between the groups and, within each discipline, according to the resources and expertise of the project personnel. Coordination of teams and establishing priorities is, of course, the prerogative of management.

12.2.9.2 Reliability

IEEE defines software reliability as "the probability that software will not cause the failure of a system for a specified time under specified conditions. The probability is a function of the inputs to and use of the system, as well as a function of the existence of faults in the software" [7]. Using this definition, expectations of reliability must be based on how the system is to be used and for what length of time. At NASA, many of our satellites fly for several years —

often beyond their originally intended life spans. Thus reliability of software must support the expected lifetime plus any extensions. The condition under which software is expected to perform is dictated by the satellite's stated mission.

IEEE continues by defining software reliability management as "the process of optimizing the reliability of software through a program that emphasizes software error prevention, fault protection and removal, and the use of measurements to maximize reliability in light of project constraints such as resources, schedule and performance" [7]. This definition puts the burden of reliability not just on the testing phase, but on the entire life cycle, to ensure that errors are prevented starting in the requirements phase by determining the quality of such attributes as phrasing, completeness, and clarity. Throughout the life cycle, errors should be detected and removed using such techniques as code walkthroughs and inspections. Relevant measurements should be used at all phases to ensure the effectiveness of all assurance activities. In the testing phase, reliability can be evaluated using one of the many reliability models. These models, however, must be applied with very strict rigor to ensure accuracy.

Thus, another of SQA's responsibilities is to ensure that considerations of software reliability are continuously promoted and evaluated throughout the life cycle. At each life-cycle phase, SQA needs to monitor the processes that are being employed, thereby ensuring the greatest number of errors are detected and removed as early as possible within the life cycle. Many techniques and models are used in conjunction with reliability, and it is the responsibility of the SQA organization to ensure that they are applied correctly.

Just as you cannot test quality into a product, neither can you do so with reliability. You must build it in from the start. Reliability also impacts safety, and a system cannot be deemed safe if it is not also reliable. NASA is working with reliability experts to determine how these concepts can be appropriately adapted and applied in a cost-effective manner on our space missions.

12.2.10   Lesson 10: Independent Verification and Validation (IV&V) is an Important Tool within SQA

Independent verification and validation (IV&V) is defined by three components: it must be independent technically, managerially, and financially from both the development organization and the project's chain of command. IV&V must prioritize its own efforts, identifying where to focus its activities. It must have access to and a means of reporting information to the program management, and the budget for these efforts must be allocated and controlled by the program. Control must remain independent of the development organization to avoid limiting its effectiveness and to eliminate any conflicts of interest.

Verification is the process of determining whether or not the products of a given phase of the software development cycle fulfill conditions that were set by the previous phase. Other considerations include whether or not a product is internally complete, consistent, and correct enough to support the next phase. Validation is the process of evaluating software throughout its development process to ensure compliance with agreed-upon software requirements. When asked "Are we building the product right?" we are talking about verification; whereas the question "Are we building the right product?" is really addressing validation.

At NASA, software IV&V is defined as a systems engineering process employing rigorous methodologies for evaluating the correctness and quality of the software product throughout the software life cycle. Without SQA, IV&V is expensive and somewhat less effective. Where SQA is a broad "blanket" across the project and oversees all ongoing process and product activities, IV&V focuses on only those processes and products determined to have the highest risk. Therefore, IV&V teams should conduct in-depth evaluations of very specific and select areas. IV&V is not required on all projects. Rather, it is another tool to be utilized when appropriate — one that can provide a high value added when used properly [13].

12.2.11   Lesson 11: Hardware ≠ Software!

The influence of hardware quality assurance is evident in the community of SQA practitioners. Not only do hardware-intensive systems and hardware-related concerns predominate, but also hardware-based thinking and assumptions. Two such hardware mindsets relate to time and operating conditions. Software, however, is built with different constraints and considerations. NASA has grappled with these differences and the best approach for managing them while implementing very similar versions of hardware and software quality assurance. At GSFC as well as other NASA centers, these two activities reside in one department, which allows the two groups to work together in a more integrated fashion.

The major difference between hardware and software quality assurance has to do with the differences in their fundamental natures and the way in which each manifests failure. Experience shows that hardware generally fails from manufacturing defects, from poor quality of materials or fabrication, overload, physical deterioration and wearing out, fatigue, or burn out.

Software, unlike hardware, does not wear out. Generally, it fails because of unrecognized design problems, lack of testing, or changes in the operating environment. Software presents different behavior with respect to fault and error identification rates. In this case, the error rate is at its highest level at integration and test. As testing progresses, errors are identified and removed. Detection and removal continues at a slower rate during its operational use. The total number of latent system errors continually decreases. This representation assumes, however, that no new errors are introduced while attempting to fix others.

Even though software has no moving parts and does not physically wear out as does hardware, it does outlive its usefulness and becomes obsolete [2]. What is clear is that the hardware approach to reliability must be different from the approach needed for software reliability.

NASA has learned that quality assurance engineers for hardware should not perform SQA. The tools, techniques, focus and knowledge required are very different. Unfortunately, it is often assumed that the disciplines are interchangeable. This results in poor, if any, SQA. GSFC employs both software and hardware assurance engineers who work together on missions and projects for their success.

12.2.12   Lesson 12: Risk Management is NOT Optional

Risk is a daily reality on all projects, and continuous risk management should become just as routine. It should be ongoing and comfortable, and neither imposed nor forgotten. Like any good habit, it should fit seamlessly into the daily work. NASA worked with the US Navy and the Software Engineering Institute at Carnegie Mellon University to develop a process-based risk management course for government use. NASA then incorporated specific aspects into its aerospace projects.

During the course taught at NASA, various tools and methods are demonstrated that work for any project. The key is to adhere to the principles, perform the functions, and adapt the practice to fit the project's needs. As with so many other practices, continuous risk management is not a "one size fits all" solution, and NASA projects are encouraged to tailor the risk management in order to maximize effectiveness. By tailoring, organizations adapt the processes and select the methods and tools that best fit their project management practice and their organizational culture based on experiences with previous projects.

Software risk management is important because it helps avoid disasters, rework, and overkill, but, more important, because it stimulates win - win situations. The objectives of software risk management are to identify, address, and eliminate software risk items *before* they become threats to success or major sources of rework. At NASA, good project managers are of necessity good managers of risk.

There are a number of definitions and uses for the term risk. In fact, no single definition is universally accepted. However, what all definitions have in common is agreement that risk has two characteristics: *uncertainty*: an event may or may not happen; *loss*: an event has unwanted consequences or losses. Therefore, risk involves the likelihood that an undesirable event will occur, and the severity of the consequences of the event, should it occur.

At NASA, we focus on continuous risk management that can be applied to any development process: hardware, software, systems, and so on [13]. It provides a disciplined environment for proactive decision making to:

- Assess continually what could go wrong (risks)
- Determine which risks are important
- Implement strategies to deal with those risks
- Assure and measure the effectiveness of the implemented strategies

Risk management procedures must not be allowed to become "shelfware". To be effective, processes must become part of regularly scheduled product management. It requires identifying and managing risks routinely throughout all phases of the project's life. The result is a cost-effective implementation within the project [13].

12.3   Conclusion

SQA is faced with many challenges, starting with a definition of quality for software. There needs to be a common understanding as to what high quality software really is. The final definition is most usually influenced by the environment of the software usage. There are many aspects of SQA, from those within the phases of the software development life cycle to those that span multiple phases, i.e., safety, reliability, and IV&V. SQA must pay special attention to the beginning of a project — the requirements phase — and ensure that SQA does not become a synonym for testing. They are not the same things. Metrics should be a key tool for quality assurance engineers with which to evaluate the quality of the products. Finally, risk management is required on all projects; however, it is not the responsibility of SQA to manage the risks. Rather, SQA must ensure that everyone on the project is identifying and managing them. At NASA, SQA is applied to all projects at levels deemed appropriate and cost effective based on experience from previous missions and projects.

References

1. Department of Defense (2001) Practical software and systems management V 4.2, http://www.psmsc.com/ (accessed 21st April, 2003)
2. Gillies A.C. (1997) Software quality, theory and management. International Thomson computer press, London, UK
3. Hammer T., Huffman L., Rosenberg L. (1999) Doing requirements right the first time. Cross Talk, 12: 20-25
4. International Committee on Software Engineering Standards (SPICE) (1992) Software process assessment. JTC 1/SC7, http://www.sqi.gu.edu.au/spice/suite/ (accessed 21st April, 2003)
5. IEEE Std 610.12-1990 (1990) Glossary of software engineering terminology. Institute of Electrical and Electronics Engineers
6. IEEE Std 730 (1998) Standard for software quality assurance plans. Institute of Electrical and Electronics Engineers
7. IEEE Std 982.2-1988 (1988) Guide for the use of standard dictionary of measures to produce reliable software. Institute of Electrical and Electronics Engineers
8. ISO 9003-3-1991 (1991) Quality management and quality assurance standards - Part 3: Guidelines for the application of ISO 9001 to the development, supply and maintenance of software. International standards organization, www.iso.ch (accessed 21st April, 2003)

9. Kitchenham B., Pfleeger S.L. (1996) Software quality: the elusive target. IEEE Software 13: 12-21
10. NASA-STD 7120.5, Program and project management processes and requirements, NASA
11. NASA-STD-8719.13A (2001) NASA software safety standard. NASA
12. Rosenberg L., Gallo A., McCoy J. (2001) Generating high quality requirements. AIAA Aerospace conference, San Jose, CA
13. Rosenberg L., Gallo A. (2002) Software quality assurance at NASA. In: Proceedings of IEEE Aerospace conference, Big Sky, Montana
14. Rosenberg L., Hyatt L. (1996) Developing a successful metrics program. In: CD-ROM Proceedings of the 8th annual software technology conference, Salt Lake city, Utah, http://satc.gsfc.nasa.gov/support/ICSE_NOV97/iasted.htm (accessed 21st April, 2003)
15. Rosenberg L., Godfrey S. (2002) Implementing CMMI at NASA's Goddard space flight center. In: Proceedings of the software engineering process conference, Denver, CO, USA
16. Schulmeyer G.G., McManus J.I. (1998) Handbook of software quality assurance. Prentice Hall PRT, NJ, USA
17. Software Engineering Institute (SEI) (1991) Capability maturity model. Carnegie Mellon University, USA
18. Wilson W., Rosenberg L., Hyatt L. (1996) Automated quality analysis of natural language requirement specifications. In Proceedings of 14th annual Pacific Northwest software quality conference, Portland, Oregon, USA, pp. 140-151

Author Biography

Dr. Linda H. Rosenberg serves as the Chief Scientist for Software Assurance for Goddard Space Flight Center, NASA in the Office of Systems Safety and Mission Assurance Directorate and is the former division chief of the Software Assurance Technology Office. Dr. Rosenberg is a recognized international expert in the areas of assurance, metrics, requirements, and reliability and serves on IEEE program committees in these areas. She has presented papers/tutorials and chaired sessions at many international conferences and also serves as a reviewer. Dr. Rosenberg is an adjunct professor at University of Maryland, Baltimore in the Masters/Doctoral Program. Dr. Rosenberg holds a Ph.D. in computer science, an M.E.S. in computer science, and a B.S. in mathematics.

13 Making Software Engineering Competence Development Sustained through Systematic Experience Management

Klaus-Dieter Althoff and Dietmar Pfahl

Abstract: Applying systematic experience management to innovative e-learning approaches provides means for more efficient and effective competence development of software professionals – on-the-job, on-demand, and geographically distributed. Adequately packaged experience provides the starting point for the preparation and design of learning resources and for efficient reuse. Systematic evaluation during usage helps improve the quality of learning resources and identify best practice use cases, which then can be exploited to proactively offer best-matching learning resources in a given learning setting. By improving e-learning through integrated experience management, eventually qualification programs for the software workforce will develop longer lasting effects and thus will be considered more sustained by the responsible management levels. Inspired by an innovative system for collaborative learning in software organizations (CORONET) in this chapter, we extend a state-of-the-art experience factory scenario for learning software organizations suggesting the so-called "3P integration" concept. This integration concept considers for context modeling not only processes and projects (2P integration), but also the involved persons. This chapter is directed at software practitioners who are interested in innovative e-learning and experience management approaches, and researchers who aim at integrating the potentialities of both fields.

Keywords: CORONET, DISER, E-Learning, Experience factory, Experience management, Knowledge management

13.1 Introduction and Background

Success of software development projects largely depends on the quality of the workforce. Therefore, competence development of the people involved is a crucial issue for any software organization. Systematic competence development can be supported by knowledge management (KM) and e-learning (EL). During the last decade, both KM and EL have experienced many innovations (Sects. 13.1.1 and 13.1.2) but are still largely unconnected.

In this chapter, we propose the integration of collaborative EL with KM based on concepts of the well-known experience factory (EF) approach [11]. The starting point for our proposal is a recently developed, working example of an innovative EL system for collaborative learning in software organizations, CORONET, that integrates KM elements (Sect. 13.2). The CORONET system provides functionality for knowledge sharing, on-the-fly creation of new learning resources during learning sessions, and the creation of learning networks [26] that establish sustained interpersonal relationships and thus interconnect individual learning with group learning. Although CORONET supports all elements of the knowledge creation and delivery cycle [44], i.e., knowledge identification, evaluation, storage, structuring, and dissemination, CORONET is still too limited. In particular, there is no systematic methodological guidance of learners and knowledge providers on how to perform experience learning. In other words, there is a high risk that software competence development, which in CORONET is mainly based upon the establishment of long-lasting interpersonal relationships, is not yet as effective as it could be if experience management (EM) methods and tools were integrated. In Sect. 13.3, we present proven effective and efficient EM concepts that, when integrated with the CORONET system, will make competence development more sustained. That is, EL systems like CORONET will create a longer lasting impact of learning by systematically evaluating the effectiveness of learning resources in various contexts, and by proactively offering efficient guidance on how to provide and how to select best-matching learning materials. Taking the EF framework as a starting point, we illustrate how innovative EL that yet partly integrates KM methods and tools can be further enhanced through extended EM (Sect. 13.4). This is exemplified in the vision of the 3P integration approach for software process learning, an important scenario for systematic software process improvement (SPI). Traditionally, EM-based software process learning within an EF organization is characterized by packaging and reusing knowledge and experience about *process* and *project* information (2P integration). By adding a third dimension, the *people* dimension, software process learning becomes more flexible because of personalization, and eventually proactive provision of needed learning resources to individual software engineers in specific learning situations.

The following sections are directed towards both software practitioners who are interested in innovative EL and EM approaches, and researchers who desire to integrate the potential of both fields. Sections 13.2 and 13.3 present recent developments and proven concepts in EL and EM, while Sect. 13.4 presents the vision of integrating state-of-the-art approaches in EL and EM. Finally, Sect. 13.5 concludes with a discussion of the value of the proposed integration for KM research in general.

13.1.1   The State-of-the-Art in Experience Management

EM is becoming an increasingly important subdomain of KM. It defines and develops methods for structuring and handling experience of experts on a particular subject. Software engineering is a highly dynamic field in terms of research and knowledge, and it depends heavily upon the experience of experts for the development and advancement of its methods, tools, and techniques. For example, the tendency to define and describe "best practices" or "lessons learned" is quite distinctive in the literature [2] (Chap. 12 by Rosenberg in this book for typical representations of lessons learned [48]). As a consequence, in the software engineering field the EF was introduced that was explicitly responsible to systematically deal with experience. An EF is a logical or physical infrastructure for continuous learning from experience and includes an experience base (EB) for the storage and reuse of knowledge. The EF approach was invented in the mid 1980s [10]. As practice shows, it is substantial for the support of organizational learning that the project organization and the learning organization are separated [11].

The initial example of an operating EF was the NASA Software Engineering Laboratory (SEL) [46]. EF applications have been developed in the USA and in Europe [4, 56]. The large number of successful EF applications gave rise to study learning software organizations, in order to improve the methodology of building and running an EF [49]. This also includes the definition of related processes, roles, and responsibilities and, last but not least, the technical realization. The most detailed methodology for the build-up of an EF/EB on project knowledge also for the presentation of the according processes is given in [56].

EF is increasingly emerging towards a generic approach for EM as an organizational structure for reuse of knowledge and especially experience. This also includes applications that are independent from the software engineering domain. Examples of this include supporting the continuous improvement process in hospitals [5], the field of help-desk and service support [55], and the management of "non-software" projects [15]. Future trends in the scope of EF include detailing of all necessary policies, validation, and empirical evaluation [13, 56], gaining experience with the technical realization of huge EFs [45], integration with the according business processes [6], and the operation of EFs [41].

In the areas of cognitive science and artificial intelligence, case-based reasoning (CBR) emerged in the late 1970s and early 1980s as a model for human problem solving and learning [50, 51]. In artificial intelligence, this led to a focus of knowledge-based systems on experience (experience knowledge, case-specific knowledge) in the late 1980s and early 1990s, mostly in the form of problem-solution cases [9]. For the last several years there has been a strong tendency in the CBR community [3] to develop methods for dealing with more complex applications. One example is the use of CBR for KM [1], another is its use for software engineering (Chap. 9 by Shepperd in this book [52]). A very important issue here is the integration of CBR with EFs: Since the mid 1990s CBR has been used both on the organizational EF process level and the technical EB implementation level [7, 35, 57]. This approach has become more and more established [3, 14, 36].

In the 1980s and 1990s, various approaches in economic and social sciences as well as in business information systems, which explicitly dealt with knowledge as a resource of increasing importance, merged under the notion of KM [39, 47]. In spite of the high number of approaches and their heterogeneity, two main categories can be identified. On one hand, there are process-oriented approaches, which are based mainly on communication and collaboration; on the other hand product-oriented approaches, which are based on documentation, storage, and reuse of enterprise knowledge. While the former use techniques from computer supported collaborative work and workflow management, the latter build on information technology tools for documenting knowledge. These include database systems, repository systems, hypertext systems, document management systems, process modeling systems, knowledge-based systems, case-based reasoning systems, and so on [55]. From a more general perspective, it can be stated that product- and process-oriented approaches are still not integrated. Usually they are used independently from each other, or as alternatives. As a first step forward, deep integration (that is one that has foundation in cognitive sciences) of EF and CBR approaches has been achieved [3, 56].

13.1.2   State-of-the-Art in E-Learning

Computer-supported learning and teaching can be traced back to the theory of behaviorism initiated by Thorndike, and its first practical implementation in the form of so-called "programmed instruction" in the early 1950s [54]. Derived from this original work and its extensions, e.g., the inclusion of decisions, and thus the possibility of multiple paths instead of simple "linear programs" [19], computer aided instruction (CAI) emerged in the 1970s. Important for the success of CAI was the ability to separate learning methods (practice and examination, tutoring, simulation, etc.) from the subject matter contents. This separation allowed for transferring similar learning methods to various contents. The modular structure of CAI systems, consisting of a presentation module and separate modules for learner response analysis, learning method, and data administration, facilitated the flexible combination of these modules into so-called computer based training (CBT) systems. Not advantageous, however, was the strict hierarchical structuring of learning units and the limitations this implies on the workflow of a learner. Most current CBT systems still rely on the old concepts and thus can only be successfully applied when restricted knowledge about subject matter facts and methods is to be trained.

Traditional CBT systems have neither an "understanding" of the contents to be delivered to the learners, nor do they have information about the varying levels of knowledge and training progress of the learners. The first reaction to these limitations was the attempt in the early 1980s to rely on artificial intelligence approaches. This led to the concepts of intelligent computer aided instruction (ICAI) and intelligent tutoring systems [17, 53]. The main achievement of ICAI consisted in adding an expert module to the training system, which derives correct solutions to given problems and compares them to the answers supplied by the learner. The results of these comparisons are stored in a learner model and are analyzed in order to derive the individual behavior and knowledge accumulation of the learners. Based on these data, individually customized learning strategies can be selected for each learner.

Modern concepts for organizing and representing complex knowledge for the purpose of learning and training have their origins in the 1970s when the first hypertext media were developed. The hypertext idea is based in work done during the early 1940s when information units ("cards") were assembled into "knowledge maps" [16]. Well-known computer-based systems were NoteCards [25] or Hypercard [21]. A card can be accessed through its name or a link in another card. The hypertext approach strictly distinguishes between structure and content: a hypertext machine administers the cards and their relationships, and a database administers the contents of the cards. Unfortunately, the development of "hypermedia networks" turned out to be difficult consuming and for a long time no adequate authoring systems were available. On the other hand, the usage of established hypertext systems was quite successful and became very quickly supported by browsers that provide search and presentation functionality for hypertext information. By adding audio and video functionality hypertext systems were quickly enhanced to hypermedia systems. Today, hypertext and hypermedia form the basis of the World Wide Web (WWW), which provides a common platform for practically all modern e-learning systems.

The possibilities of the new hypermedia (virtual) learning spaces offer new opportunities for learning. Learning can happen at any time and at any place, synchronously and asynchronously, in a self-learning mode or in cooperation and collaboration with peers, in a self-driven (constructive) mode, or guided by tutors and predefined curricula. These new possibilities are of particular importance for the concept of lifelong learning, where the border between private and professional competence and skill development becomes fuzzy.

The new technologies that facilitate and support lifelong learning threaten the traditional distinction between producers of learning contents and consumers of learning contents. In the knowledge-sharing information society every learner can evolve from an information consumer to an information producer, by producing new information offers that others can consume. E-commerce is one of the new business areas where this idea has been most fruitful. In addition, the new educational systems — either public or private — will be deeply affected by the overlapping of production and consumption of learning contents. The traditional roles of learners and teachers will eventually disappear [23]. For industrial organizations this translates into the following vision of professional lifelong learning:

1. Everybody is a knowledge worker, i.e., everybody consumes and produces knowledge.
2. The various learning processes of knowledge workers — both self-directed or guided by others — are deeply supported by constantly evolving knowledge networks.
3. For individual knowledge workers it becomes less important to privately "store" professional subject matter-related knowledge. The possibility to access repositories of learning resources (people and content — from simple files to sophisticated, adaptive courseware) makes this obsolete.
4. The emergence of so-called communities of practice [58] will become crucial because they guarantee that new knowledge is transformed into content and that existing knowledge (and associated contents) is continuously updated according to the needs of professional life [4].

In order to adequately support content producers, state-of-the-art EL systems must offer functionality that supports selection, structuring, adaptation, personalization, and improvement of learning contents. In particular, this requires the ability to give detailed and adequate description of contents with metadata, modularization of contents, and generation of content variants with various instructional strategies. It also includes development of (self-)tests for learners, provision of feedback from the learners to the content providers, for instance, in the form of annotations, and provision of complex semantic structures that help to reuse and (semi-)automatically integrate existing content modules into larger content structures such as learning courses.

In order to adequately support content consumers (i.e., learners), a state-of-the-art EL system needs to provide powerful communication and personalization tools. In particular, this includes functionality that facilitates synchronous (chats) and asynchronous (discussion forums) interaction among learners and between learners and teachers. In addition, it includes functionality for annotating and linking learning resources in private or public workspaces.

All in all, it has become clear during the last years that modularization, annotation, information retrieval, and the combination of synchronous and asynchronous communication require the extensive application of KM techniques and methods to EL systems [20]. In particular, automatic and semiautomatic retrieval of information for problem solving, and the proactive offering of learning contents for preparation for new tasks can be addressed with innovative techniques and methods stemming from EM research. In the next section, we present a recent research prototype, the CORONET system [8, 43], which offers many KM features that a state-of-the-art EL system should possess.

13.2   Towards Integrating E-Learning and Knowledge Management

The essence of the e-learning system CORONET is its focus on collaborative methods that aim to improve the competence development of software engineers and managers. The CORONET system promotes and supports the development of sustained interpersonal relationships in combination with comprehensive functionality for creating, accessing, annotating, extending, and exploiting knowledge assets, sharing knowledge for use and reuse, and learning from others and with others. In this way, CORONET helps to establish learning networks in which people of equal and different competence levels practice both individual and group learning, experience-based learning, learning with multiple activities and resources, and knowledge sharing.

13.2.1   The E-Learning Methodology CORONET-Train

Collaborative learning is generally characterized by the goal of augmenting and optimizing the shared knowledge of a group or community, but it is also meant to support individual knowledge development. This is reached by cooperatively working on a project, negotiating on the learning goals and problem definitions, and collectively constructing knowledge in the group. To realize collaborative learning processes, a learning community has to be established. Learning communities are characterized by four factors: an individual and collective learning process, experienced-based learning, learning with multiple activities and resources in the group, and sharing of knowledge. A learning culture is practiced that is focused on the active participation of every group member. In this context, the group members are not all learning the same contents at the same time; rather, they are developing their knowledge and skills according to their own needs and interests, but in a way that the whole group can profit from afterwards. So, different learning interests and the development of different kinds of expertise are accepted and actively supported.

CORONET-Train offers three classes of methods, each method consisting of a set of processes and activities:

1. Learning methods: Five methods (case-based learning, theme-based learning, Web-based training, Web-based tutoring, and knowledge sharing) define learning processes[1] and activities that are adequately tailored to specific learning situations and learning needs of software engineers.
2. Knowledge transfer methods: Three methods (training, tutoring, mentoring) define processes and activities that subject matter experts can apply in order to disseminate their know-how and help software engineers satisfy their learning needs.
3. Knowledge engineering methods: Four methods (authoring, structuring, administration, management) define processes and activities that are needed to develop, structure, and maintain learning resources, to setup and maintain the software infrastructure, to administer the users of the infrastructure, and to introduce and manage the learning environment.

A learning scenario is an implementation of one or more CORONET-Train methods or parts of them (i.e., processes and their activities). In a learning scenario, processes and activities are adapted to a particular learning situation and supporting software infrastructure. The purpose of learning scenarios is to organize and maintain relationships among individuals involved in a learning situation by defining the sequence of tasks and their associated actions, which have to be performed in order to reach a learning objective.

---

[1] In CORONET-Train, the term "learning process" defines a sequence of learning activities. This differs from the usage of the term "learning process" in educational science, where it refers to the internal processing of information by a learner.

13.2.2   The E-Learning Infrastructure WBT-Master

The platform WBT-Master provides CORONET users with the adequate functionality needed to perform selected learning scenarios, including:

1. E-learning (EL) functionality: learning courses; learning goals; structured discussion forums; virtual classrooms; brainstorming sessions; mentoring sessions; progress tracking, testing and certification.
2. Knowledge management (KM) functionality: knowledge cards; knowledge domains; personal desktop; content taxonomies.

Conventional Web-based training (WBT) systems utilize HTML documents as learning resources. Ordinary Internet hyperlinks (references) are used to create such navigable data structures as courses, chapters, books, and so on. Typically, various WBT tools such as annotations, e-mail, discussion forums, and personal bookmarks are used to add additional value to the basic documents published on the WWW. WBT-Master considerably extends this state-of-the-practice technology [29] in the following way.

1. In addition to existing data structures based on hypermedia links, it introduces composite learning resources such as learning units, learning goals, knowledge cards, mentoring sessions, knowledge domains and more.
2. WBT-Master enables synchronous and asynchronous communication and collaboration between distributed teams and team members. This includes discussion forums, brainstorming sessions, chats, annotation facilities, and so forth.
3. In addition to especially prepared training materials, anything that is part of the stored organizational knowledge, such as technical documents, presentations, or the experience of employees, can be used as learning resources via the Internet or intranet. The system essentially supports the involvement of human subject matter experts as learning resources.
4. Since all information services operate with unified data structures, results of any collaboration (discussion sessions, brainstorming sessions, annotations, question - answer dialogues, etc.) can be seen as new training material and can be reused by others.

13.2.2.1   Collaborative Learning with WBT-Master

By using WBT-Master, knowledge workers (learners) in a software organization can perform a broad range of collaborative learning scenarios as described by the methodology CORONET-Train.

1. Web-based training: An experienced knowledge worker acting as a trainer conducts training sessions on a regular basis. In collaboration with a courseware author the trainer develops a learning course related to a specific subject matter and makes an announcement on the WBT-Master server [24].

Potential learners may access the announcement board and subscribe to a particular training session.

2. Web-based tutoring: This scenario is similar to the Web-based training scenario. The principal difference is that after having analyzed the subject matter, the tutor or trainer does not trigger the development of courseware, but instead collects a number of heterogeneous documents (text files, slide presentations, simulations, etc.), which can be used for the training session. The tutor uploads the documents to the WBT-Master server and defines a special training schedule recommending which document should be accessed at each particular stage of the training session, and what actions are expected from a learner working with the document.

3. Web-based mentoring: The starting point of this scenario is that knowledge workers (individual learners or a group of learners) need to solve a particular problem. The learners have a stable partnership with an experienced knowledge worker who can act as a mentor. The mentor is supposed to help the learners acquire new knowledge in the related subject matter area. The mentor can access the server to initiate a special one-to-many synchronous communicational session (a so-called mentoring session) with interested learners [30]. The mentor explains the problem solution by guiding the mentoring session. The mentor may select a document which is automatically visualized on the learners' screens, provide an explanation (audio or video) attached to the document, or request the learners to perform an action that may be monitored from the mentor's screen. Similarly, the learners may provide comments on the shared document or ask questions related to it.

4. Web-based knowledge mining: Knowledge workers need learning material on a particular subject matter to acquire additional knowledge. They are aware of a knowledge network supported by the WBT-Master server, containing relevant information about documents or subject matter experts. The information is structured by means of knowledge cards, which can be used by the knowledge workers to find relevant learning resources, work through relevant materials, and communicate with experts and with others working on similar materials.

5. Web-based knowledge delivery: Knowledge workers need to acquire knowledge on a particular subject matter in a long-term perspective. They are aware of a WBT-Master server that contains relevant information and is periodically updated by the subject matter experts. The knowledge workers access the server to configure their personal profiles in such a way that relevant learning resources are automatically delivered to their personal desktops and they are automatically notified about new learning resources. Communication with subject matter experts and peers working on similar learning resources is possible via the desktop.

6. Web-based collaborative problem solving: A number of knowledge workers need to solve a particular problem. They are aware that the WBT-Master server can facilitate a so-called "brainstorming session". A moderator is selected to initiate and organize the brainstorming session to elaborate a solution to the problem. Other knowledge workers that join later can catch up with the problem solving process asynchronously from the recorded session.

7. Web-based gathering and integration of personal knowledge: An experienced knowledge worker needs to gather know-how and experience from other experts on a particular topic (e.g., a specific software process), and would like to present this knowledge in the form of a training resource. Typical examples of this application are collaborative document writing or cooperative courseware authoring [22, 34]. The expert group selects a moderator and discusses the topic via a structured discussion forum, and works cooperatively to develop relevant documents through shared folders. The subject matter experts write contributions, attach documents from their local drives, or provide references to relevant documents available from the Internet. Finally, the structured discussion (or selected components of it) is converted into a homogeneous HTML document or a new learning unit.

8. Web-based virtual classroom: A virtual classroom is used for highly interactive and intense training courses in which a trainer/tutor wants to retain the human element of interaction while relying upon an IT infrastructure. The Virtual Classroom can be seen as a working place for the trainers/tutors in which they prepare training sessions for a group of trainees. For each training session, a trainer/tutor creates a new classroom library by selecting the necessary learning resources and moves them to the trainees' computers. Trainers/tutors can also describe the learning paths to be followed by the trainees in setting up a classroom curriculum.

13.2.2.2   Knowledge Management with WBT-Master

The corporate memory, or experience base (EB), of a software organization may be seen as a combination of resources and operations applicable to such resources. The operations allow users to access and create new resources, or to add an additional value to existing resources. The WBT-Master platform works with the corporate memory by offering the possibility to access and process huge collections of documents, portals, on-the-fly material (i.e., annotations to documents, contributions to discussions, question - answer dialogues, and so on) and personal knowledge of individuals in the organization. The resources of the corporate memory can be seen as basic learning resources. Basic learning resources may be organized into composite structures that serve to accomplish a particular learning or problem-solving task. Learning resources combined into a composite structure may be seen as a new learning resource. In other words, learning resources may always be reused by a member wise inclusion of these resources into other ones.

WBT-Master Content Structuring Paradigms
WBT-Master supports a hierarchy of content structuring paradigms, and is based on sound principles of multilevel data modeling [28]. The overall content structuring model is defined as three levels of content abstraction:

1. Basic elements or indivisible chunks of multimedia information (documents, portals, questionnaires): Basic elements can be seen as actual pieces of

information presented in internationally recognized data-encoding formats. For example, basic elements can be HTML documents, WinWord or PDF files, PowerPoint presentations, plain GIF images, and so on. No interdocument relationship is supposed to be defined on this level.

2. Logical composites (learning units, learning goals, discussion threads): Logical composites combine a collection of basic elements and other logical composites into a navigable structure. It can be primitively seen as a collection of hypermedia links that are separated from a document content and combined as a new entity called a logical composite. It should be noted that such composites deal with interdocument relationships and cannot affect a document content.

3. Semantic composites (i.e., Knowledge Cards, Knowledge Domains, Content Taxonomies): Semantic Composites provide a semantic structuring of server content as such. For example, any basic element and logical composite can be attached to special knowledge cards. In this case, materials get a special meaning defined by the card and can be inferred as so-called best-match training resources for users interested in this or another related topic [32]. Similarly, basic elements and logical composites may be put into a number of content taxonomy folders and accessed by browsing the semantic net [33].

Document Repositories
Alternatively to logical and semantic content structures supported by WBT-Master all basic elements and logical composites are stored as files into so-called physical repositories on the server. A particular repository is created by the server file management system as a directory possibly containing files and other subdirectories. While WBT-Master logical and semantic composites may be accessed only by means of the system tools, the WBT-Master repository may be accessed as ordinary directories by means of content management tools (say, for example, by means of a file browser locally or by means of an FTP client remotely).

WBT-Master supports five types of repositories: shared files (public level), group resources (restricted to defined groups of knowledge workers), on-the-fly material (group level), personal files, and personal bookmarks.

Knowledge Cards
Knowledge cards offer a simple but practical way of accessing preferred learning resources. A knowledge card is the description of a specific concept. For example, a semantic entity "requirements inspection" may be seen as a knowledge card. knowledge cards may be combined into a semantic network using just one type of relationship: "is a part of" (the inverse relationship may be called "consists of"). For example, the knowledge card "perspective based reading" (PBR) [12] may be related as "is a part of" to the knowledge card "requirements inspection".

The semantic relationships essentially define a graph structure (as opposed to just a hierarchy). For example, the same knowledge card "PBR" may be defined as a part of "quality assurance", "verification techniques", etc. Moreover, there may be knowledge cards defining areas of personal interest, say "expertise of Mr./Ms. XY" which may also refer to the previously mentioned card PBR etc.

Each knowledge card may provide access to a number of associated learning resources. For example, a learning course "PBR techniques" may be associated with the knowledge card "PBR", other learning units, learning goals, discussion forums, documents, etc. may be associated with the same knowledge card. Moreover, WBT-Master considers other users ("peer helpers") to be learning resources. Thus, people may be associated with a knowledge card, too.

Whenever content providers contribute to the server with new materials, they are supposed to associate them with one or more knowledge cards or create a new knowledge card and place it into a proper position within the semantic network. This could also be done by a specially designated role, i.e., the knowledge engineer.

The semantic net defined by the set of knowledge cards offers the possibility to infer learning resources using semantic relationships. Whenever a user accesses a knowledge card, the system infers all learning resources that are associated with this particular knowledge card and with knowledge cards related to it. The advantage is that knowledge workers are not supposed to browse through countless learning resources but can simply browse the semantic net consisting of previously defined knowledge cards.

Knowledge Domains

The main purpose of knowledge domains is to create and maintain well-structured repositories. The knowledge domain concept allows for imposing different types of data structures on top of existing collections of learning resources, or — seen from another point of view — for reusing learning resources in different contexts [31].

A knowledge domain can be defined as a set of documents belonging to a number of predefined semantic categories, where each semantic category is linked to a set of learning resources that are instances of the category. The definition of a semantic category includes the definition of a number of attributes, which are properties of instances of the semantic category. An attribute is a standard key-value pair. A value of an attribute is defined to be of a specified type, i.e., a value may be a string, a number, or a selection from a list of possible values. For example, the category "author" may have two associated attributes: name (string) and e-mail address (string). Similarly, the category "module" may have just one associated attribute — programming language (selection from a list of languages).

The knowledge domain schema defines common properties of all the category instances. Any resource may be inserted (stored) into a particular knowledge domain as an instance of a predefined category. For example, if a new instance of the category "module" is created, the system automatically requests to select a programming language (attribute predefined for the category), and to provide references to the module author and a particular project (relationships predefined for the category).

13.2.3 Open Issues with CORONET

As we have shown above, the EL system CORONET supports to a certain extent all elements of the knowledge creation and delivery cycle, from knowledge identification via knowledge structuring to knowledge dissemination. However, as evaluations have demonstrated [43], there is not sufficiently effective guidance of learners and knowledge providers for efficient reuse of existing learning resources, and in particular for capitalizing upon experience from using learning resources in various contexts, i.e., experience learning. In the next section, we present proven innovative EM methods and tools that, if integrated with EL systems such as CORONET, will make software competence development more sustained by creating a longer lasting impact of Web-based training at the workplace and (collaborative) learning on the job.

13.3   Recent Innovations in Experience Management

Several methodologies have been introduced that can be used for developing experience management (EM) applications [14, 56], also called experience based information systems (EBIS). The most detailed methodology for the build-up and operation of EBIS is design and implementation of software engineering repositories DISER . It consists of the following nine main steps (Fig 13.1):

1. Developing a vision for the EBIS
2. Setting goals
3. Setting subject areas
4. Defining usage and filling scenarios
5. Modeling the experience ontology
6. Implementing the EBIS
7. Going online with the EBIS
8. Maintaining the EBIS
9. Integrating existing and generating new knowledge

DISER usually starts with developing a vision for the EBIS. This means going through all the following eight steps on a rather abstract level. Such a vision explicates in particular, where the experience transfer can be supported by the EBIS. Based on the vision, concrete goals are defined that are to be achieved. This occurs with consideration of the interests of the stakeholders. With each of these goals appropriate success criteria are associated that allow a measurement of the progress concerning the goals. By vision and goals, in the next step, relevant topics, which can contribute to achieving the objectives, are identified and selected. As soon as objectives and relevant topics are known, the acquisition and use of experience can be described by scenarios. Through the scenarios, the need for information is captured in more detail. This allows for the development of a representation pattern for experience (ontology), which is usually implemented based on a rapid application development approach. Based on the prototype system the continuous operation of the EBIS is prepared, including business process integration, evaluation, and maintenance, as well as the integration of available knowledge. DISER includes the creation of a top-down rationale for the implementation (pattern and knowledge acquisition plan). This rationale contributes to the understandability of the EBIS by ensuring tractability from the components of the ontology and its related knowledge acquisition plan over scenarios and relevant topics to the objectives of the EBIS.

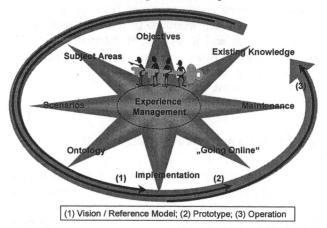

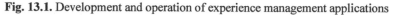

Fig. 13.1. Development and operation of experience management applications

In the following sections we focus our presentation on two steps of the DISER methodology, that is, the scenario of software process learning and the framework for experience base (EB) maintenance. Both elements were only recently described in full detail. If applied, they considerably improve the current state of the practice of EM. More importantly, both elements are ideal candidates for resolving the open issues of the e-learning (EL) system CORONET. The process learning scenario, if implemented in CORONET, provides guidance on how to systematically deal with experience captured by the various knowledge engineering functions implemented in WBT-Master. The EB maintenance framework will help to keep under control the continuously growing repository of documented knowledge and experience, that is learning resources (LRs) in the form of learning courses, learning goals, and so on, and lessons learned (LLs) in the form of discussion threads and annotations.

13.3.1   Experience-Based Process Learning

One important characteristic of experience is that it is to a high degree context dependent [56]. In software engineering a very natural context is that of the project in which the respective software is developed. Thus, experience can be captured while such a project is running or, for example, during project wrap-up. For this kind of experience the context, that is, the characteristics of the respective project, also has to be documented [15], because clues are required where to reuse the stored experience.

Another kind of context of special importance for software organizations is the respective business process an experience can be associated with. Examples for such business processes at Fraunhofer IESE are "industrial project acquisition", "conference participation planning", or "project performance". As a consequence, captured experiences are associated with the project(s) they occurred in as well as with the respective business process. This reflects the current state of the art in EM [6, 56]. We also call this kind of experience modeling the 2P-integration approach of EM.

As with projects, specific management is required for a software organization's business processes. With process learning we denote the activity of an organization to learn about its processes and process modeling techniques. Process learning includes creating and sustaining process models that are accepted by an organization's members, adapted to organizational changes on demand, and continuously enriched with experience from the operating business of the organization. Thus, process learning offers a natural opportunity for experience capture. We denote this combination as experience-based process learning.

In practice, experience-based process learning can be implemented using an electronic discussion forum. It offers a software organization's members an opportunity to participate in discourses about the respective process models. Completed discourses and comments are analyzed and summarized to improve the discussed process models and to capture lessons learned from the participants. This approach can be supported using text-mining techniques, as currently done in the indiGo project [4].

13.3.2 Experience Base Maintenance

This section presents the DISER framework for EB maintenance and explains how it is handled within an EBIS. The following, broad definition of maintenance is used: The goal of maintenance is to preserve and/or improve the value of an EBIS for the respective organization [41]. The main driving force of maintenance is the experience factory (EF) team. The EF team either performs the maintenance activities themselves or distributes them among other organization members.

Compared to a dedicated, full-time organizational unit performing maintenance, the distribution of maintenance and the often part-time basis of the EF team demand both increased coordination and tracking of the execution of maintenance activities and capture of the knowledge needed during maintenance. The second point also allows delegation of parts of the maintenance activities to lower ranking members of an organization. In the long run, the effects of personnel turnover in the EF team are minimized. However, one needs to take the different forms of maintenance knowledge into account: quality knowledge, maintenance process/procedure knowledge, and maintenance decision knowledge.

Quality knowledge describes how the quality of the EBIS is measured and the current status of the system with respect to quality as well as the rationale for the definition of quality [40]. Quality knowledge deals with quality aspects of the EBIS as a whole, that is, the EB's content and conceptual model and the retrieval mechanisms, usability of the user interface, and so on. An example of content-related quality knowledge is a definition of measures for the utility or value of single experiences (cases) [42]. There are several types of quality knowledge that are related as follows: The measures define what data is collected. The data collection is performed automatically or manually by respective data collection procedures. The collected data is analyzed using predefined models or procedures. The results of the analyses can be used for justifying an EB and as input for decisions about maintenance [41, 42].

Maintenance process and procedure knowledge define how the actual maintenance activities are performed. The actual maintenance can be performed as a mix of automatically and manually performed activities. For the automatically performed activities (maintenance procedures), tool support by components of a case-based reasoning (CBR) system or separate tools is required. The remaining activities have to be performed manually (maintenance processes). To improve guidance for the maintainers, descriptions of these processes are provided (e.g., detailed description of the acquisition of new cases through collecting cases, reviewing these cases, and publishing them in the case base, see DISER [56] and INRECA methodology [14] for examples). To combine manual and automatic maintenance, a maintenance process can have automated subprocesses or steps, which use input from or provide input for manually performed steps.

Maintenance decision knowledge links the quality knowledge with the maintenance process knowledge. It describes the circumstances under maintenance processes/procedures should be executed or checked for execution. Such maintenance knowledge can be described in an informal manner as maintenance policies [38], which define when, why, and how maintenance is performed for an EBIS. The "why" addresses not only the reason for maintenance but also the expected benefits of the maintenance operation, which should be related to the objectives of the EBIS or to the general goal of maintenance (i.e., to preserve and improve the EB's value [41]). Since these objectives are typically very highlevel, it is not very meaningful to address the EB objectives directly. Instead, we use a refinement of the objectives: the quality criteria from the evaluation program or the recording methods. The "how" is a combination of maintenance processes and procedures with additional steps as "glue".

One solution to coordinating experience and capturing the relevant maintenance knowledge is the evaluation and maintenance of software engineering repositories (EMSIG), which is a subpart of the DISER framework [41]. This framework includes a method and a technical infrastructure and is currently being developed and employed for various EBISs. The evaluation component supports analysis of the content and usage of services, and is responsible for the quality and value issues and deals with the "why" of maintenance. The results of these analyses provide the basis and input for making maintenance decisions. The maintenance assistance component supports the decision-making task by exploiting the evaluation in order to propose change requests (i.e., basic maintenance activities to be done). This deals mainly with knowledge issues and the "what" of maintenance ("what" to do for "what" knowledge/experience) and has to consider the "why" (justification from evaluation in the form of expected benefits versus expected maintenance effort). To support the task of learning about maintenance, typical tasks or patterns of maintenance activities are identified and captured ("distill maintenance guidelines"). These maintenance guidelines can be used for generating change requests automatically. The maintenance management component supports the task of organizing maintenance and, thus, is responsible for handling the change requests in an appropriate order. When a change request is executed, the maintenance primitives component provides the methods, techniques, and/or tools to perform the basic maintenance activities as demanded by the change request.

13.4   Integrating Experience Management with E-Learning

In this section we present our vision on how state-of-the-art e-learning (EL) systems like CORONET can be further improved by applying systematic experience management (EM) using the innovative DISER methodology. In particular, the process learning scenario and the experience base (EB) maintenance framework described in Sects. 13.3.1 and 13.3.2, respectively, are well-suited to resolve open issues of CORONET. These include lack of guidance on how to efficiently and effectively capitalize upon feedback and experience, and lack of control over the continuously growing repositories of learning resources (LRs) and lessons learned (LLs).

But we will go even one step further than simply transferring the 2P-integration approach of process learning to CORONET. In the 2P-integration approach a two-dimensional context (project and process information) is used to determine the best-matching resources to be offered to a knowledge worker in a specific (work or learning) situation. However, not every software engineer has the same qualifications, interests, and needs. Therefore, a third context dimension, the "person" dimension needs to be considered. Based on this insight, and since EL quite naturally puts its main focus on the people in a software organization, we extend the 2P-integration approach to a 3P-integration approach, capturing the project, process, and person dimensions of software development.

13.4.1   The 3P-Integration Approach

Using effective and efficient software project management as the subject matter, Fig. 13.2 offers a scenario that illustrates the 3P-integration approach to experience-based working and learning.

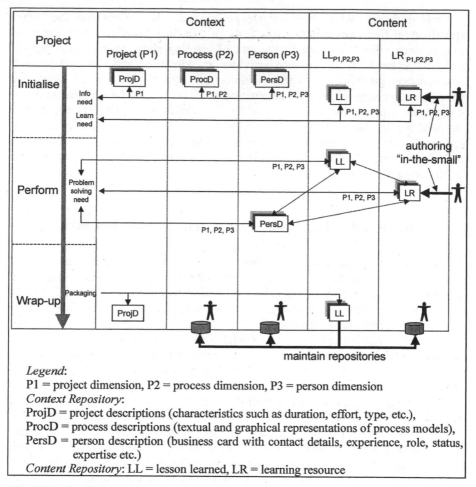

Fig. 13.2. The 3P-integration approach

In the scenario, we differentiate between three phases: project initialization, project performance, and project wrap-up. We consider two types of content (experiences or LL and LR) and three types of context (project (P1), process (P2), and person (P3)). The scenario describes how these types of content and context can be used to satisfy information and learning needs of the project initialization phase, problem-solving needs of the project performance phase, and packaging needs of the project wrap-up phase. This nicely exemplifies how an integrated EM and EL approach can support management of software projects and learning about (and for) software project management.

13.4.1.1 Project Initialization

At project start, software engineers may have two types of needs: information needs and learning needs.

In order to satisfy their information needs, involved roles: that is project manager (PM) retrieve all relevant information, such as:

1. Descriptions of similar projects: Similarity is based on current project (attribute P1); example: Publicly funded EU project with research partners X, Y, Z, and industry partners A, B, C,
2. Descriptions of related processes: Relationship is based on current project (attribute P1) and process (attribute P2); example: Process for detailed planning, which might vary according to project type
3. Descriptions ("business cards") of related persons (e.g., subject matter experts): Relationship is based on current project (attribute P1), process (attribute P2), and person (attribute P3); example: All experts for detailed planning with experience in similar projects. Since PM is an expert in CPM and PERT, no expertise is needed on that, but since PM has no experience with cost estimation, expertise on that is needed.

In order to satisfy their learning needs, involved roles (i.e., PM) may:

1. Retrieve all related LLs (e.g., offering guidelines, tips and tricks, and so on).
2. Retrieve all related LRs (e.g., offering short Web-based training courses and explanations with an adequate instructional design). It should be noted that the presentation of the LRs depends on the personal characteristics of the PM, e.g., learning style and competence level. If adequate LRs are not available as-is, they can be generated either (semi-)automatically [18] or by "authoring in-the-small" [22].

13.4.1.2 Project Performance

While the project is running, information and learning needs can be satisfied since they occur in the same way as during project initialization. When problems occur that cannot be resolved by reading the process description, there are three possibilities to get help:

1. Retrieval of a solution to the same or similar problems that occurred in the past (LL)
2. Retrieval of related learning materials (LR), suited to the context and the personal learning style
3. Retrieval of contact information to relevant experts (PersD)

The prioritization of the retrieved information is based on a set of rules, for instance, generally experts should not be bothered with questions if the problem can be solved by consulting an LL or a by refreshing the knowledge by self-learning with an LR.

13.4.1.2   Project Wrap-Up

At the end of the project, a new project description (ProjD) and a set of lessons learned (LLs) are generated. In a simple setting, the LLs are derived from wrap-up interviews. In a more advanced setting, they can be (partly) derived from annotations on project descriptions, process descriptions, person descriptions, LLs, and LRs (see also Sect. 13.3.1). Based on the analysis of the LLs, existing ProDs, PersDs, and LRs are updated, and/or new ProcDs, PersDs, and LRs are created.

13.4.2   Secondary Considerations and Outlook

To base competence development of software engineers exclusively on reading the related process documentation and learning from experience of previous (similar) experience (e.g., packaged into tips and tricks) is not always sufficient. There are two reasons for that:

1. Complexity: Processes, methods, or tools are sometimes very complex and thus difficult to apply correctly from the beginning; thus, in order to avoid mistakes during application (e.g., from misunderstanding) some sort of initial practice in a training situation can be beneficial.
2. Motivation: Theoretical knowledge about processes, methods, and tools is often too boring to be acquired by simple reading of the related documentation; thus, in order to avoid mistakes during execution (e.g., from omission) some sort of motivational training that activates the learner can be beneficial.

Thus, it is not sufficient to only offer best-matching LLs in real work situations, but it is actually necessary to provide adequate LRs at the right time and with little search effort. In order to do so, the following research problems have to be tackled:

1. Which parts of a process description (and associated methods and tools) need to be trained/taught before their first application?
2. How must the training material be prepared in order to be most effective?
3. How and when do training materials have to be delivered to be most effective?
4. How can learning materials (i.e., their content, their presentation, and their delivery) be adequately adapted to the personal profiles (previous knowledge, preferred learning style, etc.) of software engineers?

Even though pure EM without EL is insufficient — as we have argued above — we believe that most of these questions can be answered by systematically applying the 3P-integration approach. Once the problems have been resolved, new LRs can be generated by reusing authentic project experience (as captured in LLs), for instance, real application examples, typical mistakes, tips and tricks, and enriching them with didactically relevant enhancements (e.g., explanations, exercises, tests). As soon as an initial set of LRs has been defined and stored in a learning resource base (LRB), the LRs associated with a particular process description can be treated in the same way as the process description itself, that is, they can undergo the same maintenance cycle of packaging, evaluation, selection, and processing as LLs that are stored in an EB.

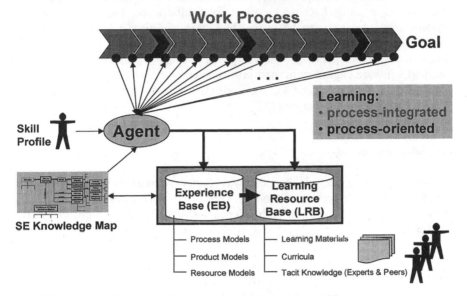

Fig. 13.3. Active guidance of software engineers through e-coaching

Eventually, experience-based EL systems like CORONET, will switch from reactive to proactive [27]; that is, instead of requesting a software engineer to retrieve adequate LRs as a learning need occurs (pull strategy, process-oriented learning), the EL environment automatically offers adequate LRs as soon as it detects a potential need during the performance of a particular development process by the software engineer (push strategy, process-integrated learning). The automatic offering of adequate LRs as the need occurs can be called "e-coaching". Fig. 13.3 visualizes the interplay between process-oriented and process-integrated learning as well as the use of a combined EB and LRB to support e-coaching.

13.5   Summary and Conclusion

Integrating experience management (EM) and e-learning (EL) provides a combination of continuous learning and problem solving with experience-based preparation, usage, and improvement of learning resources (LRs). Packaged experience in the form of lessons learned (LLs) provides the starting point for the design of LRs. Systematic EM according to the DISER method provides guidance on how to incorporate and maintain LRs in an experience-based information system. The combination of EM and EL offers several benefits for the user:

1. First, there is no need for the user to decide on one approach or the other, since both can be used in an integrated fashion.
2. From the EL perspective, LRs can be based on already available experience. In addition to reusing LRs and collecting feedback on them, a continuous improvement process can be established, thus yielding a longer-lasting and deeper learning effect (sustained learning).
3. From the EM perspective, a new type of content (LRs) can be offered to support software engineers in their professional work. The LRs supplement the packaged work experience (LLs), and thus further strengthen case-based, situated, and authentic learning [37].

Acknowledgement

The work presented in this chapter was partly supported by the European Commission (EU Project CORONET, Grant No. IST-1999-11634) and the German Ministry of Education and Science (BMBF Project indigo, Grant No. 01AK951A).

References

1. Aha D.W., Becerra-Fernandez I., Maurer F., Muñoz-Avila H. (Eds.) (1999) Exploring synergies of knowledge management and case-based reasoning. In: Papers from the AAAI 1999 workshop (Tech. Report WS-99-10), AAAI Press, Menlo Park
2. Aha D., Weber R., (eds.) (2000) Proceedings of the workshop on intelligent lessons learned systems at 17th national conference on AI (AAAI-00). American association for artificial intelligence, Menlo Park, CA, WE-00-03, ISBN 1-57735-118-5
3. Althoff K.-D. (2001) Case-based reasoning. In: Chang, S.K. (Ed.), Handbook on software engineering and knowledge engineering. Vol. 1 "Fundamentals", World scientific, Singapore, pp. 549-588
4. Althoff K.-D., Becker-Kornstaedt U., Decker B., Klotz A., Leopold E., Rech J., Voss A. (2002) The indiGo project: enhancement of experience management and process learning with moderated discourses. In: Perner, P. (Ed.), Data mining in e-commerce, medicine and knowledge management, Springer, Berlin Heidelberg, New York
5. Althoff K.-D., Bomarius F., Müller W., Nick M. (1999) Using a case-based reasoning for supporting continuous improvement processes. In: Proceedings of German workshop on machine learning, Technical report, Institute for image processing and applied informatics, Leipzig, Germany
6. Althoff K.-D., Decker B., Hartkopf S., Jedlitschka A., Nick M., Rech J. (2001) Experience management: The Fraunhofer IESE experience factory. In: Proceedings of industrial conference on data mining, Institut für Bildverarbeitung und angewandte Informatik Leipzig
7. Althoff K.-D., Wilke W. (1997) Potential uses of case-based reasoning in the experience-based construction of software systems. In: Bergmann R.,W. Wilke W. (Eds.), Proceedings of the 5th German workshop in case-based reasoning, Center for learning systems and applications, University of Kaiserslautern, Germany

8. Angkasaputra N., Pfahl D. (2002) The CORONET system: a methodology-driven infrastructure for collaborative learning at the workplace. In: Proceedings of LLA'02: workshop week of special interest groups machine learning, intelligent tutorial systems, and adaptivity and user modeling in interactive systems of the GI (German Computer Society). Hannover, Germany, pp. 20-26

9. Bartsch-Spörl B. (1987) Ansätze zur behandlung von fallorientiertem erfahrungswissen in expertensystemen. KI, 4: 32-36

10. Basili V.R. (1985) Quantitative evaluation of software methodology. In: Proceedings of the First Pan-Pacific computer conference, Melbourne, Australia, Key note address

11. Basili V.R., Caldiera G., Rombach H.D. (2001) The experience factory. In: Marciniak J.J. (Ed.), Encyclopedia of software engineering, vol.1 John Wiley and Sons, New York, pp. 511-519

12. Basili V.R., Green S., Laitenberger O., Lanubile F., Shull F., Sorumgard S., Zelkowitz M.V. (1996) The empirical investigation of perspective-based reading. In: Empirical software engineering 1: 133-164

13. Basili V.R., Shull F., Lanubile F. (1999) Building knowledge through families of experiments. IEEE transactions on software engineering, 25: 456-473

14. Bergmann R., Breen S., Göker M., Littich M., Manago M., Traphöner R. (2003) Developing industrial case-based reasoning applications: the INRECA methodology. In: State of art survey, LNAI series, 1612, Springer, Berlin Heidelberg, New York

15. Brandt M., Ehrenberg D., Althoff K.-D., Nick M. (2001) Ein fallbasierter ansatz für die computergestützte Nutzung von Erfahrungswissen bei der Projektarbeit. In: Buhl H.U., Huther A., Reitwiesner B. (Eds.), Information age economy, Procedings of 5th internationale tagung wirtschaftsinformatik, Heidelberg, Physica, pp. 251-264

16. Bush V. (1945) As we may think. In: Atlantic monthly, pp.101-108

17. Carbonell J.R. (1970) AI in CAI: An artificial intelligent approach to computer assisted instruction. In: IEEE transactions on man machine systems 4: 190 ff.

18. Caumanns J. (2000) Automatisierte komposition von wissensvermittelnden dokumenten für das World Wide Web. Ph.D. thesis. Cottbus technical university, Germany

19. Crowder N.A. (1959) Automatic tutoring by intrinsic programming. In: Lumsdane A.A., Glaser R. (Eds), Teaching machines and programmed learning, National education association, Washington D.C., USA

20. Dietinger Th., Gütl Ch., Maurer H., Pivec M., Schmaranz K. (1998) Intelligent knowledge gathering and management as new ways of an improved learning process. In Proceedings of WebNet 98, Charlottesville, USA, pp. 244-249

21. Goodman D. (1987) The complete hypercard handbook. Bantam Books, New York, N.Y., USA

22. Grützner I., Angkasaputra N., Pfahl D. (2002) A systematic approach to produce small courseware modules for combined learning and knowledge management environments. In: Proceedings of 14th international conference on software engineering and knowledge engineering, New York, pp. 533-539

23. Gunzenhäuser R., Herczeg M. (2001) Lehren und Lernen im Zeitalter der neuen digitalen Medien. In: i-com, 0/2001, Germany

24. Grützner I., Pfahl D., Ruhe G. (2002) Systematic courseware development using an integrated engineering style method. In: Natural and artificial intelligence systems organization: networked learning in a global environment, challenges and solutions for virtual education. World congress proceedings, Millet, ICSC-NAISO academic press

25. Halasz F.G. (1988) Reflections on notecards: seven issues for the next generation of hypermedia systems. Communications of the ACM, 31: 836-852
26. Harasim L., Hiltz S.R., Teles L., Turoff M. (1995) Learning networks: a field guide to teaching and learning online. MIT press, Cambridge
27. Heinrich E., Maurer H. (2000) Active documents: concepts, implementation and applications. Journal of universal computer science 6: 1197-1202
28. Helic D., Maglajlic S., Scherbakov N. (1999) Educational materials on the WEB: data modeling approach. In: Proceedings of 22nd international symposium on multimedia and hypermedia systems, Rijeka, Croatioa, pp. 139-142
29. Helic D., Maurer H., Lennon J., Scherbakov N. (2001) Aspects of a modern WBT system. In: Proceedings of international conference on advances in infrastructure for electronic business. Education, science, and medicine on the Internet, SSGRR 2001, CD-ROM publication (ISBN: 88-85280-61-7), paper 38
30. Helic D., Maurer H., Scherbakov N. (2001) Mentoring sessions: increasing the influence of tutors on the learning process in WBT Systems. In: Proceedings of World conference of the Web society, Charlottesville, USA, pp. 515-519
31. Helic D., Maurer H., Scherbakov N. (2001) Knowledge domains: A global structuring mechanism for learning resources in WBT systems. In Proceedings of world conference of the Web society Charlottesville, USA, pp. 509-514
32. Helic D., Maurer H., Scherbakov N. (2001) Accessing best-match learning resources in WBT environments. In Proceedings of world conference on educational multimedia and hypermedia, Charlottesville, USA, pp. 206-212
33. Helic D., Maurer H., Scherbakov N. (2001) Creating and maintaining semantic nets of learning resources in a WBT environment. In: Proceedings of 24th international symposium on multimedia and hypermedia systems, Rijeka, Croatia, pp. 136-143
34. Helic, D., Maurer H., Scherbakov N. (2002) Aspects of collaborative authoring in WBT systems. In: Proceedings of the international conference on advances in infrastructure for electronic business, Education, science, and medicine on the Internet, SSGRR 2002w. CD-ROM publication (ISBN 88-85280-62-5)
35. Henninger S. (1995) Developing domain knowledge through the reuse of project experiences. In: Samadzadeh M. (Ed.), Proceedings of the IEEE European design automation conference, Brighton, Andleterre, pp.186-195
36. Kalfoglou Y., Menzies T., Althoff K.-D., Motta E. (2000) Meta-knowledge in systems engineering: panacea or undelivered promise? The knowledge engineering review 15: 381-404
37. Kearsley G., Shneiderman B.(1999) Engagement theory: A framework for technology-based teaching and learning. URL http://home.sprynet.com/~gkearsley/engage.htm (accessed 20th April, 2003)
38. Leake D., Wilson D. (1998) Categorizing case-base maintenance: dimensions and directions. In: Smyth B., Cunningham P. (Eds.) Advances in case-based reasoning LNAI, Springer, Berlin, Heidelberg, New York, pp. 196-207
39. Lehner F. (2000) Organizational memory-Konzepte und Systeme für das organisatorische Lernen und das Wissensmanagement. Carl Hanser Verlag
40. Menzies T. (1998) Knowledge maintenance: the state of the art. The knowledge engineering review, 14: 1-46
41. Nick M., Althoff K.-D., Tautz C. (2001) Systematic maintenance for corporate experience repositories. Computational intelligence 17: 364-386

42. Nick M., Feldmann R. (2000) Guidelines for evaluation and improvement of reuse and experience repository systems through measurement programs. In: Proceedings of the 3rd European conference on software measurement, Madrid, Spain, 1-11

43. Pfahl D., Trapp S., de Teresa J., Oliveira J., Stupperich M., Rathert N., Molu R., Scherbakov N., D'Ambra J. (2002) CORONET final report. Fraunhofer IESE, Technical Report no. 045.02/E. URL: http://www.iese.fhg.de/coronet/ (accessed 20th April, 2003)

44. Probst G., Romhardt K. (1998) The components of knowledge management - a practical approach (German). URL: www.cck.uni-kl.de/wmk/papers/public/Bausteine/ (accessed 20th April, 2003)

45. Rech J., Decker B., Althoff K.-D (2001) Using knowledge discovery technology in experience management systems. In: Proceedings of the workshop on Maschinelles Lernen (FGML01), GI-workshop Lernen–Lehren–Wissen–Adaptivität (LLWA01), Universität Dortmund, 8.-12. Okt. 2001

46. Rombach H.D., Ulery B.D. (1989) Establishing a measurement based maintenance improvement program: lessons learned in the SEL. In: Proceedings of the conference on software maintenance, New York, USA, pp. 50-57

47. Romhardt K. (1998) Die Organisation aus der Wissensperspektive - Möglichkeiten und Grenzen der Intervention. Wiesbaden: Gabler Verlag

48. Rosenberg. L.H. (2003) Lessons learned in software quality assurance. In: Aurum A., Jeffery R., Wohlin C., Handzic M. (Eds.), Managing software engineering knowledge. Springer, Berlin Heidelberg New York

49. Ruhe G., Bomarius F. (Eds.) (2000) Learning software organizations - methodology and applications. Springer, Berlin Heidelberg New York, LNCS 1756

50. Schank R.C. (1982) Dynamic memory: a theory of learning in computers and people. Cambridge university press, Cambridge, UK

51. Schank R.C., Abelson R. (1977) Scripts, plans, goals, and understanding. Lawrence Erlbaum Associates, Hillsdale, New Jersey, USA

52. Shepperd M. (2003) Case-based reasoning and software engineering. In: Aurum, A. Jeffery R., Wohlin C., Handzic M. (Eds.), Managing software engineering knowledge, Springer, Berlin Heidelberg, New York

53. Sleeman D., Brown J.S. (1982) Intelligent tutoring systems. Academic press, London, UK

54. Skinner B.F. (1954) Science of learning and the art of teaching. In: Harvard educational review, 2: 86-97

55. Stolpmann M., Wess S. (1998) Optimierung der Kundenbeziehungen mit CBR systemen-Intelligente Systeme für E-Commerce und support, Addison Wesley Longmann (Business and Computing), Bonn, Germany

56. Tautz C. (2000) Customizing software engineering experience management systems to organizational needs. Ph.D. thesis, University of Kaiserslautern, Stuttgart, Fraunhofer IRB Verlag.

57. Tautz C., Althoff K.-D. (1997) Using case-based reasoning for reusing software knowledge. In: Leake D., Plaza E. (Eds.), Case-based reasoning research and development, Second international conference on case-based reasoning (ICCBR97), Springer, Berlin Heidelberg New York, pp. 156-165

58. Wenger E. (1998) Communities of practice: learning, meaning, and identity. Cambridge university press, New York, USA

Author Biography

Dr. Klaus-Dieter Althoff received his diploma in mathematics and operations research from Aachen University of Technology, his Ph.D. in computer science and his Habilitation (post-doctoral degree) in computer science both from the University of Kaiserslautern. His past and current research interests include learning organization, organizational memory, experience factory, systematic improvement, knowledge acquisition, modeling, management, maintenance, evaluation, machine learning, case-based reasoning, data mining, and knowledge discovery. He was involved in a number of international and German events on learning software organization, case-based reasoning, knowledge acquisition and management, and machine learning as a co-chair, program committee member, and co-organizer. Currently he is competence manager for Systematic Learning and Improvement at Fraunhofer IESE.

Dr. Dietmar Pfahl heads the Certifiable Education and Training (CET) department of the Fraunhofer Institute for Experimental Software Engineering (IESE), Kaiserslautern, Germany. His past and current research interests include software process improvement, change management, simulation-based learning, collaborative learning, and the integration of e-learning with knowledge management. Before joining Fraunhofer IESE in 1996, he was a research staff member with the German Aerospace Research Establishment (DLR), and a software engineering consultant with Siemens Corporate Research. Dr. Pfahl received a M.Sc. in applied mathematics and economics from the University of Ulm, and a Ph.D. in computer science from the University of Kaiserslautern.

Part 4
Practical Guidelines for Managing Software Engineering Knowledge

Ross Jeffery

This part of the book concerns the last part of the technology infusion process—that of taking the processes, tools, or techniques and using them in an industrial setting. Few organizations have documented significant experience with explicit knowledge management in the software engineering domain. Those that have experience have not necessarily revealed the elements that provided positive returns and those that did not.

To illustrate the difficulties in this area we discuss recent experience in Australia. Some four years ago we constructed an approach to managing electronic documents in a software R&D organization [1]. In this project we developed the databases and search tools to allow software developers in the organization to search all electronic documents and e-mails for relevant experiences that would assist in their current tasks. The feedback from users of the facility was positive, with comments indicating that advantages of the environment included saved time and the ability to find documents that previously had been unlocatable. Despite this, the facility was disabled. We believe this was because the system was not supported by senior management in the organization rather than because of lack of support at the lower organizational levels. Regardless of the reason, the experiment must be considered a failure, as the system did not survive. Practical guidelines for managing software engineering knowledge need to include technical, sociological, and organizational issues if we are to understand the criteria for industrial success. In Part 4 we begin the necessary broad-ranging discussion of these various aspects of knowledge management in software engineering.

Part 4 includes four chapters founded on industrial experience with software engineering knowledge management. It is obvious that in these four chapters we are not able to address all of the technical, organizational and social issues that will be confronted in industry. Rather, we provide experience that exists at this point in time and that may inspire further investigation of the issues in other organizations.

In order to provide a more general framework for the chapters in this part of the book, we first provide an outline of a software engineering experience repository that has been established over the last two years within a small software development organization in Sydney. We use this example because the experience repository developments within this organization have been driven by the needs of the organization and its staff and as such, the example provides insights into both needs and solutions for the particular context described. It is a possible framework within which we can position the following chapters. The experience repository is used regularly in this organization and provides a positive return on investment. This is not to say, of course, that the experience could be successfully transferred to other organizations without change.

Allette Systems is a small software organization with 20 to 30 employees developing Web applications for customer organizations (not simple web sites) and also doing text markup for electronic database creation of large text databases. This example concerns the system development side of the business but not the markup side. As a part of a general process improvement initiative within the company work began several years ago in assessing their processes and suggesting necessary changes. Early recommendations resulted in the establishment of a time recoding system to improve the cost identification and cost recovery aspects of the business. Once this was established a more general investigation of the software processes revealed a need to improve the documentation process within the organization. This improvement aspect was addressed by creating a descriptive process model of the software process in use. A custom-built generator was then used to create HTML, which generates a web-based desktop process model for task guidance. The next element added to this was the use of a tool (Pageseeder from Weborganic, see www.allette.com.au), which facilitated comment and discussion on the content of the process model. Finally, the structure was added to allow experiences, checklists, templates and examples to be added to the system. Thus at this point in time the organization has a defined process, the ability to store comments and experiences with this process, examples of documents, code and other lifecycle artifacts, and templates of documents needed during the process. Usage data collected on the repository and interviews with staff indicate consistent use of the repository, especially code fragments, and a high level of user satisfaction with the facility.

However, the approach taken in the Allette example is different from that taken in the "experience factory" work. The assumption at Allette is that organizational participants will provide relevant experiences if provided with an appropriate storage and retrieval structure. The structure provided in this instance is the process model framework rather than a database and search facility framework, as was the case in the R&D organization [1]. There is no formal experience management or experience organization. We have no knowledge though on how this would scale up to larger organizations.

The objective of Part 4 is to provide a selection of articles presenting practical experience with knowledge management in software engineering. The chapters provide illustrations of how the challenges of knowledge management have been addressed in a number of organizations and in different contexts within those organizations.

There are four chapters in Part 4. In Chap. 14, "Practical Guidelines for Learning-based Software Product Development", Rini van Solingen, Rob Kusters and Jos Trienekens address the issue of establishing learning in an ever-changing software development environment. They argue that since the software development processes and products evolve at a fairly rapid pace it is necessary to facilitate learning through the use of control loops and feedback. In this way people can correct mistakes and be supported in learning from their own experience. They propose three types of loops:

1. A product quality loop, which provides feedback to the individual on compliance of their product with use demands
2. A process quality loop, which compares expected and actual process performance
3. A process - product loop that analyses the ability of the selected process to produce the required product quality

They then consider what needs to be done to establish these loops, but leave the question of how to establish them up to the particular context. In this way the practical questions such as how to measure product quality goals or how to model cost/quality tradeoffs can be implemented based on the specific needs within the usage context.

In Chap. 15, "In-project Learning by Goal-oriented Measurement", Rini van Solingen considers the goal question metric paradigm in the context of in project learning. Readers are probably familiar with his earlier GQM book [2] which documents the industrial application of GQM. In this paper he outlines the GQM approach to measurement, describes how knowledge acquisition is used in defining the measurement program, how feedback to the developers is facilitated through the measurement process, and then provides an industrial example of the use of GQM and its place in learning.

Chapter 16, "e-R&D: Effectively Managing and Using R&D Knowledge" by, Christof Ebert, Jozef De Man and Fariba Schelenz describes the process improvement initiative at Alcatel and how it supports knowledge dissemination in Alcatel. They describe, through examples from Alcatel, how explicit and tacit knowledge can be shared and the use of both team management and knowledge management.

In Chap. 17, "Knowledge Infrastructure for Project Management", Pankaj Jalote discusses how Infosys Technologies encodes and captures project experience for use on future projects. The process infrastructure, including templates and checklists is created and measurement is used to capture data on prior projects. Experience from people is also captured in the "body of knowledge" and stored in a database. This chapter describes a system with similarities to that of Allette as outlined above.

References

1. Jeffery R., Koenneker A., Low G. (1999) Lessons learned from the failure of an experience base initiative using a bottom-up development paradigm. In: Proceedings of NASA software engineering workshop, December, Greenbelt, Maryland, USA
2. Solingen R. van Berghou, E.W. (1999) The goal/question/metric method: a practical guide for quality improvement. McGraw-Hill, Spain, ISBN 0077095537

Editor Biography

Ross Jeffery is Professor of Software Engineering in the School of Computer Science and Engineering at University of New South Wales (UNSW) and Director of the Centre for Advanced Software Engineering Research (CAESER) at UNSW. He is the founding chairman of the Australian Software Metrics Association (ASMA). He was also instrumental in creating the Australian Conference on Information Systems. He has served on the editorial board of *IEEE Transactions on Software Engineering*, and he is associate editor of the *Journal of Empirical Software Engineering*. He has also been on the steering committee of the IEEE and ACM International Conference on Software Engineering. He is a founding member of the International Software Engineering Research Network (ISERN).

14 Practical Guidelines for Learning-Based Software Product Development

Rini van Solingen, Rob Kusters and Jos Trienekens

Abstract: Software products are developed in environments that are far from stable. People, processes and technology are continuously changing and renewed. As such, it is important to make learning an integrated part of software development in order to get a grip on such continuous changes. Integrating learning activities and processes into the daily practice of software product development is, however, not easy. In this chapter it is proposed that such learning can be facilitated by means of control loops. With such control loops, software development teams receive feedback on their own performance, which enables them to correct mistakes, control their output, and thus enables learning on their working processes. In this chapter a model of control loops is presented that works with embedded software product development. Practical guidelines are presented to facilitate in-practice learning with these loops.

Keywords: RPM model, Requirements engineering, Process engineering, Measurement engineering, Control loops, Feedback

14.1   Introduction

Life today is heavily dependent on software. Examples of software applications include word processors, spreadsheets, e-mail and Internet applications. There is, however, also a large amount of software incorporated in electronic products. Such products include mechanical, hydraulic and electronic machinery with processors and embedded memory chips. These chips contain certain control instructions, which are termed "software". Software for such products is commonly known as embedded software' and the product is termed an "embedded product". Examples of embedded products include cellular phones, televisions, microwave ovens, petrol-pumps, cars and payment terminals. Embedded products range from single products to mass-produced items, one dollar products to one million dollar products, single-user to thousand-user products, product life times of three months to several decades, single input and output to multiple input and output products. The role of software in embedded products and services is increasing tremendously. Software development is becoming *the* most effort-consuming task during the development of embedded products. For the example of a television set, the effort spent to develop a new generation of televisions has been shown to account for more than 70% of software development resources [23]. Or consider cellular phones: research has indicated that the software in cellular phones shows an increase by a factor 10,000 over the last 12 years [17].

The increase in software application in embedded products implies a rigorous change in the development of these products. There is a shift happening from mainly hardware product development to mainly software product development. This change has a high impact on organizations that develop embedded products. Past knowledge of hardware development is becoming obsolete, while knowledge of software development is found lacking.

The quality of embedded products is a relevant topic as more and more embedded software is incorporated in life-vital applications. In order to achieve quality software, the emphasis on embedded product quality is often refocused onto its development process. This is because quality is neither something that happens by accident, nor can it be brought in afterwards [11, 15].

In order to keep up with the trend of ever-increasing amounts of software in embedded products with the increasing demand for better software in shorter cycles, the embedded software industry needs to increase their development capabilities to keep up with these demands. Increasing embedded software development capabilities can be done in three ways:

1. Increasing professionalism by adopting best practices from other organizations and market domains. An example of such an approach is the Capability Maturity Model [15], which is a collection of industrial best practices for software management.
2. Hiring better skilled people. This is especially relevant in periods of economic downturn when highly skilled people become available.
3. Increasing learning skills by installing organizational learning processes that support bottom-up learning from project to project. The embedded product industry can learn to manage the new situation by increasing their focus on learning to improve and be successful.

The first and second strategies are described in many other publications and are therefore not addressed in this chapter. This chapter focuses on the third strategy: learning from one's own practices.

14.2 Learning During Embedded Product Development

Recent research has indicated that learning is crucial to survive in the embedded software product development market [28]. Integrating practical learning activities and learning processes into daily practice is not easy. This is caused by the fact that learning is just a secondary objective during product development. First priority is given to day-to-day activities such as matching customer demands, meeting deadlines, producing deliverables, responding to change requests, and so on. Learning can, however, become part of the normal process by ensuring that the appropriate information is provided at appropriate events, to the appropriate persons.

In order to do this, it is proposed that group learning within embedded software development teams can be facilitated by means of control loops. With such control loops, development teams receive feedback on their own performance, which enables them to correct mistakes, control their output, and as such enables them to learn from their own work. Control loops are powerful mechanisms for integrating learning into software development. It is, however, important to make sure that the right control loops are installed. Software product developers should receive the right feedback, on the right activities, at the right time and in the right way.

The main three control loops addressed in this chapter are [28]:

- *Loop 1*: The product quality loop, which enables control over software product quality. This is achieved by analyzing the difference between required product quality and actual product quality. This control loop ensures that developers receive feedback on whether the product they have made complies with user demands.

- *Loop 2*: The process quality loop, which enables control over process effectiveness. This is achieved by analyzing the difference between expected process performance and actual process performance. This control loop ensures that developers receive feedback on the effectiveness of the actions they take in their process.

- *Loop 3*: The process - product loop, which analyses the ability of the selected development process in achieving the required level of product quality. This control loop ensures that the selected software development process (and the actions chosen in this process) results in a product that complies with its requirements. As such, early feedback is provided on the effectiveness of the development process with respect to the final product. This last loop facilitates a negotiation process between the required product quality and the feasible product quality within the selected process, duration, cost, risk, and so on.

Please note that there is a distinction between a control loop and a feedback loop. A control loop provides a means to take action and to have control of certain events. A feedback loop provides information on certain activities and therefore information from which to learn. In this model we address control loops; however, feedback is an important means to gain control. The learning effects are, however, on the control level ("single-loop learning" [1]). High-level learning ("double-loop learning" [1]) is not directly triggered by these control loops, although it might happen.

These three control loops can only be implemented if certain activities or processes are in place to enable information flow to function as a feedback cycle. For embedded software product development this means installing at least the following three engineering processes [28]: software product requirements engineering (SPRE), software development process engineering (SDPE) and software measurement program engineering (SMPE). This is visualized in Fig.14.1. The arrows in this figure show the direction of the processes SPRE, SDPE, SMPE and their outcomes.

- *SPRE*: Software product requirements engineering is the process of collecting the wishes of software product stakeholders and transforming these wishes into a product quality specification. The outcome of SPRE is a product quality specification.

- *SDPE*: Software development process engineering is the design of a measurable development process model for the development of a specific software product fulfilling the product quality specification. The outcome of SDPE is a software development process model.
- *SMPE*: Software measurement program engineering is the design and implementation of a set of process, product and resource metrics, used to evaluate software product quality and process - product relationships. The output of SMPE is a set of product and process measurements.

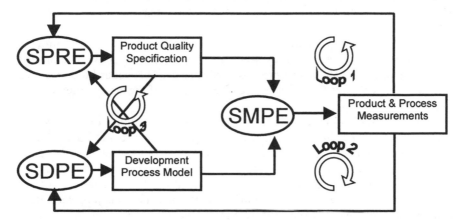

Fig.14.1. Model for embedded product development control loops

These three processes and control loops imply that an embedded product development organization will at least:

1. Ensure that it specifies what product quality actually means
2. Make a detailed project plan that includes all detailed actions taken
3. Use measurement to evaluate whether actions had intended effects

The activities listed in Fig. 14.1 are not uncommon for embedded product development. Mostly, product requirements are documented, project plans are made, and several measurements are made. As such it may mean that parts of the proposed control processes are already installed in practice. However, often the required level of detail is not installed, meaning that adaptations and expansions need to be made. Product quality requirements have to be specified in an unambiguous and measurable way, the project plan should describe the specific actions taken with their intended effects, and the measurements made should enable evaluations of the product and the process.

For each of these three processes, SPRE, SDPR, and SMPE, a set of ten practical guidelines is presented. These guidelines were developed over a period of several years in both scientific, and industrial research projects (see e.g. [28, 31, 22]). This set of 30 guidelines supports embedded industry by the implementation of learning activities in their projects. These learning activities directly contribute to the product under development because they install the control loops.

14.3   Guidelines for Model Application in Practice

A conceptual model was presented in the previous section on the control of embedded product quality through the implementation of three control loops that enable learning. Additional support is required to facilitate the use of this model in practice. This support is provided through a set of guidelines for each of the three processes. These guidelines originate from multiple sources, including literature and experience from applying the conceptual model in industrial projects.

The guidelines mainly focus on the three engineering processes with less emphasis on the control loops. This is because if the guidelines are followed, the loops will be implemented automatically, and the three processes are linked to each other and use each other's outputs as input.

The guidelines in this chapter mainly describe 'what' should be done and point to the tasks and activities that are part of each of the engineering processes. These guidelines do not present 'how' this should be done, because it is assumed that "how guidelines" largely depend on the specific context in which they are applied. These guidelines have been validated in a set of case studies; for details on the validation, experiences and cost/benefit analysis see [28].

14.3.1   Guidelines for Software Product Requirements Engineering

Software product requirements engineering (SPRE) is the process of collecting the wishes of product stakeholders and transforming these wishes into a product quality specification. The product quality specification is used for two purposes:

- To design a development process that will produce the specified product quality within the constraints of the development project
- To evaluate compliance of the final product to the product quality requirements

The guidelines for software product requirements engineering are:

R.1. Identify all stakeholders for the product, and involve each stakeholder in the requirements engineering process.
R.2. Let stakeholders state their product quality wishes in their "own terminology", and transfer those wishes into (standard) engineering quality terminology.
R.3. Use experience with a similar type or older version of the product that already exists as input to the creation of a product quality specification.
R.4. Make a distinction between essential, stringent and additional wishes.
R.5. Requirements engineering should be considered a negotiation process during which decisions are made on the level of satisfying product quality wishes.

This negotiation process should discuss both functional and nonfunctional product wishes.

R.6. Communicate rejection or selection of a product quality wish to the stakeholders.

R.7. Handle the abstract concept of product quality by subdividing quality into operational attributes.

R.8. Specify the (relative) importance of product quality attributes for a new product, and visualize this in a product quality profile (PQP).

R.9. Specify product quality requirements in measurable terms.

R.10.   Show the trade-off between quality demands and the cost/effort incurred to realize these demands.

These guidelines are described in detail in the next section.

R-1: Identify All Stakeholders for the Product, and Involve Each Stakeholder in the Requirements Engineering Process

Each product goes through several stages as it is designed, produced, transported to the customer, installed, used, repaired and recycled. For each of these stages in the product life-cycle, different 'users' of the product can be distinguished. However, the way in which the product is used and its related quality needs will differ depending on the users. We propose a modeling technique, which distinguishes product users as being 'stakeholders', with every stakeholder possessing one or more responsibilities (roles) [20, 21]. For each product, a model can be made that identifies the stakeholders and their interrelationships. This guideline is based on the assumption that making a quality product implies addressing the specific needs of specific stakeholders.

A stakeholder is defined as an identifiable person, or homogeneous group of people that has a legitimate interest in the degree of quality of the product. A role is defined as an area of responsibility of a stakeholder, determining the view of the type and degree of quality required [20]. Ideally each stakeholder is involved in the process of requirements engineering. The way in which the stakeholders are consulted can be different, depending on the best way to capture their knowledge.

R-2: Let Stakeholders State Their Product Quality Wishes in Their 'Own Terminology', and Transfer Those Wishes into Standard Terminology

Stakeholders have implicit ideas and needs for product quality. In order to prevent formulation problems, it is recommended that stakeholders express their product quality wishes in their own language. This has several benefits. First, stakeholders can express their implicit needs more easily. Second, many stakeholders have neither experience with standard quality terminology, nor are they always willing to learn it. Furthermore, it prevents stakeholders from having their own interpretations of a standard terminology, and mistakes are prevented. However, when stakeholders state their wishes in their own terms, these wishes have to be transferred to engineering quality terminology, such as ISO 9126 [16], that can be understood by software developers.

R-3: Use Experience with a Similar Type or Older Version of the Product as Input for the Creation of a Product Quality Specification

If an older version of the product or a similar type of product is already used in practice, experience with this product can be a valuable reference for requirements engineering ("anchoring and adjustment" [5]). This guideline resembles the concept of "product families" (see e.g. [7]), which is based on the notion that the next generations of products have a close resemblance and are based on previous generations.

Such experiences can lead to expressions such as "reliability should be equal to the previous version", "usability needs to be higher" and "the functionality was fair but needs some specific expansions". Such references make it clear what developers need to focus on. Experiences with older versions of a product are also an excellent source to find out the way in which a stakeholder uses the product.

R-4: Distinct between Essential, Stringent and Additional Wishes

Not every product quality wish is equally strong. It is recommended to make a distinction between:

- Essential wishes that must be addressed by the product. Without addressing these strong demands the product will be useless
- Stringent wishes, for which it is highly recommended that they are addressed. However, under certain conditions it is possible to ignore such wishes
- Additional wishes that are neither essential nor stringent, but it can be beneficial if they are addressed

This distinction supports requirements engineering because it indicates the level of negotiation that is possible for each wish. To support the selection of stringent and additional wishes, it is recommended that their relative importance be made explicit through assigning priorities and noting the arguments for these priorities.

R-5: Requirements Engineering Should Be Considered as a Negotiation Process During Which Decisions Are Made on the Level of Satisfying Product Quality Wishes. This Negotiation Process Should Discuss Both Functional and NonFunctional Product Wishes

Based on the total set of stakeholder product quality wishes, a selection will be made from this set. The decision to which extent a certain product quality wish will be satisfied is a complex negotiation process. Criteria that play a role in the acceptance or rejection of a wish include costs, benefits, technological feasibility, effort involved, time to market, level of contradiction with other wishes, or risks. It is advisable not to limit this negotiation only to the quality aspects of a product. The functional demands also need to be discussed, because functional and nonfunctional wishes are related. This negotiation process also addresses investment issues, because decisions need to be made as to where to invest resources for the product.

This negotiation process alone is not part of requirements engineering. It is done iteratively with process engineering, because process engineering provides insights on the costs and time issues for each specific product quality requirement. This negotiation process goes on continuously throughout a project. When additional requirements are formulated, which is the case for almost every software development project, again trade-offs and negotiations will be made. Ideally, a product quality specification is made once and never changed, but this is rarely the case in practice.

R-6: Communicate Rejection or Selection of a Product Quality Wish to the Stakeholders

Given that there is a process during which all product quality wishes are evaluated and a decision is taken to accept or reject a wish, the outcome of this decision process must be communicated. The main reason for this is that our approach addresses product quality explicitly. The decisions taken should therefore also be made explicit and communicated to the people involved.

Furthermore, this communication is necessary to manage the expectations of stakeholders. Stakeholders implicitly expect that wishes be fulfilled once they have been stated. This creates high expectations. If the product is delivered and does not comply with these wishes, stakeholders will be disappointed and perceive the product as being of low quality. If the decisions on the level of satisfaction required of a certain product's quality are communicated, a stakeholder has the opportunity to adapt expectations, early on in the product development process.

R-7: Handle the Abstract Concept of Product Quality by Subdividing Quality into Operational Attributes

Quality has many dimensions. These dimensions are termed 'quality attributes' when considering a product. In order to make the abstract concept of quality more operational, it should be specified in terms of operational quality attributes. Even though these attributes might have multiple meanings, they are at least more concrete than the general term 'quality'. For software product quality, the ISO 9126 standard for the division of product quality into the attributes of functionality, reliability, usability, efficiency, maintainability and portability is suggested [16].

R-8: Specify the (Relative) Importance of Product Quality Attributes for a Product, and Visualize This in a Product Quality Profile (PQP)

If product quality is specified in terms of product quality attributes, it is recommended that these be visualized in a product quality profile (PQP). A PQP visualizes the product quality along with the product quality attributes. The sum of all quality wishes belonging to a specific class indicates the maximum level of quality. If the product complies to all wishes, it is experienced as high-level quality by all stakeholders. The subset of wishes that is selected during the tradeoff with other conditions is specified in the product quality profile. A PQP visualizes which targets are set, but does not indicate priorities. Setting priorities is done during the negotiation process and is carried out iteratively with process engineering.

R-9: Specify Product Quality Requirements in Measurable Terms
Ideally, product quality targets are specified as objectively as possible; therefore it is recommended that product quality be specified in measurable terms [2, 11]. By specifying requirements measurably, explicit goals become available, and the performance gap between target and actual quality can be monitored. The benefit of this is that the way in which these targets are fulfilled is left open, creating possibilities for variation and control by the developers. After all, requirements engineering specifies 'what' to build, and not 'how'.

R-10: Show the Trade-Off between Quality Demands and the Cost/Efforts Incurred to Realize Those Demands
The results of the trade-off of quality to cost and effort should be made explicit and communicated. The highest level of quality is often not the objective for embedded products. High quality costs money and often only a few customers require that high level and are therefore willing to pay for it. Making a trade-off means investigating, each wish, how it can be addressed it and what it costs. This involves looking at the process and the available resources capable of addressing each wish. Furthermore, addressing certain wishes may have impacts on time to market, i.e. development duration. Balancing wishes with the costs incurred involves an iterative process between requirements and process engineering.

14.3.2   Guidelines for Software Development Process Engineering (SDPE)

Software development process engineering is the design of a measurable development process for the development of a specific product that complies to the product's quality specification. A development process consists of a set of actions with explicit expected effects on product quality. During process engineering a set of process actions are selected that contribute to the required product quality. These process actions are then assembled into a product-specific development process model. A process action is an action taken to achieve an explicit expected effect. Process engineering can also be seen as configuring and tuning a situated software development process, based on the product quality specification. The guidelines for software development process engineering are:

P.1. Only start with process engineering if the stakeholders' wishes for product quality are made explicit.
P.2. Make explicit the set of essential process actions and the set of supplementary process actions.
P.3. File the expected effect of process actions on product quality in an experience base.
P.4. For each specific product, develop a separate development process model that makes explicit the set of process actions taken to control product quality.
P.5. Consider that the effects of a specific process action can be both positive and negative, and that they can be different for different projects because context factors vary.

P.6. Estimate whether the selected set of process actions is capable of complying to the product quality targets.

P.7. Use the information in the experience base for the selection of process actions.

P.8. In order to improve and learn, innovate by introducing new process actions with which no experiences exist.

P.9. Make explicit the learning objectives for the application of certain process actions.

P.10. Revise the development process model when significant changes occur.

P-1: Only Start with Process Engineering If the Stakeholders' Wishes for Product Quality Are Made Explicit

The main objective of process engineering is to configure a product specific development process. This can only be done if the implicit needs from the stakeholders are made explicit and process engineering depends on the results of requirements engineering. The exact product quality targets are, however, set iteratively with requirements engineering because deciding on the targets is always a trade-off between aspects such as feasibility, time to market, effort, costs, and so on. Process engineering enables estimation of what product quality will be when using a certain process within certain conditions. Completed iteratively with requirements engineering, a development process is designed and the product quality targets are set.

P-2: Make Explicit the Set of Essential Process Actions and the Set of Supplementary Process Actions

Configuring a development process for a specific product never starts from scratch. Every organization has its own "standard way" of doing projects and its own 'standard' set of processes. This set of essential process actions is always taken in development projects and must be made explicit. In addition to this it must be made explicit what the experiences (expectations) are of the impact of each process action on product quality.

Besides a set of essential process actions that are always taken, there is also a set of supplementary process actions that can be taken if the specific situations demand it. This supplementary set must also be made explicit, together with the expected effects on product quality.

P-3: File the Expected Effect of Process Actions on Product Quality in an Experience Base

The essential and supplementary process actions that people in the organization use and the effects of these process actions on product quality should be modeled explicitly and stored in an experience base. This experience base is a dynamic and evolving storage medium in which new experiences and measurements with effects of process actions can be stored and adapted based on new insights. The experience base is also consulted to support decision making during process engineering. For the set up of such an experience base and how it can be structured, we refer to the literature [2, 10, 13, 14].

P-4: For Each Specific Product, Develop a Separate Development Process Model that Makes Explicit the Set of Process Actions Taken to Control Product Quality

The presented approach is based on the assumption that there is no one best way of making a quality product, because product quality depends on the specific needs of all stakeholders and the context in which it is being developed and used. In line with this assumption, every product requires its own development process to achieve the specific product quality. This process needs to be made explicit.

Process actions need to be made explicit at several different moments of development, e.g. during project planning when the intended set of process actions is defined, during project execution if certain process actions are omitted or added, and after project finalization when it becomes clearer what the right set of process actions should have been. Making these process actions explicit means identifying, for each process action, the time when it should be taken, how these should be taken, using which technique, by whom, with what expected effect, and so on.

Practical experiences identified that process engineering resembles what is done in practice during 'project planning', although implicitly. During project planning, project managers define a development process with deliverables, deadlines and resources, that is intended to result in a product that fulfils the project targets. However, this process rarely addresses product quality explicitly. The recommendation is therefore to bring process engineering in line with the project planning work.

P-5: Consider That the Effects of a Specific Process Action Can Be Both Positive and Negative, and That They Can Be Different for Different Projects, Because Context Factors Vary

Process actions that influence a specific goal in one area might decrease the effectiveness of the development process in another. This is often overlooked. It is recommended to always consider the multiple effects of process actions. Do not only focus on the product quality attribute that requires improvement, but also consider the effects on the other product quality attributes. This ensures that an increase of product quality in one attribute does not imply a decrease in another. It is recommended to consult the development team for conditions in the project that had a clear influence on the effects of the process action [14, 4].

P-6: Estimate Whether the Selected Set of Process Actions Is Capable of Complying to the Product Quality Targets

Making an estimate of the product quality that a certain development process is likely to deliver is recommended. This estimated product quality can be compared with the product quality targets to identify whether the selected set of process actions is sufficient, or whether corrective action should be taken. This corrective action could be changing the set of process actions, changing the product quality targets, or both. Expected effects for this set of process actions can be retrieved and final product quality can be estimated.

P-7: Use the Information in the Experience Base for the Selection of Process Actions

If a change has to be made to the selected set of process actions, the experience base can be consulted to find those process actions that address the specific quality attribute. These changes can be twofold: additional process actions will need to be selected, or selected process actions will need to be omitted. It should therefore be possible to consult the experience base to find process actions that have a positive or negative impact on a specific quality attribute.

P-8: In Order to Improve and Learn, Innovate by Introducing New Process Actions with Which No Experiences Exist

The experience base, with models of process product relationships needs to be expanded with information on new process actions. Not every project will be suitable for experimenting with innovative process actions on which hardly any knowledge is available. For example, a product with high product performance requirements will not necessarily be favorable for experimenting with a new technique that focuses on product efficiency. This has to do with the risk involved in learning [24]. It is recommended that every project be assessed for the possibility of experimenting with new process actions to learn their effects on product quality.

P-9: Make Explicit the Learning Objectives for the Application of Certain Process Actions

It has been identified that learning should be a direct objective in process improvement programs. For process engineering, this implies that the learning objectives are stated explicitly and defined for specific process actions. On these process actions the objective can be, for example, to identify what the effects are on product quality, what the conditions are under which these effects occur, or to monitor whether the intended effects occur and what the reasons for discrepancies are.

P-10: Revise the Development Process Model When Significant Changes Occur

The main product of process engineering is a development process model that indicates which process actions are taken, at what time, with what amount of effort and by whom. This development process model is the main deliverable that ensures that the development process is capable of addressing the product quality targets. It should therefore be complete, correct and consistent with the work carried out in the development process. This process model is not static, as it evolves over time, based on changes in the project. As the development process model makes explicit 'how' the product is developed, it is essential to keep this model up to date during project execution, especially since measurement program engineering depends on this process model.

14.3.3   Guidelines for Software Measurement Program Engineering (SMPE)

Measurement program engineering is the design and implementation of a set of process, product and resource metrics to evaluate product quality and process - product relationships. During measurement program engineering, metrics are defined, collected and analyzed for two purposes:

- To evaluate the compliance of embedded product quality with the stated product quality targets
- To evaluate the effects of a certain process action on product quality, when used within a specific context in a specific way

Measurement program engineering can also be seen as the process that provides feedback on the effectiveness of the process actions, and therefore facilitates learning. The guidelines for software measurement program engineering are:

M.1.   Prepare developers for participating in measurement programs.
M.2.   Know what the product quality targets, process model and learning objectives are before starting measurement program engineering.
M.3.   Measurement program engineering should be goal-oriented to ensure that a limited but relevant set of measurements is collected.
M.4.   Specify expectations (hypothesis).
M.5.   Analyze and interpret measurement data regularly, which is preferably done by those people who performed the actual measurements.
M.6.   Focus analysis and interpretation of the measurement data on a specific process action, the overall process or to the product quality targets, but not on the performance of individuals.
M.7.   Assign dedicated resources to support the development team in measurement program engineering.
M.8.   Evaluate the differences between actual and target product quality.
M.9.   Evaluate the effects of process actions.
M.10.   Store in the experience base the knowledge of the effects of a process action within a specific situation.

M-1:   Prepare Developers for Participating in Measurement Programs

Measurement of software processes and products is not something that can be immediately done. Experiences has shown that to carry out software measurement successfully, the development context including the developers should be prepared [2, 12, 8, 29]. This is a finding from the software engineering field and from learning literature, which clearly emphasizes the establishment of a learning environment before learning occurs [25, 9, 26, 27].

While both software engineering and learning literature recommend the preparation of an organization and its people for measurement programs, neither field states explicitly what this preparation consists of. During the application of these ideas in industry, this has been done by presenting the benefits of measurement in other environments, and by making the exact impact of measurement for the developers explicit. The developers are told up front what their involvement will look like, what they need to prepare and carry out, the time it will take and what benefits it will bring. Furthermore, it is arranged that the developers are always in control of the work and direction of the improvement program.

M-2: Have Product Quality Targets, Process Model and Learning Objectives Available When Starting Measurement Program Engineering

Measurement program engineering can only start whenever the measurement goals are defined. These goals are stated in the product quality targets and learning objectives that result from both requirements and process engineering. With product quality targets, it is possible to measure the conformance of the actual product quality with targets during product development. The learning objectives specify which process actions need to be measured and the purpose of these measurements. The process model specifies the process actions taken and the sequence of activities in the project.

M-3: Measurement Program Engineering should be Goal-Oriented, to Ensure That a Limited but Relevant Set of Measurements is Collected

Measurement should be driven by goals [2]. This has the benefits that measurements are only collected toward an explicit stated purpose and that only necessary measurements are taken. This limits the costs (and burden) of measurement and help measurement on only those process and product aspects of interest. Refining goals into metrics is a difficult process, but specifying an intermediate level of questions can facilitate this, which simultaneously provides a framework for the interpretation of these measurements [3]. Operational support for using goal-oriented measurement (GQM) is described in the literature [29].

M-4: Specify Expectations (Hypothesis)

In order to increase the learning effects of measurement, it is necessary to make explicit what the expectations for the measurements are. These hypotheses need to be defined before the measurements are taken. Discrepancies between hypotheses and actual values trigger causal analysis of such differences and support in learning the effects of process actions [6, 2, 30]. Without the specification of hypotheses, learning effects tend to be much lower.

M-5: Analyze and Interpret Measurement Data Regularly, which is Preferably Done by Those People who Performed the Measurements

Measurement data should be interpreted in context [2]. This means that those people who have knowledge of the context in which the data was collected, ideally those who actually collected the data, should carry out the analysis of measurements. In order to support the group learning aspect of measurement, analyzing and interpretation of measurement data should be done in groups. A way in which this can be implemented is organizing so-called feedback sessions in which the measurements are presented to the development team, who then draw conclusions about the measurements, make decisions or take action [18, 19, 29].

As developers tend to have a positivistic attitude and people have the general tendency to look for the first plausible interpretation, the opposite interpretation is often overlooked. It is therefore useful that someone takes the devil's advocate role during the interpretation of measurements and challenges the interpretations from opposite viewpoints [30].

M-6: Focus Analysis and Interpretation of the Measurement Data on: A Specific Process Action, the Overall Process, or on the Product Quality Targets, But Not on the Performance of Individuals

Interpretation should also be done toward the measurement goals. If the intermediate level of questions is used this interpretation is much easier, because the measurement data should provide answers to these questions [29]. The measurements are always taken to support a learning process. As such, these measurements may not be used to judge people [15, 12, 30], because this will directly block the learning process of the people, and as a consequence the complete improvement program might fail.

M-7: Assign Dedicated Resources to Support the Development Team in Measurement Program Engineering

The development team will have both project and learning objectives. The project objectives are often much more concrete, and attainment of these objectives is possible in shorter time. In the case of deadlines or project pressure, there is a risk that the learning objectives will be put on hold. To tackle this risk, it is recommended that the effort of the development team be limited to involvement only in those elements of measurement program engineering that add to the learning process. The non-learning tasks can be performed in parallel by other dedicated resources.

M-8: Evaluate Differences Between Actual and Target Product Quality

One of the reasons that measurement program engineering is carried out is to evaluate the conformance of the final product with product quality targets. The product is therefore measured and evaluated to see whether differences between the actual and target quality of the product exist.

If it is indicated during measurement program engineering that there is a negative gap between actual and expected effects of a set of measures, corrective action should be taken. This corrective action can be:

- Taking additional actions to influence the specific quality attributes
- Altering the product quality targets to the current product quality

This last option should not be overlooked. Product quality is always a tradeoff decision between time and cost. In many situations it might be acceptable not to spend time and money to make improvements when the product quality level is lower than the target. This depends on the market situation, competition, or financial situation. The only recommendation is to make this decision an explicit one, and to analyze the consequences of not improving product quality toward the targets.

M-9: Evaluate the Effects of Process Actions
The other purpose of measurement program engineering is to identify and learn the effects of process actions on product quality. Process actions are taken with an explicit purpose in mind; however, it cannot always be guaranteed that these effects actually occur, because these effects depend on several (possibly unknown) conditions. In cases where there is a high dependency on the effectiveness of a process action, it can be decided that measurements are required to monitor its results. These measurement results have to be analyzed and compared with the expected results (hypothesis). In the case of discrepancies, it is necessary to identify the causes (conditions) for these flaws. When it is clear that a certain process action does not give the intended effect, or produces unexpected side effects, corrective action can be taken.

M-10: Store in the Experience Base the Knowledge of the Effects of a Process Action within a Specific Situation
When the goals of a measurement program are attained, a great deal of learning has occurred. Such knowledge must be stored [24] in the experience base of process - product relationship models. Besides the effects of a certain process action on product quality, context information also needs to be stored in the experience base. Context information includes information on the specific situation in which the effects occurred. Such information is necessary for future decision making, because it helps in making an estimation of the likelihood that a process action will give a certain effect, and therefore supports in the estimation of product quality during process engineering. If context factors largely resemble a past situation, it is more likely that the same effects will occur then when all context factors are different. This context information is equally as important as the information on the effects on product quality themselves.

14.4   Conclusions

Learning is to be a key skill in software engineering as it is performed in ever-changing innovative situations. Therefore, individual and group learning seems is vital for successful software development. In this chapter an approach has been introduced that enables learning during embedded product development by the implementation of three control loops. Practical guidelines are presented and described in detail, outlining how each of these approaches can be installed in practice. For experiences with industrial application and validation of the presented approach and guidelines, we refer to [28]. So far, experiences have been positive, though further work should be done to continue developing guidelines for increased learning during product development. The work presented in this chapter has been developed for embedded systems environments. Some of the concepts and guidelines could also be relevant for non-embedded domains; but this has yet to be investigated.

References

1. Argyris C. Schön D.A. (1978) Organizational learning: a theory of action perspective, Addison-Wesley, Harlow, UK
2. Basili V.R., Rombach H.D. (1988) The TAME project: towards improvement oriented software environments. IEEE transactions on software engineering, 14: 758-773
3. Basili V.R., Weiss D.M. (1984) A methodology for collecting valid software engineering data. IEEE transactions on software engineering, SE-10: :728 - 738
4. Birk A., Järvinen J., Solingen R. van, (1999) A validation approach for product-focused process improvement. In: Proceedings of the 1st PROFES conference, Oulu, Finland, pp. 22-24
5. Davis G.B. (1982) Strategies for information requirements determination. IBM systems journal, 21: 4-30
6. Entwistle N. (1981) Styles of learning and teaching. John Wiley and Sons, West Sussex, UK
7. Erens F.J. (1996) The synthesis of variety: developing product families. Ph.D. thesis, Eindhoven University of Technology, Netherlands
8. Fenton N.E., Pfleeger S.L. (1996) Software metrics: a rigorous and practical approach. Thomson Computer Press, London, UK
9. Garvin D.A. (1993) Building a learning organization. Harvard business review, pp. 81-91.
10. Genuchten M. van (1991) Towards a software factory. Ph.D. thesis, Eindhoven University of Technology, The Netherlands
11. Gilb T. (1994) Principles of software engineering management. Addison-Wesley, Harlow, UK
12. Goodman P. (1993) Practical implementation of software metrics. McGraw-Hill, London
13. Hamann D., Järvinen J., Birk A., Pfahl D. (1998) A product process dependency definition method. In: Proceedings of the Euromicro 98 workshop on software process and product improvement, Västerås, Sweden
14. Hamann D., Järvinen J., Oivo M., Pfahl D. (1998) Experience with explicit modeling of relationships between process and product quality. In: Proceedings of the 4th European software process improvement conference, Monte Carlo
15. Humphrey W.S. (1989) Managing the software process. SEI series in software engineering, Addison-Wesley, Harlow, UK
16. ISO 9126, Information Technology, Software product evaluation: quality characteristics and guidelines for their use, ISO, 1991 and Part I: Quality model, International organization for standardization, FCD 1998
17. Karjalainen J., Makarainen M., Komi-Sirvio S., Seppanen V. (1996) Practical process improvement for embedded real-time software. Quality engineering, 8: 565-573

18. Latum F. van Oivo M., Hoisl B., Ruhe G. (1996) No improvement without feedback: experiences from goal oriented measurement at Schlumberger. In: Proceedings of the 5th European workshop on software process Technology, Lecture notes in computer science, Springer, Berlin Heidelberg New York, 1149: 167-182
19. Latum F. Solingen R. van, Oivo M., Rombach D. H., Hoisl B., Ruhe G. (1998) Adopting GQM-based measurement in an industrial environment. IEEE Software, 15: 78-86
20. Kusters, R.J., Solingen R. van, Trienekens, J.J.M. (1997) User-perceptions of embedded software quality. In: Proceedings of the Eighth international workshop on software technology and engineering practice, London, UK, pp. 184-197
21. Kusters R.J., Solingen R. van, Trienekens, J.J.M. (1999) Identifying embedded software quality: two approaches. Quality and reliability engineering international, 15: 485-492
22. PROFES (1999): Various Authors, PROFES User Manual, User Manual of the PROFES improvement methodology, ISBN 3-8167-5535-6
23. Rooijmans J., Aerts H., Genuchten M. van, (1996) Software quality in consumer electronic products. IEEE Software, 15: 55-64
24. Schneider K., Hunnius J.P. von, Basili V.R. (2002) Experience in implementing a learning software organization. IEEE Software, 19: 46-49
25. Senge P.M. (1990) The leader's new work: Building learning organizations. Sloan management review, 3: 7-23
26. Senge P.M. (1990) The fifth discipline: The art and practice of the learning organization. New York, Doubleday books, ISBN: 0385260954
27. Senge P.M., Roberts C., Ross R.B., Smith B.J., Kleiner A. (1994) The fifth discipline fieldbook: Strategies and tools for building a learning organization, NB-publishing, London, UK
28. Solingen R. van (2000) Product focused software process improvement: SPI in the embedded software domain. BETA Research Series, Nr. 32, Downloadable from: http://alexandria.tue.nl/extra2/200000702.pdf, Eindhoven University of Technology, (accessed 20th April, 2003)
29. Solingen R. van, Berghout E.W. (1999) The goal/question/metric method: a practical guide for quality improvement of software development. McGraw-Hill, Spain, ISBN 0077095537
30. Solingen R. van, Berghout E., Kooiman E. (1997) Assessing feedback of measurement data: relating schlumberger RPS practice to learning theory. In: Proceedings of the 4th international software metrics symposium, Albuquerque, Canada, pp. 152-164
31. Trienekens J.J.M., Kusters R.J., Solingen R. van (2001) Product focused software process improvement: concepts and experiences from industry. Software quality journal, 9: 269-281

Author Biography

Dr. Ir. Rini van Solingen is a principal consultant at CMG, a worldwide software product and service supplier. Within this role, he has specialized in software product and process Improvement. He has been a senior quality engineer at Schlumberger/Tokheim and was head of the Quality and Process Engineering department at the Fraunhofer IESE. Dr. van Solingen has over 100 publications, is a frequent speaker at international conferences and is author of the software measurement book: *The Goal/Question/Metric method* (http://www.gqm.nl/).

Prof. Dr. Rob Kusters is professor of ICT and Business Processes at the Dutch Open University in Heerlen where he is responsible for the master program Business process and ICT. He is also an associate professor of IT Enabled business process redesign at Eindhoven University of Technology, where he is responsible for a section of the program in management engineering and is an associate member of the research school BETA, which focuses on operations management issues. His interests include enterprise modeling, software quality and management.

Dr. Ir. Jos Trienekens is an associate professor at TU Eindhoven (TUE) in the area of ICT systems development and a senior researcher at Kema Registered Quality in the Netherlands. At TUE he is responsible for a research program, on ICT-driven business performance. He is also an associate member of the research school BETA at TUE which focuses on operations management issues. Dr. Trienekens has published various papers in books, journals and international conference proceedings, has joined several international conferences as a PC member and as organization committee member, and has experience as project partner in several European projects.

15 In-Project Learning by Goal-oriented Measurement

Rini van Solingen

Abstract: Measurement is often advocated as a means to get a better grip on software development. Measurement implements a method to gain knowledge of what is happening, and therefore is in fact a learning process. The most common method for software measurement is the Goal/Question/Metric approach (GQM). In the GQM method a systematic approach is represented for tailoring and integrating goals to models of the software processes, products, and quality perspectives of interest, based upon the specific needs of the project and the organization. By using GQM, metrics are defined from a top-down perspective, and analyzed, and interpreted from the bottom up. This interpretation process is a group learning process. GQM trees of goals, questions, and metrics are built on knowledge of the experts in the organization: the developers. Knowledge acquisition techniques are used to capture the implicit models of the developers built during years of experience. Those implicit models give valuable input to the measurement program and are often more important than the available explicit process models. By measuring daily practices of software development, GQM supports learning processes within software projects.

Keywords: GQM, Goal/Question/Metric, Measurement, Industrial experience, Management

15.1   Introduction

As with any engineering discipline, software engineering requires a measurement mechanism for feedback and learning. It is rarely recognized that the main objective of software development is in fact learning. To support and control software development, it is often advocated to use measurement. By measuring events and entities, information becomes available to control quality, development time, cost, and so on. Measurement is used as a source of information to gain knowledge, which is in fact also nothing more than learning.

Measurement supports the creation of a corporate memory and helps to answer of practical questions during software projects. It helps in project planning (e.g., How much will this project cost?), determining strengths and weaknesses (e.g., What is the frequency of severe failures?), providing a rationale for technology evaluation (e.g., What is the impact of UML on project duration?) and evaluating quality of processes and products (e.g., What is the reliability of this system in the field?). During a project, measurement assists to assess progress, to take corrective actions, and to evaluate the effectiveness of such actions.

In order to be effective measurement must be [16]

1. Focused on specific goals
2. Applied to all life-cycle products, processes, and resources
3. Interpreted based on characterization and understanding of the organizational context, environment, and goals

This implies that measurement must be defined from the top down. It must be focused, based on goals and models, and serve a certain specific interest. A solely metric-driven, bottom-up approach will not work because there are many observable characteristics in software (e.g., time, number of defects, complexity, lines of code, severity of failures, effort, productivity, and defect density). Without a goal-oriented focus established in advance, there is a chance that wrong interpretations will be made since important issues influencing conclusions have not been measured. Therefore, it is important to define beforehand what will be done with measurements, which goals are focused on, and which specific measurements need to be available to allow the drawing of conclusions. A context-specific selection of metrics and guidelines on how to use and interpret these metrics should be made, based on the models and goals of that environment. This chapter introduces practical examples on how to perform measurement within software development projects, and how to install software measurement feedback processes that maximize learning effects.

15.2   The Goal Question Metric Approach

The most common and popular mechanism for goal-oriented software measurement is the Goal Question Metric (GQM) approach [3, 4, 6, 15]. This approach is based upon the assumption that an organization must first specify the goals for itself and its projects, to allow measurement in a purposeful way. It must then trace those goals to the data that is needed to attain those goals operationally, and finally, but most important, it must provide a framework for interpreting the data with respect to the stated goals. Thus it is important to make clear what informational needs the organization has, so that these information needs can be quantified if possible and be analyzed toward the goals.

GQM defines a certain goal, refines this goal into questions, and defines metrics that should provide the information to answer these questions. By answering the questions, the measured data defines the goals operationally, which can be analyzed to identify whether or not the goals are attained. Thus, GQM defines metrics from a top-down perspective and analyses and interprets the measurement data from the bottom up, as shown in Fig. 15.1. Since the metrics were defined with an explicit goal in mind, the information provided by the metrics should be interpreted to answer the questions and compare these answers with the stated hypotheses. Finally, when all questions are answered it can be analyzed whether or not the measurement goal is attained.

The result of the application of the GQM approach is the specification of a measurement environment targeting a particular set of issues and a set of rules for the interpretation of the measurement data. The resulting measurement model has three levels: the conceptual level, the operational level, and the data level.

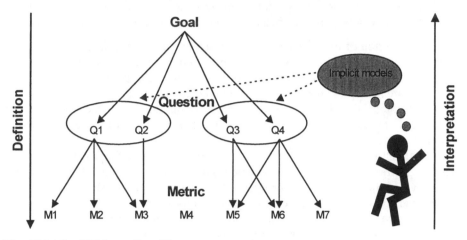

Fig. 15.1. The GQM paradigm [3]

15.2.1 Conceptual Level

A measurement goal can be defined for several objects, for a variety of reasons, with respect to various models of quality, and from various points of view, relative to a particular environment. Measurement goals should be defined in an understandable way and should be clearly structured. For this purpose, templates are available that support the definition of measurement goals by specifying *purpose* (what object and why), *perspective* (what aspect and who), and *context* characteristics [16]. One such template is illustrated in Fig. 15.2.

Analyze	The object under measurement
For the purpose of	Understanding, controlling, or improving the object
With respect to	The quality focus of the object that the measurement focuses on
From the viewpoint of	The people that measure the object
In the context of	The environment in which measurement takes place

Fig. 15.2. GQM goal definition template [16]

Objects of measurement can be classified into three groups [8]:

- *Products*: Artifacts, deliverables, and documents that are produced during the system life cycle; e.g., architectural specifications, code, or test suites.
- *Processes*: Software-related activities normally associated with time; requirements process, testing, interviewing, and so on.
- *Resources*: Items used by processes in order to produce their outputs such as software developers, project managers, hardware, software, and office space.

The definition of formal measurement goals is the first step in the definition of a measurement program. These measurement goals should be derived from the improvement goals that are assumed to be available. All people participating in the measurement program should be involved in the definition of measurement goals. Without this involvement, people's commitment to the measurement program is at risk, as it may no longer be clear to them why measurement is applied.

A distinction is made between "measurement goals" and "improvement goals". GQM specifies and supports measurement goals. These are goals that specify the objective of the measurement program. These goals can and should be derived from and based on improvement goals. Improvement goals address clear objectives to change certain aspects in an organization, for example, quality increase, cost reduction, reduced time to market, and risk reduction. Measurement goals in themselves do not increase quality or reduce development effort. They do, however, support in providing the required knowledge and information to take direct action toward these objectives. GQM supports learning about software development in an organization, and therefore supports learning "how" and "where" to improve. GQM programs provide support in integrating learning activities into the daily software process.

15.2.2   Operational Level

A set of questions is used to refine a goal into more detail by explicitly defining information and knowledge requirements for attaining such a goal. Questions try to characterize the object of measurement (product, process, resource) with respect to a selected topic and from the selected viewpoint.

It is important to specify an expected answer for each question. These so-called "hypotheses" reflect the current implicit models of the people in the measurement program. Comparison of real measurements with these hypotheses creates deep understandings of implicit knowledge and assumptions, and therefore greatly contributes to the learning effects of GQM. Without the specification of these hypotheses, learning effects of measurement are largely reduced [17].

15.2.3   Data Level

A set of metrics is related to every question in order to answer it quantitatively. Measurement data can be

- *Objective*: Measurements depend only on the object that is being measured and not on the viewpoint from which they are taken, e.g., the number of versions of a document, or staff hours spent on a task, or the size of a program.
- *Subjective*: Measurements depend on both the object that is being measured and the viewpoint from which they are taken, e.g., readability of a text, or level of user satisfaction.

15.2.4   Acquiring Knowledge for Building Measurement Programs

GQM trees of goals, questions and metrics are built on the knowledge of the people in an organization. Consequently, these people need to be involved in setting up GQM programs, which include capturing knowledge of software engineers and other representatives. Therefore, knowledge acquisition techniques applied to make the implicit models of the developers built during years of experience need to be made explicit. Those implicit models can then give valuable input into the measurement program.

To support making these implicit models more explicit, one can use so-called abstraction sheets [11]. The use of abstraction sheets during interviews provides a structured approach to focus on relevant issues regarding the measurement goal and to prevent issues from being overlooked. An abstraction sheet summarizes the main issues and dependencies of a goal as described in a GQM plan and is subdivided into four sections. The four sections of an abstraction sheet are [11]:

- *Quality focus*: What are possible metrics to measure an object of a goal, according to the project members?
- *Baseline hypothesis*: What is the project member's current knowledge with respect to these metrics? His or her expectations are documented as baseline hypotheses of the metrics.
- *Variation factors*: Which (environmental) factors does a project member expect to be of influence on the metrics?
- *Impact on baseline hypothesis*: How could these variation factors influence the actual measurements? What kind of dependencies between the metrics and influencing factors are assumed?

An example of an abstraction sheet is given in Fig. 15.3. Hypotheses are grouped in the two lower sections of the abstraction sheet and are related to the corresponding questions in the other sections. The four sections can be checked for consistency and completeness, because mutual relations between the sections exist. For example, for every quality focus, there should be at least one baseline hypothesis, and possibly some variation factors. Also, for every variation factor there should be at least one Impact on the hypothesis. These variation factors are explicitly important since they focus on those issues that influence the object under measurement. This prevents wrong conclusions from being drawn due to events occurring outside the scope of measurement.

Object	Purpose	Quality Focus	Viewpoint
Delivered Product	Understanding	Reliability and its causes	Project Team

Quality Focus	Variation Factors
Number of failures: • by severity • by detection group • number of faults • by module	Level of reviewing

Baseline Hypotheses (estimates)	Impact of Variation Factors

Distribution of failures:
• By severity:
   • Minor 60%
   • Major 30%
   • Fatal 10%
	The higher the level of reviewing, the fewer minor failures will be detected after release

Fig. 15.3. Example abstraction sheet [16]

15.3   Feedback of Software Measurement Results

Feedback of measurement data and the associated analysis of this data by the software engineers is done in so-called feedback sessions [10]. Feedback sessions are meetings of all software development team members and GQM team members in which the measurement results are discussed. Outcomes of a feedback session are interpretations, conclusions, decisions, and actions. Feedback sessions are typically carried out in industrial measurement programs through the following steps:

- *Preparing a feedback session*: Preparing feedback sessions concerns the processing of collected data into presentable and interpretable material. The GQM plan provides the basis for preparing feedback sessions. That is feedback material should support answering the questions as defined in the GQM plan, and based on these answers, one should be able to conclude whether the defined measurement goals are attained. The GQM team primarily carries out the preparation for feedback sessions.
- *Holding a feedback session*: Feedback sessions are held approximately every six to eight weeks. They typically last about 1.5 to 2 hours, but no more than 3 hours. Sessions that are any longer are seen as counter productive. This time is sufficient to discuss some 15 to 20 slides (containing graphs and tables) [15]. In principal, a software development team should run a feedback session alone. They analyze, interpret, and draw conclusions regarding the measurements, and translate their conclusions into action points. After all, they are the experts with respect to the object under measurement. The software development team should focus on evaluating action points from earlier sessions, interpreting measurement data with respect to the questions and goals as defined in the

GQM plan, and translating interpretations into conclusions and action points. The GQM team should avoid interpreting the data themselves. Their role is to challenge a software development team, for example, by offering alternative interpretations [17]. Furthermore, the GQM team provides support and may, for example, provide meeting reports. Feedback sessions are a delicate phase in a measurement program since mutual trust among all participants is, an essential element of a feedback session. Through focusing on identified goals, questions, and metrics, the discussion will start on the basis of facts.

- *Documenting results of a feedback session*: After the feedback session, the GQM team writes a meeting report containing all relevant observations, interpretations, conclusions and action points that were formulated during the session. It is advised to follow the rule that the software development team 'owns' the measurement data and therefore decides on distribution of both data and reports to, for example, management. When the GQM team wants to inform higher management, the GQM team only uses particular, often aggregated results and asks for permission to do so. In order to reuse measurement results and experiences in future measurement programs, the results of a measurement program should be documented in such a way that they are easily accessible and understandable.

The concept of organizational support for GQM measurement programs distinguishes a software development team and a GQM team [16]. This GQM team supports a software development team by carrying out all tasks in a measurement program that do not need to be performed by the software engineers. As such, the engineers only provide their input and participation when necessary, leaving their workload in measurement relatively low. Our research indicates that the amount of time spent by a software development team on a measurement program is limited to 2% of their time, and is even reduced to less than 1% for teams with GQM measurement experience [5]. Beside the benefits limiting the participation effort of the software engineers, the other benefit of measurement is that this two-team structure facilitates continuation. Both teams depend on and trigger each other, which results in a continuous process. The software development team triggers the GQM team with data and requests for aggregated results. Likewise, the GQM team triggers the software development team with requests for measurement data and interpretations of feedback material.

The second point is the observation that the main purpose and outcome of measurement programs is *learning* [17]. Measurement programs are performed to increase understanding and control, and to optimize practices [2]. This is all centered on collecting information to increase knowledge, which is nothing more than learning. Considering that improvement and measurement should be learning processes, this immediately leads to the recommendation of exploring learning theory to identify how measurements can be performed better through increasing the learning effects. In the past few years we have performed research and explored learning theory and formulated practical guidelines on increasing measurement learning effectiveness [17]. Measurement programs can only be successful when the participants actually learn [18]. Realizing that learning is an important objective of measurement, learning theory is explored in order to understand how learning takes place within industrial measurement programs and how this learning can be encouraged. Learning deals with expanding knowledge and changing behavior [9]. Elements of learning theories were also included in feedback sessions and led to two particular findings: model of the learning process between software development team and GQM team, and a list of learning enablers that stimulate group learning within measurement programs. These two products are elaborated upon in the following sections.

15.3.1   Learning Model for Development Team and GQM Team Interaction

In this section we position the guidelines from learning theory into a model of feedback sessions. Based on learning theory of student - teacher interactions [7], a model is proposed regarding development - GQM team interaction. This model is depicted in Fig. 15.4 and describes the learning process that a software development team and GQM team go through. The model illustrates that the results of a feedback session are significantly influenced by the organization of the feedback process.

The model of feedback sessions contains two loops. One loop represents the learning process of the software development team, the other the learning process of the GQM team. Both loops contain two types of impact: short-term and long-term changes. A GQM team possesses specific characteristics that define the feedback. The software development team (also with specific characteristics) has a particular perception of this feedback. The results of a feedback session are improvements that are made explicit through interpretations, conclusions, and action points. These improvements influence the software development team and GQM team, as well as the short-term and long-term changes. A more detailed description of this model is given in [17]. Multiple case studies have been carried out to validate this model.

The previous knowledge of the software development team with respect to the measured process is captured by building the measurement program based their knowledge of the process, and through interviews for the definition of the GQM. Measurement data is normally of great concern to software engineers since this information is often accessible to other departments and represents their performance.

The GQM team members provide the feedback: they process the data and prepare it for analysis and interpretation. Also, they guide the feedback process and assist software engineers in their analysis and interpretation of the data. An important requirement that needs to be fulfilled to succeed in the measurement program is that a high level of mutual trust and cooperation between the two teams must exist. Therefore, it is argued that a GQM team should be independent of the software development team and have no interest in the data that a software development team gathers. To be able to guide and support the measurement program, the GQM team needs to have an adequate level of background knowledge of the processes and products that are being measured. This is an important prerequisite if this team is to question and challenge the interpretations made by the software development team. It is also a prerequisite in the sense that respect from the software development team is required. The GQM team should regard themselves as facilitators of learning and be improvement-oriented in guiding the measurement programs. If they are, they not only assist in improving the processes of the software development team, but also learn how to improve their own work. Enthusiasm for the measurement programs is required to create a good atmosphere during the definition of the GQM plan as well as during the feedback process.

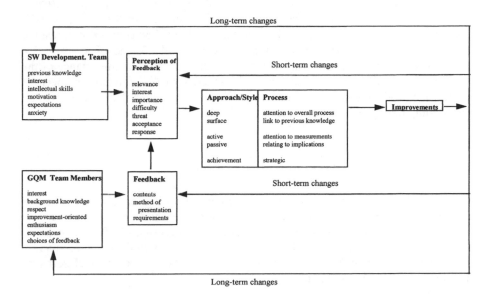

Fig. 15.4. Conceptual model of learning in a feedback session [17]

The following elements are pertinent to the feedback process. The contents of the feedback sessions should be based on the measurement results and the GQM plan. Presented material should be limited in quantity and provided regularly. The concept of relating new knowledge to available knowledge is an integral part of GQM measurement. The emphasis on relating new and existing knowledge is a fundamental prerequisite for the interpretation of measurement data. During the presentation, much attention needs to be given to these aspects. In presenting results, they should be related to the goals and questions and also to their recorded expectations (hypotheses). Learning through feedback is primarily achieved through discussion of the data presented. This way, it is an explicit conversation between people. Although it is clear that this statement is primarily aimed at educational environments, it applies equally well to the material that is presented in the feedback process. Relevance is primarily determined by a measurement process and a correct refinement of goals into questions and metrics. When the right processes are measured (those that require improvement according to a software development team), and the right data is gathered that indicates possible improvements, the relevance of the measurement program is normally high.

Carrying out a measurement program with a central role for the software development team also implies that the software development team guards the relevance. The relevance of feedback is primarily the GQM team's responsibility as the GQM team is expected to process the data and prepare it for interpretation. This relevance can be achieved by relating the processed data back to the GQM plan, in which the objects that are considered relevant by the software development team are stated. The perception of the interest of the feedback itself is considered equally important: it is important for the GQM team to convince the software development team of the importance of feedback and of the software development team's contributions to the feedback process. The importance of the feedback process lies in the fact that the knowledge of the software engineers is shared and used to improve the processes. This gives the members themselves an opportunity to improve the processes in a way they consider effective.

15.3.2   Learning Enablers for Feedback Sessions

Based on learning theory, the most prominent learning enabling factors for feedback have been identified. This paper does not have sufficient space to describe the complete analysis of these enablers as described in [9, 12, 13]. For this analysis we refer to [14]. The learning enablers will be subsequently described, together with what the enabler means within the context of software development. These enablers are:

- *Climate of openness*: A climate of openness addresses the establishment of an environment in which there is free flow of information, open communication, sharing problems and lessons learned, and open debate of ways to solve problems. Such a climate or "learning culture" could seem a simple concept, however, it is difficult to establish in practice. Research has indicated that current structures for control and management in organizations tend to disable such climates of openness and thus decrease the commitment of their people [1, 14]. The intrinsic motivation of people is especially crucial for establishing a creative and learning-oriented environment. Practical actions that managers can take to increase the intrinsic motivation of people are grouped in terms of challenge, freedom, resources, work group feature, supervisory encouragement, and organizational support [14]. A climate of openness appears to be one of the most crucial prerequisites for organizational learning. This requires a context in which people are willing to learn from their mistakes and discuss underlying causes and models for these mistakes.
- *Scanning for knowledge*: In the broadest sense, this means that there should be a continuous search for knowledge that could be relevant or applicable in the

specific learning situation. Scanning for knowledge from previous products, competitors' products, similar products, or new methods is an important input to the requirements phase of a software project. Preferably, software product requirements should not be built from scratch. Carrying-out a post-mortem analysis to find out whether a certain used process model was adequate is also a good source of knowledge (to increase learning effects).

- *Information on context and current state of the system*: Learning adds knowledge to an existing situation and can be influenced by external factors. Information is needed on the context and current state to learn appropriately and to select the best-suited additions. Here, the retrieval of information on the context and the current state of the product and the project is essential. Making processes explicit, measuring the performance of processes, or the current state of the product and its quality is useful to enable learning.
- *Team learning*: Team learning is an important part of an organizational learning process. Learning is established within groups that work together toward a shared vision and mutual objectives. Joint formulation of learning objectives, information sharing, discussion, and drawing of conclusions takes place within team learning. Team learning can be used to find out a good way in which product requirements need to be specified so that the final product complies with them. It is also important that software development teams learn the behavior of different development processes. Measurement is a powerful mechanism to enable this group learning.
- *Modeling of the system under control*: In order to control a system, a model needs to be created from this system and its influencing factors. This can be done through process modeling, and the modeling of relationship between the product requirements and process.
- *Possibilities for control*: In order to steer a process toward the required outcomes, possibilities for control should be available. This means that during a software project (corrective) action can be taken whenever necessary.
- *Involved leadership*: Managers should articulate vision, take part in the implementation of ideas, and be actively involved in the learning processes. The role of a manager for the establishment of organizational learning, and motivating the people in the organization is crucial. In a learning organization, managers and their roles are largely different to traditional management styles. The largest differences are that the manager is a designer of the learning organization, a teacher of the view on reality, and a steward for the people [13].
- *Explicit goal definition*: In order to have clear targets toward learning, particular goals should be defined and made explicit. Learning processes are of benefit if it is clear what the goals are and in which area learning is required to attain such goals. Expectations (hypotheses) must be explicitly specified with regards to the attainment of these learning goals, because expectations can be compared to actual values and reasons for differences can be identified.
- *Monitoring performance gap*: Monitoring the difference between target and actual situations is an important prerequisite for learning. It supports the identification of what is going well, and what needs improvement. Through this

performance monitoring, people get feedback on their way of working and learn where to improve. Monitoring a possible performance gap is not only done for the product, but also for the development process. The performance of process actions should be monitored, and if differences exist between expected and real effects of process actions, corrective action can be taken.

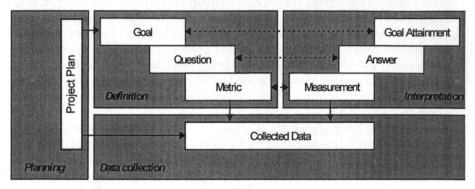

Fig. 15.5. Phases of GQM application [15]

15.4   Application of the GQM Approach in Practice

In this section, the application of GQM is clarified through the presentation of an industrial project. The industrial project used as the example developed both software and hardware for a real-time low-end cashing system in an international company. This company develops and services systems for retail petrol stations. This project was a second (incremental) release of a system, so a considerable part of the software was reused from an earlier release. At the end of the project, the cashing system contained over 70,000 source lines of C-code. The software development team consisted of a project leader, two hardware engineers, and two software engineers. This project spanned a total of two years. For more information or details on this specific measurement program see Fig. 15.5 [15]. The approach used for implementing GQM in this project was the GQM method, which is a practical set of steps, over four phases [15];

1. The planning phase, during which a project for measurement application is selected, defined, characterized, and planned, resulting in a project plan.
2. The definition phase, during which the measurement program is defined (goal, questions, metrics, and hypotheses are defined) and documented.
3. The data collection phase, during which actual data collection takes place,
4. The interpretation phase, during which collected data is processed with respect to defined metrics and turned into measurement results, which provide answers to the defined questions. After this goal attainment can be evaluated.

The planning phase is performed to arrange all prerequisites to make a GQM measurement program a success, by focusing on training, management involvement, and project planning. During the second phase, the definition phase, all GQM deliverables are created, based on input from the project and organization. This input is collected by means of structured interviews, reading documentation or other knowledge acquisition techniques. During the definition phase the measurement goal, all questions, related metrics, and expectations (hypotheses) of the measurements are made explicit and documented in a set of reports. When all definition activities are completed, actual measurement can start. During this data collection phase measurements are collected and stored in a measurement database. Then the "real work" can start using the measurement data in the interpretation phase. During the interpretation phase, the measurements are used to answer the stated questions, and these answers are again used to see whether the stated goals have been attained. Comparisons between hypotheses and actual results facilitate deep learning [14].

The first step in the definition process is the definition of a measurement goal. The people participating in the measurement program should be involved in the definition of these measurement goals. Without this involvement, people's commitment to the measurement program is at risk, as it may no longer be clear to them why measurement is applied, and motivation is negatively influenced. In this project the above-introduced measurement goal template was filled out, which is depicted below. The measurement program goal on product and process reliability [15] was to

- Analyze the: delivered product and development process
- for the purpose of: understanding
- with respect to: reliability and its causes
- from the viewpoint of: the software development team
- in the following context: the cashing system project

Based upon this goal, the following set of questions and measurements were specified in close cooperation with the specific software development team. It may appear that certain questions or metrics are not in line with what some readers might expect. This is because a measurement program is defined and matched to the specific information and knowledge requirements of the specific team. As such, questions and metrics are always different from one environment to the other. The learning effects, however, match exactly to the current level of knowledge.

- Q1: What is the distribution of failures after delivery?
  - M1:   Number of failures per calendar month
- Q2: What is the distribution of failures across severity classes?
  - M2:   For each failure: severity class (fatal, major, minor)
- Q3: What is the distribution of faults after delivery?
  - M3:   Number of faults per module
  - M4:   Number of KSLOC per module
- Q4: What is the relation between module reuse and reliability?

- M3:   Number of faults per module
- M4:   Number of KSLOC per module
- M5:   For each module: amount of reuse (100%, <20%, >20%, 0%)
- Q5:   What is the relation between module complexity and reliability?
  - M3:   Number of faults per module
  - M4:   Number of KSLOC per module
  - M8:   Cyclomatic complexity per module
- Q6:   What is the detection effectiveness of internal groups?
  - M1:   Number of failures per calendar month
  - M9:   Percentage of failures per internal groups that find defects
- Q7:   What is the distribution of failure handling effort?
  - M10:   Effort per failure for finding the underlying fault
  - M11:   Effort per fault for repair and testing
  - M12:   Process phase in which the fault was introduced

For three of the above questions (Q1, Q2, and Q4) detailed measurements results will be presented and elaborated in the way they were presented and discussed in several feedback sessions [16].

15.4.1   Question 1: What is the Distribution of Failures after Delivery?

Figure 15.6 illustrates the amount of failures reported by the project. The number of failure reports on this product approached zero towards the end of development. A chart like this not only indicates reliability of the product, but also shows effects of detection events. For example, in April of the first year a novice user test was performed, and the number of failure reports was high. Without this test, the number of failures would probably be lower; however, they were likely to be found in later stages. Another peak is shown in November, when the first field release was prepared. During the integration phase several failures were detected. The relatively low number of failures during July and August of year 1 reflect the summer holidays.

Note that therefore the software development team can only interpret such charts, as an outsider might have concluded that the product was becoming reliable. This is a general rule: only the people in the software development team can interpret measurement data, as they have all the knowledge of what happened. Someone outside the project can of course prepare such charts, as long as this person does not draw any conclusions.

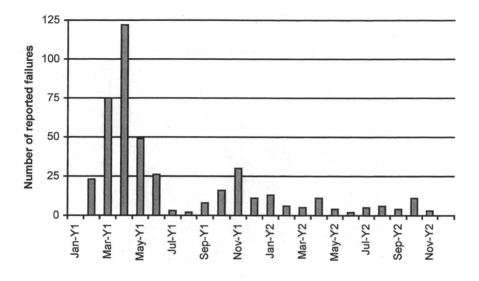

Fig. 15.6. Number of failure reports on product under development

15.4.2   Question 2: What is the Distribution of Failures over Severity Classes?

The software development team considered the severity of a failure as an important aspect of reliability. The more fatal a failure, the more negatively it impacts reliability. For example, it is not acceptable to find fatal failures after the release of a system to the field, while some minor failures may be acceptable (for this project). Therefore, the GQM plan contained a "severity" classification for failures, which defined three classes for severity of a failure:

- *Fatal failures*: For example, the system failed, executed wrong transactions, or lost transactions
- *Major failures*: For example, the system refused legitimate transactions, or produced redundant outputs with small impact on performance
- *Minor failures*: For example, aesthetic problems such as misspelling or output formatting problems

Figure 15.7 illustrates the distribution of failures over time based on severity category. The hypotheses as the software development team stated them in February of year 1 are also presented in this chart. The percentage of fatal failures stabilized at around 25%, while the expected number of fatal failures was 10%. The software development team had learned how failures were distributed by severity, and this knowledge could be used in future projects. These numbers could also be used in future projects to plan failure repair.

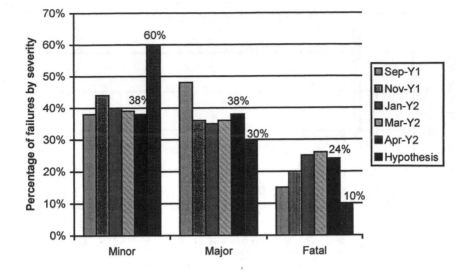

Fig. 15.7. Number of failures per severity category

15.4.3 Question 3: What is the Relation between Reuse and Reliability?

The software developed in this project was largely reused from a previous release. Figure 15.8 shows that the fault density (number of faults per thousand source lines of code) decreased linearly as the amount of reuse increased. Distinctions were made between existing faults and new faults. New faults were introduced during changes or additional development, whereas existing faults were already in the software before it was reused. The number of newly introduced faults decreased when the amount of reuse increased. When more than 20% of the code was reused this resulted in five time fewer new faults compared to complete new development. In all completely reused modules, no faults were identified. The software development team learned that it was beneficial to reuse (parts of) modules during development. Reusing only the structure of an existing module also resulted in increased reliability.

Conclusions on reuse drawn by the software development team were

- Reuse is a useable method for fault prevention and detection. This is a remarkable learning point by the project, since by reusing they also detected faults still included in other systems. So, not only did the current system become more reliable, but other systems also became more reliable.
- Most of the faults in partially reused modules are detected before release. This is caused by the lower confidence level of engineers in partially reused modules than in personally developed modules. This is a remarkable social learning

aspect. The team concluded that they were much more critical testers toward reused software than to their own developed software, which resulted in even higher reliability of the reused modules.

- Reuse results in lower fault density. The measurements clearly showed a strong impact on reliability by means of reuse. The software development team advocated an increase in the amount of reuse strongly after that, both in their own as well as in other projects, as a means of improving reliability.

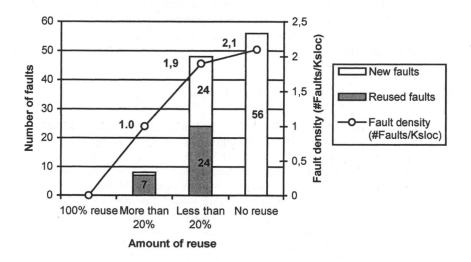

Fig. 15.8. Fault densities of modules categorized by amount of reuse

These measurement results were used to convince managers and engineers of the effectiveness of reuse, and could also be used to promote reuse elsewhere in the organization. Productivity improvements caused by reuse were not considered in this measurement program on purpose. The reliability increase caused by reuse was learned from this measurement program, so other projects did not have to learn this again.

15.5   Conclusion

The GQM approach is a mechanism for defining and interpreting operational and measurable software engineering goals. It can be used in isolation or, better still, within the context of a more general approach to software quality improvement. GQM has evolved in the past years to become the de facto standard for the set-up of software measurement programs. The GQM approach combines in itself most of the current approaches to measurement and generalizes them to incorporate processes and resources as well as products. This makes it adaptable to different environments, as confirmed by the fact that it has been applied in many organizations [15, 16].

Although rarely explicitly considered in industry, the main objective of software measurement is in fact learning. Without learning, there will be no increased understanding and therefore no improvement. In this chapter, learning theory was used to identify possibilities of increasing the learning effectiveness of feedback sessions. The outcome of this investigation was presented in a model of a software development team — GQM team interaction that describes both the learning processes of a software development team and a GQM team. Furthermore, several enablers were introduced that support learning in measurement programs.

References

1. Amabile T.M. (1998) How to kill creativity. Harvard business review, 76: 77-87
2. Banker R., Slaughter S. (1997) A field study of scale economies in software maintenance. Management science, 43: 1709-1725
3. Basili V.R., Weiss D.M. (1984) A methodology for collecting valid software engineering data. IEEE transactions on software engineering, SE-10: 728-738
4. Basili V.R., Rombach H.D. (1998) The TAME project: towards improvement-oriented software environments. IEEE transactions on software engineering, SE-14: 758-773.
5. Birk A., Solingen R. van, Järvinen J. (1998) Business impact, benefit, and cost of applying GQM in industry: an in-depth, long-term investigation at Schlumberger RPS. In: Proceedings of Metrics'98, Bethesda Maryland, 93-96
6. Briand L.C., Differding C.M., Rombach, H.D. (1996) Practical guidelines for measurement based improvement, ISERN 96-05
7. Entwistle N. (1981) Styles of learning and teaching, John Wiley and Sons, West Sussex, UK
8. Fenton N.E., Pfleeger, S.L. (1996) Software metrics: a rigorous and practical approach. Thomson computer press, London, UK
9. Garvin D.A. (1993) Building a learning organization. Harvard business review, pp. 81-91.
10. Latum F. van, Oivo M., Hoisl B., Ruhe G. (1996) No improvement without feedback: experiences from goal oriented measurement at Schlumberger. In: Proceedings of the 5th European workshop on software process technology, Lecture notes, Springer, Berlin Heidelberg New York, 1149: 167-182
11. Latum F. van, Solingen R. van, Oivo M., Rombach H. D., Hoisl B., Ruhe G. (1998) Adopting GQM based measurement in an industrial environment. IEEE Software, 15: 78-86
12. Nevis E., DiBella A., Gould J. (1995) Understanding organizations as learning systems. Sloan management review, 36: 73-85
13. Senge P.M. (1990) The fifth discipline: The art and practice of the learning organization, Doubleday, New York, USA

14. Solingen R. van, (2000) Product focused software process improvement: SPI in the embedded software domain. Ph.D. thesis, Eindhoven University of Technology, Netherlands, ISBN 90-386-0163-3
15. Solingen R. van, Berghout E.W. (1999) The goal/question/metric method. McGraw-Hill Publishers, ISBN 0077095537
16. Solingen R. van, Basili V.R., Caldiera G., Rombach H.D. (2002) Goal question metric (GQM) approach. In: Marciniak J.J. (Ed.), Encyclopedia on software engineering, John Wiley and Sons, West Sussex, UK
17. Solingen R. van, Berghout E., Kooiman E. (1997) Assessing feedback of measurement data: relating Schlumberger practice to learning theory. In: Proceedings of IEEE 4th international software metrics symposium, 152-164.
18. Ulrich D. (1998) Intellectual capital = competence x commitment. Sloan management review, 40: 9-20

Author Biography

See Chapter 14

16 e-R&D: Effectively Managing and Using R&D Knowledge

Christof Ebert, Jozef De Man and Fariba Schelenz

Abstract: This chapter describes a process improvement initiative at Alcatel called e-R&D. It deals with systematically and continuously disseminating knowledge throughout the organization and embodying it in new products and services. e-R&D can be broken into three implementation tracks: strengthened process capability, visibility and workflow integration. These three tracks and their impact on knowledge management are explained in the chapter and are illustrated with examples and lessons learned. Focus is given to organizational learning as one component of knowledge management, and underlined with tool support that facilitates such learning.

Keywords: Collaborative product commerce, e-R&D, Software process improvement, Managing process diversity, Workflow management,

16.1 Introduction

Effectively managing knowledge is a mandatory driver for business success in software-dominated product development. To keep software development competitive, Alcatel put in place an orchestrated process improvement with underlying engineering tools. This initiative is called e-R&D. One important aspect of e-R&D is illustrated within this chapter. It deals with systematically and continuously creating knowledge, disseminating it throughout the organization and embodying it in new products and services. Knowledge management thus will be characterized from the three perspectives of products, processes and projects.

Why do we map knowledge management on products, processes and projects, primarily? The great majority of today's technology-based companies has overloaded their R&D project pipelines and don't have the visibility of impacts across the various tracks. A little bit of processes tuning, improving project management, or getting some visibility on new product introduction can no longer cure this. The allure of new, high-margin products, combined with the delayed impacts of resource allocation decisions, seduce product managers into starting more projects than their development resources can handle. Similar manufacturing during the 1980s, the perceived "software factories" must focus simultaneously on all three dimensions.

Why do we call managing these assets "e-R&D"? For two reasons: effectively managing and using product, process and project assets necessarily fit into the wider range of Alcatel's business process improvement and corporate e-business initiatives. The term e-R&D also means enabling of interactive R&D processes and increasingly collaborative work across the globe.

What is the vision behind e-R&D? The vision of the e-R&D initiative is to provide outstanding R&D performance. This is achieved through the three elements of e-R&D, namely accountability, process improvement and technology effectiveness. *Accountability* targets management practices and is one of Alcatel's values. *Process improvement* considers the variety of R&D processes and how to improve our process capability based on available experiences and process assets. *Technology effectiveness* leverages on accountability and process improvement and looks into providing the right innovative technology to address our customers' needs.

e-R&D can be broken into three implementation tracks:

- Strengthened process capability
- Visibility
- Workflow integration

These elements are centered on a standardized product life cycle (Fig. 16.1). For well-orchestrated product launch, development, post-launch and discontinuance, all functions of the enterprise must play a part in developing and executing an integrated plan. The potential for growth as well as replacement must be assessed based on a common framework.

Strengthened process capability is the key to e-R&D. If you do not know where you are and where you want to go, change will never lead to improvement. For several years, Alcatel has implemented the world-renowned Capability Maturity Model (CMM), originally issued by the Software Engineering Institute [23]. This model provides a framework for process improvement and is used by many software development organizations. It defines five levels of process maturity plus an improvement framework for process maturity, and as a consequence quality and predictability.

Knowledge management must be linked to business. We thus included within e-R&D the CMM with a strong focus on business objectives and metrics for follow-up of change implementation. Take as an example a mobile phone design. Since this is a commodity good, we focus primarily on targets such as return rates. Defects increase return rates and reduce brand loyalty. Both have devastating business impacts. The business division responsible for Alcatel's mobile phones therefore looks carefully at that objective. Design reviews are centered on reducing return rates and check on not only manufacturing aspects, but also on how design decisions impact usability. Knowledge and experience from past projects (and failures) is embedded into the underlying design processes.

How do engineering tools appear? Processes without adequate tool support remain theoretical. Our objective is to improve visibility in engineering and to master a variety of workflows and external interfaces related to R&D. e-R&D must bridge the needs of process improvement with tool support. Naturally, workflow management and knowledge management are closely related in such highly collaborative environments as described here. Process-related knowledge builds the nucleus toward automating and reusing artifacts, thus reducing cycle time and rework.

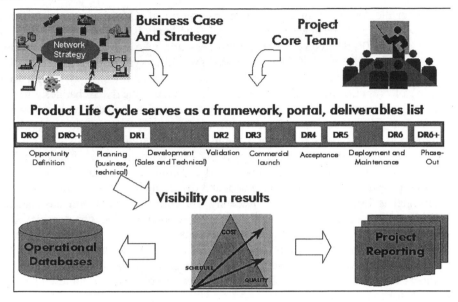

Fig. 16.1. e-R&D drives R&D improvements along the life cycle

Key terminology in this chapter is briefly explained here. A process is a sequence of steps performed for a given purpose, for example, the software development process. The process follows the guidance provided by enterprise or business unit policies. A work product or artifact is the outcome of a process. It can be intermediate and internal to a process or it can be delivered to another process.

The product life cycle (PLC) summarizes on a high-level the phases between a product's inception and its phase-out. The Capability Maturity Model (CMM), has been the de facto standard of software process improvements. In this context, we do not distinguish between hardware and software systems regarding business processes and the underlying management processes in portfolio and project management.

The chapter is organized as follows: Sect. 16.2 describes the environment in which we operate. Sect. 16.3 briefly introduces the topic and background of knowledge management (KM) in software engineering. It also covers some results available from other studies and solutions. Sect. 16.4 covers integrated management of process diversity, for both concepts and tool support. Sect. 16.5 introduces the concept of return on knowledge and how to select the appropriate solutions for effective knowledge management. Finally, Sect. 6 concludes with our own concrete results, which we achieved over the past years.

16.2   Case Study Setting

To cover the full depth of the possible integration of KM concepts, this chapter focuses on a single business unit in Alcatel. The study is based on experiences in the Alcatel 1000 S12 voice switching business unit in Alcatel's voice networking business. The Alcatel 1000 S12 is a digital switching system that is used in over 50 countries world-wide, with over 180 million installed lines. It provides a wide range of functionality (line concentrators, small local exchanges, transit exchanges, international exchanges, network service center, and intelligent networks) and scalability (from small remote concentrators to large local exchanges). Its typical size is over 4.5 million source statements (in a Pascal-like language), which are customized for network operators. In terms of functionality, S12 covers almost all areas of software and computer engineering. This includes operating systems, database management and distributed real-time software.

Alcatel is ISO 9000 certified. Recently the entire business unit has reached CMM level 3. The activities and results described in this chapter played a dominant role in achieving this. The concepts of e-R&D are currently being reused more across Alcatel. In terms of effort or development cost, the share of software is increasing continuously and is currently in the range of 90%. The projects vary in size between a few person-years and more than a hundred person-years (broken into increments).

More than 2000 R&D engineers work in this business unit globally. In such a large business unit operating in several geographically distributed development centers, the need for effectively managing process diversity arises earlier than in a small and co-located unit.

Having one PLC across Alcatel allowed us to dig deeper and identify policies and templates for the decision process, as well as to anchor a variety of functional detailed processes, roles and infrastructure tools. We definitely recommend starting with a generic PLC plan then continuing on a more detailed level, rather than in the opposite direction. This top-down approach applies for the entire discussion around business process reengineering and e-commerce introduction. Start with a generic (business) process, apply it in pilots and product lines in order to improve on business processes, and then allow specific tailoring.

Our vision was centered on visibility in engineering and mastering a variety of workflows and external interfaces. This need is pictured in the environment that we wanted to support (Fig. 16.2). A variety of workflows together describe how software engineering artifacts are gradually generated. Some are internal to engineering, while others are at the boundary to other functions. They all have their own tool environments, which often overlap. Many of these tools are proprietary, mostly legacy and surely not originally intended to work with each other or to be managed externally.

The need for workflow management stems from the heterogeneity of those tools and the detailed processes overlap considerably, such as login procedures, document management and product data management. The system described in this paragraph is build upon one instance accessible via an intranet to all engineers of the business unit who share similar needs, processes and tools. When scaling up to a broader corporate level, we maintain the notion of instances per product line, as this is where the greatest coherence and synergies can be achieved.

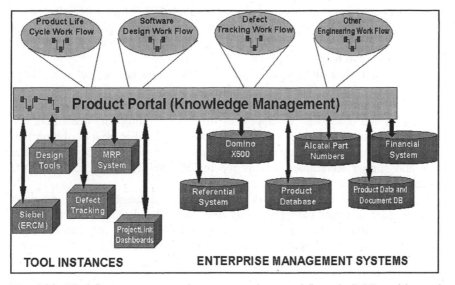

Fig. 16.2. Workflow management integrates various workflows in R&D and beyond and allows access to a diversity of shared and partially legacy tools environments

16.3   Knowledge Management in Software Engineering

Knowledge management usage gained a lot of momentum during the 1990s. Eighty percent of the largest global enterprises now have KM projects [14]. Moreover, KM reached the software engineering community late in the 1990s. Typically knowledge was not managed before, but was randomly collected and lost in the graveyards of corporate document vaults that were incompatible with each other. Increasingly KM has gained ground as a discipline that needs dedicated attention, not only from a functional but specifically from a cross-functional perspective [9].

Two recent publications deal with this subject and provide of evidence about how to link KM experiences into software organizations [3, 21]. Most references, however, are still more on the theoretical side and do little to answer practical questions from day-to-day project business. In this section we try to approach the state of the practice, and in the next section we show what was implemented in Alcatel to address initial KM questions related to software engineering.

How will KM help software organizations? KM provides modes and techniques to deal with the different kinds of software engineering related knowledge, namely:

- Know-how (processes, interfaces, technologies, infrastructure)
- Know-what (projects, project characteristics, predictions, relationships)
- Know-why (products, product lines, product dependencies, portfolios)

The goal of KM is to improve the organizational skills of an enterprise on all hierarchical and functional levels through better usage and deployment of skills and knowledge of its resources. It is a management activity, and as such is goal-oriented, planned and monitored [3, 18, 21].

KM requires a clear definition of its context, scope and objectives. These parameters are closely linked to business objectives of the respective organizational entity. A software development team might be interested in identifying which checklist to apply to improve coding or peer reviews. Department leaders in software organizations are interested in skill evolution that is aligned with future technology needs. They might also insist on deploying peer reviews and similar techniques to improve maintainability and become experts dependent on experts.

A project management team could be interested in learning from previous projects in order to better manage quality and reliability. Product line managers are interested in improving the portfolios they are responsible for, and the right baselines and evolution paths are agreed upon and implemented to serve an ever-changing market.

Business unit and business division senior managers are interested in seeing operational performance and in improving on allocation of resources and restructuring their own operations. Customers are interested in project performance or service request management to reduce cycle times until they get solutions that serve their own operational needs. Stakeholders and financial analysts want to get fast insight into strategy and how the roadmaps satisfy the strategies. Finally, corporate management might have the need to relocate product lines or reassess strategic focus, and thus need a summary on all portfolios. Knowledge in a technology-driven company thus builds up hierarchically, starting from very basic software engineering practices.

In this section we deal with knowledge identification, dissemination and preservation within software engineering organizations applied to the previously described e-R&D model. KM has to support knowledge identification, dissemination and preservation by providing a framework that encourages knowledge growth and reuse in the organization. This framework should be pragmatic. It should address concrete use cases of the initial target communities and then gradually grow to capture more use cases. Use cases could be "support of a project manager to retrieve information from past projects that apply to her current own project".

Instruments to solve this problem are workflow management, collaborative tools, document management, Web-based training or portals for access to information. All these tools help with learning and embedding knowledge into its operational usage. We have linked such instruments within e-R&D, starting from a process perspective, and growing to product and project dimensions.

KM must bring together process, product and project knowledge from a learning perspective. The answer we investigate here is primarily centered on enabling R&D organizations to more effectively handle knowledge within the daily operational activities. Often information is reused, but with high redundancies or manual overhead. At times, the redundancies create rework as things are not done right the first — or even errors that remain in the product. An example is product requirements and business case information. If this information is not shared between stakeholders at the beginning of a project, the development could end in gold plating or it could have the wrong focus.

Being able to not only reuse information but also to embed the respective processes into integrated workflows for specific tasks generates immediate returns by making engineers more flexible. Consider the time and effort necessary to move engineers from one project to another. Having standard KM around a standard product life cycle reduces the learning curve to real technical challenges, instead of organization overheads. We should, however, be aware that KM is not reduced to workflow management, which we treat as a facilitator for effective KM.

Knowledge management systems offer different perspectives to allow for instance navigation based on work products, roles or processes. Technological innovation and successful new products are the results of well-oiled relationships and tightly choreographed teamwork, whether among the different business units or divisions of a corporate enterprise, or between autonomous and geographically far-flung enterprises.

The product life cycle (Fig.16.1) shows the global view of the processes. With its many embedded hyperlinks, it allows navigating with a few clicks to the final element the reader is interested in. Usability is key, rather than formalism and hierarchy.

Processes must be easily accessible for the practitioners and managers. They must integrate seamlessly. By focusing on the essence of processes, integrating processes elements with each other and providing complete tools solutions, organizations can tailor processes to meet specific needs and allow localized and problem- or skill-specific software practices, while still ensuring that basic objectives of the organization are achieved. This is what we call managed process diversity.

Practitioners do not look for heavy process documentation, but rather for process support that exactly describes what they have to do at the moment they have to do it. Modular process elements must be combined according to a specific role or work product to be delivered. Still, the need for an organizational process, as described by CMM L3 is strongly emphasized and reinforced [23]. To bridge this gap, different approaches have been described recently for managing process diversity [15, 6, 4].

Having the concepts for managing process diversity within the software development, the next step is to seamlessly integrate R&D workflows, such as software development or software maintenance, with their (e-)business counterparts, such as customer relationship management or service request management. Given the current focus on collaborative product commerce (CPC), specifically from an end-to-end perspective, engineering processes must integrate with the related or interfacing business processes. Examples include configuration management for software artifacts belonging to a single product line and reused in a variety of products, and how they relate to the overall product data management. Alternatively, software defect corrections and how they relate to overall service request management must be considered as part of the enterprise CRM solution. Product life cycles, though necessary as a foundation, are insufficient if not integrated well with non-software related business processes.

Figure16.2 details how such factors not only characterize the project complexity and thus the management challenges, but also how they determine the level of process integration and workflow management. Various project factors determine different approaches to manage the involved software processes. A good overview on the need for workflow systems and integrated process management is provided in [2].

Since the late 1980s, the software engineering community has achieved a good understanding of processes and their interaction, which was primarily driven by the CMM. The CMM is not a process model as such, but a listing of the capabilities that an organization must have to be effective in instituting a software or R&D process. This framework, though software-specific in its terminology, is fully open toward hardware- and systems engineering on its level 2.

With knowledge about basic requirements of software processes and their interaction, CASE methods and processes can finally merge into what is called workflow systems or process models [2]. These process models have much in common with each other (e.g. Fusion [5], WSSDM [11], RUP [13], and OPEN [10]). The Object Management Group standardizes a Software Process Engineering Metamodel (SPEM) [19]. Current major integrated software engineering development environments try to scale across individual process steps and process artifacts [6].

A key step toward disseminating process knowledge is workflow automation. Although individual tools can increase productivity by a few percentage points, the non-automated portions become critical bottlenecks [22]. Workflow management systems offer different perspectives to allow for instance navigation based on work products, roles or processes. Navigation is realized with HTLM hyperlinks as shown in Fig.16.3. A life-cycle picture shows the global overview of the processes, and many embedded hyperlinks allow navigating with a few clicks to the final element of interest.

The entry level is a product catalogue, which is accessible from different points. We call it the entry level of the portal, as it is a good starting point for different functions that have specific questions related to one dedicated product. Examples include non-R&D functions, such as marketing (e.g., How far is a product from its delivery?), security (Where are certain protocols or components embedded that might cause security threads?) or procurement (How much royalties do we have to pay in a certain region?).

The right side of Fig.16.3 shows the hierarchical access to increasingly specific product and project information. Since these layers are themselves portals, they are also accessed from specific project or R&D levels. Process-specific knowledge is depicted on the left side of Fig. 16.3. Starting from the common PLC, it indicates how a specific product-line manages process diversity, depending on products, project size, resources and other criteria. If we draw a horizontal line through the middle of Fig. 16.3 we get basically a view of what is standardized and thus broadly introduced by e-R&D, and what is product-line specific and thus tailored or instantiated according to specific needs.

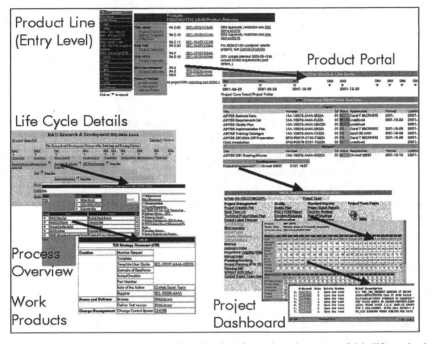

Fig. 16.3. Selecting the life cycle and navigating through an instance of this life cycle down to a work product

Instead of the software engineering-specific solutions outlined above, a tool for product life-cycle management, enterprise resource management (ERM) or customer relationship management (CRM) could also theoretically satisfy the needs specified in Sects. 16.1 and 16.2. For this reason we started to evaluate the tools and solutions landscapes that developed during the timeframe between 1999 and 2001. Knowing that it would take us at least two years to build such environment, and also being aware that it would certainly scale up towards the entire company of around 20,000 R&D engineers, we looked carefully towards commercial solutions.

While product life-cycle management tools interwork with many HW design and manufacturing tools, they only recently started to look into specific software engineering environments. Examples include MatrixOne, Agile or PTC, which try to interwork with specific software engineering tools, such as Rational's Clear-DDTS. More generic ERM tools would not sufficiently support software engineering on the more specific workflows. CRM environments integrate with defect tracking tools, but not beyond. Their scope is limited to various front-end processes. However, all mentioned tools could be extended, as they are event-driven.

The business case concerns the benefit of creating an object request broker to give to such tools an open interface that allows interworking with legacy and proprietary tools. However, the transactional interface between such tools does not adequately support the fine-grained integration of data we want to achieve while avoiding as much as possible replication of data. For examples, the product life cycle view must include data from the PDM system, the software documentation system, the defect tracking system, the personnel database (for the actors), the process assets library, and the authorized tools list, all in one view.

16.4   Practical R&D Knowledge Management

To benefit from improved business processes, the different functions of the enterprise plus potential external partners (e.g. outsource manufacturing) need to agree on uniform processes and practices. They need to apply common access to knowledge, performance metrics and decision-making protocols. They need to share information, communication and underlying resources.

The barriers to such harmonization and cooperation are not to be underestimated. They range from language barriers to time zone barriers to incompatible technology infrastructures to clashing product line cultures and "not invented here" syndrome. An obvious barrier is the individual profit and loss responsibility that in tough times means primarily to focus on current quarter results and not to invest in future infrastructures. Providing visibility is perceived a risk, because incumbents become accountable – which indeed is the objective – and more subject to internal competition.

We will show in this section how we dealt with such difficulties within R&D and project management of business unit for voice switching. Our focus here is on the processes and technologies that facilitated the growing amount of knowledge sharing and knowledge management in the three mentioned dimensions of product, process, and projects.

The perceived conflict between organizational process and individual tailoring can be resolved by a tailorable process framework, which we introduced in the impacted product lines over the past two years. This framework is fully graphically accessible and allows the selection of a process applicable for components as well as an entire product based on selecting the appropriate parameters characterizing the project. The framework allows automatic instantiation of the respective development process and product life cycle, and a project quality plan or specific applicable metrics, based on modular process elements such as role descriptions, templates, procedures or check lists, which are hyperlinked with each other.

Usability of any workflow support system is determined by the degree to which it can be adapted or tailored toward the projects' needs. There are organizational and project-specific environmental constraints, which make it virtually impossible to apply the workflow system out of the box. Most commercially available workflow systems therefore offer some adaptation of a standard workflow to a project-oriented instance, which ensures that each single activity supports the project targets [5, 10, 11, 13]. Adaptation is achieved by offering a set of standard workflows, which are selected (e.g. incremental delivery versus grand design; parallel versus sequential development; development versus maintenance). On a lower level, work products are defined or selected out of a predefined catalogue. Some models distinguish among mandatory and optional components [10]. Most of them are implemented based on object-oriented paradigms that allow building of classes of process elements and (limited) inheritance in cases where hierarchical refinement is offered.

Process diversity is not managed at an organizational level by current commercially available frameworks, but is delegated to the lowest level of application in a project. Before the start of a project, the models are adapted following the above-mentioned criteria. Rudimentary guidelines are available; however, often the workflow systems are not seen as a self-contained product, but require extensive additional consulting to create the right tailoring.

When we evaluated such systems, users from different projects provided the feedback that the workflow systems are fine as they come out of the box, but after tailoring and embedding all sorts of legacy in terms of tools, methods or templates, they tend to become less flexible and finally end in a fragmented and isolated process mess. What may be right for green field development and start-ups that do not want to spend money developing their own software processes is not adequate for an organization with already defined processes and a mature tools environment involving legacy systems.

A small example shows this trade-off. To successfully deliver a product with heterogeneous architecture and a mixture of legacy components built in various languages, certain processes must be aligned on the project level. This holds for project management, configuration management and requirements management. Otherwise, it would, for instance, be impossible to trace customer requirements that might affect several components through the project life cycle. On the other hand, design processes and validation strategies are so close to the individual components' architecture and development paradigms that any standard would fail as would all standards for one design or programming methodology that failed in the past. To make the puzzle complete, for efficiency reasons, the manager of that heterogeneous project or product line surely would not like it if within each small team the work product templates or tool-based workflows were redefined.

Such low-level process change management is exactly the point where current workflow systems for unified processes fail. Though these workflow systems offer lots of functionality from various application use cases, they do not do a good job of integrating process needs on the above-mentioned levels into a hierarchy with guided selection.

With these observations and practical experiences in mind, two years ago we started at Alcatel an approach to provide to the users on all levels with a standard workflow management framework with the opportunity to integrate different processes [7, 8]. We call it a framework because it offers process elements that can be linked on several hierarchical levels, starting from the life cycle down to phase descriptions and finally ending on the level of procedure (Fig. 16.3).

Many vendors offer platforms for enterprise portals with flexible mechanisms to display information from various sources including legacy systems, but these systems fail to offer the support for integration and organizational tailoring we want to achieve [16]. We therefore decided to build the integration layer ourselves based on simple and generally supported Web standards, creating the necessary flexibility in a situation where not all requirements of the software engineering workflow management were already known. The resulting architecture is simple yet effective (Fig. 16.4).

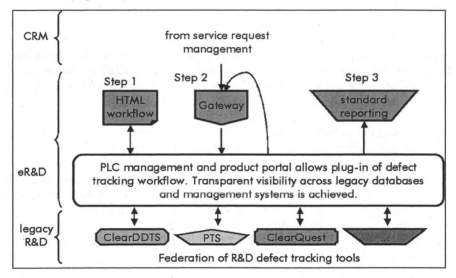

Fig. 16.4. Three-tier architecture indicating the product in between the front-end business processes and the back-end functional (legacy) environments. Example shows service request management and its link to R&D defect management

We distinguish three tiers, in which the top describes the front-end, which is typically a business process such as service request management. Such business process has interfaces with R&D that used to be achieved predominantly manually. Since there was no business case to remove all the legacy R&D tools, despite the fact that we could gradually introduce standard suites for new products, we needed to build a translation tier between the R&D processes, respective tools and the business processes. We call this tier e-R&D since it describes the electronic R&D workflows by aggregating R&D processes and work product management. e-R&D is governed by the product life cycle, thus ensuring a stable interface between R&D and external business processes.

On top of the needs summarized in Sect. 16.1, we realized that within a business unit, the similarities of processes would allow a more reuse-oriented selection of processes on top of the corporate product life cycle. Our needs for managing process diversity within a business unit were as follows:

- Reinforce the concept that process change management must be based on process reuse
- Focus on the *essence* of state-of-the-art software engineering paradigms and process description techniques
- Ensure maintainability and defined tailoring of workflow according to needs of the project: project size, involved components, continuously improving quality and efficiency goals which are often are specified contractually
- Support all types of development projects in the switching and routing sector: platform change, new development of a generic product, small customization projects (which is the majority of effort spent in this business division)
- Facilitate reuse of processes and, where applicable, underlying technology and tools by providing clear interfaces between the different layers of a process description
- Provide means for scalability, for instance, what starts as a small prototype or pilot project may later integrate with a larger product development

In a first step, we agreed on the factors that define the sets of processes and process elements that should be subject to tailoring and those that should be invariant. These two classes can be identified if practical experiences with process diversity are balanced with the need to keep control on project and product management:

- Invariant processes that would be unchanged across the various components and projects (e.g. project management such as planning and tracking, configuration and build management, requirements management, traceability, system test, qualification test)
- Processes and process elements that are tailored according to a specific development paradigm (e.g. design process, templates, guidelines, estimation rules, process metrics, project quality plan, validation and verification techniques, defect prevention actions)

In the next step, we investigated which criteria would determine selection of a specific process. We identified the following criteria that determine the layout of processes:

- The project size in terms of effort (we use three types to avoid too many choices)
- The product type (for instance, whether it is a generic R&D project, or a customization or maintenance project or a prototype)
- Specific component criteria (e.g. design paradigm, programming language, development platform, industrialization parameters related to market introduction and customer interfaces)
- The process edition (the process is subject to configuration management, especially for big projects that overlap with ongoing improvement activities)

The tool itself was built entirely open to both external business processes and legacy R&D processes, strictly following the three-tier architecture described above (Figs. 16.2, 16.4).

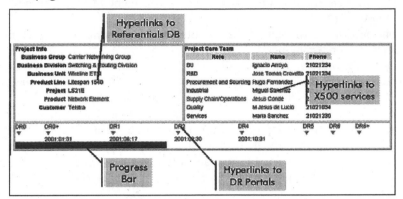

Fig. 16.5. Hyperlinks facilitate integration with other tools and processes. This instance shows the project dashboard that is automatically set-up and pre-populated upon approved project

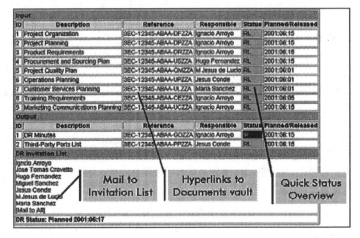

Fig. 16.6. The concrete instance of one work product, role, or milestone allows linking toward vaulting systems, metrics, reports, etc. This instance shows a milestone with all necessary details

To facilitate deployment across Alcatel, interfaces to corporate databases were recently added (Figs. 16.5, 16.6). To support organizational tailoring, the organizational structure is included automatically from the corporate reference database where this information is maintained. All person-related information is also kept up to date through an automatic link into the corporate directory services, which are also used as the basis for a common authentication mechanism.

16.5   Knowledge Management Return on Experience

In order to define a successful KM program, it is mandatory to choose the right KM model. The knowledge management model is linked to the business strategy, the knowledge management organization, the knowledge management concept and the type of knowledge (Table 16.1)

- The productivity model results in sharing knowledge and avoiding redundancy by using electronic databases, filled with documents and best practices (explicit knowledge). This model fits well for the implementation of a cost reduction business strategy.
- The quality model concentrates on best practices through sharing of explicit process frameworks. This is an ideal model to implement a business strategy based on specialization.
- The creativity model emphasizes the integration and combination of knowledge. This model is essentially needed to implement a business strategy oriented toward innovation.

Table 16.1. Choosing a knowledge management model

Business strategy	Knowledge management model	Knowledge management organization	Knowledge management concepts	Knowledge type
Cost reduction	Productivity	Sharing avoid redundancy	Information base	Explicit
Specializat ion	Quality	Best practice	Common processes	Explicit
Innovation	Creativity	Integration and combination of knowledge	Dynamic knowledge	Tacit

According to Alcatel's experience, most KM programs use a combination of the above-mentioned KM models, because only 10% of the existing knowledge is explicit knowledge, and 90% tacit knowledge. Explicit knowledge is knowledge that can be formalized, described and stored in an organized way in databases, allowing sending of targeted information to users according to profiles. Tacit knowledge is knowledge accumulated through experience. It is in individuals; it is alive and evolving, sometimes even unconsciously. Concretely this means that to share tacit knowledge we need other mechanisms than electronic databases. Tacit knowledge is transferable in working communities through exchange, workshops and on-the-job-training. Parts of tacit knowledge can be captured by communities of experts and written down in order to share with a larger number of people.

Another important aspect is the use of appropriate tools to implement the chosen KM model (Fig. 16.7). As described in Sect. 16.4, we have selected several different tools to embed into e-R&D and thus integrate explicit and tacit knowledge.

The tools need also to take into account the dynamic aspect of knowledge. Documents, reports and guidelines are easy to share but are quickly outdated. An important part of a KM program consists of setting up and keeping alive knowledge flows through communities and processes.

Knowledge sharing is a new way of working, and therefore new reflexes need to be trained. First comes the reflex of looking for existing knowledge before starting a new task, and second, the more difficult reflex, to bring one's own contributions to enrich the knowledge base in return.

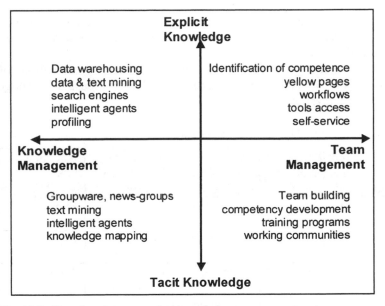

Fig. 16.7. Choosing the appropriate knowledge management system

As with any improvement program, successful KM programs are the ones that are measured and followed up by the management. Quantitative measures give feedback on the number of people, number of documents, number of processes, number of ideas, and number of downloads. What remains more difficult are qualitative measures like how much value has been created by the process of reuse, what new competencies and expertise have been built-up in the organization and what is its value. In the conclusions we address our own results on the returns observed.

16.6   Conclusions

We consider knowledge a crucial resource that drives Alcatel's future success, which must therefore be managed carefully. Sustained knowledge management is a prerequisite to maintaining a competitive advantage. Customers today are less tolerant than ever of poor-quality software and delayed deliveries. To maintain market share, software companies are finding that it is no longer sufficient to have the most innovative product without acceptable quality or to miss the agreed delivery deadlines.

When looking into the different dimensions of knowledge within R&D, we could distinguish

- Product knowledge, i.e. knowledge about how products are developed, their internal technology and how they relate to network elements, standards, protocols, and the like. Feature content, components and interfaces contribute to this dimension. Especially in telecommunications, which is characterized by particularly rapid technological change and uncertainty in an environment that often integrates technologies of more than five different decades, product knowledge is the key success factor for a solution supplier.
- Process knowledge, i.e. knowledge of business processes, workflows, responsibilities, supportive technologies and interfaces between processes. Within software engineering — unlike hardware engineering — this aspect of KM is often neglected. As a result, elements don't scale up, and performance decreases.
- Project knowledge, i.e. knowledge about the underlying parameters in terms of resources, functional and attribute requirements, work products, budget, timing, milestones, deliverables, increments, quality targets and performance parameters. Project knowledge is closely linked with product and process knowledge as it glues together these two other dimensions and ensures that we can finally deliver a product.

KM relates to cost management. Technology can be individually sufficient and perfectly fitting to a dedicated product, while still not positively affecting productivity and throughput of the entire organization. We found out for instance, that at a given time a state-of-the-art commercial configuration management system was introduced for different products in parallel without knowledge from each other.

Dedicated improvement objectives were in each case defined and used to guide the introduction, but the set up, the definition of procedures, roles or delivery mechanisms and even the link to standard metrics and standard problem management was reinvented in each case. Certainly mere documentation of processes is not the target of e-R&D, as this should happen before.

Synergy as it is intended within most companies cannot grow with such a lack of organizational learning. Nevertheless, we should emphasize the experience that synergies are limited to that can be effectively reused and shared. These boundaries vary and are typically strongly limited at the product line level (i.e.

similar products), and again appear at the corporate level (e.g. common customer front end, common PLC, etc.).

e-R&D drives productivity improvement and thus frees resources for innovation. The business case combines several aspects:

Improved quality: We can directly address the customer needs by linking dedicated improvement objectives, such as return rate, via CMM to process changes in R&D. Over the past several years, Alcatel proved substantial field quality improvements and defect reduction. Two-digit improvements are feasible if the CMM is applied and closely followed up in engineering projects.

Reduced cycle time: The efficiency and effectiveness of engineering processes directly influence engineering cycle time. For instance earlier defect detection means faster and more comprehensive defect correction. A defect found during development costs less than 10% of effort to correct compared to its detection during testing. Utilizing a consistent product life cycle and process repository is a necessary condition for reducing cycle time. These repositories reduce the friction of unclear interfaces and responsibilities and cut rework because of inconsistent assumptions and cut retrieval time for specific documents and work products. One of our product lines was able to cut cycle time to almost half after giving emphasis CMM and product life cycle (Fig. 16.8).

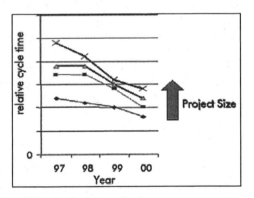

Fig. 16.8. Cycle time reduction as a consequence of strong focus on process improvement and product alignments

Improved engineering flexibility: With decreasing size and duration of projects, engineers need to be flexible to quickly start working in a new environment. While technical challenges cannot be reduced, the organizational and administrative overhead must be managed and limited. Alcatel relies on a consistent product life cycle across the company to ensure that we can deliver solutions independently of the origin of the components. In a company the size of Alcatel, it is key to align working environments and the development process in order to reduce the learning curve when starting a project.

Reduced overhead: Links to the management system with its process and role descriptions and to document templates are embedded in the workflow support system, presenting engineers with immediate process support when and where they need it. Long process descriptions are replaced by pictorial overviews and automated interfaces. For example, clicking on a work product name activates an interface to a document management system, and administrative data such as the document number are automatically derived from the project context.

Improved communication: Information is presented in a consistent way for all projects, avoiding replication of data and reducing search time. The PLC view of the workflow system provides a "dashboard" with immediate visibility on key data and responsibilities, contributing to an increased awareness of accountability.

Increasing alignment of processes and tools: With process asset libraries linked to tools, we are able to filter out and evaluate scenarios of how process change affects tools, or where tool changes would influence processes. So-called "best-practices" can be communicated with related tools and procedures to increase engineering effectiveness and to allow learning from the best in class around Alcatel. Interfaces to tools and their user guides can now be embedded in the process support environment.

Faster ramp-up time and skill management: Increasingly, project roles and also specific work product templates or process-related roles are standardized and can be reused, thus facilitating more consistent skill and human resource management. Transferring products to another location, as is today often the case, is facilitated by standardized role descriptions and workflows. Ramp-up time is shorter with new engineers responsible for such transferred products.

e-R&D has successfully grown in Alcatel from one product line to gradually cover the entire company. Today e-R&D concepts are being introduced in all product lines in order to stimulate organizational learning and improvements. With this initiative, R&D is fully included in Alcatel's e-business evolution.

References

1. Boehm B. (1996) Anchoring the software process. IEEE Software, 13: 73-82
2. Bolcer G.A., Taylor, R.N. (1999) Advanced workflow management technologies. Software process practice and improvement, 4: 125-171
3. Chang S.K. (2001) Handbook of software engineering and knowledge engineering. World Scientific, Singapore
4. Cockburn A. (2000) Selecting a project's methodology. IEEE Software, 17: 64-71
5. Coleman, D. et al. (1997) Fusion update Part II: architecture and design in the next generation of fusion. Fusion Newsletter Vol. 5.3. Palo Alto, www.hpl.hp.com/fusion/, (accessed 22nd August2002)
6. Deck M. (2001) Managing process diversity: while improving your practices. IEEE Software, 18: 21-27
7. De Man J. (1997) Process improvement through the Intranet. In: Proceedings ITU Telecom interactive, Geneva

8. De Man J (2000) A lightweight process-centered project support environment: motivation, implementation and experience. In: Proceedings world multiconference on systemics, cybernetics and informatics, Orlando, Florida, USA, Vol. 9
9. Edwards J.S. (2003) Managing software engineers and their knowledge. In: Aurum A., Jeffery R., Wohlin C., Handzic M. (Eds.), Managing software engineering knowledge, Springer, Berlin Heidelberg, New York
10. Graham I. (1997) The OPEN process specification. Addison-Wesley, Readings, MA
11. IBM Object Oriented Technology Center (1997) Developing object oriented software. Prentice Hall, Englewood Cliffs, UK
12. Jensen B.D. (1995) A software reliability engineering success story - AT&T's definity PBX. In: Proceeding of the IEEE 6th international symposium on software reliability engineering, Toulouse, France, pp. 338-343
13. Kruchten P. (1999) The rational unified process. Addison-Wesley, Reading, MA, USA
14. Lawton G. (2001) Knowledge management: ready for prime-time? IEEE Computer, 34: 12-14
15. Lindvall M., Rus I. (2000) Process diversity in software development. Guest editor's introduction to special volume on process diversity, IEEE Software, 17: 14-18
16. Lindvall M., Rus I. (2003) Knowledge management for software organizations. In: Aurum A., Jeffery R., Wohlin C., Handzic M. (Eds.), Managing software engineering knowledge, Springer, Berlin Heidelberg New York
17. McConnell S. (1998) Software project survival guide. Microsoft Press, Redmond, WA
18. Oliver G.R., D'Ambra J. Toorn, C. van (2003) Evaluating an approach to sharing software engineering knowledge to facilitate learning. In: Aurum A., Jeffery R., Wohlin C., Handzic M. (Eds.), Managing software engineering knowledge, Springer, Berlin Heidelberg New York
19. OMG Object Management Group (2001): Software process engineering metamodel specification, http://www.omg.org/docs/ptc/01-11-01.pdf (accessed 21st April, 2003)
20. Perry D.E., Siy H.P., Votta L.G. (1998) Parallel changes in large scale software development: an observational case study. In: Proceedings of IEEE 20th international. conference on software engineering, Kyoto, Japan, pp. 251-260
21. Rus I., Lindvall M. (2002) Knowledge management in software engineering. Special issue of IEEE Software, 19: 26-38
22. Sharon D., Anderson T. (1997) A complete software engineering environment. IEEE Software, 14: 123-127
23. Software Engineering Institute (1995): The capability maturity model - guidelines for improving the software process, Addison Wesley, Boston, MA, USA

Author Biography

Christof Ebert is Alcatel's Director of Software Coordination and Process Improvement in Paris, France. He is a senior member of IEEE and *IEEE Software* associate editor-in-chief. He has published extensively on software engineering-related topics and lectures at conferences and university. He holds a Ph.D. with honors from the University of Stuttgart.

Jozef De Man is Manager of Software Coordination and Process Improvement of Alcatel, based in Antwerp, Belgium. As a project leader, he is responsible for introducing globally and further elaborating of the concepts of the managed process diversity as described in. He was the original lead designer of the mentioned automated process interface model. He is a Distinguished Member of the Alcatel Technical Academy and professor at the University of Ghent, Department of Industrial Management.

Fariba Schelenz is Director of Knowledge Management with Alcatel's Network Service Division, specializing in large turn-key projects, and has been based in Paris, France for five years. She graduated from the Technical University Berlin and from INSEAD (France). She has given conference lectures and university courses on strategic impact of new technologies, business process improvement, and knowledge and project management.

17 Knowledge Infrastructure for Project Management

Pankaj Jalote

Abstract: In any organization, past experience plays a key role in improvement and management. How effectively past experience can be leveraged depends on how well this experience is captured and organized to enable learning and reuse. Systematically recording data from projects, deriving lessons from it, and then making the lessons available to other projects can enhance this reuse. In this chapter we discuss three key approaches for organizing and using past experience and how they are employed in Infosys Technologies, a large software house that has been assessed at level 5 of the CMM. First, we discuss the process infrastructure that encapsulates the past experience in the form of processes and supporting templates and checklists. Second, we discuss the process database that contains metrics from past projects. Finally, we discuss the body of knowledge system that is used to record experience of people in problem solving in a variety of areas. We also briefly discuss how this knowledge infrastructure is used for managing a project.

Keywords: Project management, Metrics, Process assets, Knowledge infrastructure, Software development

17.1 Introduction

An organization is a cohesive entity that has some mission or defined goals. The organization (or the people in it) performs some tasks to achieve these goals. Knowledge helps perform these tasks better, faster, and cheaper. The main goal of knowledge management is to help reduce cost, reduce cycle time, or improve quality through the effective use of knowledge. In an organization that is in the business of software development, since the main assets are the intellectual capital, knowledge management is particularly important [14].

Knowledge can be external, i.e. knowledge produced by people outside the organization. This type of knowledge resides in books, journals, magazines, and so on. Knowledge can also be internal, i.e. the knowledge that is created primarily within the organization, largely through experience and experimentation. Generally, the goal of knowledge management within an organization is to manage the internal knowledge of the organization (creation of which uses external knowledge.) Leveraging experiential knowledge is the focus in the experience factory model [1] and is envisaged at the higher levels of the Capability Maturity Model (CMM) [15]. In this paper we focus on the management of internal knowledge, particularly the knowledge that is useful in project management, i.e. use of which can make project management more effective.

Suppose in a software organization, there exists a "super" project manager who consistently executes projects successfully, whose estimates are generally on target, and who seems to avoid the "fire-fighting" mode most of the time. Clearly, this project manager has acquired the knowledge to properly perform the various tasks associated with project planning and execution through experience.

Clearly, the organization will want this experience to be available to other project managers so they can also execute projects successfully. One way to achieve this is to have the super project manager available as a "consultant" to other project managers. This approach is not scalable. Having knowledge reside with an individual also has other undesirable side effects. The goal of knowledge management (for project management purposes) is to preserve and leverage experience of individuals, such as this super project manager, for the benefit of all project managers.

Hence the basic objective of knowledge management is to compile and organize internal knowledge such that it resides in systems and is available for use by project managers. Consequently, the key elements of knowledge management are collecting and organizing the knowledge, making it available through some knowledge infrastructure, and then using the knowledge to improve the execution of projects.

The centerpiece of a knowledge infrastructure for project management is the processes and related process assets. Processes describe how different tasks are to be executed and encapsulate the knowledge the organization has for efficiently performing that task. Process assets are documents that aid in the use of processes. Besides process and process assets, metrics knowledge from past projects is invaluable for new projects — both for planning and project monitoring. Hence, another key element in knowledge infrastructure for project execution is the process database which keeps the summary of the past projects. Process assets and process databases capture the key elements but still leave some things uncaptured. Hence a system to capture the rest of the knowledge that may be of use is needed. We discuss these three elements of knowledge infrastructure in the rest of this paper. These elements are based on how they are supported at Infosys, a large software house that has been assessed at level 5 of the CMM. Further details on these are given in [8, 10].

17.2   Process Specification and Process Assets

A process-oriented approach for project execution forms the foundation, or the backbone of any knowledge management system. Without defined processes for executing different tasks, it is not even possible for a project manager to ask the question "How can I use past experience to perform this task better?" This is because implicit in this question is the existence of some method that the project manager is to use and that he wants to improve! Hence the centerpiece of any knowledge management system for project execution is the set of processes defined to perform different tasks in a project.

And what is a process? Technically, a process for a task is comprised of a sequence of steps that should be followed to execute that task. For an organization, however, the processes recommended for use by its engineers and project managers are much more than a sequence of steps—they encapsulate what the engineers and project managers have learned about successfully executing projects. Through the processes, which cover engineering as well as project management tasks, the benefits of experience are conferred to all, including a newcomer in the organization. These processes help managers and engineers emulate past successes and avoid the pitfalls that lead to failures. Hence, processes are the main means of packaging and reusing past knowledge.

For an organization, the standard processes that have to be followed by a project have to be properly specified and documented. Different approaches are possible to precisely and succinctly specify a process. At Infosys, processes are organized in a top-down manner. A process consists of stages or phases, in which a stage (phase) consists of activities, and each activity could be further broken down into subactivities. The formal process definition specifies the top three levels only, and further details are specified as checklists. The definition for each stage generally follows the entry, task, verification, and eXit (ETVX) model [12], and specifies the following:

1. Overview: A brief description of the stage
2. Participants: All the participants that take part in executing the various activities in the stage
3. Entry criteria: the pre-requisites that must be satisfied before this stage can be started
4. Inputs: All the inputs needed to execute the stage
5. Activities: List of all activities (sometimes also important sub-activities) that are performed in this stage
6. Exit criteria: The conditions that the outputs of the stage must satisfy in order to consider the stage as completed
7. Outputs: All the outputs of the stage
8. Measurements: All the measurements that must be done during the execution of the stage
9. Special verification
10. References

With a specification like this for each stage, the dependence between stages is explicitly specified in the form of entry criteria. The order in which the stages are presented in the process definition is merely for documentation convenience. Note that this specification captures past experience not only about the sequence of steps that should be used, but also about entry and exit criteria that should be satisfied, what measurements to take, what outputs should be produced, and so on.

At Infosys, various processes are specified. These include processes relating to both the engineering tasks of the project, as well as the tasks related to project management. For example, for a development project, the recommended life-cycle process is specified as the development process. There are other processes for different types of projects, for example, the reengineering process and the maintenance process. The project management process, which covers project planning as well as project monitoring and closure, is the main management-related process. There are other supporting processes, like the configuration management and review process.

A process specification encapsulates an organization's experience in form of "successful recipes". Process descriptions, however, are generally succinct and do not give detailed steps on how to execute different tasks or how to document their outputs. In order to facilitate the use of processes on projects, guidelines, checklists, and templates usually provide useful support. These together are called *process assets* and are generally present in many high-maturity organizations [9].

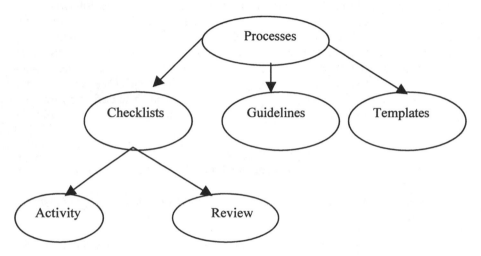

Fig. 17.1. Process and process assets

Guidelines usually give rules and procedures for executing some step in the process. For example, a step in project planning process is "estimate effort". But to actually execute this step, a project manager will need some guidelines. Checklists are usually of two types; activity checklists and review checklists. An activity checklist is, as the name suggests, a list of activities that should be done while performing a process step. The purpose of review checklists is to draw the attention of reviewers to the defects that are likely to be found in an output. Templates essentially provide the structure of the document in which the output of a process or a step can be captured. The relationship between process and these assets is shown in Fig. 17.1.

The main purpose of these process assets, which capture specific aspects of organizational knowledge, is to facilitate the use of processes and to save effort. For example, creating a document with a template can be so much easier and less time consuming than creating it from scratch. These assets also help improve the quality by minimizing the number of defects injected by providing proper guidelines and activity checklists, and by catching the injected defects early by aiding reviews. It should be clear that to derive full benefits from a process-oriented approach for project execution, process assets are extremely important. At Infosys, all guidelines, checklists, and templates are available on-line and are regularly updated. A sample of some of the process assets that are used in project management is shown in Table 17.1.

Table 17.1. Process assets for project management

Guidelines	Checklists	Templates/Forms
• Effort and schedule estimation guidelines • Group review procedure • Process tailoring guidelines • Defect estimation and monitoring guidelines • Guidelines for measurements and data analysis • Risk management guidelines • Guidelines for requirement traceability • Defect prevention guidelines	• Requirements analysis checklist • Unit test and system test plan checklists • Configuration management checklist • Status report checklist • Requirement review checklist • Functional design review checklist • Project plan review checklist • Code review checklist for C++	• Requirements specification document • Unit test plan document • Acceptance test plan document • Project management plan • Configuration management plan • Metrics analysis report • Milestone status report • Defect prevention analysis report

In the context of knowledge management, the guidelines for process tailoring deserve special mention. Any defined process will not apply to all situations and all projects. Tailoring is the process of adjusting a previously defined process of the organization to obtain a process that is suitable for the particular business or technical needs of a project. To allow proper tailoring of previously defined processes, tailoring guidelines are provided. These guidelines define under what conditions which type of changes should be done to a standard process. In essence, they define a set of "permitted deviations" of the standard process to suit the needs of a project. These guidelines are themselves based on experience and encapsulate the past experience of project managers regarding how to tailor the process under different circumstances. Fig. 17.2 illustrates the role of tailoring guidelines for a project. More information on the tailoring guidelines at Infosys is given in [8, 10].

In addition to these generic assets, if a project manager finds that a past project was similar in some respects, he may want to use some of its outputs. Reusing artifacts can save effort and increase productivity. To promote this goal, process assets from projects may also be collected when the projects terminate. The assets that are typically collected and made available through a separate system, include project management plan, configuration management plan, schedules, standards, checklists, guidelines, templates, developed tools, training material, and other documents that could be used by future projects

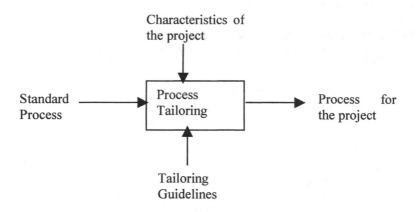

Fig. 17.2. Process tailoring

17.3   Process Database

The process database (PDB) is a repository of process performance data from projects, which can be used for project planning, estimation, analysis of productivity and quality, and other purpose [7]. The PDB consists of data from completed projects and forms the quantitative knowledge about experience in project execution. As can be imagined, to populate the PDB, data is collected in projects, is analyzed, and then is organized for entry into the PDB [6]. Many high-maturity organizations have some form of process database [9]. Here we discuss what the PDB at Infosys contains. We do not discuss how measurements are done in projects, and refer the reader to [8, 10] for more information.

Overall, the data captured in the PDB at Infosys can be classified into the following categories:

- Project characteristics
- Project schedule
- Project effort
- Size
- Defects

Data on project characteristics consists of the project name, the names of the project manager and module leaders (so they can be contacted for further information or clarifications about the project), the business unit to which the project belongs (to permit business-unit-wise analysis), the process being deployed in the project (which allows analysis for different processes to be done separately), the application domain, the hardware platform, the languages used, the DBMS used, a brief statement of the project goals, information about project risks, the duration of the project, and the team size.

The data on schedule is primarily the expected start and end dates for the project, and the actual start and end dates. The data on project effort includes data on the initial estimated effort and the total actual effort, and the distribution of the actual effort among different stages, e.g. project initiation, requirements management, design, build, unit testing, and other phases. This data is useful in estimating the effort or the schedule of a new project.

The size of the software developed may be in terms of lines of code (LOC), the number of simple, medium, or complex programs; or a combination of these. Even if function points are not used for estimation, a uniform metric for productivity may be obtained by representing the final size in function points. The final size in function points is usually obtained by converting the measured size of the software in LOC to function points, using published conversion tables. Size data is always required for comparison purposes and for building models.

The data on defects includes the number of defects found in different defect detection activities, and the number of defects injected in different stages. Hence, the number of defects of different origins found in requirements review, design review, code review, unit testing, and other phases is recorded. (The detailed data on reviews, however, is kept in a separate review database, which is used for analyzing the review process and setting suitable guidelines for controlling reviews [8].) Defect data can be used for quality planning for a project and evaluating the effectiveness of the various quality activities, when performed in the project.

This information in the PDB allows a project manager to obtain data on "similar" past projects — information that is most often sought by project managers when planning a new project. With this type of information, a project manager can search and find information on all projects that focused on a particular business application, used a particular database management system, operating system, hardware, language, etc., was of certain size or duration, and so on. The screen that can be used by project managers to generate this report is shown in Fig. 17.3.

How is the data for the PDB obtained from projects? As part of the standard process for executing projects, project personnel are required to enter data on effort, defects, and schedule. There are tools for each of these. For schedule management, most projects use Microsoft Project, in which all the tasks and milestones are enumerated, along with their dates and the resources of each task. For effort collection, an in-house tool called the weekly activity report (WAR) system is used. The WAR system for a person shows all the tasks assigned to their, and requires the person to enter the hours spent on the different tasks every day. To ensure consistency in usage, codes are specified for various activities. Every week, each person has to submit their WAR, which is then used for analysis. For defect tracking and analysis, a PC-based commercial tool called the defect control system was earlier used, but has now been replaced by a Web-based in-house tool. For defects, predefined categories exist for severity, type, stage of injection, stage of detection, and so on. More details about data collection are given in [8, 10].

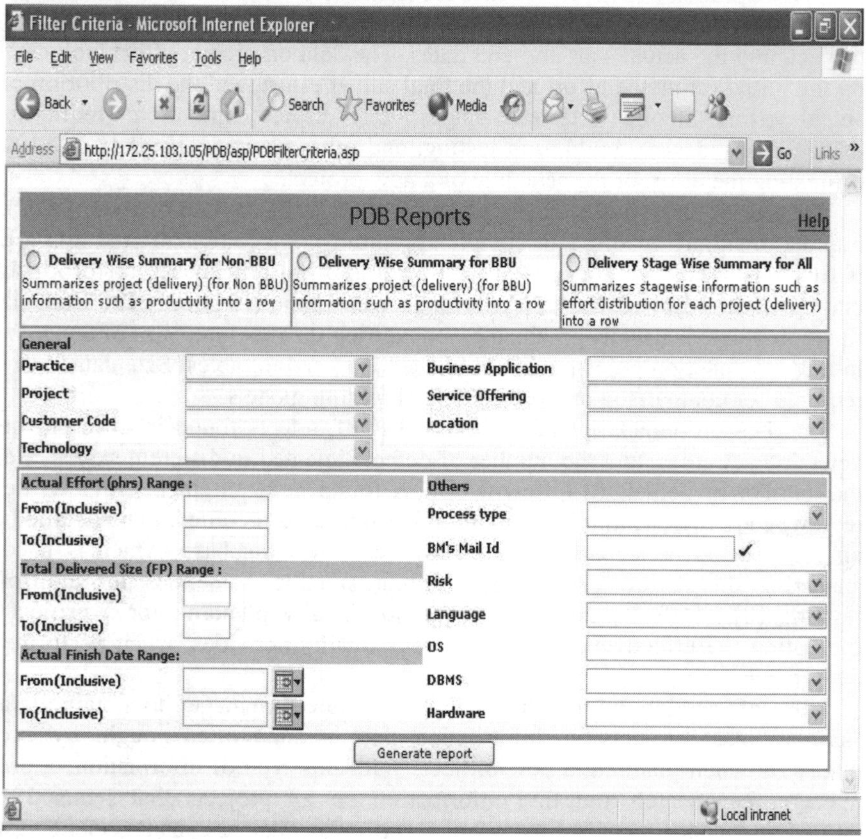

Fig. 17.3. Screen for generating reports from process database

At the end of the project, the raw data on effort, schedule, defects, and size is analyzed and summarized during a postmortem analysis [2, 3, 4], whose objective is to derive lessons from the project based on what worked and what did not. That is, the purpose of having an identified completion analysis activity, rather than just saying, "the project is done", is clearly not to help this project, but to help future projects by leveraging the "lessons learned" in this project. This type of learning can be effectively supported by analysis of data from completed projects. At Infosys, it is done as part of project closure analysis. After closure analysis, the results are packaged in a manner such that they can be used by others through the PDB. Packaging is an important step in knowledge management and is also a key step in the quality improvement paradigm [1]. Full examples of closure analysis reports are given in [8, 10]. The relationship between projects and PDB is shown in Fig. 17.4.

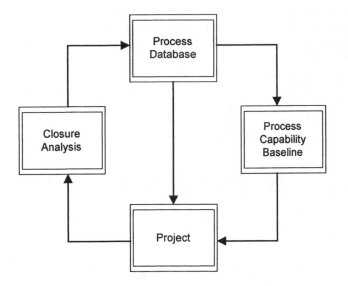

Fig. 17.4. Process database and closure analysis

The data from the PDB can also be used to understand the capability of the process in quantitative terms. The capability of a process is essentially the range of expected outcomes that can usually be expected if the process is followed. In other words, if a project follows a process, the process capability can be used to determine the range of possible outcomes that the project can expect. A process capability baseline (PCB) is the snapshot of the capability of the process. At Infosys, the PCB specifies the capability of the process for parameters like delivered quality, productivity, effort distribution, defect injection rate, defect removal efficiency, defect distribution, and so forth.

The PCB is essentially a summary of knowledge about process capability. This knowledge can be used in various ways in project management. For example, productivity data can be used to estimate the effort for the project from the estimated size, and distribution of effort can be used to estimate the effort for the various phases of the project and for making staffing plans. Similarly, defect injection rate can be used to estimate the total number of defects a project is expected to have, and the distribution of defects can be used to estimate the defect levels for different defect detection activities. The overall defect removal efficiency or quality can be used for estimating the number of defects that may be expected after the software is delivered and can be used to plan for maintenance. The PCB also plays an important role in overall process management within the organization.

17.4   Body of Knowledge

Though the processes and process assets capture experience related to how different tasks should be done, they still leave information that cannot be generalized or "processized". For example, this might be specific information about how to use a particular tool, how to "get around" some problem in a new compiler, how to tune an application. It is hard to put a process assets-like framework on such knowledge. To capture this type of unstructured knowledge, some other mechanism is needed. At Infosys, another system called the body of knowledge (BOK) is used to encapsulate experience. Now this system has been enhanced with other knowledge management initiatives into a knowledge shop (K-Shop) [13].

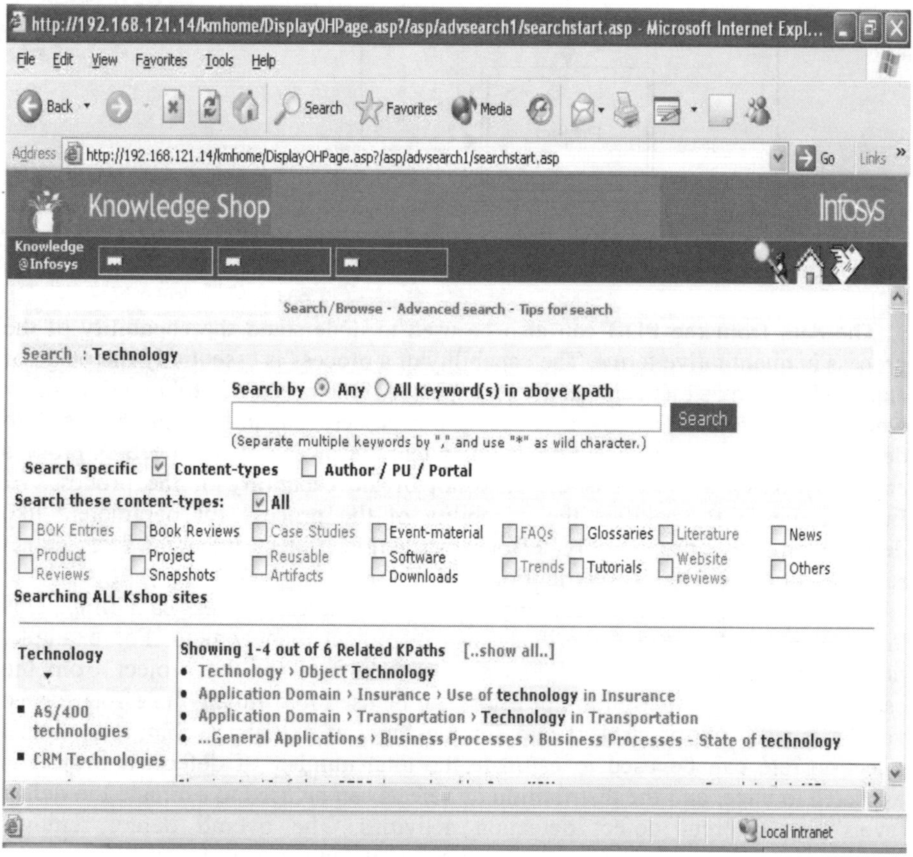

Fig. 17.5: Search screen for the K-shop

The knowledge in the BOK, which is primarily in the form of articles, is organized by different topics. Some of the topics are requirement specification, tools, build, methodologies/techniques, design, testing, quality assurance, productivity, and project management. In the BOK system, articles relating to "lessons learned" and "best practices" are posted. Tutorials and articles on trends are also available. The BOK system is Web-based, with its own keyword or author-based search facility. The top-level screen of the K-shop is shown in Fig. 17.5.

Any member of the organization can submit an entry for inclusion in the BOK. A template for submitting a BOK entry has been provided. Each submission undergoes a review, which focuses on usefulness, generality, changes required, and so on. and an editorial control is maintained to ensure the quality of the entries. Financial incentives are provided for employees to submit to BOK, and the department that manages the BOK actively pursues people to submit. To further the cause, submission to the BOK is also one of the factors that is considered during the yearly performance appraisal. A quarterly target for BOK entries is set for the organization.

In addition to the K-shop, there is also a people knowledge map [13]. This system details the skills and expertise of the different people in the organization. Using this, a project manager can quickly identify and contact specialists. This is referred to as competence management in [14]. Such a system helps speed up learning through informal knowledge transfer between people. It also helps the organization identify areas where it is lacking the necessary skills and where expertise needs to be built.

17.5   Use of Knowledge Infrastructure in Projects

We briefly discuss how these elements of the knowledge infrastructure are used in projects. The user is referred to [8, 10] for more details. The main use of this knowledge is in project planning and project monitoring. During project planning, a number of tasks need to be performed for which some elements of this knowledge infrastructure are used.

For planning the process that should be used in the project, and for performing the different tasks in the project, processes and process assets are used extensively. All projects use one of the defined standard processes and use the defined guidelines for tailoring the process. During the execution of the project, guidelines, checklists, and templates are used heavily for most of the tasks. During reviews, review checklists are used. It is fair to say that for most of the major tasks, projects rely heavily on past experience in the form of checklists, process, and templates.

During project planning, once the process planning is done, some of the key tasks are effort and schedule estimation, risk management planning, and quality planning. In Infosys, for many of these tasks there are guidelines that specify how these tasks are to be done. These guidelines are such that they explicitly make use of past data from process database or the PCB.

We can get a sense of the usage of these elements from their access figures. The overall quality system documentation, which contains all the main documents, is accessed about 4,000 times each month. Within this documentation, many of the templates like the ones for CM plan, unit testing plan, or project management plan are accessed about 100 to 200 times each month; the common processes (like the CM process, project management process, or development process) are accessed about 100 to 200 times each month; various estimation guidelines are accessed about 150 times each month; the metrics analysis spreadsheet is accessed about 150 times per month; a typical programming language standard is accessed about 100 time a month, and a typical checklist is accessed about 50 to 100 times a month. The PCB, which summarizes the data in the PDB and which is used heavily for estimation, is accessed about 1,500 times each month.

The metrics infrastructure is also used for project monitoring. As discussed earlier, metrics data on size, effort, schedule, and defects is collected regularly in projects. These data are regularly analyzed to evaluate the health of the project. These evaluations include actual versus estimated analysis for effort and schedule. For some quality activities also where defect predictions are made, similar analysis is done. Earlier, these analyses were done through reports that were generated at milestones. Now an integrated project management (IPM) system has been developed that integrates all the tools for collecting different metrics. Based on the data, it generates a project health report on demand. Hence, the health of the project can be checked at any time. The IPM system also shows the audit and review reports. The top-level screen of the IPM system is shown in Fig. 17.6.

Metrics from the project give up some numbers about the various parameters being measured. But interpretation of these numbers require past experience. For example, when is the measured attribute, "too large" or "too small" to deserve management intervention requires past experience? At Infosys, guidelines have been provided for evaluating various parameters. For example, thresholds have been set based on past experience on how much deviation of actual from planned is acceptable [8].

Similarly, when using statistical process control for controlling the process, control limits need to be set. Setting of these limits require past data on the process execution. We refer the reader to [5, 11, 16] for concepts related to statistical process control and control charts. At Infosys, analysis of data in the PDB and review database is

used for setting these limits. Further details on this can be found in [8].

What is the cost of this entire knowledge infrastructure? At Infosys, most of this infrastructure is managed by the software engineering process group (SEPG), whose strength is about 0.5% of the engineering staff strength (but the SEPG also does other tasks besides managing this infrastructure.) In addition, task forces from across the organization are formed for limited periods for special initiatives that are needed from time to time. This overhead, clearly, is quite small for an organization. However, there is also a small overhead in using these systems, entering the data, doing data analysis, and so on. This cost is hard to measure. However, we suspect that it is no more than an hour or so per person per week.

Regarding the benefits, we have already mentioned the access data earlier. The benefit in using this information is also hard to quantify. However, the heavy usage seems to suggest that project managers do find it useful. The senior management also swear by it — without these systems they feel that the large number of projects being executed at Infosys cannot be kept in tight control.

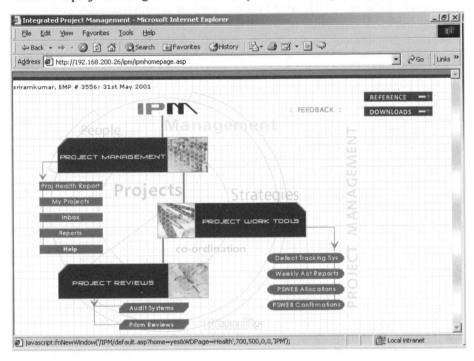

Fig. 17.6. Integrated project management system

17.6   Summary

The main purpose of knowledge infrastructure for project management is to leverage past experience of the organization to improve the execution of new projects. To achieve this objective, the knowledge infrastructure has to compile and organize internal knowledge such that it resides in systems and is available for use by project managers. Consequently, the key elements of building knowledge infrastructure are collecting and organizing the knowledge, making it available through systems, and reusing it to improve the execution of projects. In this chapter we discussed three main knowledge management systems that are used at Infosys; processes and process assets, process database, and body of knowledge.

The centerpiece of a knowledge management set up for project management is the processes and related process assets. Processes describe how different tasks are to be executed and encapsulate the knowledge the organization has for efficiently performing that task. Process assets are guidelines, checklists, and templates to support the use of the processes. With processes and process assets, past experience can be effectively used by a new project as help is available on how to execute a task, how to review it, how to document the output, and so on

Besides process and process assets, metrics knowledge from past projects is invaluable for new projects, both for planning and for project monitoring. Hence, another key element in knowledge management for project execution is the process database, which keeps the summary of the past projects. The process database is a repository of process performance data from projects that can be used for project planning, estimation, analysis of productivity and quality, and other purposes. The required metrics from a project are captured through various tools as the project proceeds. The captured data is also used for monitoring a project through the integrated project management tool.

The process assets and the process database capture the key elements but still leave some things "uncaptured". Hence a system to capture the rest of the knowledge that may be of use is needed. The body of knowledge system preserves such knowledge. It is a Web-based system with its own keyword or author-based search facility. The knowledge in BOK is primarily in the form of articles describing best practices, lessons learned, "how to", and so on for a range of topics.

In the end, it is worth pointing out something that perhaps is quite obvious; The knowledge captured in various systems is dynamic and keeps changing. In the software world, the change is even more rapid. Hence, maintaining the knowledge and keeping it current by enhancing it, adding more useful knowledge, and removing information that is not of use is a task that has to be undertaken within the organization. In other words, knowledge management is not free. However, the gains from the use of knowledge captured in these systems should pay many times more than the cost of setting and maintaining these systems.

References

1. Basili V.R., Rombach H.R. (1994) The experience factory. In: Marcianac J.J. (Ed.), Encyclopedia of software engineering, John-Wiley and Sons, West Sussex, UK
2. Birk A.; Dingsoyr T.; Stalhane T. (2002) Postmortem: never leave a project without it, IEEE Software, 19: 43 -45
3. Chikofsky E. J. (1990) Changing your endgame strategy. IEEE Software. 7: 87, 112
4. Collier B., DeMarco T., Fearey P. A. (1996) Defined process for project postmortem review. IEEE Software, 13: 65-72
5. Florac W.A., Carleton A.D. (1999) Measuring the software process - statistical process control for software process improvement. Addison Wesley, SEI Series on software engineering, Boston, MA, USA

6. Grady R., Caswell D. (1987) Software metrics: establishing a company-wide program, Prentice Hall, Englewood Cliffs, UK
7. Humphrey W. (1989): Managing the software process, Addison-Wesley, Harlow, UK
8. Jalote P. (1999) CMM in practice - processes for executing projects at Infosys, Addison-Wesley, SEI Series on software engineering, Boston, MA, USA
9. Jalote P. (2000) Use of metrics in high maturity organizations. In: Proceedings of 12th software engineering process group conference, SEPG 2K, Seattle, USA
10. Jalote P. (2002) Software project management in practice. Addison-Wesley, Harlow, UK
11. Montgomery D.C. (1996) Introduction to statistical quality control. John Wiley and Sons, West Sussex, UK
12. Radice R.A., Roth N.K., O'Hara A.C., Ciarfella jr. W.A.(1985) A programming process architecture. IBM systems journal, 24(2), p.79
13. Ramasubramanian S., Jagadeesan G. (2002) Knowledge management at Infosys. IEEE Software, 19: 53-55
14. Rus I., Lindvall M. (2002) Knowledge management in software engineering. IEEE Software, 19: 26-38
15. Software Engineering Institute (1995) The capability maturity model - guidelines for improving the software process. Addison Wesley, Harlow, UK
16. Wheeler D.J., Chambers D.S. (1992) Understanding statistical process control. SPS press, ISBN: 0945320132, Knoxville, TN, USA

Author Biography

Pankaj Jalote is Professor and Head of the Department of Computer Science and Engineering, Indian Institute of Technology, Kanpur, India. He was formerly an assistant professor in the Department of Computer Science at the University of Maryland, College Park, where he also had a joint appointment with the Institute of Advanced Computer Studies. He obtained his B. Tech. from IIT Kanpur and his Ph.D. in computer science from University of Illinois at Urbana-Champaign. From 1996 to 1998, he was Vice President (quality) at Infosys Technologies, a large Bangalore-based company providing software solutions worldwide, where he spearheaded Infosys' successful transition from ISO to CMM Level 4.

Index

Druck: Strauss Offsetdruck, Mörlenbach
Verarbeitung: Schäffer, Grünstadt